D1616927

Travel and Ethics

Despite the recent increase in scholarly activity regarding travel writing and the accompanying proliferation of publications relating to the form, its ethical dimensions have yet to be theorised with sufficient rigour. Drawing from the disciplines of anthropology, linguistics, literary studies and modern languages, the contributors in this volume apply themselves to a number of key theoretical questions pertaining to travel writing and ethics, ranging from travel-as-commoditisation to encounters with minority languages under threat. Taken collectively, the essays assess key critical legacies from parallel disciplines to the debate so far, such as anthropological theory and postcolonial criticism. Also considered, and of equal significance, are the ethical implications of the form's parallel genres of writing, such as ethnography and journalism. As some of the contributors argue, innovations in these genres have important implications for the act of theorising travel writing itself and the mode and spirit in which it continues to be conducted. In the light of such innovations, how might ethical theory maintain its critical edge?

Corinne Fowler lectures in Postcolonial Literature at the University of Leicester, UK.

Charles Forsdick is James Barrow Professor of French at the University of Liverpool, UK.

Ludmilla Kostova is Associate Professor of British Literature and Cultural Studies at the University of Veliko Turnovo, Bulgaria.

Routledge Research in Travel Writing

EDITED BY PETER HULME, *University of Essex*, and TIM YOUNGS, *Nottingham Trent University*

Travel and Ethics
Theory and Practice

Edited by Corinne Fowler, Charles Forsdick, and Ludmilla Kostova

Routledge
Taylor & Francis Group
NEW YORK   LONDON

First published 2014
by Routledge
711 Third Avenue, New York, NY 10017

Simultaneously published in the UK
by Routledge
2 Park Square, Milton Park, Abingdon, Oxon OX14 4RN

*Routledge is an imprint of the Taylor & Francis Group,
an informa business*

© 2014 Taylor & Francis

The right of Corinne Fowler, Charles Forsdick, and Ludmilla Kostova to
be identified as the authors of the editorial material, and of the authors for
their individual chapters, has been asserted in accordance with sections 77
and 78 of the Copyright, Designs and Patents Act 1988.

Library of Congress Cataloging-in-Publication Data

Travel and ethics : theory and practice / edited by Corinne Fowler, Charles
Forsdick, & Ludmilla Kostova.
    pages cm. — (Routledge Research in Travel Writing ; 7)
    Includes bibliographical references and index.
  1. Travelers' writings—Moral and ethical aspects. 2. Travel writing—
History. 3. Literature and morals. 4. Postcolonialism—Social
aspects. I. Fowler, Corinne, editor of compilation. II. Forsdick,
Charles, editor of compilation. III. Kostova, Ludmilla, editor of
compilation.
  PN56.T7T676 2013
  809'.93327—dc23
  2013003051

ISBN13: 978-0-415-99539-9 (hbk)
ISBN13: 978-0-203-76409-1 (ebk)

Typeset in Sabon
by IBT Global.

 SUSTAINABLE FORESTRY INITIATIVE Certified Sourcing www.sfiprogram.org SFI-01234 SFI label applies to the text stock

Printed and bound in the United States of America
by IBT Global.

Contents

Introduction
Ethics on the Move

Charles Forsdick, Corinne Fowler,
and Ludmilla Kostova

TRAVEL WRITING SCHOLARSHIP

The study of travel writing has emerged rapidly over the past three decades as a thriving cross-disciplinary field that has made an increasingly active contribution to the internationalization of research practices in the humanities and social sciences. The area of research has been consolidated by the development of those institutions and structures on which the sustainability and further development of the diverse activity federated under such a title depends: journals, textbooks and other reference works, scholarly associations, and book series.

Studying travel writing allows the student or researcher the flexibility to draw on a range of other disciplines, theories, and concepts; at the same time analyzing a textual form that is inherently transcultural permits critical dialogues that are themselves often powerfully comparative and cross-cultural. Travel writing has long been an object of academic inquiry, although customarily reduced to source material in fields such as history and geography. Those who studied the form as a genre in its own right tended to focus on individual travel writers, or to be interested in the importance of the travelogue to the history of the book. Scholars such as Percy Adams underlined the centrality of travel writing to the emergence of modern European literature,[1] privileging the links between such texts and a key genre such as the novel. Nonetheless, the relative assumptions of literary value allocated to each literary form, and the generic hierarchies that accordingly emerged, seem for a long time to have impeded the wider consideration of travel narratives as a literary form in their own right.

Contemporary attention to travel writing can be traced to wider shifts in humanities scholarship in the postwar period. The challenge to a well-established canon in literary studies, and the associated prizing open of a wider range of fields to subaltern—or at least less dominant—voices, permitted attention to be directed to source material previously dismissed as paraliterary or journalistic—and relegated to the library stacks alongside many other examples of the "great unread". The rejection of generic and hegemonic canonicity—and by association that of archival authority—in favor of recovering alternative voices, or other (hi)stories "from below", permitted both the excavation of forgotten texts and the creation of new approaches to other material around which critical orthodoxies had crystallized.

Although often cited as a foundational text in postcolonial studies, Edward Said's *Orientalism* is perhaps more accurately understood as the text that triggered—through its contribution to the field of colonial discourse studies—renewed interest in the travelogue as a literary form worthy of attention in its own right.[2] Said's work managed to crystallize a series of intellectual currents that lent themselves to study of this cultural form, evident also in the work of anthropologists such as Talal Asad and James Clifford,[3] as well as in the more general focus among early postcolonial critics on the practices of constructing and controlling difference that Gayatri Spivak dubbed "othering". Simplifying such critical approaches, Terry Eagleton sees in them the risk of an intellectual dead-end:

> The bad news is that otherness is not the most fertile of intellectual furrows. Indeed, once you have observed that the other is typically portrayed as lazy, dirty, stupid, crafty, womanly, passive, rebellious, sexually rapacious, childlike, enigmatic and a number of other mutually contradictory epithets, it is hard to know what to do next apart from reaching for another textual illustration of the fact.[4]

While Eagleton's critique is pertinent for certain reductive approaches to colonial discourse, according to which scholars comb travel narratives to identify and confirm preexisting sets of stereotypes, such a presentation is more a parody of studies in travel writing than an accurate reflection of the activity the field has allowed. Eagleton does not, for instance, reflect the more attenuated attention to the historically and geographically grounded approaches to the textualization of travel that is evident in some of the earliest responses to Said—notably, those of Dennis Porter.[5]

The rapid expansion and evolution of studies in travel writing in the anglophone academy resulted in a clear move from an emphasis on colonial discourse in the 1980s toward an active and nuanced engagement in the 1990s with the complexities of the wider discourses of cultures and travel. While other national traditions of studies in travel writing evolved along different lines, with many French scholars focusing, for instance, on questions of intertexuality and genericity, English-language research tended to draw on postcolonial criticism and gender studies to foreground issues of identity and voice. Mary Louise Pratt's *Imperial Eyes*, which appeared in 1992,[6] encouraged increasing attention—through its development of notions such as the "contact zone" and the "travelee" (the person who inhabits the culture through which the traveler passes and who is accordingly "traveled over")—to the dynamics of travel writing, foregrounding attention to such phenomena as autoethnography and the instability of identity as examined in the work of Clifford. A series of major texts have been published over the past two decades, suggestively positing the creative potential of the encounter of travel writing with other key fields in the contemporary humanities and social science research, such as gender studies,[7] translation studies,[8] and ecocriticism.[9]

Although many of these approaches contain an implicitly ethical dimension and are often even motivated by a loosely ethical imperative to challenge dominant voices and explore alternative modes of intercultural contact and communication, the open, active, and enabling engagement of studies in travel writing with questions of ethics remains largely undeveloped despite the potential of such work to reinvigorate the field and to expand the range of audiences with which it can speak.

TRAVEL WRITING AND ETHICS

At the close of the twentieth century, one of the few studies of travel writing to focus exclusively on ethics was published. Syed Manzurul Islam's *The Ethics of Travel: From Marco Polo to Kafka* levels a by now familiar charge at travel writing[10]—namely, that it communicates more about the traveler than about the country being visited.[11] Islam's essay for this volume responds to travel writing's evolving forms. In his earlier study, however, he wrote, "All these intrepid travelers, despite moving so much and so far in space did not seem to have traveled at all."[12] Islam's critique is leveled at a "sedentary" mode of travel, a mode that he argues has furthered the Orientalist project by drawing clear distinctions between traveler and travelee. For Islam, as for so many scholars of travel writing today, the process of othering that ensues from this distinction represents the genre's most unethical and enduring feature. Islam's book focuses on the extent to which travel writing from the thirteenth century to the late twentieth both internalized and perpetuated a false "logic of difference", a logic that is embedded in the very metaphor of travel itself (p. 5). Islam's concern in the book is the extent to which this metaphor views the travelee as though she was a "daughte[r] of the soil" (p. 5). It is this connotation of spatially bounded cultural subjectivity at the site of travel, he argues, that gives rise to misleading notions of essential belonging and essential difference (p. 5). Islam holds that this apparent "fixity of location", seemingly confirmed by factors such as the physiognomic difference between traveler and travelee, is grounded in Kantian philosophy, which mobilizes a circular and self-confirming logic, reinforcing the Cartesian "duality of *res cognitans* and *res extensa*" (p. 9). Following Said, then, Islam shares with later scholars a sense that colonialism itself is founded on these perceived cultural boundaries (p. 55). Travel writing is thus always already implicated in the imperial project.

Despite the pessimism of Islam's assessment, his study prefigures the quest of recent scholarship to understand how travel writers have attempted to, in his words, "overcome" the genre's unethical orientations (p. 9). Inspiring the later formulation of "dwelling-in-travel"[13] Islam argued that the traveler "dwells by moving" these rigid boundaries in ways that transcend individualism (p. 10). He advocates ethically informed modes of travel, which he characterizes as "nomadic" rather than "sedentary", whereby the traveler's sense of self uncongeals (p. 11). Ethical travel as Islam defines it, after Martin Heidegger, initiates a psychological and philosophical journey to "the primordial condition of existence itself" (p. 12). "Only to a dweller [in travel] is the Being of being revealed" (p. 12) laying bare unethical processes of representation and contradicting the apparent cultural boundedness of beings in particular space. In this schema, the travelee cannot be reductively contained as "an object of" the traveler's "knowing gaze" (p. 13).

There is by now an established body of work on travel writing as a genre that problematizes and thematizes cultural difference. Following a sustained period of scholarly pessimism inspired by the postcolonial critique of travel narratives' imperialist orientations, scholars began to sound more optimistic notes about travel writing's ethical dimension. In particular, critics have expressed growing discomfort—along the lines of Eagleton's comments on the risks of an intellectual *impasse*, cited above—with the apparently tireless and at times self-congratulatory ethical interrogation to which travel narratives have been subjected. This has given rise to a more systematic, site-specific, and nuanced brand of scholarship. Initially focused on modernist travel writing,[14] this line of inquiry investigates travel writing's capacity to be less culturally arrogant and complicit with prevailing political orthodoxies than ethical—especially postcolonial—critiques of the 1990s, had hitherto supposed. The debate continues, receiving further modifications in relation to specific sites of travel such as Afghanistan.[15] While Islam is troubled by travelers' intransigence, then, recent scholarship has considered the genre's capacity to "make it move", to quote Tim Youngs on the ficto-critical travel writing of Stephen Muecke.[16]

However, this more optimistic scholarly approach is rarely incautious. A case in point is Youngs's forensic examination of Muecke's work, which he discovers to be underpinned by European, rather than aboriginal, intellectual traditions.[17] Nonetheless, optimism is a salient feature of contemporary studies in travel writing. Nowhere is this more apparent than in recent investigations into the politics and poetics of form.[18] Formal experimentation has proved a fruitful avenue of inquiry, yielding insights into travel writing's capacity for transforming itself from, in the words of Bill Ashcroft, "an aggressive form of knowledge-making to a mode of reflection".[19] As scholars such as Stephen Levin, Julia Kuehn, and Paul Smethurst have argued, formal experimentation can indicate the presence of "disordering anti-structures" in narratives of travel.[20] These anti-structures, Smethurst suggests, enable a form of cultural critique or a metacommentary on the genre of travel writing.[21] Smethurst does in fact warn that innovation in form often reflects aesthetic and commercial imperatives rather than ethical considerations. Even so, the essays in Smethurst's edited collection all attend closely to hybrid forms written in a range of languages and in various historical periods. Similarly, attention has been paid to what Arjun Appadurai calls "the 'technoscapes' of contemporary globalization", which have the potential to effect further innovations of form.[22] However, it is advisable to exercise caution in this regard. Since the deeper structures of inequality have remained largely unaltered by the development of information and communication technologies, it seems wise to be skeptical about celebratory analyses of its democratizing capacity.[23]

The most recent approaches to travel and ethics have attended closely to contemporary travel writing's engagement with the dilemmas that arise in a late capitalist era of globalization. Both Stephen Levin and Debbie Lisle stress the need to take such engagements seriously.[24] Levin's study *The Contemporary Travel Novel: The Aesthetics of Self-Fashioning in an Era of Globalization* focuses on a subcultural trend in adventure travel writing that he defines as the "literature of negation".[25] Observing its "failed identification" with the cultural and economic conditions of mass society, Levin argues that these narratives reveal sustained resistance to the present social order even if this resistance operates only at the level of fantasy.[26] Levin's conclusions are complemented by the insights of a longitudinal study conducted by Richard Wilkinson and Kate Pickett, whose book *The Spirit Level* ignited fierce political debate across the Atlantic and beyond.[27] Published in the same year as Levin's study, the book provides compelling evidence to support the contention that people consistently experience anxiety about self-serving materialism as though it were only a "private ambivalence" toward the age.[28] Levin's study explores precisely this phenomenon in relation to post–World War II travel novels.

Heralding a post-1975 renaissance in travel writing, Lisle similarly believes that the genre increasingly exhibits profound anxieties about late twentieth-century globalization. As Lisle is careful to point out, this does not mean that travel writing has revoked its "colonial vision".[29] Rather, she contends that its increasing emphasis on empathy and commonality indicates the copresence (with colonial viewpoints) of a "cosmopolitan vision", albeit one that falls short of the democratic and emancipatory values that it appears to endorse.[30] However, by offering "*incomplete* articulations of power that offer compelling moments of resistance", Lisle argues, such writing provides fertile ground for scholarly investigations into critical debates about global politics.[31] In a similar spirit of inquiry, Claire Lindsay has productively examined the prevalence of "affective identification" in anglophone and Spanish-language narratives (see Chapter 3 of the present volume). Maureen Moynagh, meanwhile, has examined "political tourists" and their expressions of solidarity with fellow travelees.[32] Once again, Lindsay and Moynagh each present their discussions in highly qualified terms. These qualifications alone testify to the enduring currency of the postcolonial critique of the genre's imperialist orientation.

What makes Lisle's text particularly relevant to the present volume is that she addresses the important issue of finding criteria that would enable us to "judge between competing representations of difference in travel writing . . . within a poststructural framework" and so between "*better* or *worse* travelogues".[33] Rejecting as erroneous the claim that poststructuralism "leads to ultimate relativism", she follows philosopher Simon Critchley in maintaining that the genre "has *always* been anchored by ethical and political discriminations" but has tended to "collapse the distinction between the ethical and the political . . . between what 'is' and what 'ought' to be the case".[34] Lisle further draws upon David Campbell's conception of "a politically committed ethos of criticism" that precludes the possibility of politically and ethically situated subjects ever "standing outside the world in order to judge it" by universal and seemingly objective ethical norms.[35] On this basis she concludes that "a travelogue can be judged as 'good' to the extent that it acknowledges, addresses and engages with its ethical and political responsibility to the other".[36] Given this, Lisle is concerned about the absence of "*political reflexivity* and *critical thought*" in most contemporary travel writing but nevertheless looks forward to more authors resisting the received codes of the genre and addressing the ethicopolitical dimension of cultural encounters.[37]

As noted above, ethical interpretations play an important role in both contemporary literary studies and historical studies. Scholars have long debated the stance of the historian in writing and teaching history. A selective approach to such debates conducted within the discipline of history could help us better understand the position of the travel writer, who—as Chapter 2 of this volume discusses—often poses as a kind of historian. Moreover, it could encourage reflection on the critic's own interpretative strategies.

In literary studies, the preoccupation with ethics has taken a variety of forms. In particular, scholars have stressed the importance of literary narratives for moral philosophy. In *Ethics, Literature and Theory*, Wayne C. Booth argues that "the thick descriptions and narrative shapings of literature provide an untapped resource for philosophers".[38] A similar claim could be made for travel narratives, especially if we take into account the open admission of a famous practitioner of the genre, William Dalrymple, who claims that "the travel writer [can] use the techniques of the novel—develop characters, select and tailor evidence".[39]

Following Wayne C. Booth, some scholars have opted for rhetorical approaches to literary narrative, with James Phelan, among others, conceiving narrative as "an event" in its own right rather than merely as "a representation of events".[40] Phelan further draws attention to relations among authors, narrators, and audiences in texts.[41] On the whole, his analysis of narrative strategies and attitudes inscribed in texts may help us produce more nuanced and sensitive readings of travel narratives by encouraging reflection on authorial agency and, particularly, on authorial responsibility and its limits. Significantly, the critic has also commented on the reader's ethical stance with respect to the literary text. In his view, she "does bring values to the text, but [ideally] remains open to having those values challenged and even repudiated".[42] Her stance vis-à-vis the travel narrative may be in many ways similar. Ideally, travel writing could challenge the reader's preconceptions and actively engage her values and judgments by transforming abstract notions about life elsewhere into specific stories focusing on palpable experiences.[43]

The relationship between travel writers and their critics also has distinct ethical implications. In his introduction to *The Best Travel Writing 2010: True Stories from around the World*, Dalrymple expresses considerable hostility to critics of the genre who, in his view, are not sufficiently sensitive to the traveler's position as an outsider "setting out alone and vulnerable on the road".[44] Academics, he avers, ignore the traveler's insecurity and accuse him (quintessentially *him*) of Orientalism and cultural imperialism.[45] However, despite his intransigent attitude to academics, Dalrymple appears to have taken his cue from some of the criticisms that have been leveled at travel writers. Thus, both his recent book *Nine Lives*,[46] and the texts of other writers that he values (for instance, Christopher de Bellaigue's *Rebel Land: Unraveling the Riddle of History in a Turkish Town*[47]), do their best to problematize what Lisle has called "authorian sureness".[48] The critic juxtaposes the stance of the sure-footed narrator in travelogues to unreliable narrators in fiction and is skeptical about the ability of travel writers to move away from that stance because "the genre relies so heavily on the logic of identity/difference".[49] Through their focus on people rather than places,[50] however, Dalrymple and de Bellaigue have managed to project images of themselves as struggling to understand the "characters" they represent and being faced with unanticipated results.

Read in terms of Phelan's rhetorical theory, the narratorial selves that the two travel writers construct signify that they have chosen to "limit" their "guidance" of their audience and to "transfer" some of their own "authorial responsibility" to their readers.[51] By "exercising the responsibility" that has been "transferred" to us we may participate, however vicariously, in the narrators' attempts to make sense of the motives, choices, and acts of the "characters" that they portray and thus understand some of the challenges that travel writers face as they undertake to represent cultural difference.

Apart from illustrating the genre's elasticity, and hence its ability for survival, texts such as the ones briefly considered above illustrate the possibility of an alliance between the practices of criticism and travel writing. By taking critics' unflattering comments seriously, travel writers can move away from the genre's imperialist legacy and produce narratives that will explore, more effectively, "the extraordinary diversity that still exists in the world under the veneer of globalization".[52]

This volume contains thirteen essays that address theoretical questions pertaining to the ethics of travel and, for the most part, challenge or extend earlier postcolonial engagements with travel's mechanisms and representations. In Chapter 1, Michael Cronin explores the emergence of language-centered travel writing, whereby language itself provides the raison d'être for travel. Cronin examines the travel accounts of Mark Abley, Pamelo Petro, and Helena Drysdale, arguing that this new current in late modern travel writing reveals how language is a site of recurring anxiety over the future survival of linguistic diversity. His essay explores the inherent contradiction of a travel account that is centrally concerned with the threat to minority languages and yet is itself written in a major global language. Endangered languages, he argues, are deemed to evoke radically different worldviews and yet the writers of these travel narratives are ultimately unable to resolve the tension between upholding linguistic diversity and providing a commentary on the incommunicable and untranslatable nature of the languages that are the subject of their narratives.

Chapter 2, by Gillian Jein, presents a further examination of travelees' opacity. Her chapter offers a combined focus on French travel in the United States and Jean Baudrillard's 1986 travelogue *America*,[53] which postcolonial critics have condemned for its neoimperialist, narcissistic, and eschatological tendencies. Countering the "virulence" of this critique, Jein distinguishes between legislative and interpretative travel writing practices to identify what she sees as an important shift in late twentieth-century travel writing. While she argues that the former renders "othered" social space as legible and knowable, interpretative spatial practices reflexively foreground its ultimately untranslatable nature. Jein argues that Baudrillard's narrative clearly presents itself as a record of knowledge and yet undermines this with a form of poetic mapping whose ironic, hyperbolic, and aphoristic dimensions ultimately challenge its own authority in ways that challenge our collective ability to know "America" at all.

The next two chapters examine the ethics of travel writing in practice. In Chapter 3, focused on Paraguay, Corinne Fowler asks whether particular narrative strategies—such as overt fictionalization and alternative forms of narrative focalization—can promote what Claire Lindsay terms "affective identification" on the part of the reader with the travelee.[54] Fowler's essay focuses on Paraguay as a site of travel that overwhelmingly figures in European and Australian travel accounts as an irrational yet enticing utopia populated with "biddable" women and idle men. In the first half of her chapter, Fowler argues that generations of travelers—and a handful of fiction writers—have projected a range of anxieties about modernity and social disorder onto Paraguay. Moving beyond merely identifying and sourcing these salient patterns of representation, however, the second half of the chapter examines the extent to which particular narrative modes might potentially combat these tendencies, concluding that particular techniques of fictionalization and focalization are amenable to promoting "affective identification" on the part of the reader with Paraguayan travelees. In Chapter 4, Laurie Hovell McMillin explores—through her own self-reflexive account of "dwelling-in-travel"—the difficulties of representing the contested history of Sri Lanka's civil war. Her concluding paragraphs represent a practitioner's response to Syed Islam's endorsement of ethically informed modes of travel (discussed above), whereby the traveler's sense of self uncongeals.[55] Writing of herself in the third person, McMillin notes that the experience of travel in Sri Lanka ultimately—and productively— left her without "a stable place from which to think and act".

In Chapter 5, Charles Forsdick examines Victor Segalen's early twentieth-century practical and theoretical writings on travel *Essai sur L'exotisme* and *Equipée*.[56] Forsdick takes as his starting point Pratt's notion of the "traveler" and "travelee", and argues that Segalen's writings challenges the potential rigidity of Pratt's binary by means of his concept of *exotisme*. By constructing a certain type of traveler as an *exote*, he argues, Segalen does not merely present a radical contrast to the thinking of his contemporaries but may also be seen to challenge a postcolonial engagement with the mechanisms and representations of travel. Forsdick concludes that this aesthetics of diversity depends on unstable identities and may therefore be read as containing traces of a postcolonial ethics of travel.

In Chapter 6, meanwhile, Jopi Nyman fills a gap in the study of the ethical parameters of travel by focusing upon the role of animals in travel narratives. The author begins by drawing attention to the tendency of early travel writers to populate distant lands with monstrous animals as well as with threatening humans. However, he notes that animals became marginalized in travel narratives due to the emergence of practices such as big game hunting in Africa and India. Nyman divides his analysis of the role of animals in travel writing into two parts. In the first part he examines texts shaped, to a lesser or to a greater extent, by discourses of colonialism, such as Ernest Hemingway's *Green Hills of Africa* and Gerald Durrell's *Overloaded Ark*.[57] In the second part of the chapter, Nyman concentrates on two recent travel narratives, Brian Payton's *In Bear Country: A Global Journey in Vanishing Wilderness* and Linda Spalding's *The Follow*,[58] which go beyond the traditional representation of the animal as other and overtly display an ethical attitude toward animals. In the author's view, such narratives challenge the animal's naturalized role as other while also illustrating the openness of the travel genre to new themes and approaches.

In Chapter 7, Anthony Carrigan concentrates on the ethical problems associated with an increasingly globalized mass tourism since—as he points out—many forms of late twentieth-century tourism exploit wealth's unequal distribution, perpetuating practices such as displacing local people or unfair labor practices. Focusing on writings about tourism in the Caribbean and the Pacific Islands and promoting a comparative approach to compatible sites of travel, Carrigan argues that these literatures communicate a shared sense of postcoloniality in the face of the exploitative aspects of globalized tourism.

In Chapter 8, Alasdair Pettinger sheds new light on an established prac-tice in anglophone travel writing: when travelers visit places where the lan-guage or dialect is different from that of their assumed readers, they resort to the kind of "translation" that simplifies their interactions with the local people and may even conceal their inability to communicate effectively with them. Pettinger details the late twentieth-century travels of Europeans and North Americans to Haiti, one of the world's poorest countries. His chap-ter explores a parallel phenomenon: the negotiation of economic differences that may prove as difficult and confusing for travelers as conversations in a foreign language. Pettinger draws attention to the ethical implications of representing such negotiations in travel narratives. Taking into account the fact that contemporary travelogues are frequently marketed together with guidebooks in bookstores and may therefore act as "conduct books" that shape the expectations and behavior of other travelers, he concludes that travel writers "have a certain ethical responsibility to be more reflective on their own circumstances and privilege".

In Chapter 9, Ludmilla Kostova examines *Street Without a Name: Childhood and Other Misadventures in Bulgaria*, a genre-bending text by Bulgarian-born writer Kapka Kassabovas, who has chosen English as her medium of expression. Kostova examines the conditions of the book's engendering—especially the role played by the publisher in the process of shaping it as, in Misha Glenny's words, an "autobiographical travelogue".[59] She likewise looks at Western and Bulgarian responses to the book as well as at Kassabova's own commentary upon it and her avowed aim of chang-ing the received image of the country of her birth. The narrative persona that the writer fashions for herself in *Street Without a Name*[60] is analyzed within the context of present-day ideas of cosmopolitanism and is further linked to the emergence of a distinctive postnational migrant middle-class identity in the aftermath of the collapse of communism in Eastern Europe. What makes Kassabova's travelogue particularly relevant to this volume is that it disrupts "the logic of identity/difference" on which, according to Debbie Lisle, the travel genre is based and this has distinct ethicopo-litical implications.[61] In her exploration of those Kostova is not guided by any universal principles of judgment but instead poses a number of spe-cific questions about Kassabova's responsibility to her intended audience of anglophone readers and the presence or absence of "political reflexivity and critical thought" in her text.[62]

In Chapter 10, Alex Drace-Francis engages with the ongoing debate about the ethical position of the traveler vis-à-vis the others that she represents. His focus is on Romanian texts, composed between 1702 and 1858, and on the construction of a Romanian cultural identity. He questions critical inter-pretations that stress rigid divisions between Europe's East and West, and represent Western travelers as figures solely involved in acts of "cultural hege-monization" and Eastern travelees as the passive objects of their "mapping". Instead Drace-Francis concentrates on cultural interactions and mutual perceptions. In the texts he discusses, Romanian authors either describe British and French travelers or respond to such travelers' writings about their country or people. In addition, Drace-Francis foregrounds the *dynamics* of Romanian perceptions of the Western traveler. In the course of a century and a half, he argues, such perceptions "grew from a state of relatively indifferent curiosity to one of fierce indignation", with the traveler finally becoming "the object of satire as well as the source of reproach". Drace-Francis thus presents travel writing as part of an "entangled history" of Europe marked by complex cases of mutual (mis)recognition rather than by simplistic polarities.[63]

In his first return to the subject of travel and ethics since his 1988 study *The Ethics of Travel*, Syed Manzurul Islam devotes Chapter 11 to the contention of Michel Hardt and Antonio Negri, in their book *Empire*,[64] that we now live in a time where the elements that once marked our difference—be it our culture, race, tradition, nation-state, or whatever tied us to a particular location and to a distinctive ways of being—have disappeared. Islam contests this view, arguing that, despite the increasing globalization of capital, there remain zones of difference that are inhabited by the poor and destitute. These zones offer pathways of travel toward genuine difference. He tackles the question of how such difference is to be represented with reference to Alfonso Lingis's *The Community of Those Who Have Nothing in Common*;[65] Brad Newsham's *Take Me with You: A Round-the-World Journey to Invite a Stranger Home*;[66] and Pico Iyer's travel narratives *Sun After Dark* and *The Global Soul: Jet Lag, Shopping Malls and the Search for Home*.[67] Islam concludes that the question of travel and ethics remains very much alive purely on the grounds that the relative differences that divide the world have not disappeared.

In Chapter 12, Jan Borm proffers a much needed discussion of travel writing, ethics, and pedagogy. The author reflects upon key ethical issues involved in teaching American travel writer Gretel Ehrlich's book *The Cold Heaven: Seven Seasons in Greenland* to a group of French students and on the feedback that some of them subsequently provided. Uppermost in the students' responses is a preoccupation with the perceived contrast between the 'minimalist' Inuit lifestyle and Western materialism and acquisitiveness. They likewise stress the ethical imperative of preserving Inuit culture's distinctive features. In closing, Borm highlights the positive role that travel writing can play in pedagogic programs by enhancing students' understanding of cultures that have been traditionally marginalized and thus stimulating them to reshape their mental maps and recognize their responsibility to and for various others.

Bringing the book to a close, Graham Huggan's Chapter 13 examines the contention that cultural criticism is undergoing a "Gothic" period, characterized by densely theoretical work on trauma, mourning, and late-capitalist "wound culture".[68] Huggan observes that a key term, here, is *spectrality*, which is tied to Jacques Derrida's surreptitious counterphilosophy of "hauntology" and the ubiquitous figure of the ghost.[69] Taking the late W. G. Sebald's contemplative exploration of travel's poetics as his case study, Huggan asks what role ghosts have to play in contemporary travel writing. This poetics, he argues, is hampered by the unbearable weight of the past upon the present. Huggan suggests that Sebald's writing is haunted in several senses, both oscillating between the realms of the dead and the living and preoccupied with the traumatic memory of multiple disintegrated worlds. The nostalgic impetus to travel, he argues, "ultimately registers a longing for the journey to end all journeys, the 'journey beyond'".

Taken collectively, the essays herein assess key critical legacies from a range of parallel disciplines to the ethics debate so far. Of equal significance to the contributors to this volume are the ethical implications of the form's parallel genres of writing, such as ethnography and journalism. As some of the essays argue, innovations in these genres have important implications for the act of theorizing travel writing itself and the mode and spirit in which it continues to be conducted. In the light of such innovations, this volume asks how ethical inquiry into narratives of travel might best maintain its critical edge.

NOTES

1. Percy G. Adams, *Travel Literature and the Evolution of the Novel* (Lexington: University of Kentucky Press, 1983).
2. Edward W. Said, *Orientalism: Western Conceptions of the Orient* (London: Routledge, 1978).
3. Talal Asad, ed., *Anthropology and the Colonial Encounter* (London: Ithaca Press, 1973); James Clifford, *The Predicament of Culture: Twentieth-century Ethnography, Literature, and Art* (Cambridge, MA: Harvard University Press, 1988).
4. Terry Eagleton, *Figures of Dissent: Reviewing Fish, Spivak, Žižek and Others* (London: Verso, 2002), p. 19.
5. Dennis Porter, "*Orientalism* and Its Problems", in Francis Barker, Peter Hulme, Margaret Iversen, and Diana Loxley, eds., *The Politics of Theory: Proceedings of the Essex Sociology of Literature Conference* (Colchester: University of Essex, 1982), pp. 179–93; Dennis Porter, *Haunted Journeys: Desire and Transgression in European Travel Writing* (Princeton, NJ: Princeton University Press, 1991).
6. Mary Louise Pratt, *Imperial Eyes: Travel Writing and Transculturation* (London: Routledge, 1992).
7. Sara Mills, *Discourses of Difference: An Analysis of Women's Travel Writing and Colonialism* (London: Routledge, 1991).
8. Michael Cronin, *Across the Lines: Travel, Language and Translation* (Cork: Cork University Press, 2000).
9. Graham Huggan and Helen Tiffin, *Postcolonial Ecocriticism: Literature, Animals, Environment* (London: Routledge, 2010).
10. Syed Manzu Islam, *The Ethics of Travel: From Marco Polo to Kafka* (Manchester: Manchester University Press, 1996).
11. Tim Youngs, "Making It Move", in Julia Kuehn and Paul Smethurst, eds., *Travel Writing, Form, and Empire: The Poetics and Politics of Mobility* (London: Routledge, 2009), pp. 148–66.

12. Islam, *The Ethics of Travel*, p. xvii; hereafter page numbers will be cited parenthetically in the text.
13. On "dwelling-in-travel", see James Clifford, *Routes: Travel and Translation in the Late Twentieth Century* (Cambridge, MA: Harvard University Press, 1997), p. 44.
14. Andrew Hammond, "Memoirs of Conflict: British Women Travellers in the Balkans," *Studies in Travel Writing* 14, no. 1 (2010): p. 184.
15. Corinne Fowler, *Chasing Tales: Travel Writing, Journalism and the History of British Ideas about Afghanistan* (Amsterdam: Rodopi, 2007).
16. Youngs, "Making It Move".
17. Youngs, "Making It Move".
18. Julia Kuehn and Paul Smethurst, eds., *Travel Writing, Form, and Empire: The Poetics and Politics of Mobility*.
19. Bill Ashcroft, "Afterword", in Kuehn and Smethurst, eds., *Travel Writing*.
20. Stephen Levin, *The Contemporary Anglophone Travel Novel: The Aesthetics of Self-fashioning in the Era of Globalisation* (London: Routledge, 2008). See also Kuehn and Smethurst, eds., *Travel Writing*.
21. Paul Smethurst, "Introduction," in Kuehn and Smethurst, eds., *Travel Writing*, p. 3.
22. Ashcroft, "Afterword", p. 236.
23. Jairo Lugo-Ocando, "Democratic Practices and Information and Communication Technologies: A Cross-National Study" (PhD diss., University of Sussex, 2004).
24. Levin, *Contemporary Anglophone Travel Novel*; Debbie Lisle, *The Global Politics of Contemporary Travel Writing* (London: Cambridge University Press, 2006).
25. Levin, *Contemporary Anglophone Travel Novel*, p. 2.
26. Levin, *Contemporary Anglophone Travel Novel*, p. 3.
27. Richard Wilkinson and Kate Pickett, *The Spirit Level: Why Equal Societies Almost Always Do Better* (London: Allen Lane, 2009).
28. Wilkinson and Pickett, *Spirit Level*, p. 4.
29. Lisle, *Global Politics*, p. 3.
30. Lisle, *Global Politics*, p. 5.
31. Lisle, *Global Politics*, p. 23; emphasis in the original.
32. Maureen Moynagh, *Political Tourism and Its Texts* (Toronto: University of Toronto Press, 2008), p. 211.
33. Lisle, *Global Politics*, pp. 262–63; emphasis in the original.
34. Lisle, *Global Politics*, p. 263.
35. Lisle, *Global Politics*, p. 264.
36. Lisle, *Global Politics*, p. 265.
37. Lisle, *Global Politics*, p. 265; emphasis in the original.
38. Wayne C. Booth, "Foreword", in Stephen K. George, ed., *Ethics, Literature and Theory: An Introductory Reader* (London: Rowman and Littlefield, 2005).
39. William Dalrymple, "Introduction", in Sean O'Reilly, James O'Reilly, and Larry Habegger, eds., *The Best Travel Writing 2010: True Stories from around the World* (London: Amazon Media 2010), Kindle e-book, Location178.
40. James Phelan, "Rhetoric/Ethics," in David Herman, ed., *The Cambridge Companion to Narrative* (Cambridge: Cambridge University Press, 2007), p. 203.
41. Phelan, "Rhetoric/Ethics", p. 208.
42. Phelan, "Rhetoric/Ethics", p. 212.

43. Phelan makes a similar remark about the transformation of readerly perceptions of slavery through an ethical engagement with Sethe's choice in Toni Morrison's 1987 novel *Beloved*. See James Phelan, "Sethe's Choice: *Beloved* and the Ethics of Reading", in *Ethics, Literature, Theory*, p. 312.
44. Dalrymple, "Introduction", Location 189.
45. Dalrymple, "Introduction", Location 188.
46. William Dalrymple, *Nine Lives: In Search of the Sacred in Modern India* (London: Bloomsbury, 2010).
47. Christopher de Bellaigue, *Rebel Land: Unravelling the Riddle of History in a Turkish Town* (London: Penguin, 2011).
48. Lisle, *Global Politics*, p. 269.
49. Lisle, *Global Politics*, p. 261.
50. Dalrymple, "Introduction", p. 236.
51. Phelan, "Rhetoric/Ethics", p. 312.
52. Dalrymple, "Introduction", p. 237.
53. Jean Baudrillard, *America*, trans. Chris Turner (London; New York: Verso, 1988).
54. Claire Lindsay, *Contemporary Travel Writing of Latin America* (London: Routledge, 2010), p. 112.
55. Islam, *The Ethics of Travel*, p. 11.
56. Victor Segalen, *Equipée* [1929] (Paris: Gallimard, 1983); Victor Segalen, *Essay on Exoticism: An Aesthetics of Diversity*, trans. Yaël Rachel Schlick [1955] (Durham, NC: Duke University Press, 2002). First published as *Essai sur l'exotisme*.
57. Ernest Hemingway, *Green Hills of Africa* (London: Arrow, 1994); Gerald Durrell, *The Overloaded Ark* [1978] (London: Faber and Faber, 2010).
58. Brian Payton, *In Bear Country: A Global Journey in Vanishing Wilderness* (London: Old Street, 2007); Linda Spalding, *The Follow* (London: Bloomsbury, 1998).
59. Misha Glenny, "'Mum, Why Is Everything So Ugly?'" *Guardian*, 5 July 2008, p. 6.
60. Kapka Kassabovas, *Street Without a Name: Childhood and Other Misadventures in Bulgaria* (London: Portobello, 2009).
61. Lisle, *Global Politics*, p. 206.
62. On the significance of political reflexivity and critical thought in travel writing, see Lisle, *Global Politics*, pp. 265–66.
63. On travel writing on Europe as a "model of entangled history", see Wendy Bracewell, "The Limits of Europe in East European Travel Writing", in Wendy Bracewell and Alex Drace-Francis, eds., *Under Eastern Eyes: A Comparative Introduction to East European Travel Writing* (Budapest: Central European University Press, 2008).
64. Michael Hardt and Antonio Negri, *Empire* (Cambridge, MA: Harvard University Press, 2001).
65. Alfonso Lingis, *The Community of Those Who Have Nothing in Common* (New York: John Wiley, 1994).
66. Brad Newsham, *Take Me with You: An Around-the-World Journey to Invite a Stranger Home* (London: Bantam, 2002).
67. Pico Iyer, *Sun after Dark* (London: Bloomsbury, 2005); Pico Iyer, *The Global Soul: Jet Lag, Shopping Malls and the Search for Home* (London: Bloomsbury, 2001).
68. Gail Jones, "Mourning, Australian Culture, and the Stolen Generation," in Judith Ryan and Chris Wallace-Crabbe, ed., *Imagining Australia: Literature and Culture in the New World* (Cambridge, MA: Harvard University Press, 2004), p. 27.

69. Jacques Derrida, *Specters of Marx: The State of Debt, the Work of Mourning, and the New International*, trans. Peggy Kamuf (New York: Routledge, 1994), p. 28.

1 Speech Acts
Language, Mobility, and Place

Michael Cronin

John Steinbeck knows that companionship demands speech. Even when the companion is his dog Charley, the question of human speech seems inescapable. What is also inescapable is that human speech is plural and, in the case of Charley, Steinbeck's travel mate on his odyssey through the United States, this plurality makes a difference:

> He [Charley] was born in Bercy on the outskirts of Paris and trained in France, and while he knows a little poodle-English, he responds quickly only to commands in French. Otherwise, he has to translate and that slows him down.[1]

In a multilingual world, language and language difference is an inevitable feature of travel.[2] How travelers deal with the fact of languages other than their own, or radically distinct varieties of their own language, has clear implications for their capacity to engage with or interpret the realities they encounter. From an ethical standpoint, it is no less apparent that language contact has two distinct impacts, one representational, the other instrumental. The representational impact relates to the ability of the travel writer to represent the thoughts, values, and experiences of others, who do not speak his language, in the language of the writer. Pronouncements about the lives and habitats of others, however strong or tenuous the truth claims, do suppose an access to knowing that must, however, take account of post-Babelian realities. The instrumental impact is the impact of travel itself on language communities. In other words, if the travel writer is the practitioner of a major world language, to what extent is he as traveler complicit in global linguicide that may see up to 90 percent of the more than six thousand languages in the world disappear by the end of the century?[3] Mass travel has long been acknowledged as a significant pull factor in language shift and language death, so how do major world language travelers face up to the sociolinguistic consequences of their own traveling practices?[4]

In this essay I explore contemporary travel accounts—written in a major world language, English—that seek to engage with language difference not as a by-product but as an object of travel. That is to say, the accounts take language itself—or rather, languages—as the primary motive for traveling. Inevitably, ethical concerns, which range from species destruction to the legitimacy of political violence, are a recurrent feature of the narratives as they probe the current state and future prospects of the world's languages. The inevitability is partly a function of how the language variousness of the world is constructed. Published within six years of each other by major English-language publishers, Pamela Petro's *Travels in an Old Tongue: Touring the World Speaking Welsh*,[5] Helena Drysdale's *Mother Tongues: Travels through Tribal Europe*,[6] and Mark Abley's *Spoken Here: Travels among Threatened Languages* all take minority languages as the structural theme of their travels.[7] The accounts become part travelogue, part crusade, as the travelers try to come to terms with the unpalatable realities of language decline.

PLACE

In describing her rationale for visiting some countries and not others, Helena Drysdale explains that shortage of space prevented her from including the Irish, Welsh, Scots, Luxembourgois, Sorbs, and Galicians, and that "I also had to cut out Romanies and Jews, on the grounds that I was investigating speakers of language that were rooted to a place, and the relationships between them and that place."[8] For her part, Pamela Petro, an American Welsh-language learner, wonders how Welshness or Welsh identity might be defined, and concludes,

> Truth is, there's no formula in the world for gauging Welshness, no recipe that calls for three stereotypes mixed with five pints of beer that will cook up a Welsh person. Except . . . except perhaps enthusiasm for the place, and a simple wanting to be there. The only reason I say I felt "more Welsh" is that on the basis of an evening's talk (pretty paltry evidence, I admit), I seem to like Wales better. I miss the salty dampness and the bumpy landscape and the fruity smell of life lived near big, manure manufacturing animals.[9]

Mark Abley, considering wrangling over orthography in Mohawk communities in Canada claims that "Mohawks feel an intense loyalty to their own place. But the rivalries between those places stands in the way of a united language. Nobody wants to feel that his or her own speech, so jealously guarded against the encroachments of the outside world, is being shoved aside in favour of somebody else's dialect."[10] Language is seen to define place, and places are inextricably bound up with forms of speech. The placedness of language is variously expressed. For Drysdale, it reveals itself in the many Sami words for lichen or a list of Sardinian foodstuffs in Sard. For Abley, it is the plethora of words for flora and fauna in the

Australian aboriginal language Wangkajunga, for which there are no English equivalents. But of course, the places are not just any kind of place, they are particular kinds of places. They are generally peripheral, remote, or marginal so that the frequently endangered state of the languages becomes conflated with the physical peripherality of the speakers. The landscape and the tongue become one in a topography of dispossession.

Pure movement is not likely to endear readers if there are no moments to punctuate kinesis. Travel demands the immobility of place if only to make sense of mobility itself. Language in the interaction between movement and place can, of course, occupy two positions. On the one hand, it is language that allows meanings to circulate in a place between speakers, within a community, and beyond that to other speakers and other places. The very act of writing a travel account partakes of the circulatory capacity of language. Other speakers, at other times and in other places, can read what you have to say. On the other hand, language becomes the quintessential expression of a specific group of speakers in a specific place. It is precisely the noncirculatory nature of language that defines its sociocultural raison d'être. Drysdale's assertion that although she did not speak Breton, "I would have thought it was the language of the fields and fishing boats" captures what she sees as the inevitable fit between territory and utterance.[11] The dual nature of language, the two positions it can occupy in the dialectic between movement and place, sets up a fundamental ethical tension in the language-centered accounts that is never fully resolved.

Abley, Petro, and Drysdale are all animated by a concern for the loss of language diversity. In traveling the world (Petro, Abley) or Europe (Drysdale) they repeatedly insist on the irrevocable loss to world culture that would be represented by disappearance of the world's many languages. Speaking of the Kimberly region in Western Australia, Abley notes that of the thirty different languages, only three are spoken by children: "It's as though twenty-seven sphinxes are crumbling away before our eyes."[12] Traveling is testimonial, a bearing witness to the fragility of human constructions of immeasurable complexity. The difficulty is that the very process that allows the reportage of loss, seemingly unfettered mobility, is also the process that construes minority languages in a particular way and ultimately imprisons their speakers in a teleology of extinction.

The Swiss travel writer Nicolas Bouvier, commenting on the nature of travel, argued that it rested on the fundamental dyad, *s'attacher, s'arracher* (to become attached/to become uprooted).[13] The travel writer moves on but the travelees stay put. It is indeed this basic urge to keep on moving that brings writers to the genre in the first place, as Drysdale, author of *Alone through China and Tibet* (1986), *Dancing with the Dead* (1991), and *Looking for George* (1996) makes clear in her utopian vision of a restless world:

> I wanted our restless life to last for ever. I would lean back and envisage
> a future in which everyone lived on the road—the ultimate in the free

movement of peoples. Cities would be deserted; our descendants would hardly believe that there was once an era of static living, in which people were shackled to one place, often for their entire lives.[14]

If "being shackled to one place" is seen as a precondition for linguistic survival, then a profound ambivalence will shadow any attempt to enthuse over the linguistic benefits of place. So when Drysdale meets Tiziana, a speaker of Sard, she feels that the young woman has one overriding desire, to leave the island as soon as possible. The writer herself gives expression to this desire by admitting that after listening to polyphonic singing in a church and coming close to the cultural and linguistic "epicentre of the island" that she "couldn't wait to escape".[15] Similarly, when she meets Kamberi, an Albanian doctor from Macedonia in the village of Vranjovce, she feels that he "faced being stuck here for ever".[16] The movement that brings the writer to celebrate and validate language diversity in situ, the championing of various forms of *s'attacher*, provokes an equally resistant strong desire to *s'arracher*, to give voice to a deep suspicion about all forms of *s'attacher*. In order to understand what the origins and the consequences of this ambivalence are as they relate to travel and language, it is worth considering language and travel in a broader framework of cultural analysis.

One of the most common icons of the global age is not surprisingly the globe itself. From shots of the blue planet suspended over abyssal darkness courtesy of the Apollo space missions to the sketchy outline of the earth on notices encouraging hotel customers to reuse their towels, images of the planet are increasingly common in the contemporary imaginary. Seeing things from a distance is as much a matter of subjection as observation. Occupying a superior vantage point from which one can look down on a subject people or a conquered land is a staple of colonial travel narratives.[17] There is a further dimension to the question of distance described by Tim Ingold in which he draws a distinction between perceiving the environment as a "sphere" or as a "globe".

For centuries, the classic description of the heavens was of the earth as a sphere with lines running from the human observer to the cosmos above. As geocentric cosmology fell into discredit and heliocentric cosmology came into the ascendant, the image of the sphere gave way to that of the globe. If the sphere presupposed a world experienced and engaged with from within, the globe represented a world perceived from without. Thus, in Ingold's words, "the movement from spherical to global imagery is also one in which 'the world', as we are taught it exists, is drawn ever further from the matrix of our lived experience".[18] In the movement toward the modern, a practical sensory engagement with the world underpinned by the spherical paradigm is supplanted by a regimen of detachment and control. As images of the globe proliferate, often ironically to mobilize ecological awareness, the danger is that these images themselves distort our relationship to our physical and cultural environment by continually situating us at a distance, by abstracting and subtracting us from our local attachments and responsibilities. However, it is precisely such an ability that is often construed as a basic requirement for both national, and more latterly, global citizenship.

It is the capacity to look beyond the immediate interests of the clan, village, or ethnic grouping that creates the conditions for a broader definitions of belonging at a national or indeed global level. Bronislaw Szersynski and John Urry argue, for example, that "banal globalism", the almost unnoticed symbols of globality that crowd our daily lives, might be "helping to create a sensibility conducive to the cosmopolitan rights and duties of being a 'global citizen', by generating a greater sense of both global diversity and global interconnectedness and belonging".[19] But Szersynski and Urry ask the following questions: "[I]s this abstraction from the local and particular fully compatible with dwelling in a locality? Could it be that the development of a more cosmopolitan, citizenly perception of place is at the expense of other modes of appreciating and caring for local environments and contexts?"[20]

In opposition to the figure of the citizen, we find the notion of the "denizen", which has been propagated notably by the nongovernmental organization Common Ground, where a denizen is deemed to be a person who dwells in a particular place and who can move through and knowingly inhabit that place. Therefore, Common Ground dedicates itself to encouraging the proliferation of vernacular, ideographic, and connotative descriptions of local places that can take the form of place myths, stories, personal associations, and celebrations of various kinds.[21] In a sense, what traveling in and through a world of languages does is to bring into sharp relief the tension between the traveler as citizen speaking a global language and the inhabitant as denizen speaking a local language. Petro expresses the attendant doubts when she claims that "I feel we English-speakers are weightless and language is our wings. We circle the globe in a tail-wind of convenience, but from our bird's eye viewpoints can't tell our destinations from our points of departures."[22]

DECLINE

Self-doubt aside, what the dovetailing of physical and linguistic mobility results in is a careful scaling of social development and historical sensibility. Minority language speakers are not only stuck in a particular place but also in a particular mode of development and in a particular relationship toward time itself. Describing her arrival on the island of Corsica, Drysdale comments, "Corti was astonishingly rundown. Yellow stucco façades on the main street were crumbling; their back regions were little more than stacks of stones with plumbing tacked on. Many shops were boarded up."[23] Stand still long enough and everything begins to decay and rot. The decline of language is mirrored in the decrepitude of its speakers and their environments.

When a region offers evidence of a contrary development, as in Catalonia, the occasion is one not of celebration but of disappointment. Noting the spread of high-rise residential developments throughout the region, Drysdale claims, "It was happening throughout Catalonia. I was beginning to look at everything with a premature nostalgia. Catalonia was a victim of its success. I couldn't warm to it."[24] The traveler as global citizen is implicated in the "denial of coevalness" observed by Johannes Fabian,[25] where at one end of the scale we find the advanced late modern Western traveler and at the other the premodern or lapsed modern denizen. It is because of their position on this scale that the minority language speakers have a sense of long-range historical memory that appears touchingly anomalous to the schismatic time traveler of late modernity. Encountering a Breton-language enthusiast, Drysdale points out, "He referred to events of the ninth century as if they happened last week."[26] The important qualification in these English-language accounts, however, is that they speak to an internally differentiated West. That is to say, it is not simply a question of Westerners stereotyping non-Westerners but of the use of language in motion to position other Westerners differently.

The recurrent ethical dilemma for these travel writers is that they want through their testimonies to make an eloquent plea for the value of linguistic diversity. In order to articulate their case and stress the uniqueness of the languages observed, they have to argue for a close correlation between language and place, which also has the added structural and narrative advantage of allowing the writers to go and describe these places. However, the placedness of the speakers puts them beyond the pale of schismatic modernity and global mobility. Their defining attribute becomes a mark of their belatedness. Time stands still and minority language speakers become the prisoners of the picturesque landscapes lovingly articulated in their disappearing languages. As the travelers (with the exception of Petro in Wales) do not spend radically extended periods of time in any of the places they describe or at least nothing like the time necessary to learn any of the minority languages they encounter, the world becomes once again a picture or a set of pictures, as time cedes place to space, and diversity alliteratively echoes decline.

Charles Forsdick, in his analysis of French travel literature in the twentieth century, notes that the perceived decline of diversity is one of the most common preoccupations of the literature. Travelers go to far-off places, tell their readers that the "exotic" is an illusion, that everywhere has now become much the same and the writers themselves are the last witnesses of differences which are about to disappear forever:

> The implicit sense of erosion [of diversity] that characterizes certain nineteenth-century and earlier twentieth-century attitudes to the distinctiveness of individual cultures may, in its more extreme manifestations, have bordered on apocalypticism; but the transfer from

generation to generation of such renewed prophecies of entropic decline uncovers the pervasive and conservative tendency according to which transformation is cast as death and loss.[27]

Forsdick draws a comparison with Raymond Williams's analysis of the trope of the decline of rural England, which Williams saw less as a precise event happening at a specific moment in time than as a "structure of feeling" running through English writing for centuries. In other words, though the notion of the decline of diversity may be differently accented depending on whether the context is the triumph of the Fordist factory or the predatory designs of globalizing Goliaths, there is a sense in which the theme of the imminent demise of diversity is akin to a recurrent structure of feeling as proposed by Williams.[28]

Things are always getting worse, and the cultural critic, like the despairing travel writer, can only report on a world that is about to lose its distinctiveness and leave us adrift in a "standardized world". Chris Bongie, discussing the terminal pessimism of Claude Lévi-Strauss's *Tristes Tropiques* on the future of diversity, observes,

> Dire visions such as these however, most often resemble each other not only in their pessimism but also in their propensity for deferring the very thing that is being affirmed: although humanity is settling into a "monoculture", it is at the same time still only *in the process of*, or *on the point* of, producing a "beat-like" mass society.[29]

There is no time like the present to tell us about all that is soon to be past. The attraction of the entropic, of course, is that it does away with the historic. Indeed, Thomas Richards sees the scientific origins of the concept of entropy as a convenient means of ensuring the end of history, "As a myth of knowledge, entropy, like evolution, would seem to place history outside the domain of human activity. Because it transfers agency from human beings to physical principles, it ostensibly represents a pessimistic relinquishing of all possibilities of social control."[30] So, are late modern English-language travel accounts on minority languages obsessed with threnodies of loss? Is the entropic the default condition for a politics of cultural despair?

When Mark Abley goes in search of the Native American language Yuchi he is taken by his informants Richard and Henry to the house of Josephine Keith, the youngest fluent speaker of Yuchi. As Abley explains,

> Yuchis, as ever, are harder to find. At last we crossed a bridge over Polecat Creek and turned hard right onto a gravel road that swung past farmland and juvenile woodland. Richard leaned forward and said, "We're arriving at the last household in the world where Yuchi is spoken every day."[31]

A historical analogue is provided by a story of Alexander von Humboldt being presented in Brazil with a parrot whose language no one could understand. The reason for this was simple. The bird spoke the language of the Atures people, and "[t]he Atures language had died out among humans. It was last heard coming from a bird's beak."[32] Australia, in Abley's account, is peopled by speakers of language, who in certain cases find that their only remaining interlocutor is a sibling living many miles away. Petro is frequently frustrated in her global attempts to find communities of Welsh speakers, and Drysdale's most common complaint is the vanishing traces of the languages she has come to observe. It is indeed the parlous state of minority languages that provides an ethical justification for travel as the writers repeatedly invoke the decline-of-diversity trope.

Abley quotes a remark by Massachusetts Institute of Technology linguist Ken Hale, "'Losing any one of them [languages] is like dropping a bomb on the Louvre,'"[33] to convey a sense of the scale of cultural loss as the result of worldwide language attrition. So what travels into languages become is a form of salvage archaeology, last dispatches from the frontiers of speechlessness. There are cases mentioned that frustrate the entropic momentum—Welsh, Catalan, Faroese—but they serve mainly to highlight the hopeless plight of the great majority of speakers of lesser-used languages. The overwhelming evidence points to imminent extinction.

POLITICS AND CULTURE

If the role of the travel writer is to report on the scale of the catastrophe, at what point does description cede to explanation or interpretation sideline dismay? Petro, Drysdale, and Abley all advance explanations as to why many languages are in an endangered state that involves everything from the impact of the logging industry to the social niceties of exogamous marriages. However, the accounts share a collective antipathy to forms of the political, which eventually places history outside the domain of human activity in keeping with the entropic paradigm. Abley, for example, notes, "I didn't go looking for politics. I didn't want to write about politics,"[34] but confesses that in the presence of Canadian Mohawks the subject was hard to avoid. Drysdale, discussing one of her informants, Madame Herault, claims, "Madame Herault was passionately Provençal, but it was culture, not politics."[35] Petro observes that in Lampeter in Wales, "To become a 'learner', I grasped early on, was to take a political stand. If you're Welsh, that is; I'm still not sure what it implies for Americans."[36] The reluctance to engage with the political is expressed in a canon of distaste where activism is duly lauded but militancy is always suspect. The difficulty is that the two activities are not always easily distinguishable, particularly for the traveler passing through, so that one community's activist quickly becomes another's fanatic.

When Drysdale finally crosses over the border from the Spanish Basque country into France, the relief is palpable: "I felt lighter myself, happy to leave a sombre, oppressive culture for something more frivolous, more chatty."[37] As with a later trip to Corsica, the environment is uniquely fore-boding, the sense of imagined violence darkening the perception of the people and the place. In Brittany, links are discovered between Basque sep-aratists and Breton autonomists. Petro, for her part, is ever watchful for an unwelcome political edge to her engagement with Welsh speakers abroad. In her encounter with Keith, a Welsh speaker in Singapore, physiognomy is the giveaway: "Keith's eyes narrow in a dangerous way when he says that England is economically prejudiced against Wales. 'Still,' he says, 'we'll have home rule in ten years, mark my words.'"[38]

In the absence of the political, the inevitable recourse is to a pseudo-anthropology of type. Thus, the subtitle of Drysdale's account is *Travels through Tribal Europe*, and when she describes the efforts of Corsican women to end political violence she bemoans the fact that, "as in Northern Ireland, ancient hatreds would continue to tear the place apart".[39] Atavism, not circumstance, becomes the driving factor in situations of language con-flict. "Ancient hatreds" firmly situate present-day tensions in the premodern and the prehistoric, where neither politics nor reason have a purchase in the maelstrom of emotion that compels the benighted prepolitical unit of the tribe to repeat the blood sacrifices of the house gods. With politics explic-itly disavowed, situation ethics gives way to a fine-boned morality that has the enlightened traveler prompt to condemn and less ready to explain. The failure is all the more striking in that power is often invoked in historical analyses but is conspicuously absent from contemporary descriptions of language tensions (a noticeable exception being Drysdale's description of present-day Belgium). As a result, hostility between minority and majority language speakers becomes naturalized into an essentialist predisposition rather than analyzed in terms of clear discrepancies of state power, eco-nomic resources, sociopsychological vulnerabilities, and so on.

When the reader is reassured that Madame Herault's interest in Proven-çal has to do with culture, not politics, the travel writer reveals a kind of culturalist credo that has become the common currency of many contem-porary encounters with the languages and cultures of others. That is to say, culture itself has assumed a foundational role in contemporary society. If, in previous ages, God or nature was seen as the ground on which all else rested for its meaning, in the postmodern age, it is culture that is summoned to the basement of epistemic and ontological coherence.[40] The sense that culture goes all the way down satisfies the essentialists who see culture as a set of immutable attributes passed from one generation to the next. Con-versely, the notion that anything can be understood as a cultural construc-tion cheers the relativists who can disassemble the handiwork of national chauvinists. The primary difficulty is that both camps explicitly or implic-itly subscribe to culturalist readings of social and historical phenomena that have the signal disadvantage of marginalizing structural questions in political discourse and analysis. In other words, whereas formerly racial or class difference was invoked to justify exclusion and inequality, it is now culture that is recruited to justify surveillance and marginalization. "They" are not like "us" not because they eat differently or dress differently or speak differently. The differentialist racism of societies becomes culturalized.

This is one of the reasons why a common response to the highly mediated and mythologized "crisis" of multiculturalism ("ghettos" as the sleeper cells of terror) is to focus on the cultural shibboleths of integration—notably, language and citizenship tests—designed to elicit appropriate cultural knowledge. Petro, Abley, and Drysdale indeed all give accounts of the attempts by governments in historically different periods to force language change as a means of shoring up citizenship claims most notably in the educational systems of France, Britain, Australia, and the USA. However, the point about citizenship tests is not that most British, German, Danish, or Dutch citizens would fail them. That is not what they are there for. The purpose is explicitly performative. The aim is to subject migrants to the public gaze, where the state can be seen to exact a particular form of linguistic or epistemic tribute.

What is crucial to note is that "integration" that is held up as the telos of the tests is not a static but a dynamic category, one that can be indefinitely reframed depending on the exigencies of the moment. That is to say, if the other becomes too well "integrated", if she enthusiastically embraces the language, institutions, and habitus of the host society, she becomes equally suspect as the "fifth column", the "enemy within" who dissimulates treachery through feigned assimilation. The sense of the labile nature of integration is inadvertently referred to by one of Petro's acquaintances, Liz Shepherd, a diplomat working for the British embassy in Thailand. Petro receives a fax message from Shepherd that reads, "'I did try Ambassador Morgan for you, but he's out of the country at the moment. Pity—he's a great character, and nationalistic in the nicest possible way'".[41] The ambassador has integrated into mainstream British, English-language culture, but "nationalistic in the nicest possible way" suggests acceptable levels of difference, a line not to be crossed that would trouble the always provisional, irenic prospect of integration.

The murderous forensics of anti-Semitism in European history fed precisely off the highly volatile reconfiguration of what it meant to be "integrated". Therefore, the question that might be asked is whether the "culturalization" of difference, deeply seductive to the practitioners of a literary genre like travel writing, is not complicit in a less than ethical depoliticization of the public sphere. As the social theorist Alana Lentin has noted,

> Many theorists, artists, musicians and writers have emphasised the fluidity of cultural identities. But without challenging the underlying reason for why culture dominates our understandings it is unlikely that

this will have a significant impact in the realm of politics and policy making. Thinking culturally about difference is the default for not talking about "race", thereby avoiding the charge of racism. But the need for such a substitute obscures the fact that the hierarchy put in place by racism has been maintained.[42]

In the instances of language suppression discussed by Abley in his Australian and North American travels, settler racism has clearly affected the fortunes of indigenous languages. However, it is Lentin's broader contention that thinking culturally about difference becomes a way for not thinking about all kinds of other things, and this is particularly pertinent to travels through the territories of endangered or minority languages. The axiomatic inclusion of language as a feature of culture, comparable to a local cheese or a distinctive wine, means that the speakers are almost invariably deprived of agency as there is no structural analysis in the present moment as to what it is they can do apart from withering away in their picturesque surroundings. In the words of the critic Seamus Deane, they have no option but to "stay quaint and stay put".[43]

COMMUNICATION

A difficulty faced by the travel writer who explicitly tackles the subject of language difference in travel is how to communicate that difference. The problem is compounded in the case of a dominant global language like English by ethical concerns around the imperialist pretensions of the language. Abley, as he moves through the language space of others, is particularly sensitive to the predatory presence of the language of his narrative, English. Comparing English to the Native American language Yuchi, Abley claims that "modern English is the Wal-Mart of languages: convenient, huge, hard to avoid, superficially friendly, and devouring all rivals in its eagerness to expand".[44] One of his informants in the Yuchi-speaking community, Richard, has an even darker reading of the Wal-Mart metaphor:

> "At Wal-Mart," he said, "you can still buy the stuff that smaller stores used to sell. Languages aren't like that. Languages are unique. English doesn't sell the other merchandise—it eliminates the other merchandise."[45]

Tourism, as Abley notes in the case of Welsh, is one of those practices that puts minority languages under even greater pressure. This makes traveling through the medium of English ethically problematic, as the traveler is less small store owner and more a part of the Wal-Mart sales force. Drysdale is explicit about the linguistic and ethical dilemma for the travel writer caught between the desire for contact and the reality of difference. In Greece, she wants to speak to a group of women foraging for edible leaves but does not know their language:

> For all my rejoicing in the diversity of Europe's languages, here I was faced with the reality of their exclusiveness. They rendered me frustrated, alienated, confused, physically handicapped. Not that this was the language's fault; it was my own.[46]

Language is crucial in establishing the types of contacts that are necessary to provide information and human insight for the travel writers. A global language like English permits global movement, but the ethical end stops are the perceived linguistic destructiveness of that global mobility (Abley on English-language tourism) and the real-world limits to the global reach of an international vehicular language (Drysdale in Greece).

It is partially in response to these dilemmas that Petro conceives of her travel project from a different perspective. Finding that as an American anglophone learning Welsh in Wales it was very difficult not to slip back into the dominant language, English, she resolves to travel the world to speak Welsh with other Welsh speakers. She chooses destinations where the other language is not English in the hope that Welsh will function as an effective lingua franca. In other words, in Petro's case, global travel is not to enhance the position of English but to bolster the status of Welsh. It becomes, in a sense, a search for a global solution to a local problem. The project is rendered problematic by her lack of full proficiency in the Welsh language and by the fact that many of the Welsh people she meets are either fully anglophone or are bilinguals who know more English than Petro does Welsh. However, even apart from the circumstantial difficulties of specific Welsh-language contact, Petro is forced to reflect on the nature of global language use and her position as a speaker of American English.

She notes that learning Welsh as an outsider, she has no "birthright antagonisms" and that, "I am most me, most American—enterprising, optimistic, composite—when I'm trying to anchor myself with words in someone else's home, and in motion all the time".[47] Off in search of Welsh, what she frequently finds are particular perspectives on English. She argues that she sometimes feels to be American "is to be blank, without a nationality or language" and she wonders, "Is this because America is such a polyglot culture that it contains pieces of everywhere else, or because American culture in the late twentieth century is so monolithic and transcending that it *is* everywhere else?".[48] At one level, what Petro articulates is the Wal-Mart dystopia of Abley, the transcendent, universal language that defines everywhere else. At another, she implies that it is the polyglossic background to American culture—and by extension, the language—that makes it uniquely poised to describe the world.

That this self-perception is not confined to Americans is evident in Drysdale's musings on cultural and linguistic difference where she claims, "being a typically British hybrid, I could never belong anywhere" and "perhaps it is that hybrid quality that gives the British—or at least the English—a natural dislike of homogeneity".[49] What is worthy of note is not the dubious sociolinguistic or sociocultural truth value of the claims but the construction of two major anglophone cultures as the sites of hybridity and openness, a construction precipitated by the conjoined experience of "motion" and language difference. In a sense, for all the paeans to language diversity, and notwithstanding a nervousness around the omnipresence of English, English emerges as more open house than closed shop. Paradoxically, travels by English speakers in and among minority languages tend not to diminish the status of majoritarian anglophone language and culture but serve instead to enhance it.

One means of capturing minority language difference in majority language narrative is lexical exoticism.[50] The communicative ambition of the majority language is tempered by the untranslatable residue of the minor. In northeastern India the Boro language provides Abley with a list of words that have no equivalent, which must be paraphrased, in English: "*onguboy*: to love from the heart, *onsay*: to pretend to love, *onsra*: to love for the last time".[51] It is the very resistance to translation that constitutes the unique identity of these languages and becomes a further argument for the importance of their retention and development. For Drysdale and Petro it is less the limits to translation that announce difference than the material presence of the other language. So the names of countries visited and subheadings appear in both English and Welsh in Petro's *Travels in an Old Tongue*, and Drysdale in *Mother Tongues* regularly includes excerpts from texts or isolated words in the languages of the regions she visits. Indeed, for Drysdale, the phonic substance of language makes it admirably fit for certain purposes. In Brittany, she notes,

> I bought a dictionary full of wonderful no-nonsense words like *gwinkal*, "to kick", *gortoz*, "to wait for", *didamall*, "blameless", *trimiziad*, "quarter". It looked blunt and humorous. It sounded not sophisticated like French or intellectual like German, but ancient, peasant like. It wore sabots.[52]

What is important is not so much the eccentric personification of language as the underlying commitment, present in all accounts, to versions of linguistic relativism. That is to say, languages are deemed to involve radically different ways of seeing the world, and even if the words have equivalents, the lifeworlds of speakers inhabiting different languages are inescapably various. It is the language itself that shapes the world in which they dwell. Therein lies the problem for the traveler sensitized to language. If languages do hold within them distinct worlds of experience and sensibility, then how much can the traveler be said to understand? Does the championing of language diversity and the celebration of linguistic uniqueness, a comprehensible ethical stance, deftly undermine any representational function for the travel account by suggesting, in fact, that what is essential about these worlds of communication cannot be communicated? It can be argued that what the language trails reveal is not the visual transparency of the globe but the linguistic opacity of its denizens. Like Steinbeck's companion, the only hope of late modern travel writers is to try and translate, then worry aloud about what ultimately gets lost on the way.

NOTES

1. John Steinbeck, *Travels with Charley: In Search of America* (London: Penguin, 1997), p. 7.
2. Michael Cronin, *Across the Lines: Travel, Language, Translation* (Cork: Cork University Press, 2000); Carmine G. Di Biase, ed., *Travel and Translation in the Early Modern Period* (Amsterdam: Rodopi, 2006); Loredana Polezzi, ed., "Translation, Travel, Migration," special issue, *The Translator* 12, no. 2 (2006): 169–88.
3. David Crystal, *Language Death* (Cambridge: Cambridge University Press, 2000).
4. Daniel Nettle and Suzanne Romaine, *Vanishing Voices: The Extinction of the World's Languages* (Oxford: Oxford University Press, 2000).
5. Pamela Petro, *Travels in an Old Tongue: Touring the World Speaking Welsh* (London: HarperCollins, 1997).
6. Helena Drysdale, *Mother Tongues: Travels through Tribal Europe* (London: Picador, 2001).
7. Mark Abley, *Spoken Here: Travels among Threatened Languages* (London: Heinemann, 2001).
8. Drysdale, *Mother Tongues*, p. 13.
9. Petro, *Travels in an Old Tongue*, p. 192.
10. Abley, *Spoken Here*, p. 174.
11. Drysdale, *Mother Tongues*, p. 832.
12. Abley, *Spoken Here*, p. 35.
13. Nicolas Bouvier, *L'Usage du monde* (Paris: Payot, 1992), p. 136.
14. Drysdale, *Mother Tongues*, p. 80.
15. Drysdale, *Mother Tongues*, p. 291.
16. Drysdale, *Mother Tongues*, p. 326.
17. Mary Louise Pratt, *Imperial Eyes: Travel Writing and Transculturation* (London: Routledge, 1992), p. 216.
18. Tim Ingold, *The Perception of the Environment: Essays in Livelihood, Dwelling and Skill* (London: Routledge, 2000), p. 211.
19. Bronislaw Szerszynski and John Urry, "Visuality, Mobility and the Cosmopolitan: Inhabiting the World from Afar", *British Journal of Sociology* 57, no. 1 (2006): 113–31.
20. Szerszynski and Urry, "Visuality, Mobility and the Cosmopolitan", p. 123.
21. See the Common Ground website, "Common Ground" <http://www.commonground.org.uk>.
22. Petro, *Travels in an Old Tongue*, p. 166.
23. Drysdale, *Mother Tongues*, p. 260.
24. Drysdale, *Mother Tongues*, p. 222.
25. Johannes Fabian, *Time and the Other: How Anthropology Makes Its Object* (New York: Columbia University Press, 1986), p. 35.
26. Drysdale, *Mother Tongues*, p. 383.
27. Charles Forsdick, *Travel in Twentieth-century French and Francophone Cultures: The Persistence of Diversity* (Oxford: Oxford University Press, 2005), p. 205.

28. Raymond Williams, *Politics and Letters* (London: New Left, 1979), pp. 156–65.
29. Chris Bongie, *Exotic Memories: Literature, Colonialism and the Fin de Siècle* (Stanford, CA: Stanford University Press), 1991, p. 40, emphasis added.
30. Thomas Richards, *The Imperial Archive: Knowledge and the Fantasy of Empire* (London: Verso, 1993), p. 103.
31. Abley, *Spoken Here*, p. 80.
32. Abley, *Spoken Here*, p. 206.
33. Abley, *Spoken Here*, p. 126.
34. Abley, *Spoken Here*, p. 182.
35. Drysdale, *Mother Tongues*, p. 20.
36. Petro, *Travels in an Old Tongue*, p. 95.
37. Drysdale, *Mother Tongues*, p. 201.
38. Petro, *Travels in an Old Tongue*, p. 166.
39. Drysdale, *Mother Tongues*, p. 257.
40. Terry Eagleton, *After Theory* (London: Allen Lane, 2003).
41. Petro, *Travels in an Old Tongue*, p. 193.
42. Alana Lentin, "The Problem of Culture and Human Rights in the Response to Racism", in Gavan Titley, ed., *Resituating Culture* (Strasbourg: Council of Europe, 2004), p. 99.
43. Seamus Deane, *Celtic Revivals: Essays in Anglo-Irish Literature* (London: Faber, 1985), p. 110.
44. Abley, *Spoken Here*, p. 56.
45. Abley, *Spoken Here*, p. 79.
46. Drysdale, *Mother Tongues*, p. 311.
47. Petro, *Travels in an Old Tongue*, p. 109.
48. Petro, *Travels in an Old Tongue*, pp. 165–66, emphasis in the original.
49. Drysdale, *Mother Tongues*, p. 389.
50. Cronin, *Across the Lines*, pp. 40–41.
51. Abley, *Spoken Here*, p. 124.
52. Drysdale, *Mother Tongues*, pp. 384–85.

2 From Legislative to Interpretive Modes of Travel
Space, Ethics, and Literary Form in Jean Baudrillard's *America*

Gillian Jein

I confess that in America I saw more than America; I sought the image of democracy itself, with its inclinations, its character, its prejudices and its passions, in order to learn what we have to fear or to hope from its progress.

—Alexis de Tocqueville, *Democracy in America*

Long live the Fourth World, the world in which you can say "Right, utopia has arrived. If you aren't part of it, get lost!", the world that no longer has the right to surface, the disenfranchised, who have no voice and are condemned to oblivion, thrown out to go off and die their second-class deaths.
Disenfranchising.

—Jean Baudrillard, *America*

This chapter takes the strands of space, ethics and literary form to engage with a shift in late twentieth-century travel writing, a shift that will be described here as a move from legislative to interpretive negotiations of alterity. The contextual frame is French travel in the US, while the more reduced focus of the piece is Jean Baudrillard's travelogue *America*. Baudrillard's imaginative geography forms the critical impetus for identification of this shift,[1] via which this article explores the interplay of spatial, literary, and theoretical dimensions in the text and how this interplay is indicative of an ethical tension between the social space of America—the material lifeworld of everyday contingency—and the poetry of the text's appropriation of that space.

In colonial and postcolonial scholarship, especially, postmodern travel writing has been criticized for the "othering" effects its abstract, textual dislocations potentially perform on the realities of everyday life.[2] Baudrillard's text has been dismissed out of hand as neoimperialist and symptomatic of what humanist critics such as Christopher Norris and Denis Dutton see as postmodernism's narcissistic and eschatological tendencies.[3] To take one example, Baudrillard's depiction of the desert has been accused of raising the specter of binary modernism, which critics see as proof of postmodernism's failure to allay its nostalgia for transparent sign-object relationships. Finally, the author's abstract locutions run the gauntlet of accusations as to the text's essentialism, its indifference toward minority groups in America, while the authorial voice cannot escape the banner of its white European intellectual inheritance.[4] In attempting to clarify and counter the virulence of such critique, this article distinguishes between legislative travel practices, which derive from a will to render legible the social space of the other purporting to function as a record of knowledge, and interpretive practices of space, which—in binding social space to the hermeneutic—reflexively engage in critiquing the possibility of a transparent record.[5] More particularly, what shall be addressed here is the double movement of Baudrillard's travel writing (and its dual accountability) that one might describe as a simultaneous movement of both content and form across the normative boundaries of liberal moral standards for representing the social space of the other. This movement holds in tension writing's potential to act as a record of the other, while at the same time Baudrillard's adoption of a poetic mapping consisting in irony, hyperbole, and aphorism suspends the possibility of this record's standing in for, or re-presenting, the other. Instead of record, what emerges from *America* is the self-reflexive, inverted position of the singular traveler's challenge to the categories via which we might pertain to know an authentic space that might be called "America".

Borrowing Zygmunt Bauman's terms *legislator* and *interpreter*, this double movement is articulated here in relation to a cultural shift engaged in questioning established discursive hegemonies for representing alterity. This shift is reflected in travel writing as the genre moves from a legislative modality, consistent with a narrative form that contains social space through established codified binaries, to an interpretive textual mode, a writing that reveals the contingent and constructed nature of these binaries through the use of reflexive literary forms.[6] Interpretive travel writing, then, can be considered as an emergent, self-conscious encounter with space, a representational form that recognizes the risk inherent in writing's pertaining to a transparent relationship with the real, its tendency to reduce and stabilize space. It is from this perspective, which moves away from a concern with the descriptive, that it becomes possible to reread the paradoxical poetry of Baudrillard's *America* as a critique of the legislative impulse to control social space, epitomized here in the exploration of the US as "Utopia achieved". The adoption of a poetic approach to alterity renders problematic the relationship between physical or "objective" space— the real—and the travel writer's translation of space into representational form. But it is not simply a matter of reinserting the subject into space— through this interpretive poetics the notion of space as an inherently stable entity existing a priori to cultural interference is itself cast into doubt. In a twofold move, therefore, the poetics of Baudrillard's form distorts not only the reader's potential to pretend to engage through this text with the "real" of America (a potential earnestly pursued in earlier travel writing on the

US), but, further, these textual strategies open a space of autocritique of Western value systems that presume the legibility of—and by implication, the possibility for—legislative coherence in social space.

To stay with this notion of "social space" for a moment, for many critics it is the absence of everyday America that leads them to classify Baudrillard's prose as amoral, "trite" or "frivolous".[7] If social space is understood as the arena of interaction, and thus where the travel writer engages in the ethics of relationships with the other, then the substance of Baudrillard's text, in the author's subtraction from the text of a "deep America of mores and mentalities" would seem to forgo any attempt at ethical exchange.[8] However, when the text is situated within the historical context of European writing on America, and given consideration as a transfigurative critique of Western value systems, we can ask whether it is not possible to see in this text a challenge to Western modes for legislating for the other. It is, I will argue, through the absenting of social life, and its interpretive literary rendering in the travel text, that there emerges a profound moral concern about what happens to social space in the era of the simulacrum. In this reading, Baudrillard's *America* exploits travel, both formally and ontologically, as a means to unravel the distinctions between the everyday and the ideological, while the paradox and amoralism of the text's distancing of American social life suggests a critique of impulses to account universally for that life.

The concern over the "othering effects" of "postmodern" travel writing and its seeming expulsion of the "everyday" stems from the ethical turn in travel studies—a turn that is itself inseparable from the legitimacy crisis of modernist epistemologies in general and the recognition of the discursive hegemonies at play in Western travel narratives. To date, the ethics debate in travel studies has evolved largely in relation to sites of colonialist expansion and postcolonialist aftermaths in an important effort by Western scholars to come to terms with the social, political, and cultural consequences of racial subjugation and empire. The theoretical frameworks for travel studies, therefore, have been in the main elaborated with the colonial and postcolonial contexts in mind. The result is that, along with the burgeoning critical interest in the discourse of travel, there emerges a sense of guilt on the part of the West with respect to its imperial past and a burden of responsibility on the Western writer that makes it difficult to write about travel without ensnaring the text in the discursive apparatus of imperial or neoimperial forms.

In the tradition of ethical debate dating back to Immanuel Kant, the paradigms that structure ethical discourse can be divided into two kinds of duty: duty toward oneself and duty toward others.[9] For the travel writer it is the latter that is of primary concern, where this duty toward others consists in her responsibility regarding the textual appropriation of others' social space. But what is this social space? Geographers identify three interwoven aspects at work in the production of what has been termed social space, and these categories are useful for considering the ethical implications of representations of travel. These categories include the cognitive (or knowledge of space), the aesthetic (representations and expressions of space), and the moral (interrelative space). It is to be noted that all three are qualitative in character, and social space is seen to emerge here through consistent negotiation between the ideologies, infrastructures, and institutions of the dominant and the contingencies of everyday life. Through its affectation to re-present space and its discursive negotiation of alterity, the travel text is actively engaged in the wider production of these cognitive, aesthetic, and moral aspects of social space. In that it is engaged in the subjective production of space, travel writing treads a fine line between the obliteration of otherness in terms that reduce difference or, at the other extreme, the distanciation of others through the exoticization of difference. Travel, as a departure from "everyday life", is an action that initiates dimensions of experience to defamiliarize the world, but the modes via which this defamiliarization takes place, or the extent to which the unfamiliar is permitted to endure, are neither ontologically nor discursively stable. The role played by travel writing in imperial contexts, for example, in bringing that which is foreign into the familiarity of language, is central to the discursive production of hierarchical systems. Thus the reproduction of tropes, stereotype, and the assumption of authorial transparency lay out not only the historical schema according to which another culture may be read, but cognitively—and, in the case of colonial expansion, empirically—map the spaces of everyday life in terms of sameness.

It is this encoded discourse that leads us to revaluate what is at stake in the poetics of travel writing within this formerly minor genre. Paul Smethurst, in his introduction to *Travel Writing, Form, and Empire*, suggests that examining "imperial form", in its particular literary manifestation as tropes, metaphors, and other representational practices, reveals how these devices were essential to the endurance of what Michel Foucault terms the "order of things"—those foundational structures of knowledge on which imperialist discourse was erected.[10] It is through this formal mesh that the discursive production of space in terms of Western binaries becomes visible, binaries such as self/other, the West/the rest, nature/civilization, and authentic/fake. These binaries work to stabilize the strange, to reduce the potential radicality of mobility inherent in the act of travel. Through binary action alterity is demobilized and codified in terms that render it legible in accordance with imperialist necessities. It is this act of codification that, to move the form beyond the colonialist context, will be referred to here as a *legislative* mode of travel writing. Adapting Bauman's term *legislative* to describe the tradition of the intellectual as social actor whose authority gains meaning from modernity's collective belief in the Enlightenment era's grand narratives of progress and universality,[11] the designation can also be used to describe the discursive apparatus that such a worldview produces in travel writing.

To rest for a moment with the cultural context in which Bauman conceives this legislative model operating, we can elaborate to say that this model operates on the assumption of a preconceived model of a collective order according to which the other can be described and, in the case of imperial operations, according to which the social system of another culture can be shaped and administered. Bauman observes that this position leads to the "establishment of a relatively autonomous, self-managing discourse able to generate such a model complete with the practices its implementation required".[12] This model of order and its discourse perform through Western ideological formulations, gathered together under Fredric Jameson's concept of the "grand narratives": a litany consisting in the autonomous subject, its truth, its freedom, history, teleology, progress, power, economy, and sex or, as Baudrillard would say, "all the *real*'s big numbers".[13] These epistemological strategies for making sense of the world have been sundered by the rise of theory, and reframed in travel writing critique as strategies for abstractly translating alternative cultural traditions in terms applicable to Western Europe—what the anthropologist Steve Tyler names as the Hegelian and scientific fusion of horizons, "which reduces all traditions to the shape and interests of Western discourse".[14] In aesthetic terms, this worldview is revealed through the literary modulation of other cultures as quantifiable, and made manifest in travel writing as an approach to space that seeks to render alterity legible. The aim in legislative travel writing is to re-present space in terms of a stable collection of locations, sites, and situations, with the effect that the space of social life is produced in terms relative to the same. The assumption of a transparent, coherent relationship between the code of language and the exterior world, or between the sign and its referent, works to immobilize space as it brings the meaning of alterity under control. This is a mode of writing travel in which, Smethurst states, "instability and potential disorder are necessarily suppressed within the knowledge structures that give *form* to imperialist discourse".[15] Legislative travel writing consists, then, in a mode of producing space that smoothes, frames, and strategically positions other cultures within the epistemological boundaries of sameness.

It is from here that the notion of legislative travel may be connected to the ethics of engaging with the social space of others. Legislating for another is only possible when the ground from which one speaks is epistemologically stable and connected to a hierarchical or "Archimedean" position from which to speak.[16] The legislator for Bauman epitomizes the authoritative position of the Western intellectual during the modern period, a position grounded in the belief, among others, that the world was knowable, that what was yet unknown would be known and that all cultural trajectories could be plotted along the moral axis of the West's progression toward the democratic ideals of freedom and equality. However, the ethical codes pertaining to such a system situate value on the basis of exclusion, those who are not yet in the fold of this form of social life merely need to be convinced of its "truth value", or else they are, by definition, morally inferior and should remain outside. In transferring Bauman's terms to the critical terrain of travel writing, the notion of an ethical code takes on a spatial dimension as interaction with others is linked to processes of rendering alterity legible, and the imposition of a cohesive order on alterity becomes indicative of a comprehensive, unilateral vision of the world. This is a form of travel writing in which contingency and instability are suppressed in favor of the paradigms of order and synchronicity. The legislative travel narrative corresponds to an ethical engagement with space in which the social, political, and cultural elements of elsewhere are written by means of formal operations that are primarily reductionist in their relationship to the external world. Put another way, this coding paradoxically allows travel to remain stable; mobility for the most part is rendered neutral through the application of epistemological or ontological frameworks that permanently assert the hegemony of ideological discourses of Western Europe's modernity.

The extent to which the West consistently reproduced knowledge discourses that reinforced its imperialist domination of other cultures is well documented by postcolonial scholarship. But these operations are also performed internally, and for our purposes, in Western European productions of the US. From the European discovery of America onward, Western European travel writing to the US is illustrative of paradigms consistent with a worldview as to the attainability of objective knowledge, the possibility of its effective, controlled, and ethically ordered distribution, and its movement toward the universality of rational—or, in other words, design-led—society. The most succinct version of this discourse is, of course, the reformulation in terms relative to Europe of American space as the "New World". As Rob Kroes expresses it, "America is never seen as purely *sui generis*, as constituting an alien entity to be fathomed in terms of an inner logic wholly its own".[17] Europe has been crucial in producing the discursive topography of North America and determining its position within a global symbolic order. European colonization, and the appropriation of this world as "new", was, in the words of Plinio Freire Gomes, an exercise in "blank variations".[18] The insufficiency of descriptive vocabulary and the inability to map unexplored territories exploded European horizons for knowledge, and America generated a "crisis of expression";[19] its cultures, cities, flora, and fauna defied description. The appropriation of the continent as "new" is a reinvention, a wiping of the slate, a vision allowing Western Europe to resolve and order this new space through the establishment of a geometrical and discursive plane via which native America might be stripped of all prior substance.[20] In the earliest travel accounts, America is the virginal terrain for Europe's regeneration, a model space where all desirable elements for society that were spatially and temporally dispersed across the Old World could be assembled in a single place, a blank conceptual space where Europe could start again. In the bid to cope with the unknown and to eliminate the threat which this great other posed to contemporary categories of knowledge, certain key binaries establish themselves as the modes for legislating for North America, the most common of which are the poles of old/new, ideal/pragmatic, history/ahistory, deep/superficial, real/utopia, modernity/primitiveness. In later accounts dating from the modern period, these dichotomies are again mobilized, although often, depending on the traveler's ideological position, the poles are reversed. Kristen Ross, in *Fast Cars, Clean Bodies*, explains this reversal in terms of a shift in the balance of Western powers, and the migration of American consumer culture to French shores. Ross argues that while imperialist France may have dominated the nineteenth century's imagination of civilization, in the wake of two world wars, the surety of such a position was called into question, and France found itself colonized by American Fordism and commodity culture.[21]

I will take two examples. Between the wars, Paul Morand, in *New York*, describes North American space in genealogical terms, where culture can be plotted as a diachronic trajectory—New York is the progeny of London, the child whose progress will determine the future shape of cultural life in Europe.[22] The poetics of Morand's text reveal the legislative tendency, identifiable most readily in the guidebook format, to reduce social space into comprehensively prescribed units. The narrative is atemporalized via Morand's synchronic cartographic division of his experience into the respective Downtown, Midtown, and Uptown zones of the New York grid. This text appropriates social space and wipes out its contingency by mapping it in terms of the rationalist spatializations of cartography. In 1945, with the advent of the nuclear society, Jean-Paul Sartre's American essays in *Situations III* negotiated American social life in terms of an ideological grid, and identified America as an ahistorical site, devoid of Europe's identity crisis.[23] In this account, the physical space of Manhattan's grid is metaphorically transposed onto the social space of America, so that the geometry of the map is transferred to social space as cultural conformism. While more aware of his relative position, American culture is generally legible for Sartre in terms of the triumph of conformity and the technocratic reductions of capitalism. In this account, the individual is in permanent thrall to a belief in the moral purity of the "American way of life". Within the narrative, the mapping of physical space onto social space produces culture as an abstract macrostructural force, and the singularity of objects encountered is made legible in terms of an ethno-ideology, a differential reading of Europe as worldly and realistic, within a logic that describes the US as idealistic and innocent.

These examples assert the modern tendency to exploit travel as a means to reach the essential, or the core of a culture, a tendency inseparable from travel as the quest for authenticity. And in turn it is this notion of the possibility of an "authentic" space that conditions the attendant production of alterity in narrative terms. As we have seen above, this quest is bound to the view that there exists an authentic, or collective, version of "America" that can then, under the right circumstances, be experienced and contained, decoded and re-presented. But this vision of a real "America" hinges quite paradoxically on a system of comparative dyads that traditionally haunt France's ideological battlefields, so that, in looking toward America, French intellectuals have sought to validate or invalidate an identity position built on a conception of Frenchness. As Kroes observes, "reflection on America as a counterpoint to European conventions functions within a larger reflection on Europe's history and destiny".[24] The representational mode that corresponds to this legislative version of authenticity is metonymy, a reading that moves directly from singularity to a generalized diagnosis of American culture as lacking depth, history, and wholeness. While the cultural contexts framing interpretation change, the ordered schema, or what the geographer Edward Soja calls "the lure of binarism",[25] consistently enables the travel writer to legislate for the reality of the US as coherent structure, imposing on mobility the stability of narrative order. In legislative travel writing on the US, space is constructed as empirically comprehensible in accordance with the relative, historical shifts in ideological location; a framework wherein social space serves as a quantifiable backdrop against which the narrative performs its coherence.

So far we have been arguing that centric perspectives have their own *poetics*, or formal means of operating, and their own *politics*—a relation, therefore, with social space that invests these perspectives in networks of power. Connecting the ethics of this power—its relative exclusions and hierarchies that work at the cognitive, aesthetic, and affective levels within social space—to the performance of legibility in literary form allows us to look beyond the explicitly political questions of travel writing and obtain a view of travel discourse as a means of producing social space. It is time now to ask whether a dominant regime of representation of such discursive appropriations can be challenged, contested, or changed and what the poetics of such a counterstrategy might look like. If the paradigms holding together the hegemonic site are order and reduction, then it would seem that what is called for is a strategy of language that destabilizes such a system, a form of mobility that might counter such reductionism. Smethurst puts the question another way when he suggests that "if we were somehow able to reinstall a proper sense of mobility, and use this against the imposed imperial (and narrative) form in European travel writing, it might help to deconstruct that form".[26] Such a language could not simply reposition the poles of hierarchy, however, for this, as Henrietta Lidchi has demonstrated, is to rest within the logic of stereotypical association and fail to get beyond the idealized unified striations of the discursive site.[27]

The question then becomes how to instill "a proper sense of mobility" into the travel text—a mobility that would, in a negative movement, threaten the discrete components of the legislative mode while also opening out the space of otherness without seeking its closure through legibility. The installation of mobility in textual form, what I refer to here as an interpretive mode of travel, necessarily involves a consciousness and a mistrust of the operations via which legislative meaning comes to establish the integrity of its ordered interiority.[28] Only from such awareness can Western travel discourse move beyond the representational modality reposing on the subject's presumed privileged access to attributes of sameness and constancy that might be applied universally. Contrary to this presumption, a self-conscious reflexivity potentially destabilizes the subject's integrity by undermining the transparency of sign-object relations, which now becomes a problem rather than an assumption. As Bauman states, "It has suddenly become clear, that the validity of an aesthetic judgement depends on the 'site' from which it has been made and the authority ascribed to that site; that the authority in question is not an inalienable, 'natural' property of the site, but something fluctuating with the changing location of the site".[29] The coherency of the site depends on the transparency of its meaning; however, it is precisely by rendering problematic the legibility of the relationship between the word and the world that an alternative space of mobility and poetic ambivalence is allowed to appear. It is from this perspective that we may read Baudrillard's travel narrative as an interpretive dislocation of the hegemonic discursive techniques associated with modern European travel writing.

The potential resistance identified by Smethurst in mobility's deferral of boundaries raises a series of problems, however, for the context of intra-Western travel writing. Not least of these is the philosophical conundrum of how to criticize the totalizing strategies of rationalism without such a criticism, emerging as it does from a site of Western privilege, creating its own elevated totality. The answer to such a question is beyond the more modest objectives of this chapter, which are to see in what ways Baudrillard instills mobility within coda of literary form, and what kind of spatial production emerges from such mobility. Nevertheless, the ethical implications of this spatial production engage with the questions of, first, whether or not Baudrillard's literary form, based as it is on mobility and executed through the techniques of paradox, aphorism, and hyperbole, erodes the solidity of this Archimedean point, and second, what kind of social space emerges from this form.

In *America*, contrary to restrictive analogy or a claim to authenticity, the reader encounters a reflexive rendition of the journey as a collection of signs, with writing synthesizing these signs along an open-ended trajectory, whereby cognitive and aesthetic spatialities of travel are arrayed in a manner similar to that of discrete cinematic scenes. In this scenario, the American landscape is inseparable from the effect which movement produces in its continuous assemblages of scenes that refuse the contained frames of narrative description, the detail of what Roland Barthes calls *l'effet de réel*, or what Baudrillard refers to here as the "snapshot":

Nostalgia born of the immensity of the Texan hills and the sirens of New Mexico: gliding down the freeway, smash hits on the Chrysler

stereo, heat wave. Snapshots aren't enough. We'd need the whole film
of the trip in real time . . . not simply for the pleasure of remembering
but because the fascination of senseless repetition is already present in
the abstraction of the journey.[30]

Contrary to the deep structures identifiable in the legislative mode, here
the journey is inscribed in an affective schema: travel does not illuminate
or facilitate connection to the real; rather, this mobility is seen as the inau-
guration of meaninglessness, a meaninglessness that is held up against
the representational containers of what Gilles Deleuze and Félix Guattari
have called "the classical book, as noble, signifying, and subjective organic
interiority (the strata of the book)".[31] The physical movement described
here, the speed of the motorcar, finds its aesthetic equivalent in cinematic
form—both of which allow for the removal of social space, the space of
others; and the screen becomes the dominant interface between the self and
the world. This opening section, then, prepares the reader for the mode of
defamiliarization that proliferates in this work, and which is the removal
of interaction with the contingencies of social America, the abstraction of
"human-made" space, in favor of a semiotic procession through a series
of depthless landscapes. *America* is a cinematic geography of hyperreal
spaces, and in distinction from a descriptive narrative accumulation aspir-
ing to the authentic, the text accumulates a hybrid collection of poeticized,
interpretive geographies screened in dialogue with a series of theoretical
observations that are closer in form to poetry than the systemic reasoning of this sociologist's disciplinary background. Adopting the logic of cinematic form, the entire text moves in a panning gesture from the deserts of
Death Valley to the lush college campuses of California, through the streets
of New York and along the Los Angeles highways.

To think about this panning gesture in ethical terms, mobility, and in
particular, speed bears association with superficiality; a means of exploiting
place that refuses the depth of everyday life in favor of a motion that sweeps
across the territory to leave behind a series of spatial impressions. These
binaries of fast/slow, superficial/depth have their corresponding traveler
types that can be identified respectively in the distinction between tourist
and traveler, whereby the former corresponds with the fast and superficial halves of the above dyads. It is Baudrillard's impressionistic mobility
that leads Caren Kaplan to equate him with a "tourist", and within this
equation to call his long-standing binary opposing Europe to America the
reproduction of an "exhausted paradigm". However, in distinction from
the case of the tourist, where haste functions in tandem with an essen-
tializing discursivity, to confine space to its picture-postcard equivalent,
Baudrillard draws on Paul Virilio's notion of speed as a means to achieve
disappearance. Unlike traditional formulations of the polarity in which
travel (as opposed to tourism) leads somehow to a more authentic experience of place, mobility is adopted in order to displace the notion of an

authentic, or real, America. Appropriating Virilio's theorization of speed as an essential factor in postindustrial spatiotemporal experience,[32] Baudrillard adopts the momentum of the motorway as his modus operandi for experiencing "America" and the semiotic conversion of landscape to sign, which this unending circulatory form of travel facilitates. This ontological mode of spatial experience, in its technological distortion of "organic" movement, finds its literary equivalent in the poetic devices that Baudrillard adopts to disrupt meaning. And this kind of incessant movement facilitates a practice of space that, in its dependence on vacuity for its perpetuation, creates an interface between the moving subject and the world, and when translated into literary form, becomes a means via which language becomes a form of strategic resistance to the systematization processes of Western value systems.

This abstraction from the "real" and from meaning is performed through the construction of a series of binary oppositions, framed in terms of what Barry Smart refers to as "Baudrillard's fatal comparison" of America and Europe.[33] Established on the common ground of modernity, Europe's attachment to ideological models for understanding history and progress is contrasted with America's disregard for such models and its pragmatic technological and cultural realization of modernity. Baudrillard's *America* is the realized epitome of Enlightenment models under the sign of reason, unencumbered by the consecutive crises of the self and the state of Europe's long nineteenth century. According to this model, America is the pragmatic realization of the conception of freedom formalized in Europe, but spatially materialized here for Baudrillard in the landscapes of the "New World": "For us, in Europe, it was the Revolution of 1789 that set its seal upon us, though it was a different seal, that of History, the State, and Ideology. Politics and history, not the utopian, moral sphere, remain our primal scene."[34]

In this scenario, the language of opposition seems to set up a quantitative measure via which both Europe and America can be judged, while at the same time the capitalization of "History", "State", and "Ideology" alert us to the narrative status of these modern containers of value. Furthermore, as we shall explore further on, the notion of America as utopia introduces the paradoxical trope via which Baudrillard's "fatal optimism" and an aporetic ethical space become discernable.[35] Poetic paradox intervenes further to dismantle the grounding of the binary model in scientific or quantitative language: "We are still at the centre, but at the centre of the Old World. They who were a marginal transcendence of that Old World are today its new eccentric centre. Eccentricity is stamped on their birth certificate."[36] The phrase draws on the traditional distinction of "Old" and "New", but instead of legislative difference, the juxtaposing of opposites "eccentric" and "centre" pushes, in paradoxical equation, at the boundaries of sense. Rather than performing to consolidate either of the social spaces of Europe and America, these poetic formulations of Baudrillard's prose enter to disrupt the potential coherence of this comparison to any type of reality, and it becomes clear that it is this very reality that is strategically being forced toward enigma and disappearance in Baudrillard's traveling:

> I went in search of *astral* America, not social and cultural America, but the America of the empty, absolute freedom of the freeways, not the deep America of mores and mentalities, but the America of desert speed, of motels and mineral surfaces. I looked for it in the speed of the screenplay, in the indifferent reflex of television, in the film of days and nights projected across an empty space, in the marvellously affectless succession of signs, images, faces, and ritual acts on the road; looked for what was nearest to the nuclear and enucleated universe, a universe which is virtually our own, right down to its European cottages. . . . I knew all about this nuclear form, this future catastrophe when I was still in Paris of course. But to understand it, you have to take to the road, to that travelling which achieves what Virilio calls the aesthetics of disappearance.
>
> For the mental desert form expands before your very eyes, and this is the purified form of social desertification. . . . The inhumanity of our ulterior, asocial, superficial world immediately finds its aesthetic form here, its ecstatic form. For the desert is simply that: an ecstatic critique of culture, an ecstatic form of disappearance.[37]

This quotation serves as an introduction to the myriad of possible ways to approach this text, and the ethical tensions that rest irresolvable in this regard. On the one hand, if we adopt a liberal humanist position, this enigmatic disappearing act can be taken as a dismissal of all interest in the social life of America, an antihumanist obliteration of the material conditions of everyday life. Read in this way, as an indifference toward the complexities of the historicosocial condition of US culture, one could argue, along with Kaplan in *Questions of Travel*, that this emphasis on the aesthetic and ecstatic form removes from view the discourses of minorities and other socially oppressed groups. Kaplan accuses Baudrillard's *America* of reproducing the parameters of "an exhausted paradigm"—namely, the opposition of a "deep" Europe to a "superficial" America—stating that this metaphysical binary is exploited by Baudrillard to the detriment of minority discourses emerging from the female, black or immigrant communities.[38] The problem with this reading, however, is that the very taking of a position with regards to a "description" of the realities of social oppression would reinstate the paradigms of resolution that the entirety of Baudrillard's later writings works to avoid.

As an entry point into the difficult ethical conundrums of Baudrillard's refusal of the social, it is worthwhile taking a brief moment to situate *America* within the broader concerns of Baudrillard's conception of the "real". From *L'Échange symbolique de la mort* (1976) onward, Baudrillard's writing abandons the scientific apparatus of sociology and introduces a poetic, interpretive quality to his prose, a poetic quality that, drawing on the reversibilities of Friedrich Hölderlin, Baudrillard develops as a twofold strategy. On the one hand, interpretive traveling is mobilized as a challenge to the legislative language of theory that remains within the systemic project of Enlightenment and that even in its dispensation of myths remains, nevertheless, attached to the vision of a perfectible world. Rather than describe, the traveler seeks to defamiliarize the world in order to bring to light the unintelligibility and terroristic character of this belief that all can be rendered familiar. Through the language of enigma, the silent communications of juxtaposition, contradiction, irony, and hyperbole, is intimated the interpretive complexity of the world. On the other hand, Baudrillard's work poeticizes the legislative language of theory, and in doing so interrupts the discursive operations that tend toward hegemony and the clarification of social space. It is this "perfect world" that Baudrillard seeks to inveigle with enigmatic prose, and it is this entire project of perfection, the West's belief in technoscientific perfection of social life, described elsewhere by the author as "fullness", that is collapsed here onto the cognitive, aesthetic, and ethical landscapes of America.[39] *America* adopts the interpretive modes of aphorism, parataxis, parable, paradox, enigma, ellipsis, and tropes of all kinds in an effort to coax the sociological inferential diagrams of dialectic and logic to the limits of sense. The potential of travel discourse to become a tool in the ideological hegemonies of the West, and an arm in its most favored instrument of domination—modern science—is overturned here as Baudrillard sets off in search of "astral America". Landscapes flash past, elaborated through a poetics of mobility in which travel becomes not only an ontological mode of movement but also a poetic mode of experience. "Astral America" is the real-and-imagined site, what Soja would describe as a "third-space", from which to undermine legislative modalities and their concomitant production of the West as universal sign. This landscape, then, must be understood as a real-and-fictional ground for a strategic game of resistance to both the stabilizing force of legislative language and "the perfect crime"—Baudrillard's term to describe the West's efforts to bring about perfection, and epitomized in the book by the "paradisic and inward-looking illusion" of California's university campuses. The emphatic modulations of the term *America* work to distance the attainability of an "authentic" space: "For me there is no truth of America"; "America is neither dream nor reality"; "America is a giant hologram".[40] This fictional terrain provides the basis for the "mutual volitization of the status of the thing and discourse",[41] and it is from the fictional ground that the affective, ethical concerns of Baudrillard's writing emerge.

In this light, the comparison between Europe and America, rather than work toward the production of a discrete reality that can be represented in European terms, induces these binaries to expose ironically the quantitative simplicities of their own reduction. The binaries of Europe and America as respectively historical/ahistorical, cultural/acultural, and idealist/prag-matic are reproduced here, but this is not a simple combination designed to render either space more legible. Instead these legislative simplifications are complicated by an interpretive poetics that successively strips statements of their comprehensive tendencies so as to harness these binaries toward an implied critique of those same legislative tendencies. In the section "Uto-pia Achieved", for example, Baudrillard discusses the differences between American and French multiculturalism. He begins by drastically simplify-ing the postcolonial situation in France, stating, "All that happened was a transferring of the colonial situation back to the metropolis, out of its origi-nal context."[42] As an abstract locution, this statement denies history and singularity in its neat erasure of the complexities of intercultural crossing in the postcolonial situation. Language obliterates difference here as it easily maps one complexity onto another and so refuses the identity of either. Sim-ilarly, in discussing American multiracialism the author talks of an "inten-sity born of rivalry" that creates a "converging energy", a "complicity" between races, which at the same time is marked by violence and banality.[43] This generality rests on the juxtaposition of contradictory values, just as it emerges in relation to an equally paradoxical contrast with French colonial-ism, and all are merged here in an ambivalence that refuses analytical ratio-nalization. Baudrillard lauds the lack of racism in America, for example, while his heteroclite combinations tempt the reader to condemn as racist the poetic rendering of such a complex object as human interrelations. At the next turn, however, Baudrillard warns against the notion of univer-sally legislating for culture, which when "abstractly formalized . . . devours singularity just as rapidly as revolution devours its children".[44] This state-ment not only removes the ground from beneath these other comparative strands but also, through its poetic transfer of revolution as a cannibalistic metaphor for universalism, renders logical response redundant. No sooner has the traveler teased the reader with an easy maxim than he speeds on to provide another aphorism that invalidates the first. The practices of this text, rather than producing knowledge, thus exploit the corrosive qualities of irony and the ellipsis of aphorism to short-circuit meaning.

Nonsense exploits the tangibility of the binary, but it also contains within it the germ of consciousness, and an awareness of the mechanistic means via which systems of representation work to determine meaning for social space. While this self-reflexivity works to draw attention to language, it also intervenes in social space in the form of hyperbolic cultural critique. The defamiliarization of the world enacted through travel writing as poetry seems to perform in terms of a strategic response to the full emptiness of social life under the sign of the consumerist West. In a twofold operation, movement displaces the ground of authenticity, while poetry encroaches upon the linear trajectories of prosaic language. Baudrillard clarifies his project elsewhere, noting that "to escape fullness you have to create voids between spaces so that there can be collisions and short-circuits".[45] These voids are created in response to a "real" that can no longer be understood in separation from its image, the meaning of social life is inseparable from its myths, and for Baudrillard a language that seeks to clarify the world merely demonstrates the power of the idea of perfection: "For reality asks nothing other than to submit itself to hypotheses. And it confirms them all. That, indeed, is its true ruse and vengeance."[46] Precisely what is problematic in terms of reading *America* as an authentic search for America is that, as Mike Davis points out, American space cannot be dissociated from its cinematic or simulated aspects.[47] In the same way that the quest for "*the* social" cannot resist the legislative patterns of theoretical language, this space cannot be extracted from the regimes of discursive tradition that have consistently appropriated it as the best and worst that Western civilization has to offer.[48]

And so traveling America is, of necessity, a traveling through the discursive terrain of the simulacrum, which Baudrillard elaborates elsewhere as the replacement of reality with the signs of reality, where the object always already enters the world as sign. In the culture of the media-saturated West, where the sign operates not in relation to any external reference but according to its own logic, to disguise the lack of the real, what we perceive as real is always at the same time the confirmation of a hypothesis. In this scenario, social space is no longer regulated by any kind of symbolic exchange that would order relations according to some transcendental "other" that would guarantee meaning; rather, what we are faced with is a system of sign-for-sign exchange, where the sign generates value within the logic of its own self-enclosed circulation. As Baudrillard describes it, "Everything is destined to reappear as simulation. Landscapes as photography, women as the sexual scenario, thoughts as writing, terrorism as fashion and the media, events as television. Things seem only to exist by virtue of this strange destiny. You wonder whether the world itself isn't just here to serve as advertising copy in some other world".[49]

America, then, if we are not to dismiss Baudrillard's "othering" out of hand, must be read as a "fiction about a powerful fiction",[50] and the West understood here as a space entangled in the successive raveling and unraveling of its own universalizing myths, which are the ironic bind of its community. In *America*, where "the cinema is all around you outside, all over the city",[51] the production of the social space of America is inseparable from media-saturated representations of social space. In terms of an ethical ground, therefore, what Baudrillard fictionalizes in America is the morality of neoliberalism and a systemic ideology that must expunge all that does not marry well with it. The "powerful myth" that Baudrillard engages is Ronald Reagan's vision of America, in which Cold War anticommunist rhetoric is collapsed into the perceived threat to the mythologies of American individualism. It is in the sections of the book "Utopia Achieved" and "The End of US Power" that Baudrillard's poetic traveling confronts the tyranny of systemic meaning, and paradox works to close down meaning in a strategy to undermine a value system that, in its efforts to eradicate the evil from the world, must become itself terroristic. Rather than prescribe an alternative position, Baudrillard merely asks us to consider what complete security, efficiency, and legibility would look like: "[W]hat kind of a state would be capable of dissuading and annihilating all terrorism in the bud . . . ? It would have to arm itself with such terrorism and generalize terror on every level. If this is the price of security, is everybody deep down dreaming of this?"[52] The consequence of such values result in "Utopia Achieved": this paradoxical conundrum, the placement of "no place", and how Baudrillard refers to the inexplicable persistence of a "moral hysteresis" in a society as diverse and secular as the US.

The full paradoxical weight of this semantic antagonism can be read in relation to Thomas More's *Utopia* (1516), the famous depiction of an island whose coordinates fail to be heard in the moment of a sneeze, on which evil is avoided and crime prevented. In More's account, of course, the meaning of u-topia, no-place, places this perfect society within the realm of the ungraspable. Utopia must remain self-contained if it is to remain pure, and evil cannot be tolerated if it is to remain good; in More's account criminals become slaves to the Utopians. In Baudrillard's appellation of America as "Utopia Achieved", perfection is made to clash with material realization through the confrontation of two antonymic signifiers. The resulting paradox performs within Baudrillard's much-used technique of reversibility, which can be seen as a form of poetic resolution to the determinism of the concept and the exclusionary operations it necessitates. Transferring utopia to the scene of modernity equates it with the modern belief—persistent in the early years of Reagan's presidency—in the West as the center of civilization, and in its rightfulness as the absolute model for the rest of the world. "The miraculous premise of a utopia made reality" is built on the belief in the universality of Western systems, technical and human:

> The Americans are not wrong in their idyllic conviction that they are at the centre of the world, the supreme power, the absolute model for everyone. And this conviction is not so much founded on natural resources, technologies, and arms, as on the miraculous premise of a utopia made reality, of a society which, with a directness we might judge unbearable, is built on the idea that it is the realization of everything the others have dreamt of—justice, plenty, rule of law, wealth, freedom: it knows this, it believes in it, and in the end, the others have come to believe in it too.[53]

But the clarity of these value systems, inscribed in the West's increased technoscientific efforts to bring about perfection and the correspondent belief in the attainability of complete order necessitates the exclusion of all that is other to it. In many of Baudrillard's books the brutality of perfection is expressed through a reversal of Hölderlin's famous maxim, "Where there is danger some Salvation grows there too".[54] For our period, Baudrillard notes, the poles must be reversed because in the face of the Western legislative tendencies toward security, prevention, and immunity, or "the fatal excess of positivity",[55] we can no longer tolerate being victims of fate or danger. What this excess is in danger of losing, however, is alterity and singularity, and so Baudrillard's reformulation reads, "But where what saves grows, there also grows danger".[56] It is the notion of an excess of reality, security, and efficiency that Baudrillard equates here to an achieved utopia. And this legislative world is necessarily a pitiless universe:

> If utopia has already been achieved, then unhappiness does not exist, the poor are no longer credible. If America is resuscitated, then the massacre of the Indians did not happen, Vietnam did not happen. . . . The have-nots will be condemned to oblivion, to abandonment, to disappearance pure and simple. This is "must exit" logic: "poor people must exit". The ultimatum issued in the name of wealth and efficiency wipes them off the map. And rightly so, since they show such bad taste as to deviate from the general consensus.[57]

It is here that Tocqueville's discursive appropriation of America as the supreme example of a "people" governed by a moral rather than a political outlook reveals its own reductive consequence. For it is within this logic that the obliteration of Native American culture can be understood as a "natural" result of the progression of a society toward democracy. However, as Baudrillard points out, Tocqueville never draws these two strands of history together; the purity of the concept necessitates the expulsion of its material consequence, and the linearity of language can allow these two facets—the theoretical and the empirical—to remain at a distance from each other, "as if good and evil had developed separately".[58]

In conclusion, Baudrillard's hyperbolic extension of social space to the realm of Utopia can be read as a poetic attempt to resist the banality of Western universalism. His writing is an effort conceived within the fatal optimism that "the more the hegemony of the global consensus is reinforced, the greater the risk, or chances it will collapse".[59] Baudrillard's "othering" is travel conceived as a poetic, interpretive reversal of the perfect crime of legibility, pushing language to the limit of hypothesis, so as to challenge theoretical systematization through the introduction of fiction into the containers of that system. *America* is an interpretive ground that in its accumulation of the othering effects of poetry opens itself out to moral criticism but at the same time silently points to a profound concern with how the idealization of social space, its quantification and marriage to legislative language, conspires toward the eradication of difference and alterity. It is an ironic performance of space as both real and imagined, then, an irony that tyrannically judges American culture as "banal" at the same time as it exhibits its complicity in this tyranny. Baudrillard's amoral, bombastic judgements open onto a reflexive space without offering an alternative model or an idea of social justice that would replace the simulacra that encroach on social space. But, paradox is at the heart of any attempt by a Western travel writer to form a coherent ethical model via which to approach alterity, for a coherent ethics would necessarily redefine the legislative ground. Baudrillard's traveling, in its conceptual acrobatics, performs ambivalence as a mode of resistance against the epistemological categories of legislative frameworks, to open onto an aporetic ethical ground. This ground emanates from the interpretive reflexivity of the text's literary form, a form that in its negotiation of America as utopia realized reveals all the more those exclusions, beyond "the interiorized space of language" that such paradox elides.[60]

Finally, there is no doubt that power remains in circulation throughout Baudrillard's text. But this power is not holistic or integral; it is not the power of imperial certainty, but the poetic agency that through its aphoristic mobility threatens the logic of mapping language onto social space, and reengages aesthetics in modalities of resistance. In this case we might conceive of how literary form might *perform* an engagement with alterity rather than work to estrange it. This is a way of thinking that challenges us to consider what Homi Bhabha describes as "a theoretical position that does not set up a theory-practice polarity".[61] In this light, Baudrillard's defamiliarization of America can be seen to recognize the problem of attaining to a language or to a position from which to speak about the realities of social space. In an interview with Sylvère Lotringer, he qualifies the relationship between theoretical appropriation and objective reality, saying, "As long as you consider that there is such a thing as a real world, theory has a place, let's say a dialectical position, for the sake of argument. The theory and reality can be exchanged at some point—and that's ideality. . . . But I hold no position on reality. . . . The real is not an objective status of things, it is the point at which theory can do nothing".[62] Baudrillard's traveling opens out onto the ground of otherness, and on this affective ground there shifts restlessly the fiction and aporia that if we are not to confine, control, or reduce can poetically shape ethical correspondence with the world.

NOTES

1. See Edward Said, *Orientalism* (London: Penguin, 1978).
2. See, for instance, Douglas Kellner, who sees in *America* the "decline of Baudrillard's theoretical powers and the collapse of social analysis and critique—as well as politics". Douglas Kellner, *Jean Baudrillard: From Marxism to Postmodernism and Beyond* (Stanford, CA: Stanford University Press, 1989), p. 170.
3. For instance, Caren Kaplan describes Baudrillard's *America* in terms of a "world-weary cultural relativism that masks an aggressive Eurocentrism". Caren Kaplan, *Questions of Travel: Postmodern Discourses of Displacement* (Durham, NC: Duke University Press, 1996), p. 100.
4. See Denis Dutton, "Jean Baudrillard", *Philosophy and Literature* 14 (1990): 234–38; Christopher Norris, *Uncritical Theory: Postmodernism, Intellectuals, and the Gulf War* (Amherst, MA: University of Massachusetts Press, 1992); and Kellner, *Jean Baudrillard*.

5. This piece follows Mike Gane's more nuanced categorization of Baudrillard's writing as both "counter-modernist" and "counter-postmodernist", and appropriates the text to examine the ethical implication of such modes of countering for travel writing. See Gane's response to Douglas Kellner in Mike Gane, "America, the Desert and the Fourth World", in *Baudrillard: Critical and Fatal Theory* (London: Routledge, 1991), pp. 178–92.

6. Zygmunt Bauman, *Legislators and Interpreters: On Modernity, Post-modernity and Intellectuals* (Cambridge: Polity Press, 1987).

7. Dutton, "Jean Baudrillard", p. 235; Kaplan, *Questions of Travel.*

8. Jean Baudrillard, *America*, trans. Chris Turner [1986] (London: Verso, 1988), p. 5.

9. Pia Søltoff, "Ethics and Irony", in Robert L. Perkins, ed., *The Concept of Irony* (Macon, GA: Mercer University Press, 2001), pp. 265–88.

10. Paul Smethurst, "Introduction", in *Travel Writing, Form, and Empire: The Poetics and Politics of Mobility*, ed. Julia Kuehn and Paul Smethurst (London: Routledge, 2008), pp. 1–18 (at 2–3).

11. Bauman, *Legislators and Interpreters*, p. 2.

12. Bauman, *Legislators and Interpreters*, p. 2.

13. Jean Baudrillard, *The Evil Demon of Images*, trans. Paul Patton and Paul Foss (Sydney: Power Institute, 1987), p. 46.

14. Stephen A. Tyler, "The Poetic Turn in Postmodern Anthropology: The Poetry of Paul Friedrich", *American Anthropologist* 86, no. 2 (1984): p. 328.

15. Kuehn and Smethurst, *Travel Writing*, p. 2.

16. See James Clifford, *The Predicament of Culture: Twentieth-century Ethnography, Literature and Art* (Cambridge, MA: Harvard University Press, 1988).

17. Rob Kroes, "America and the European Sense of History", *Journal of American History*, December 1999: p. 1135.

18. Plinio Freire Gomes, "Blank Variations: Travel Literature, Mapmaking, and the Experience of the Unknown in the New World", in Hagen Schulz-Forberg, ed., *Unravelling Civilisation: European Travel and Travel Writing* (Oxford: P.I.E./Peter Lang, 2005), p. 89.

19. Gomes, "Blank Variations", p. 96.

20. Gomes, "Blank Variations", p. 96.

21. See Kristin Ross, *Fast Cars, Clean Bodies: Decolonization and the Reordering of French Culture* (Cambridge, MA: MIT Press, 1995).

22. Paul Morand, *New York* (Paris: Flammarion, 1930).

23. Jean-Paul Sartre, "Villes d'Amérique", pp. 93–111; "New York: ville coloniale," pp. 113–24; and "Présentation", pp. 125–32, in *Situations III* (Paris: Gallimard, 1949 [1945]).

24. Kroes, "America and the European Sense of History," p. 1135.

25. Edward Soja, *Thirdspace: Journeys to Los Angeles and Other Real-and-Imagined Places* (Cambridge, MA: Blackwell, 1996), p. 60.

26. Kuehn and Smethurst, *Travel Writing*, p. 2.

27. See Henrietta Lidchi, "The Spectacle of the 'Other'", in Stuart Hall, ed., *Representation: Cultural Representations and Signifying Practices* (London: Sage, 1997).

28. See Richard Sennett, *The Conscience of the Eye: The Design and Social Life of Cities* (New York: Norton, 1990).

29. Bauman, *Legislators and Interpreters*, p. 135.

30. Baudrillard, *America*, p. 1.

31. Gilles Deleuze and Félix Guattari, *A Thousand Plateaus: Capitalism and Schizophrenia*, trans. Brian Massumi [1980] (London: Continuum, 2004), p. 4.

32. Virilio hypothesizes that new technologies from the motorcar to the airplane to the cinematographic camera produce hitherto unheard-of perceptions of

time and space that definitively alter humanity's relationship to the real. See Paul Virilio, *Esthétique de la disparition* [1980] (Paris: Galilée, 1989).

33. Barry Smart, "Europe/America: Baudrillard's Fatal Comparison", in Chris Rojek and Brian S. Turner, eds., *Forget Baudrillard?* (London: Routledge, 1993), pp. 47–69.
34. Baudrillard, *America*, p. 76.
35. Gerry Coulter uses this term to describe Baudrillard's belief and hope that despite the proliferation of systematization in the Western world it may collapse under the weight of its own excess. See Gerry Coulter, "Baudrillard and Hölderlin and the Poetic Resolution of the World", *Nebula* 5, no. 4 (2008): p. 146.
36. Baudrillard, *America*, p. 81.
37. Baudrillard, *America*, p. 5.
38. See Kaplan, *Questions of Travel*.
39. Jean Baudrillard, *Baudrillard Live: Selected Interviews*, ed. Mike Gane (London: New York: Routledge, 1993), p. 38.
40. Baudrillard, *America*, pp. 29–30.
41. Jean Baudrillard, *Symbolic Exchange and Death*, trans. Iain Hamilton Grant (London: Sage, 1993), p. 235.
42. Baudrillard, *America*, p. 82.
43. Baudrillard, *America*, p. 82.
44. Baudrillard, *America*, p. 83.
45. Baudrillard, *America*, p. 38.
46. Jean Baudrillard, *The Perfect Crime*, trans. Chris Turner(New York: Verso, 1999), p. 99.
47. As Mike Davis states, "The ultimate world-historical significance—an oddity—of Los Angeles is that it has come to play the double role of utopia *and* dystopia for advanced capitalism. The same place, as Brecht noted, symbolized both heaven and hell". Mike Davis, *City of Quartz: Excavating the Future in Los Angeles*, 2nd ed. (New York: Vintage, 1992), pp. 19–20.
48. See note 6 in chapter 1 for more detail on the etymology of the word. A thorough investigation of the intellectual traveler and postmodern America is beyond the scope of the current chapter, and indeed merits further research. For an exploration of utopia and America, see David H. T. Scott, *Semiologies of Travel: From Gautier to Baudrillard* (Cambridge: Cambridge University Press, 2004), chap. 4. In *City of Quartz*, Davis elaborates on critiques of Los Angeles within the noir genre and demonstrates how the city was (and still is) a terrain of fervent cultural debate.
49. Baudrillard, *America*, p. 32.
50. Coulter, "Baudrillard and Hölderlin", p. 152.
51. Baudrillard, *America*, p. 56.
52. Jean Baudrillard, *Fatal Strategies: Revenge of the Crystal*, trans. Philip Beitchman and W.G.J. Niesluchowski (New York: Semiotext(e), 1990), p. 22.
53. Baudrillard, *America*, p. 77.
54. Friedrich Johann Hölderlin, "Patmos," in *Hölderlin: Poems and Fragments*, trans. Michael Hamburger (Oxford: Alden, 1990), p. 39.
55. Jean Baudrillard, *The Illusion of the End*, trans. Chris Turner (London: Polity, 1994), p. 49.
56. Jean Baudrillard, *The Vital Illusion*, ed. Julia Witwer (New York: Columbia University Press, 2000), pp. 80–81.
57. Baudrillard, *America*, p. 111.
58. Baudrillard, *America*, p. 88.
59. Jean Baudrillard, *The Gulf War Did Not Take Place*, trans. Paul Patton (Bloomington: University of Indiana Press, 1995), p. 86.

60. Baudrillard, *Symbolic Exchange and Death.*
61. Homi K. Bhabha, *The Location of Culture* [1994] (London: Routledge, 2010), p. 257.
62. Jean Baudrillard and Sylvère Lotringer, "Forgetting Baudrillard" (interview), *Social Text* 15 (1986): 140–41.

3 Fiction and Affect
Anglophone Travel Writing and the Case of Paraguay

Corinne Fowler

Travels Without My Aunt misunderstands everything about my country. It misses the whole point, the Paraguayan culture itself, where everything's going.[1]

—Javier Valiente Cabrera,
note penciled in the margin of Julia Llewellyn Smith's,
Travels Without My Aunt: In the Footsteps of Graham Greene

In a chapter of Claire Lindsay's insightful study titled *Contemporary Travel Writing of Latin America*, she questions an assertion by Debbie Lisle that the genre of travel writing remains stubbornly colonial. One of the grounds for Lindsay's interrogation is that Lisle has overlooked "a broader and more subtle consideration of form in contexts beyond the anglophone tradition with which she engages".[1] Lindsay's criticism is fully justified on one front: monolingual approaches to travel impede access to the fullest range of scholarship.[2] Usefully, though, Lindsay's observation highlights a tendency of postcolonial criticism to characterize the anglophone tradition as more colonial than its Francophone and Spanish-language counterparts. The prognosis for contemporary anglophone travel writing has tended to be gloomy at best. Especially for critics writing at the cusp of the twenty-first century, notably Steve Clark, Patrick Holland, and Graham Huggan,[3] contemporary anglophone writing seemed incapable of shrugging off its colonial legacy.[4] This pessimism has persisted despite extensive investigations into travel writing's capacity for formal experimentation and reflexivity, particularly in the context of late twentieth-century capitalism.[5] Yet, as Lindsay herself asks, surely travel writing is not always already "one way traffic", as Clark asserts?[6]

Clark's sense of "one way traffic" rests on the principle that "Europeans mapped the world rather than the world mapping them."[7] There is a lingering suggestiveness about Clark's allusion to transformational cultural remappings. In the past decades, processes of transformation have been the subject of sustained scholarly inquiry into anglophone travel writing's historically variegated relationship to various contexts of imperial domination.[8] With an eye on emerging lines of inquiry into areas such as political tourism and fictocritical travel writing,[9] now seems a good moment to revisit some of the English-language contexts in which contemporary travel writing is being produced. Are *anglophone* and *postcolonial* mutually exclusive categories when it comes to travel writing? If not, which form(s) might such narratives adopt?[10] Above all, how might fiction help or hinder this process?

TRAVEL WRITING ABOUT PARAGUAY, 1825–PRESENT

Paraguay presents very particular challenges for travel writers. Generations of European and Australian travelers, and a handful of fiction writers, have projected a range of anxieties about modernity and social disorder onto Paraguay. Most recently, too, travel writing has registered concern about environmental crisis and international terrorism. As with travel narratives about other Latin American nations, this practice of projection has typically provoked a corresponding neglect of Paraguay's cultural and material dimensions.[11] In many respects travel writing about Paraguay has much in common with dominant depictions of the entire region. Governed for centuries by the paradigm of expansion and exploration,[12] travelers to Paraguay have been preoccupied with the prospect of hidden cities of gold in landscapes often menaced by potentially cannibalistic indigenous peoples.[13] This preoccupation gives rise to a salient feature of anglophone travel narratives about Latin America more generally—namely, a persistent lack of "affective identification" with the region's inhabitants.[14] Paraguay specialists Jennifer French and Thomas Wigham assert that expressions of affinity with Paraguayans are strikingly absent from narratives about the country.[15] More specifically, they direct this charge at British travel writer John Gimlette, whose book *At the Tomb of the Inflatable Pig* is discussed at length below.[16] Gimlette's recent blog post seems to more than justify French and Wigham's concern. He writes:

> [I]t's interesting to think that a few copies of [*At the Tomb of the Inflatable Pig*] . . . will make the long voyage back to Asuncion [Paraguay's capital city]. [O]nly about a thousand Paraguayans will know what to do with it—the other five million find books either beyond their range of experience or just plain pointless . . . those bits that are bound to horrify (the bloodiest war in the history of mankind, cannibalism and the murderous piranhas) will elicit little more than a shrug. "That's the way it is", they'll say.[17]

Given Gimlette's depiction of this Central South American nation as "conjur[ing] up everything exotic and extreme in South America . . . hellish jungles, dictators, fraudsters and Nazis",[18] his sparse Paraguayan readership is perhaps little to be wondered at. A key challenge for travel writers, then, is to contrive new forms with the capacity to enact the kind of narrative manoeuvres that can promote more reflexive accounts of mutual engagements between European travelers and Paraguayans.[19] Quoting Judith Butler, Lindsay similarly draws attention to a widespread absence of "solidaristic and compassionate values" in the anglophone world, identifying this as a dominant trait of much contemporary anglophone travel writing about Latin America.

As Kevin Foster points out in his shrewd study titled *Lost Worlds: Latin America and the Imagining of Empire*, any researcher into the representational patterns of anglophone travel narratives risks "replicating the very cultural trope that it critiques—the wilful or accidental disappearing of Latin America".[20] Worse still is Terry Eagleton's contention that imagology is "not the most fertile of intellectual furrows".[21] Notwithstanding these risks, attention to the salient features of travel writing about Paraguay makes it possible to envisage, and evaluate, the potential role of fiction in promoting the kind of "affective identification" that such a setting demands.

Key textual influences on contemporary anglophone travel accounts are Richard Southey's long poem *A Tale of Paraguay*, which is focused on the Jesuit Reducciones, or missions, in the eighteenth century. The Reducciones developed into a self-financing, self-regulating protectorate for the Tupi-Guarani peoples and reflected a vision of society that intrigued and inspired subsequent generations of travelers. Despite Southey's status as poet laureate, his poem fell into obscurity soon after its publication in 1885. Another writer interested in the Jesuit Reducciones is Cunningham Grahame, whose book *A Vanished Arcadia* was published in 1901. Paraguay's tragic wars have attracted some well-known figures, notably Richard Burton, who wrote *Letters from the Battlefields of Paraguay* (1870). Joseph Conrad's novel *Nostromo*, set in the fictional Costaguana and generally acknowledged to be based on Paraguay,[22] was published ten years later in 1904; Wilfred Barbrooke Grubb's *A Church in the Wilds* (1914) features extensive land clearances in Paraguay's Chaco region. Paraguay attracted conservationists too; Gerald Durrell's 1956 *The Drunken Forest* was swiftly followed by David Attenborough's *Zooquest in Paraguay* (1959). Graham Greene's *Travels with my Aunt* was published a decade later in 1969.

This chapter refers to a number of the texts listed above, focusing primarily on their presence in the narratives of three contemporary British travel writers: Julia Llewellyn Smith, John Gimlette, and Robert Carver.[23] Greene's 1969 novel inspired the cannily marketed title *Travels without My Aunt: In the Footsteps of Graham Greene* by Julia Llewellyn Smith, an in-the-footsteps narrative that relies on Greene's novel to distil, and substantiate, a number of familiar tropes about Paraguay related to smuggling and drug dependency. Gimlette's writerly *At the Tomb of the Inflatable Pig* was well received by critics, as was Carver's *Paradise with Serpents: Travels in the Lost World of Paraguay*, in which—as Sara Wheeler writes— Carver "sets himself up as a weedy English male of the central casting variety".[24] All three travelers follow a distinctive itinerary inspired by their predecessors' fascination with the Jesuit Reducciones and Paraguay's numerous utopian settlements. Prolonged stays in Asunción's Gran Hotel are followed by trips to the capital city's tourist office (which is always empty), the British Embassy, Eastern Paraguay, and the Gran Chaco, more or less in that order. Home to many indigenous groups, Paraguay's arid Gran Chaco region provides a major pretext for depicting Paraguay as the ultimate anti-touristic destination.[25]

PROJECTING NORTHERN EUROPEAN AND AUSTRALIAN CONCERNS ONTO PARAGUAY

> One simple truth about the Southern Hemisphere is that [. . .] [t]he South is simply less ruined, less used up, less degraded by the constant crush and press of humanity.[26]

As Foster notes, for many English-speaking travelers, Latin America has provided the ideal arena for examining issues arising from "the extension, consolidation and recession of empire".[27] Latin America has enabled travelers to engage in a form of cultural critique, identifying the shortcomings of their own nations and conceiving of alternative social formations.[28] This is demonstrably the case with Paraguay, which has long triggered British and Australian national self-scrutiny as well as a focus for concerns about global overpopulation, climate change, and Western styles of governance. However, far from providing what Thomas Phillips and Foster have each described as "a blank space on the mental map of the west",[29] Paraguayan sites of travel are crammed with contradictory representations, having repeatedly figured as Eden, Arcadia, Greeneland, and El Dorado.[30]

English-speaking travelers to Paraguay have become increasingly conscious of the genre's colonial legacies. The main textual response—as opposed to a sustained textual strategy—has been to dedicate significant portions of their narratives to chronicling common portrayals of the country. The effect is to reiterate, and reinforce, the preoccupations of earlier travelers, albeit in the parodic manner associated with the traveler's sense of belatedness.[31] As a consequence, the representative practices of earlier generations continue to set the discursive agenda. Meanwhile, neglected aspects of Paraguayan experience, particularly migrant labor, contemporary politics, and popular culture,[32] are submerged beneath a vast sea of northern European and Australian concerns. Above all, the idea persists that Paraguay is "South America's Last Frontier"[33] against consumerism, overpopulation, climate change, and touristic incursion.[34] A major hurdle, then, is the production of Paraguay as a backdrop to unfolding crises elsewhere.

PARAGUAY AS EDEN AND ARCADIA

> It was stated and indeed proved that the Garden of Eden was in this
> place, in the centre of the New World, the heart of the Indian conti-
> nent, a real, physical and actual place, and that here man was created.
> Any of these trees might have been the trees of life.[35]

In 1656, a Spanish colonial administrator named Antonio de Leon Pinelo
published a religious tract titled *Paradise in the New World*, in which he
declared that heaven was located in the South American territory that was
to become Paraguay.[36] Part of this territory would later be incorporated
into the seventeenth- and eighteenth-century Jesuit Reducciones. Two early
travel accounts were instrumental in establishing Paraguay's Edenic creden-
tials: Father Martin Dobrizhoeffer's 1784 account of the country's equestrian peoples and Cunningham Grahame's *A Vanished Arcadia* (1901).[37]
The former was a source of inspiration for Robert Southey's *A Tale of
Paraguay*, which represents the country as a pre-industrial idyll:

> There, and there only, hath a peaceful lot
> Been granted, by Ambition troubled not.[38]

The sense of nostalgia conveyed by the phrase "There, and there only"
establishes Paraguay's role as a symbolic counterpart to Southey's native
Britain, which—as Foster observes—was by then in the throes of industrial revolution and indeed troubled by a working class in the clutches of
"Ambition".[39] Paraguay's Edenic qualities are communicated by its "full
supply of fruitage now mature".[40] In the sinister world of Southey's poem,
however, Paraguay's Edenic status is predicated on a bout of ethnic cleans-
ing by a rival tribe, the survivors of which are protected by the Jesuits.[41]
As Foster points out, industrialization—coupled with growing awareness
of imperial excesses—reignited sixteenth-century debates that had been
inspired by Thomas More's *Utopia*.[42] Foster observes that such debates
have underscored subsequent *nineteenth*-century quests for utopia.[43] As
he argues, *A Tale of Paraguay* is not so much about the Jesuits as about
fear of working-class protests against the hardships associated with industrialization.[44] For Southey, as for so many others, the Jesuits represented
a benevolent social order yet one that depended on the Guarani knowing
their place and "not desiring to engage/Upon the busy world's stage".[45]
Pursuing his argument further, Foster considers the symbolic significance
of the Reducciones for Graham, a far more egalitarian thinker than the
reactionary Southey. The missions enabled Graham to reflect on British
social reform around the time his narrative was published at the turn of the
twentieth century. However, Graham was not so much fascinated by the
missions' success as haunted by their ultimate failure. Although the Jesuits
amassed considerable wealth, Graham's *A Vanished Arcadia* applauds their

prioritization of moral, spiritual, and social concerns over those of profit. As Foster observes, however, Graham's narrative is particularly attentive to telling details of paternalism, such as the "twelve pairs of fetters" left behind in the ruins, offering a critique that hints at the seeds of the missions' destruction. Foster concludes that the failed missions had a critical role in fueling Graham's growing pessimism about another imperiled vision of utopia associated with European debates:

> Disillusioned by the orthodox endorsement of imperial expansion and assurance that the capitalist economy would help wean the ignorant millions from their horrid ways, Graham reached out to the Jesuit Missions of Latin America for evidence that a better way of living once existed. Yet all he finds there are echoes of his present-day disenchantment. . . . In the Jesuits' doomed defence of collaboration over competition, happiness over self-enrichment, fellowship over exploitation, Graham identifies . . . a doomed precursor of the socialism that he and other like-minded activists were struggling to bring into being.[46]

In the wake of travelers' sustained fascination with the Reducciones, John Gimlette's narrative similarly presents Paraguay as "the heart of Arcadia",[47] where "food flops . . . from cassava and orange trees . . . [and] the idea of sustenance without effort ha[s] always been appealing".[48] The concept of unearned plenty informs a related discourse—present in all contemporary writing about Paraguay—about lazy citizens, a discourse that draws on well-worn myths about "lotus eat[ing]" natives.[49] Indeed, contemporary travelers dwell almost obsessively on lotus eating and oranges, a fascination that partly derives from the writing of Graham Greene, whose 1968 *Sunday Telegraph* article demonstrates the connection between flopping fruit and Odyssean lotus eating.[50] Greene describes Paraguay as a "land of deep tranquillity . . . where windblown oranges lie ungathered along the country roads. . . . What price . . . is the lotus-eater prepared to pay for his tranquillity?"[51] Ever conscious of his forebears, Carver similarly draws attention to this trope. In the following passage, he relates "the well-worn tale of coming across abandoned orange groves, with the fruit lying at the base of the tree",[52] stumbling soon afterward upon the same archetypal scene: "here they were, all around the deserted Franciscan retreat, orange trees with fruit everywhere, on the branches and on the ground, rotting away".[53] However, as a textual response to these tropes, the passage pursues the discursive agendas of his predecessors. Carver and others draw heavily on notions of lotus eating by seizing on Paraguayans' enthusiasm for *terere* drinking,[54] a custom that commonly serves as a symbolic substitute for lotus eating.[55] In her travel narrative, Llewllyn Smith writes about Paraguayan sloth in the same vein as *Travels Without My Aunt*: "the concept of overtime does not exist in Paraguay and everything stops at four."[56] When I asked Asunseño Javier

Valiente Cabrera to read and comment on Llewllyn Smith's narrative, he penciled the following response into the margin: "she sees one person stopping at four and generalises the practice to all Paraguayans!"

It would not be possible or even helpful to detail here each and every northern European and Australian anxiety that underlies travelers' interest in Paraguay as a utopian location. However, I will briefly discuss the most recent trends in contemporary narratives, beginning with the following passage from Carver, whereby Paraguay figures as the final frontier against climate change:

> It was a real pleasure just to sit in a cane chair outside my room look-ing at and listening to the birds . . . [t]iny hummingbirds . . . rainbow coloured with iridescent green the dominant shade, hovered and darted by a hibiscus plant, long thin beaks moving inside the flowers to search for drops of water or nectar. I would sit for timeless periods, completely enraptured . . . drinking in this tranquil atmosphere. Overpopulation, pollution, the depleted environment are realities of our era; to come to . . . Paraguay was to realise how much ha[s] been lost.[57]

The reviewer Martin Davies is accurate in identifying Carver's narra-tive as offering "a vision of the Old World seen from the New".[58] Carver laments the planet's overpopulation from his deep repose within Edenic Paraguay. It is hard to agree, however, with Davies's subsequent conten-tion that viewing Europe through a Paraguayan lens "puts this book into a mould-breaking category".[59] On the contrary, journeys through Paraguay have allowed travelers to reflect critically on the Old World since the late nineteenth century.

Since their earliest European fictional representation in Voltaire's 1759 *Candide*,[60] the Jesuit Reducciones have provoked historically and ideologi-cally varied national introspections by Australian and European travelers.[61] Contemporary travelers have very much remained in dialogue with their predecessors about the Reducciones' symbolic significance. Though Gim-lette and Carver in particular have very modern takes on the missions' contemporary resonance, their discussions proceed along the tracks of their forebears. Despite their consciousness of being "heirs" to the utopian tradition,[62] the result is to produce variations on the same utopian theme. Gimlette consciously frames his account of a visit to the missions at Trinidad with the travelogue of Cunninghame Graham, from which he quotes liber-ally. Joking at the apparent incongruity of Graham's serene Guarani work-ers and the "Scottish labour party, all raw faced and tweedy",[63] Gimlette highlights what he sees as the naïveté of Graham's depiction of contented workers. He is also concerned with overturning Graham's sense that the Jesuits were indifferent to material concerns. With nothing but the "swish of grass" for company, then, Gimlette surveys the "great urban experi-ment" through which the Jesuits "watch[ed] as their neophytes turned the estates to profit".[64] This skepticism is not limited to the Jesuits, however, but extends to religious belief more generally. As he leaves the mission at Trinidad, he makes the following request to the waiting taxi driver: "Can you take me to Jesus?" "Jesus" is the name of another Jesuit mission, and the reader is reassured that "this was no plea for salvation".[65] It is a small detail, yet it indicates Gimlette's self-presentation as a time traveler from a thoroughly secular future where, at least in his mind, both religion and socialism have become anachronistic. Book-ending the twentieth century, then, Graham and Gimlette's narratives provide oblique commentaries on the respective failures of socialism and religion. However, while Graham anticipates and laments the impending decline of socialism, Gimlette's retrospective gaze at its demise is far more sanguine: "As I surveyed the great orange shell of Jesus, it was hard to feel pity . . . I console myself that had Graham lived to see more of the twentieth century and the epidemic of Utopias, he might have felt differently".[66] Despite the apparent detachment of these postmodern musings among the red sandstone ruins of the missions, however, the introduction to *At the Tomb of the Inflatable Pig* registers anxiety at the rise of yet another brand of utopianism with particular contemporary resonance: political Islam. Gimlette's narrative mourns the fall of a final frontier (as travelers have consistently perceived Paraguay) against the ugliness of the new world order defined by the terrorist threat and the War on Terror. This is apparent in the following framing analysis at the beginning of the travelogue:

> There was once a time when the ripples made by world events took many months to reach Asunción. Now the ripples come faster and faster. At least two Paraguayans were killed in the World Trade Centre outrage and the country accuses its most easterly city [Ciudad del Este] of being a focal point for Islamic extremism.[67]

There is nothing new about travelers asserting that they have boldly experienced what no traveler ever can again. However, the contemporary preoccupation with Paraguay as a final frontier is umbilically connected to utopian projects in general and the missions in particular.

Carver has his own take on the Reducciones. No socialist travel narrative, *Paradise with Serpents* draws parallels between supposedly passive Guarani people and the British welfare state:

> I thought of the Jesuit *Reducciones* often—a lost paradise, a paternalist closed system, a theocratic state: but most of all I thought of it as a precursor of the modern world, where the state, through its administration, herds the population, treating them as cattle, to be organised and milked, kept in good health and prevented from hurting themselves . . . The highest virtue in the modern European state is blind obedience to government direction: the loss of initiative, enterprise and sheer verve for living.[68]

In its function as an antidote to deadened senses and to Carver's notion of Britain's health, safety, and welfare culture, Paraguay is, once again, eclipsed by domestic concerns. A considerable portion of both Carver's and Gimlette's narratives are devoted to failed utopian visions to which Paraguay has played host. In their sense of fascination and amusement at these doomed ventures, which Gimlette repeatedly describes as "unedifying", each travel book stops short of exploring alternative modes of understanding and representing Paraguay.[69]

As the title of Carver's *Paradise with Serpents* implies,[70] the utopian coin has its flip side. Reflecting the disillusionment brought about by so many failed utopias, Paraguay's very topography is rendered in binaristic terms. While Eastern Paraguay is represented as Eden, the Chaco is generally represented as a "Green Hell". In the following passage from Gimlette, the *Rio Paraguay* symbolically slices the landscape into two symbolic opposites:

> Eastern Paraguay was now way off to the right, a lustrous, smoky-blue ribbon of hills and forests. The other way, to the left, the horizon was a thin strip of bitter reeds and backwaters, swamps and stunted black trees, each hard enough to crack an axe. This was the Chaco . . . an endless, salty desert of spines and poisons.[71]

Populated by "blood drinking Indians",[72] the "spines and poisons" of Gimlette's Chaco reflect a historical tendency to attribute all kinds of outlandish qualities to a region of Paraguay that the conquistadors deemed uncolonizable.[73] Although Gimlette demonstrates a perceptive awareness of the way in which Paraguay's failure to support Europeans' utopian visions led to its subsequent "role" as "Gomorrah",[74] his dualistic rendering of Paraguay's landscapes nevertheless gravitates toward the country's depiction as a ruined paradise. This is apparent in the following account of his visit to a disused tannin factory: "[The log factory] was an enormous cathedral of rust, yawning and groaning in the hot wind. I scrambled inside, into an oily black jungle of lubricating swamps, cables, idlers and grinding teeth."[75] As rusty monument to failed utopias and reluctant workforces, the "cathedral" provides tangible evidence of the New World's resistance to industrialization. The image of grinding teeth confirms, rather than resists, Paraguay's depiction as a Latin American Gomorrah. Though Carver also derides the "fantasy of Paraguay as Paradise",[76] his narrative inherits, rather than contests, a sense of his predecessors' thwarted hopes. He writes that "life in Paraguay is indeed far from the hopeful dreams European idealists who planned the salvation of mankind away from Old World corruptions and temptations".[77] As his narrative progresses, Carver's Paraguay becomes increasingly apocalyptic. His exit scene is a case in point: "We were away . . . the jungle and Chaco all around the city like a ring of dark glowing emerald. . . . I was out, away, free, gone. . . . *Adios and vaya con Dios Paraguay* . . . I had escaped."[78] The apocalyptic scenes of Carver's narrative lead back to Conrad's *Heart of Darkness*;

his Paraguayan river journey is a case in point: "I thought of Joseph Conrad moving by boat upriver from civilization and its ambiguities to a primal, primeval world, ancient, sparse of men, a journey back to an earlier epoch of existence."[79] While Carver does not go so far as to cry "the horror! the horror!" he does make the following pronouncement: "If Mr. Kurtz were to go back in time, to the early twentieth century, Paraguay was a good place to do it."[80] Characterized by sustained questioning of the imperial project, the "earlier epoch" to which Carver refers has provoked a rash of narratives about Paraguayan utopias, Graham's *A Vanished Arcadia* among them.[81] While travelers' anxieties have ranged from the decline of empire to climate change, then, Paraguay has retained its function as a repository for travelers' hopes and despairs.[82]

Paraguayan dystopias, too, have repeatedly served as a cautionary tale against the potential outcomes of political policies pursued at home. This is apparent in the work of Australian travel writer Anne Whitehead, whose book *Paradise Mislaid* (1997) centers on her visit to Nueva Australia, the site of another utopian settlement led by the editor of *The Worker* called William Lane, who was disillusioned by exploitative labor practices during Australia's severe depression of the 1890s. Because Lane's vision of a new socialist community excluded people on the grounds of their race, Whitehead draws parallels between Australian settlers' expulsion of local and indigenous Paraguayans and the treatment of aborigines back home. Noting that the Paraguayan-born descendents of Australian settlers are given an education from which these expulsions and their social consequences have been expunged, Whitehead uses the example of Nueva Australia to warn against repeating the mistakes of the past.[83] As Foster observes, however, it is Whitehead's preoccupation with another failed utopia, Nueva Germania,[84] that provides contemporary Australia's starkest warning. Established by Friedrich Nietzsche's sister and others, Nueva Germania was fervently committed to racial supremacist principles. As Foster asserts, "Whitehead's implicit comparison" between both Paraguay's Nueva Australia and today's Australia "presents Nueva Germania as the . . . shadow self of New Australia" and her book is a "parable" against any future return to principles of the white Australia doctrine.[85]

Travellers' preoccupation with utopias and dystopias does not always inevitably preclude moments of reflexivity and "affective identification". Australian traveler and researcher Michael Leach is notably more transparent about his visit to Nueva Australia. Published in 2002,[86] his travel essay makes no attempt to conceal that his primary preoccupation is with Australia, not Paraguay. His visit to Nueva Australia is narrated in the following terms:

> Like other Australian historians and journalists before me, this is more homage than a research trip. And I have read too much to truly witness the present. Already, I am seeing the ghosts of utopia. (p. 12)

Alert to his own tunnel vision, Leach is at pains to foreground the limits of his ability to perceive Paraguay's contemporary scenes and settings. He warns the reader about the extent to which his consciousness is drowning in historical detail. His rendering of Nueva Australia's imported landscape is a case in point: "The wide streets are peppered with gums—not entirely unusual in South America—but also, more distinctively, with silky oaks (native to Queensland)" (p. 92). Notwithstanding his motive, Leach's travel narrative is sensitive to the mindscapes of settlers whose identities—his interviewees insist—are decidedly Paraguayan. Following some difficulty locating an English-speaking descendent, Leach is finally introduced to Don Eduardo Bruce Murray, a relative of Australian settlers:

> Bruce is talking to me in his rusty, but entirely functional first language . . . The only way to describe [his accent] is *colonial*. It is extraordinary to hear the voice of Eduardo Bruce Murray, speaking an isolated English remnant, the last of an ageing few who speak nineteenth-century English in central South America. (p. 94)

Despite its familiar focus on one of the utopian settlements, Leach's narrative comes closer than any other anglophone narrative to a postcolonial sense of Paraguay. In many respects, Leach's sense that, for an Australian traveler, Paraguay is solely viewable through nineteenth-century lenses initially seems to endorse a sense that anglophone and postcolonial travel writing are mutually exclusive categories. As it unfolds, however, Leach's narrative registers a fleeting sense that the Australian colony was "colonial" in its settlement practices. It also shows a rare sense of solidarity with the Paraguayan born descendents, saluting them as part of an Australian diaspora. When the Spanish-speaking wife of an Australian descendent appeals for help with an Australian visa, Leach leaves his address "in case they want to follow up" (pp. 95–96). This sense of mutual entanglement and solidarity is expressed with a deep sense of irony about the politically charged nature of the Australian immigration system; Leach doubts that the (then) government of John Howard will recognize a non-English-speaking member of an Australian diaspora founded on socialist principles (p. 95). Despite the narrow focus of Leach's narrative on yet another utopian project, it offers a more politically engaged perspective that draws attention to its limitations as a commentary on Paraguay and its inhabitants.

POSTCOLONIAL PARAGUAY

Despite their interest in foreigners' utopian experiments in Paraguay, and with the honorable exception of Leach's hints about the "colonial" nature of Nueva Australia, contemporary travel writers are generally silent about settlers' expulsion of indigenous groups from their territories. Nowhere does

Paraguay's depiction as a *terra nullius* have more potency than in travelers' representations of indigenous peoples. Carver's depiction of the nineteenth-century settlement process lacks any sense of its colonial dimension:

> The enthusiasm with which the Paraguayan government welcomed the new Australian and New German colonies . . . is a sign of how keen they were to get new settlers to repopulate the country. There was— and indeed still is to this day—excellent fertile land, well-watered and capable of bearing good crops, simply going begging, uncultivated.[87]

Speckled with colonial phrases—"fertile land", "well-watered"—this sanitized version of the settlement process is silent about the practice of expelling indigenous groups. This expulsion was a prerequisite for selling off large portions of this land to foreign settlers and investors. As Stephen Kidd points out, however, Paraguay has historically been the least responsive Latin American country to indigenous land rights claims.[88] This history of dispossession, which fails to register in any contemporary travel account, is strikingly absent from Gimlette's visit to the Chaco. Heavily reliant on Grubb's 1914 *A Church in the Wilds*, Gimlette focuses on the way in which his predecessor "hacked into Lengua territory to the North".[89] Although the "hacking" mode in which Grubb traveled implicitly acknowledges the colonial context of his predecessor's travel account, Gimlette inherits from Grubb both the derogatory term "Lengua"[90]—referring to the Enxet people—and a resolute silence about their dispossession. In the year 1891, to which Gimlette refers, the Enxet were beleaguered by the creeping colonization of the Chaco. Six years earlier, the Paraguayan government had begun to sell off lands occupied by the Enxets to settlers, many of them British like Grubb. As a result, the Enxets' hunting and water resources were severely depleted.[91] The South American Missionary Society was at the forefront of this private land grab on a grand scale. Nevertheless, Grubb's membership in this society actually prompts Gimlette to attribute "spiritual" rather than material motives to his journey,[92] despite the fact that the South American Missionary Society was charged with the task of what Grubb himself describes as "opening up this unknown land".[93] In another passage, Grubb discusses his goals in openly pecuniary terms, noting that "by preparation of hearts and minds [the Enxet] may be led to welcome future settlers, and share with them the advantages of civilization in return for land surrendered to its service".[94] Despite this context, Gimlette's Enxet indulge in all manner of savage practices, such as aborting fetuses and "occasionally fir[ing] upon" Grubb.[95] This picture of unprovoked savagery is produced by divorcing the Exnet from the context of being under constant siege, a maneuver facilitated by their metaphorical transportation to "a state of Eden".[96] The settlement of Enxet territories was never legal and continues to be contested by their descendants.[97] Gimlette's narrative is indifferent to the plight of the landless. In fact, the presence of dispossessed indigenous people in an Asunción police station is attributed to a kind of culture crisis: "Indians camped out on the ground floors, pleading for an identity."[98] Gimlette expands on this theory a few pages later, attributing land protests to a misguided utopian quest after the manner of the Europeans, to "their deep conviction that there existed—within their finding—an earthly paradise—the Land without Evil".[99] This inherited perspective leads to a lack of solidarity with a present-day indigenous cause, the historical and colonial significance of which fails to register anywhere in his narrative.

This silence about colonial violence extends to Carver's and Gimlette's accounts of encounters between indigenous people and the Spanish conquistadors on land that was to become Paraguayan. According to Carver and Gimlette, the conquistadors encountered oversexed, promiscuous women, whom Gimlette describes as "biddable" on more than one occasion.[100] This quality, according to Carver, accounts for the tendency for Spanish military attacks to end in "org[ies]",[101] and Gimlette's depiction of the Guarani surrender at Lambare in 1537 has a similar erotic charge. Once again, "biddable" and "bare breasted" young women are sent down Lambare hill to the Spanish, whereupon the conquistadors are "devoured by their urges".[102] Gimlette concludes the section by stating that a truce was established afterward "on the rather unpromising principles of lust".[103] Neither Carver nor Gimlette conceive of these encounters as mass rape. Instead, as Gimlette reports—provided that women are included in his category of Guarani— "the Asuncion Guarani were more than satisfied with their truce with the white men."[104] The recurrent act of rape by the conquistadors, together with the salacious accounts that they spawned, perhaps account for what French and Wigham observe as a broader tendency to "voyeuristically" represent Paraguayans as "wildly" sexual. Julia Llewellyn Smith also picks up on this theme with a customary twist of Greene, hinting at a widespread sexual promiscuity that extends to Paraguayan consciousness more generally: "Aunt Augusta wallowed in the amorality of Asuncion."[105] French and Wigham further account for this tendency by pointing out that informal sexual unions were a prevalent norm following a post-independence ban on marriage between the Spanish and local women.[106]

Indeed, it is not merely these colonial contexts that have given contemporary travel narratives about Paraguay their defining literary pedigree. Graham Greene's *Travels with my Aunt* is a particularly influential text.[107] Julia Llewellyn Smith's *Travels Without My Aunt* repeatedly renders Greene's fictional claims as observable reality.[108] Travelers acquire from Greene, and—more nebulously—from his forebears a belief in Paraguay's cultural isolation and endemic corruption together with an obsession with its apparent capacity to harbor escaped Nazis and other unsavoury fugitives. In direct quotations from Greene, both Llewellyn Smith and Carver refer to smuggling as Paraguay's "national industry",[109] and wrongly describe its chilled drink—*terere*—as a "mild narcotic".[110]

Most notorious of all, however, is the handkerchief incident, featured in *Travels with My Aunt*, which is set during Alfredo Stroessner Matiauda's rule:

> *"What's happening?"*
> *"It's the National Day. Wordsworth warned me, but I had forgotten. If you go into town, carry something red."*
> *"Why?"*
> *"It's the colour of the governing party. The Liberal party is blue, but it's unhealthy to carry blue. No one does."*[111]

Famously, this ends with the protagonist's subsequent imprisonment on the basis that he has shown disrespect to Stroessner by blowing his nose on a red handkerchief. The theme of political colors is taken up by Carver, Gimlette, and Llewellyn Smith alike, often in ways that appear to verify Greene's fictional observations, as with the following passage by Gimlette: "This sort of goonery was uncomfortably close to reality [when] Asuncion erupted into political colours. . . . The street of my hotel might start the day as blue and then be red by lunchtime."[112] The sense of "goonery" and "erupti[on] into political colours" here develops Greene's theme of a politics that is more focused on colors than intelligence. In similarly disparaging yet slapstick mode, Carver dreams up a Greenesque question for the Tourism Studies exam: "Your client insists on wearing Authentic Radical blue clothes . . . at a Colorado Party National Day Rally. . . . How do you incapacitate him without causing offence?"[113] And Llewellyn Smith of course relates the same fictional episode. Alongside her account of Paraguayan politics, which similarly implies that Paraguayan attitudes to politics are characterized by a crude preference for color over policy, Valiente Cabrera's penciled marginalia simply reads: "BULLSHIT!"

FICTION AND AFFECT IN ANGLOPHONE TRAVEL WRITING ABOUT PARAGUAY

The challenges seem insurmountable. To what extent is it even possible to produce a text that promotes affective identification with Paraguayans, a text that can counter Paraguay's persistent representation as languid and insular, Edenic and apocalyptic, exotic and erotically charged? This final section considers the relationship between fiction and affect in anglophone travel narratives about Paraguay. In particular, I consider fiction's ability to promote what Lindsay, after Maureen Moynagh, terms "affective identification" with Paraguayans.[114]

First- and second-person narrative techniques are central to my discussion, which is informed by Lindsay's analysis of an anglophone Mexico-US border travelogue by Luis Alberto Urrea. In her study she argues that Urrea's modes of narrative focalization promote affective identification. First of all, Urrea plays with voice by using multiple *I* narrators. I quote part of the example provided by Lindsay. A group of Mexicans try to cross the border but run out of water:

> Mendez called them together.
> Or they called Mendez to their meeting.
> Mendez told them they were doomed if he did not go and find help.
> He told them he could make it to water, and possibly to help. It would be better if he went alone: he could move quicker . . .
> Those two chicken shits planned the whole time to book out of there and save their asses.[115]

By juxtaposing first-person narrative perspectives in this way, the travelogue is able to represent conflicting perspectives.[116] Significantly, the enabling narrative mode here is first and foremost a fictive one. As Lindsay points out, this narrative is written in a "doubly fictive" mode since most people whose perspectives are expressed in this passage die from dehydration soon after. While such approaches strain "credibility and credulity",[117] Urrea's fictive mode promotes readerly identification with the sense-making processes of a Mexican group attempting to cross the border. However, its doubly fictive mode is not excessively authoritative. Also key to promoting narrative authority in Urrea's travel book is second-person narration. Lindsay draws particular attention to a passage about dehydrated Mexicans crossing the Arizona desert while attempting to enter the US without papers: "you piss into our hands, or in whatever container you might have. You try not to dribble a single drop . . . Proteins are peeling off your dying muscles."[118] Once again, it is a fictive mode that encourages the reader to identify with the subjects of the travel account.

The use of second-person narrative reopens questions about the supposedly unethical role of fiction in travel writing. As Lindsay observes, travel writers and their critics have long been troubled by the genre's tendency to fictionalize.[119] I wish to focus particularly on the common denigration of fiction as dishonest.[120] It is of course widely acknowledged that, as Graham Mort puts it, our realities are "infused with fictional presence".[121] All discourse, authoritative or otherwise, is founded on acts of creativity and strategic invention. Nevertheless, fiction is routinely considered as diametrically opposed to rationality and truth.[122]

The present volume is titled *Travel Writing and Ethics: Theory and Practice*, and it is the latter half of the title that I address here. To investigate the role of fiction further, I produced a short travel piece based on my yearlong stay in Asunción, Paraguay, between 1998 and 1999. The piece features this journey from the perspective of an English female narrator but juxtaposes her travel account with the contrasting travel experiences of Valiente Cabrera, or "Javier", whose penciled marginalia features earlier in this essay. The piece reflects contrasting motives for travel; adventure versus economic migration.[123] Given the prevalence of economic migration for Paraguayans, focusing on Javier's journey helps to combat the sense of stasis and cultural isolation to be found in many anglophone travel narratives about Paraguay. The following passage adopts second-person narrative in the voice of Javier:

> At first you work as a waiter in a London restaurant called *Cuba Libre*. You can't believe the prices the customers pay. Or the size of the tips. You wear an apron and carry cocktails on a tray. Sometimes the women feel you up with their own boyfriends sitting right across the table from them. They call you a sexy Cuban. You tell your wife. She says it's sexual harassment and you should complain. But life's too short. And other people have to put up with worse things, much worse.

As Javier's *I* narrator implies in this narrative, sexual harassment in a London restaurant is by no means the same traumatic terrain as being a migrant without papers or water in the Arizona desert. Nevertheless, second-person narration undoubtedly encourages the reader to put himself in Javier's position and to think through the various dilemmas he experiences on his own travels to England.

Unsurprisingly, I struggled to produce a travel account that was *not* structured by dominant representations of Paraguay. Loosely autobiographical, my travel narrative fails to shrug off the obsessions of earlier travelers; it features oranges and utopian settlements. Forewarned is not therefore forearmed. In my case, knowledge that Paraguay is repeatedly depicted as languid and insular, for example, led to its counter-representation of it as energetic and outward looking. Counter-depictions risk pushing the same representative pendulum in the opposite direction.[124] The only way to tackle this, I found, was to acknowledge the enduring power of Paraguay's established representation as Edenic for my English *I* narrator but, at the same time, to displace this trope by conveying its irrelevance to Paraguayans—in this case Javier, whose more pressing concerns as a migrant living in England are juxtaposed to create multiple narrative perspectives. Since, as Mort observes, no narrative can be written in real time, be it fictional or academic, all writing necessarily "take[s] liberties" in this regard.[125] This mirrors our selective experience of reality since, as he suggests, "there is too much experience to register it all and our consciousness would simply be overloaded".[126] In my travel piece, time reflects an ethical imperative. Javier's travel experiences in England repeatedly disrupt the aesthetically orientated depiction of the English *I* narrator as she walks through the rainforest:

> The rainforest buzzes and clicks, hisses and rustles. I'm unable to distinguish the sounds, not even one. Planets wink. Fireflies flash. Frogs scream. I stoop beneath some trailing vines. But then I stop, worried

about poisonous snakes: boa constrictors, tropical rattlesnakes, ana-condas. The thickets twitch and fizz. The forest floor rumbles. I turn back, afraid. *You get a call from your mother. She was watching a government health programme about breast cancer. Afterwards she found a lump. They told her it's spread to her lymph glands and she needs radiotherapy. You send the money. You think "thank god I'm over here in England". Otherwise she might have died.*

Migrants worldwide are commonly called upon to wire money back to their families and friends. Once again, the use of second-person narrative invites the reader to put herself in Javier's position as he accrues responsi-bility for the people he left in Paraguay. It also communicates the extent to which Javier's dilemmas of travel outweigh those of the English *I* narrator. This technique ensures that his journey is presented as more vital than hers and with greater repercussions, both negative and positive.

The content, form, and style of my travel piece are inevitably bound up with issues of power and the status of fiction. I will deal with both questions in turn. The power dimensions of fictocritical travel writing are the subject of Tim Youngs's recent essay about Krim Benterrak, Stephen Muecke, and Paddy Roe's *Reading the Country: Introduction to Nomadology.* Youngs identifies the work as an "example of the Australian contributions to travel and postcolonial studies that have been largely eclipsed by the productions of the US and European academy".[127] He argues that, in terms of its formal experimentation and implicit challenge to travel writing's ongoing tendency to emphasize travelers' movement and travelees' corresponding immobil-ity, the book has succeeded in "open[ing] up and expand[ing] the often maligned genre of the travel text".[128] My travel piece similarly emphasizes both the fact of Javier's mobility as well as its curtailment in the form of visa restrictions. This consideration also informed my depiction of the rain-forest as serving contrasting functions: adventure (for the English narrator) and leisure for the Valiente Cabrera family. This is reflected in the English narrator's first encounter with the family:

> I keep my eyes to the ground, checking for scorpions. At first I'm walk-ing through a kaleidoscope of sound. But then I hear voices rising above the gargling throat of the river. Torchlight flashes through the bars of the trees. I smell an *asado.* Beef, mandioca, probably *ensalada rusa* too. Grateful, I pick my way over wet stones towards the voices. There's a hammock, a mother and father swinging side by side, their grown-up children tucking into the barbecued meat.

However, Youngs identifies a number of problems with Muecke's work that resonate with my fictionalized piece about Paraguay. Inspired as Benterrak and colleagues are by French philosophical methods of reading, for exam-ple, Youngs observes that their postmodernist attention to "fragmentation, contradiction and fluidity" risks calling aboriginal voices "into textual being by European thought, just as it was European ideas that silenced them previously".[129] Rather than representing some form of "redress", then, Youngs argues that Benterrak and others' choice of techniques may simply be "readmi[tting]" the silenced subject on "the master's terms".[130] This is an inbuilt disparity that no amount of reflexivity can resolve. By calling Javier into textual being, the travel excerpt above reflects similar inequitable processes. In this sense, then, my piece was unable to address the travel genre's imbalance of power. Notwithstanding this problem, my piece does address the historical problem that anglophone travel writing about Paraguay is characterized by a lack of affinity with the country's citizens. Following Lindsay's observations about the adoption of second-person narratives, then, the piece was able to convey a sense of Javier's contrasting travel experiences ("At first you work as a waiter"). As Lindsay argues, this relatively rare form of focalization has the power to include the reader in a process of "affective identification" as well as to highlight the uneven workings of global power.[131] As Lindsay so convincingly asserts, "conscious appeals to the fictive" specialize, more than any other mode of writing, in an affective political charge.[132] Representing Javier's migration-related dilemmas in the second person is an act of fictionalization that attempts to relinquish an informational role and promote affinity with Javier's dilemmas and experiences.

Muecke is correct in observing that fictional genres are themselves powerful discourses harnessed to particular modes of representation.[133] Accordingly, the fictional elements of my travel piece about Paraguay may be deemed problematic simply because they are predisposed to privilege aesthetic considerations in the way that Lisle asserts.[134] The following passage from my own travel piece illustrates this problem:

> Javier stops. I almost bump into him.
> "Hear that?" he said.
> And then I can. Birdsong, falling like water.
> "It's a Tinamou. Red-winged I think. You normally see it nearer the ground. They're not good fliers."
> We carry on walking. The tinamou starts up again.

In terms of its fictional function, the red-winged tinamou has a scene-setting rather than an informational purpose. The tinamou lends descriptive detail that heightens the rainforest's appeal as a site of adventure travel. The genre has an inbuilt tendency to exoticize sites of travel, and the tinamou is a clear manifestation of this tendency. Moreover, although the tinamou is commonly found in Paraguay, its appearance at this juncture is entirely fabricated. Yet—and important to note—the bird also fulfils an ethical function, setting the narrative apart from classic portrayals of Paraguay by establishing Javier the travelee as a source of knowledge on which the narrative and its readership depend. In this respect, my act of fabrication problematizes the well-worn contention—so rarely questioned in studies about travel writing—that truth telling is inherently more ethical than fictionalization. As Lindsay argues, fictionalization has a powerful affective charge. Given the self-authorizing role of truth telling in the genre of travel writing—increasingly by journalists with a professional stake in accruing rather than eschewing the power to represent—it seems crucial that fiction's ethical orientations are not overlooked.

In his essay titled "Language: Its Cultural and Intercultural Dimensions," Alvino E. Fantini observes that "[l]anguage communicates, but it also excommunicates".[135] Given the propensity of academic discourse to prematurely foreclose communication with readers beyond the academy, fictionalized travel narratives speak to the limitations of academic forms and imply a commitment to reaching new audiences.[136] As Mort points out, creative writing reflects critically on "the wider human experience of signification . . . creating . . . new configurations [and] experimenting with form whilst engaging with literary tradition". In this sense, he argues, fiction can make "an original contribution to knowledge" in accordance with established definitions of research outputs.[137] I propose that fiction's ethical potential, most particularly its affective dimension, be reconsidered with regard to the genre of travel writing. This essay thus urges travel writing scholars to reconsider fiction's status and utility for travel writing in a self-reflexive anglophone tradition.

NOTES

1. Claire Lindsay, *Contemporary Travel Writing of Latin America* (London: Routledge, 2010), p. 105. Lisle argues that, among other things, the genre's "separation of knowledge into academic and popular forms of information" is a decidedly colonial feature; Debbie Lisle, *The Global Politics of Contemporary Travel Writing* (London: Cambridge University Press, 2006), p. 25.
2. Indeed, scholars of Francophone and Spanish-language travel narratives have productively examined ways in which such writing has countered prevailing myths about specific cultures and places. See Lindsay, *Contemporary Travel Writing of Latin America*, p. 11. See also Charles Forsdick, *Travel in Twentieth-century French and Francophone Cultures: The Persistence of Diversity* (Oxford: Oxford University Press, 2005). Forsdick, among others, has explored how the writing of travelers such as François Maspero entails a very real sense of risk. Forsdick suggests that Maspero repeatedly questions the primacy of his own journey, which is frequently interrupted by competing journeys self-evidently more urgent than his own. Charles Forsdick, presentation to the panel on Travel Writing and Ethics, presented at the European Society for the Study of English Conference, Zaragoza, Spain, 9 September 2004.
3. Steve Clark, ed., *Travel Writing and Empire: Postcolonial Theory in Transit* (London: Zed, 1999); Patrick Holland and Graham Huggan, *Tourists with Typewriters: Critical Reflections on Contemporary Travel Writing* (Ann Arbor: University of Michigan Press, 2000).

4. It should be noted, however, that an established body of work focused on gendered positionality from the nineteenth century to the present has often adopted a more optimistic tenor.
5. See Stephen Levin, *The Contemporary Anglophone Travel Novel: The Aesthetics of Self-fashioning in the Era of Globalization* (London: Routledge, 2008), which examines twentieth-century travel novels and considers, among other things, their capacity for social critique. See also Lisle, *Global Politics*.
6. Steve Clark, cited in Lindsay, *Contemporary Travel Writing of Latin America*, p. 11.
7. Lindsay, *Contemporary Travel Writing of Latin America*, p. 9.
8. For a number of years, travel writing was subject to a sustained period of interrogation by postcolonial scholars interested in the genre's entanglement with imperial domination. By the late 1990s, this critique had given rise to systematic and often site-specific inquiry, which yielded a more variegated sense of the genre's relationship to prevailing political orthodoxies than postcolonial critiques of the 1990s had sometimes allowed. In particular, travel writing critics have turned to widespread evidence of experimentation in travel writing, past and present. Modernist travelers have become a particular focus of attention since, as has been convincingly argued, travel writing from this period reflects a loss "of confidence in the western gaze" signaled by an altered attitude to the act of traveling that has possibly had abiding consequences, initiating more "radical styles of writing" thereafter. See Andrew Hammond, "'The Unending Revolt': Travel in An Era of Modernism", *Studies in Travel Writing* 7, no.2 (2003): p. 184.
9. Maureen Moynagh, *Political Tourism and Its Texts* (Toronto: University of Toronto Press, 2008); Tim Youngs, "Making It Move: The Aboriginal in the Whitefella's Artifact", in Julia Kuehn and Paul Smethurst, eds., *Travel Writing, Form, and Empire: The Poetics and Politics of Mobility* (London: Routledge, 2009).
10. Studies have so far tended to focus on identifiably postcolonial writers such as Caryl Phillips and Salman Rushdie.
11. Kevin Foster, *Lost Worlds: Latin America and the Imagining of Empire* (London: Pluto, 2009).
12. Lindsay, *Contemporary Travel Writing of Latin America*, p. 3.
13. Lindsay, *Contemporary Travel Writing of Latin America*, p. 4.
14. Lindsay, *Contemporary Travel Writing of Latin America*, p. 112; Jennifer L. French and Thomas Wigham, "The Mournful Cry of the Urutau", *Midwest Quarterly* 50, no. 1 (2008): p. 38.
15. French and Wigham, "The Mournful Cry of the Urutau", p. 38. In this article French and Wigham are concerned by the accolades for a novel by US writer Lily Tuck called *The News From Paraguay*, which won the 2004 National Book Award and yet depicted Paraguay in what they consider to be a highly stereotypical manner. Nor, they suggest, has concern about this lack of affinity with Paraguayans been expressed in the English-speaking world.
16. John Gimlette, *At the Tomb of the Inflatable Pig* (London: Arrow, 2003).
17. John Gimlette, "At the Tomb of the Inflatable Pig: Letter" (1 March 2010) <www.randomhousesites.co.uk/minisites/inflatable_pig/letter.html> (11 August 2010).
18. Gimlette, *At the Tomb of the Inflatable Pig*, dust jacket blurb.
19. Lindsay, *Contemporary Travel Writing of Latin America*, p. 113.
20. Foster, *Lost Worlds*, p. 16; Lindsay makes a similar point in *Contemporary Travel Writing of Latin America*, p. 8. Travel writers such as Carver and Gimlette are also aware of this risk and yet, as I will argue, they seem unable to counter its consequences. For example, Robert Carver, *Paradise with*

Serpents: Travels in the Lost World of Paraguay (London: Harper Perennial, 2007), p. 104, observes Paraguay's status as "a locus of fantasy", and both Carver and Gimlette describe in some detail the various forms that this fantasy has taken.

21. Imagology investigates cultural representations and national stereotypes, a branch of study that is closely associated with Hugo Dyserinck. Terry Eagleton, *Figures of Dissent: Reviewing Fish, Spivak, Žižek and Others* (London: Verso, 2002), p. 2.

22. Carver asserts that Costaguana "also stands for [Conrad's native] tyrannised, oppressed Poland", representing the author's desire for a Polish war of liberation; Carver, *Paradise with Serpents*, p. 171. This is consistent with a wider tendency to project European concerns onto Latin America.

23. Carver writes that Conrad's novel *Nostromo* "was directly based on his researches into Paraguay" during the dictatorship of Solano Lopez. These, in turn, were based on George Frederick Masterman's *Seven Eventful Years in Paraguay*; Carver, *Paradise with Serpents*, p. 168.

24. Sara Wheeler, "In Stroessner's Shade", *Guardian*, 29 September 2007. Wheeler also notes Carver's preoccupation with European social ailments: "Jokes aside, an examination of these failed endeavours leads to disquisitions on European economic models, in particular the culture of dependency fostered by the welfare state and the breakdown of organic community life."

25. To cite a few instances here: "Paraguay was just an embarrassing little [airport] stop to be got over with as soon as possible" (Carver, *Paradise with Serpents*, p. 18); "[The tourist officer] jumped up from behind a dusty desk hidden under the stairwell and advanced on us with an extended hand" (Julia Llewellyn Smith, *Travels without My Aunt: In the Footsteps of Graham Greene* [London: Penguin, 2001], p. 250); "Paraguay! Why the hell do you want to go there?" (Corinne Fowler, unpublished manuscript, 1998, p. 1).

26. Carver, *Paradise with Serpents*, p. 181.

27. Foster, *Lost Worlds*, p. 13.

28. Foster, *Lost Worlds*. Foster also provides the example of Nicaragua here as a space onto which US ideological struggles were projected: "Nicaragua was endlessly reconstructed by the cultural warriors of left and right as the last frontier in the fight against Soviet totalitarianism, a genuine people's revolt against capitalism and imperialism, liberation theology in action, Godless communism personified, and so much more" (p. 16).

29. Thomas Phillips, "Heaven and Hell: The Representations of Paraguay as a Utopian Space", *European Journal of American Culture* 27, no. 1 (1998): 15–27. His observations about Paraguay are made in the following context: "Over the years, Paraguay has become [a] blank space in which to set utopias and dystopias" (p. 26). Foster, *Lost Worlds*, p. 199.

30. Travelers John Gimlette, Robert Carver, and Julia Llewellyn Smith all discuss buried treasure in their narratives.

31. See Lindsay, *Contemporary Travel Writing of Latin America*, p. 10.

32. Paul Lewis, Untitled review of *El Paraguay bajo los Lopez: Algunos ensayos de historia social y politica*, *Hispanic American Historical Review* 76, no. 4 (1999): 824–25.

33. Bonne Hamre, "South American's Last Frontier" <http://gosouthamerica. about.com/cs/southamerica/a/ParGranChaco.htm> (2 September 2010).

34. Mirroring this sentiment, reviewer Charlie Onion writes of Gimlette's book that "the outside world is impinging on Paraguay and it is, Gimlette predicts, about to change forever". Charlie Onion, Review of *At the Tomb of the Inflatable Pig*, *WAG Magazine*, 15 March 2004.

35. Augusto Roa Bastos, *Hijo de Hombre* [1960] (Madrid: Debolsillo, 1980), cited in Gimlette, *At the Tomb of the Inflatable Pig*, p. 129.

36. Phillips, "Heaven and Hell", p. 15.
37. Father Martin Dobrizhoeffer, *An Account of the Abipones: An Equestrian People of Paraguay* (Asuncion: 1784).
38. Robert Southey, *A Tale of Paraguay*, section 4, verse 5.
39. See Foster, *Lost Worlds*, p. 15.
40. Southey, *A Tale of Paraguay*, section 4, verse 5; Phillips, "Heaven and Hell", p. 17.
41. Phillips, "Heaven and Hell", p. 18.
42. Foster, *Lost Worlds*, p. 33.
43. Foster, *Lost Worlds*, p. 16.
44. Foster, *Lost Worlds*, pp. 26, 27–29. Foster also suggests that other contexts include the French Revolution, which had horrified Southey, and news of Latin American battles for independence, which Southey abhorred.
45. Southey, cited in Foster, *Lost Worlds*, p. 30.
46. Foster, *Lost Worlds*, p. 37.
47. Gimlette, *At the Tomb of the Inflatable Pig*, p. 208.
48. Gimlette, *At the Tomb of the Inflatable Pig*, p. 217.
49. Gimlette, *At the Tomb of the Inflatable Pig*, p. 122.
50. Odysseus chastises his men for "staying and munching lotus with the Lotus-eaters without thinking further of their return". Realizing its narcotic propensities, he forces them back to the ship, "lest any of them should taste of the lotus and leave off wanting to get home, so they took their places and smote the grey sea with their oars". Samuel Butler, trans., "*Odyssey*" <http://sparks.eserver.org/books/odyssey.pdf> (21 August 2009), p. 9.
51. Graham Greene, cited in Llewellyn Smith, *Travels without My Aunt*, p. 252.
52. Carver, *Paradise with Serpents*, p. 248.
53. Carver, *Paradise with Serpents*, p. 248.
54. *Terere* is an infusion of yerba maté in chilled water.
55. On a more sinister note, the consequence is to justify colonial cruelty on the grounds that Paraguayan inertia compelled it. Carver, for example, writes that the conquistadors "had to use authoritarian means—force, coercion, to get anything done"; Carver, *Paradise with Serpents*, p. 34.
56. Llewellyn Smith, *Travels Without My Aunt*, p. 264.
57. Carver, *Paradise with Serpents*, p. 57.
58. Martin Davies, review of *Paradise with Serpents*, *Independent*, 8 October 2009.
59. Davies, review.
60. As Phillips notes, Voltaire's *Candide* (1759) was the earliest fictional representation of the missions, which the protagonist visits with his companion Cacambo, during which he concludes that they are not the finest of worlds; Phillips, "Heaven and Hell", pp. 33–34.
61. As Melvin Arrington notes in an untitled review of Frederick J. Reiter, *They Built Utopia*, *Hispania* 80, no. 1 (1997): p. 71, the Jesuit province of Paraguay was established by Rome's Father General in 1604. The province covered a vast area of land, but the Jesuits later established their missions, from which the Guarani were able to keep Tupi Indians and Brazilian Paulistas at bay.
62. Carver, *Paradise with Serpents*, p. 11.
63. Gimlette, *At the Tomb of the Inflatable Pig*, p. 284.
64. Gimlette, *At the Tomb of the Inflatable Pig*, p. 284.
65. Gimlette, *At the Tomb of the Inflatable Pig*, p. 289.
66. Gimlette, *At the Tomb of the Inflatable Pig*, p. 290.
67. Gimlette, *At the Tomb of the Inflatable Pig*, p. 9.
68. Carver, *Paradise with Serpents*, p. 283. This passage is tempered by an earlier passage that presents a more celebratory reflection on the end of poverty

in Europe. "When I commented [to Paraguayans] on the legions of poor people living in the streets—the cripples, beggars, street kids, lunatics in evening dress—I was assumed to be some sort of bleeding heart socialist. Fifty years of redistributive taxation in Europe and high state employment and the welfare system had ironed out the gross visible disparities between very rich and very poor" (p. 263).

69. Gimlette, *At the Tomb of the Inflatable Pig*, pp. 303, 301.
70. The title of the book is derived from a much-quoted passage from the Spanish-born but Paraguayan-based poet Josefina Plá: "When I first came to Asunción from Spain I realised that I'd arrived in paradise. The air was warm, the light was tropical, and the shuttered colonial houses suggested sensual, tranquil lives. At night we'd go walking the streets and I'd be aware of two things; the smell of jasmine and the sound of voices in the dark. But like any paradise, this one had serpents." Plá, quoted in Carver, *Paradise with Serpents*, p. 283.
71. Gimlette, *At the Tomb of the Inflatable Pig*, p. 247.
72. Gimlette, *At the Tomb of the Inflatable Pig*, p. 299.
73. Phillips, "Heaven and Hell", p. 17. The Chaco was a perpetual source of frustration to the conquistadors since it contained no precious metals and blocked the northern route to the Andes.
74. Gimlette, *At the Tomb of the Inflatable Pig*, p. 264.
75. Gimlette, *At the Tomb of the Inflatable Pig*, p. 255.
76. Carver, *Paradise with Serpents*, p. 190.
77. Carver, *Paradise with Serpents*, p. 112.
78. Carver, *Paradise with Serpents*, p. 365.
79. Carver, *Paradise with Serpents*, p. 189.
80. Carver, *Paradise with Serpents*, p. 189.
81. Conrad's *Heart of Darkness* was first published in serialized form in 1899.
82. In his condemnation of gun ownership, for example, Carver paints Paraguay as a trigger-happy dystopia, and his description provides a clear warning to any who might consider relaxing Britain's anti-gun laws. He ventures into Asunción's streets after dark: "At dusk . . . the town centre became an ill-lit Indian-haunted place where pistoleros and whores roamed about and the police stayed mainly in their fortified barracks", accompanied by the "terrible shrieks" of apocalyptic parrots; Carver, *Paradise with Serpents*, pp. 54–55. There are many similar passages about the British National Health Service and the state of the global financial system.
83. See Foster, *Lost Worlds*, pp. 109–11.
84. The settlement was established in the San Pedro district of Paraguay, to the north of Asunción.
85. Gimlette's tour of eastern Paraguay is dominated by a compelling quest to track down two fugitives from Adolf Hitler's government: Martin Boremann and Dr. Josef Mengele, "the Angel of Death, the butcher of Auschwitz"; Gimlette, *At the Tomb of the Inflatable Pig*, p. 148.
86. Michael Leach, "Don Eduardo Is Sleeping: A Return to New Australia, Paraguay", *Overland* 169 (2001): 90–97; hereafter page numbers will be cited parenthetically in the text.
87. Carver, *Paradise with Serpents*, p. 154.
88. Stephen Kidd, "Land, Politics and Benevolent Shamanism: The Enxet Indians in a Democratic Paraguay", *Journal of Latin American Studies* 27, no. 1 (1995): 43–75.
89. Gimlette, *At the Tomb of the Inflatable Pig*, p. 305.
90. As Kidd points out, the Enxet were known locally—and in a derogatory fashion—as Lengua (Maskoy) because of their lip plates, and they were one of the two largest groups in the Chaco. Kidd, "Land, Politics and Benevolent Shamanism", p. 43.

91. Kidd, "Land, Politics and Benevolent Shamanism", p. 43.
92. The leader of the Missionary Society's earlier (1888) mission into Enxet territory, however, was the agent for the Council of Foreign Bondholders. Gimlette, *At the Tomb of the Inflatable Pig*, p. 305.
93. Wilfrid Barbrooke Grubb, quoted in Kidd, "Land, Politics and Benevolent Shamanism", p. 47.
94. Grubb, quoted in Kidd, "Land, Politics and Benevolent Shamanism", p. 48.
95. Gimlette, *At the Tomb of the Inflatable Pig*, p. 306.
96. Gimlette, *At the Tomb of the Inflatable Pig*, p. 306.
97. See Kidd, "Land, Politics and Benevolent Shamanism", p. 47.
98. Gimlette, *At the Tomb of the Inflatable Pig*, p. 111.
99. Gimlette, *At the Tomb of the Inflatable Pig*, p. 115.
100. Gimlette, *At the Tomb of the Inflatable Pig*, p. xix.
101. Carver, *Paradise with Serpents*, p. 103.
102. Gimlette, *At the Tomb of the Inflatable Pig*, p. 121.
103. Gimlette, *At the Tomb of the Inflatable Pig*, p. 121.
104. Gimlette, *At the Tomb of the Inflatable Pig*, p. 121.
105. Llewellyn Smith, *Travels without My Aunt*, p. 252.
106. French and Wigham, "The Mournful Cry of the Urutau", p. 34.
107. Graham Greene, *Travels with My Aunt* (London: Penguin, 1969).
108. This can be seen in her unlikely description of Asuncion's money changers, who generally advertise their services in Spanish with a simple *cambio!* In Llewellyn Smith's narrative, however, money changers are distinctly Greenesque, "[w]aving sheaves of guarani [notes] and mouthing 'Any US dollars?'—just as they had in Greene's day"; Llewellyn Smith, *Travels without My Aunt*, p. 250. A similar example can be found in her depiction of terere drinking: "Almost everyone carried a wooden or plastic gourd from which they sucked systematically through a plastic straw" (p. 251). Although Paraguayans customarily use metal, not plastic, straws, she reveals that this detail derives from "Greene's Czech manufacturer who tries to sell Visconti two million plastic straws on the basis that he could persuade the people to drink mate through them" (p. 253).
109. Llewellyn Smith, *Travels without My Aunt*, p. 267; Carver, *Paradise with Serpents*, p. 27.
110. Llewellyn Smith, *Travels without My Aunt*, p. 251; Carver, *Paradise with Serpents*, p. 77.
111. Greene, *Travels with My Aunt*, p. 99.
112. Gimlette, *At the Tomb of the Inflatable Pig*, pp. 103–4.
113. Carver, *Paradise with Serpents*, p. 230.
114. Lindsay, *Contemporary Travel Writing of Latin America*, p. 11.
115. Alberto Urrea, quoted in Lindsay, *Contemporary Travel Writing of Latin America*, p. 110.
116. Lindsay, *Contemporary Travel Writing of Latin America*, p. 110.
117. Ivan Callus, quoted in Lindsay, *Contemporary Travel Writing of Latin America*, p. 112.
118. Urrea, quoted in Lindsay, *Contemporary Travel Writing of Latin America*, p. 111.
119. Lindsay, *Contemporary Travel Writing of Latin America*, p. 108.
120. Lisle, cited in Lindsay, *Contemporary Travel Writing of Latin America*, p. 105.
121. Graham Mort, "Finding Form in Short Fiction", in Vanessa Gibbie, ed., *Short Circuit: A Guide to the Art of the Short Story* (London: Salt, 2009), pp. 33–49.
122. Katrina Schlunke and Anne Brewster, "We Four: Fictocriticism Again", *Continuum* 19, no. 3 (2003): 393–95.

123. Javier's parents and four of his siblings followed him to Europe soon afterward. They now live in southern Spain. As Raja Shehadeh writes in *Palestinian Walks: Notes on a Vanishing Landscape* (London: Profile, 2007), p. 9, while it is impossible to ignore the ideological projections of other nations onto a single country, it is important to promote a sense of the separate, and myriad, concerns of that country's citizens.

124. See Graham Huggan, *Interdisciplinary Measures: Literature and the Future of Postcolonialism* (Liverpool: Liverpool University Press, 2008), p. 101.

125. In recent decades, the literary text has become a channel for theoretical discovery and cultural criticism. However, as Mort argues, this has given rise to an unignorable counter-phenomenon: "the development of creative writing as an academic discipline in its own right"; Mort, "Finding Form in Short Fiction", p. 34. Increasingly funded by the Arts and Humanities Research Council, postgraduate students of creative writing undergo formal research training and typically undertake archival research, literary research, or fieldwork. Drawing on these resources, students produce a creative text and reflect critically on its modes of representation. As with formal academic theses, a successful creative PhD thesis is endowed with a critical capacity.

126. Mort, "Finding Form in Short Fiction", p. 22.

127. Youngs, "Making It Move", p. 162.

128. Youngs, "Making It Move", p. 148.

129. Youngs, "Making It Move", p. 155.

130. Youngs, "Making It Move", p. 155.

131. Lindsay, *Contemporary Travel Writing of Latin America*, pp. 113–14. Note also that Lindsay focuses on the relevance of this approach to traumatic situations—in this case, illegally crossing the Mexican border.

132. Lindsay, *Contemporary Travel Writing of Latin America*, p. 44.

133. Stephen Muecke, "Discourse, History, Fiction: Language and Aboriginal History", *Australian Journal of Cultural Studies* 1, no. 1 (1983): p. 77.

134. Lisle, cited in Lindsay, *Contemporary Travel Writing of Latin America*, p. 105.

135. I am grateful to Graham Mort for drawing my attention to this phrase in Alvino E. Fantini, "Language: Its Cultural and Intercultural Dimensions", adapted from "Language, Culture and World View: Exploring the Nexus", *International Journal of Intercultural Relations* 19 (1995): p. 147.

136. Schlunke and Brewster, "We Four: Fictocriticism Again", p. 393.

137. Mort, "Finding Form in Short Fiction", p. 23.

4   Terror

Laurie Hovell McMillin

The explosion ripped through the long distance train as it hurtled through a Colombo suburb, throwing out lumber, steel, yogurt pots, skin, bone, and hair onto the lush banana trees and palms that lined the tracks. The bomb blasts ripped jagged holes in the sides of the steel train cars, splitting the plastic seats like a machete through a green coconut. Standing on the platform at the main station two miles away, I heard a strange pop, pop, pop. I locked eyes with a fellow passenger. Another attack. A railway official bolted down the platform and some khaki-clad policemen chased him through the crowd clutching their rifles to their chests.

I went to Sri Lanka in 1984 on a fellowship sponsored by the US government to study the development of Sinhalese Buddhist identity as it centered on one man, the Anagarika Dharmapala (1864–1933). After I arrived in Sri Lanka, I became especially interested in how this figure, who died in India and felt he'd been forgotten in Ceylon, was being used by the current Sinhalese majority to ramp up Sinhalese Buddhist nationalism and solidify opposition to the Tamil insurgents. I was assigned a faculty adviser in the Buddhist Studies Department at the University of Peradeniya, near the upland city of Kandy. Professor Perera wanted me to study the ancient language of Pali so I could read the texts of the tradition and grapple with its fine philosophy. But I wanted to better understand the current conflict; I wanted to study living culture—what people today actually did and said—rather than pore over old religious texts in a library or re-split the hairs of ancient monastic debates. I switched to an adviser—a historian—who was more sympathetic to my interests. Then the university closed for vacation; soon after that the government, fearing violence, shut it down for weeks. Largely self-tutored, I read about the history and politics of the ethnic conflict for hours every day.

At the same time I was trying to get settled academically, I was trying to find my feet socially, psychically. Mostly, I was alone. I wrote dozens of letters to friends at home and waited impatiently for replies. I followed the news of the war in Sri Lanka, of terror in India: Indira Gandhi's killing in October and its violent aftermath, the Union Carbide disaster in Bhopal that killed thousands. Birds woke me long before dawn, squawking and crashing in the verdant trees outside my window. After tea, I'd start studying again and read for six hours before noon. I walked for miles just to burn up the creeping minutes of the day. I strode past rice fields and Buddhist temples, greeting school kids and monks, delighting at the surprised faces of women tending small children outside their houses. As I passed a schoolyard, a brave child might pipe up with a few words of English or the common Sinhala greeting: "Where are you going?" to which I replied in the Sinhala idiom, "Oh, I'm just going". In the afternoons I went into town. Kumar, a Tamil fruit seller, became my best friend there. He knew I loved mangoes and sent me away with pink plastic bags full of things I'd never tasted before: tiny, lemony bananas; creamy, funky durian; fleshy rambutan. Some of the local touts—young men in Western dress who had learned snatches of English—eventually learned I wasn't a passing tourist and stopped trying to sell me batiks and handicrafts, ganja and hashish. I depended on them to share a word or two.

And I followed the news. The papers were full of stories like this:

> The surprise attack was unusually well coordinated. Early last week more than 75 Tamil Tiger guerrillas . . . stormed a heavily fortified army cantonment near the northern town of Vavuniya to free 50 captured terrorists held inside. Militarily, the operation was a failure: 32 of the 50 prisoners were killed during the two-hour long battle. But the attack marked an escalation in the eight-year-old civil war that is tearing apart the island nation.

The Jayawardene governmment . . . has responded with tough antiterrorist measures. In a series of skirmishes in the past two weeks, army troops captured nearly 60 Tamil fighters and killed at least six. In earlier operations, government security forces intercepted eight boatloads of Tamils who were attempting to land on Sri Lanka's northwest coast, resulting in more than 60 deaths and six arrests.[1] The beginning of the civil war in Sri Lanka could be dated in various ways. Some say it began in July 1983, when members of the Liberation Tigers of Tamil Eelam (LTTE), a militant Tamil group, ambushed a government jeep and killed thirteen government soldiers. The country was on fire after that. Tamil shops and homes were torched. Thousands were murdered. Some believe the government provided lists of Tamil homes to Sinhalese attackers so that the terror could be carried out more efficiently. Some Tamils fought back; some were taken in and hidden by Sinhalese friends and neighbors. Many Tamils who could afford to flee the country left as soon as they could and never returned. The war had gone on from there, every attack spawning a counterattack and fresh violence.

The source of the troubles could also be dated to 1956, when the government instituted a "Sinhala-only" language policy; this policy mandated that all government and educational business be carried out in Sinhala, the language of the Sinhalese ethnic majority in the island, most of whom identified as Buddhist. Until then, English had been the lingua franca for such matters; because large numbers of Tamils were English-educated, they had occupied government and university positions disproportionate to the size of their population. The Sinhala-only policy can be seen as the government's attempt to shake off its recent colonial past, but it also effectively cut Tamils out of public life. Soon after its institution, the author of the policy, S.W.R.D. Bandaranaike, was elected prime minister on a wave of Sinhalese Buddhist nationalism. In 1959, when he deigned to listen to Tamil criticisms of the policy change, he was shot and killed by a Buddhist monk. Political struggle polarized identities, and further defined the ethnic conflict.

Still others maintained that these events were not causes but rather symptoms of a hardening of ethnic and linguistic identities that began to take shape during 150 years of British colonial rule. Or, if we go back further, perhaps a seed of the conflict can be located in the legends of the sixth-century Sinhalese Buddhist military hero Dutugemenu, who was counseled by his monk-advisers not to worry about the many deaths caused in his battle with the Tamil leader, Elara. The monks assured Dutugemenu that because all but two of the dead were not Buddhists they really did not count.[2] Or maybe the roots of the conflict were planted at the very start, when Mahinda brought a branch of the bodhi tree from north India to the island in the second century BCE, where it was planted in Anuradhapura. In any case, history was to blame, but people picked their way through that history differently, contentiously, creatively, and sometimes with murderous results.

Kandy Lake is a pretty, tree-lined body of water in the center of the upland town where I stayed. Around this lake lovers seek out private spaces. I was circumambulating the lake, my long strides whipping my lilac dress around my knees, when two touts came up behind me and asked where I was from. I turned to glance at them. I had seen one of them before, a genial, curly-headed fellow in tight jeans. The one who had spoken had delicate Sinhalese features and a mocking but friendly look. "USA," I said.

"Ah, America. Where are you going?" he asked. "You want gems? Smoke? Hashish?" I said I wasn't interested, but hoped that my expression suggested I was still willing to chat with them, to joke a bit. They were Omal and Sunil, they said, and asked my name, which I told them, and they asked where I was staying, which I didn't. I'd heard that many touts dealt and smoked heroin: "brown sugar", unrefined stuff from Afghanistan. Users just light a small hunk of it, and inhale the vapors through a piece of rolled up foil from a pack of cigarettes.

"Oh, you *nice* lady," Sunil said, meeting my eyes. I laughed, and we parted ways.

> Heroin was first introduced into the country in 1981 through the "hippie" tourists . . . [T]he consumption of heroin gradually spread to the

local population, making the island a demand driven rather than a supply driven market in the 1980s. Due to its proximity to [the] "Golden Triangle" and "Golden Crescent", Sri Lanka had become a major transit point for heroin to Europe and other Western countries on an organized scale. Heroin is routed via Sri Lanka from Pakistan or India . . . by sea by containers and mechanized fishing craft. This sea route takes two forms: from Pakistan to Mumbai (facilitated by underworld dons in the city), then to Tuticorin or Rameshwaram, and then to Sri Lanka by sea; on from Pakistan to southern India via the land route through Jaisalmer or Barmer and then by sea to Sri Lanka. A considerable amount of drugs also come from Southeast Asia transiting the Indian sub-continent.[3]

The civil war worked its way into many parts of our daily lives in Sri Lanka. In October, I went to the eastern coastal town of Trincomalee to snorkel, where I saw brilliant yellow-striped fish darting in and out of the coral. By the next week, my granting agency determined that it was too dangerous for American academic fellows like me to travel there. Jaffna and the rest of northern Sri Lanka, the base of the Tamil separatists, had long been off limits. In November, I traveled to Colombo to spend the Thanksgiving holidays with other expatriates. Someone got a turkey from the American commissary. On the holiday, however, the government imposed a twenty-four-hour nationwide curfew. Two hundred fifty Tamil terrorists near Jaffna had attacked a police station, killing twenty-nine officers, flattening the station, and martyring a number of their own.

When I'd traveled to India several years earlier, various authorities had cautioned me about how to behave. Watch what you do with your feet. Don't walk alone after dark. Dress modestly. Following these rules, they said, would prevent cultural misunderstandings and help me live in South Asia as South Asians live. And I had tried to follow some of those rules while in India. Don't make eye contact, our teacher said; be careful not to hold a person's gaze too long—it's not the way it's done. So I dutifully averted my eyes while walking down the street, turned quickly away from strangers and vendors, and learned to drop my gaze from my Indian teachers and members of my host family. The rules were meant to protect me from unwanted attention and misunderstandings, but I found that they also led me to shut down. More than that, when I turned my gaze away, it turned in on me; I lost my bearings and got stuck inside my head. I wasn't willing to repeat this in Sri Lanka: I had come to believe, to "know" in the deepest part of me, that the eyes were a point of possible connection, a place where two humans—even if they were vastly different from each other—might meet. As I understood things, I couldn't be a complete person without the chance of that mutual recognition. I hadn't traveled halfway around the world to hold myself in abeyance, I told myself: I wanted to find out what other people were like, to meet and chat with them, to know something of how they saw the world.

Anyway, it seemed a joke to try to minimize my difference; there were so many ways I clearly wasn't part of the culture: I lived alone, was paid in dollars, had an American passport, and that all brought privileges. I had no servants, I drank beer, and took long walks just for the heck of it, and no one—no father, no husband, no teacher—had anything to say about it.

I tried to be respectful, of course, but there were other cultural codes I just could not accept, especially the divisions of caste and class that guided local mores. I knew this could lead people to misunderstand or even shun me, but I made a conscious decision to risk it. I didn't always recognize, however, that breaking these rules could lead to risks for others; my conversations with the "houseboy" who worked for my landlady got him sacked; he wasn't supposed to talk to the "white lady guest". But I had to talk to him: for me, not to do so would have meant that I bought the classist ideology—that I *did* consider myself superior. I didn't recognize, however, that in asserting my equality with others and insisting on interacting with them I was also taking advantage of my status as privileged white woman. I wanted to claim that I was no better than anyone else, and at the same time I asserted that I could opt out of prevailing systems—that I, in effect, was above them. In any case, I was adamant: I was staying in Sri Lanka for nine months, and I wasn't going to keep myself locked up.

In this way I became friendly with Kumar the fruit man, the library doorman, and the touts, Omal and Sunil, Raju and Mohamed. Sunil and I often joked with each other when we met on the street; he'd trail me in the market when he wasn't "working", intervening with a shopkeeper when he thought I was being overcharged. He and Omal told me stories about their work: directing tourists to selected shops and guesthouses, selling small amounts of dope, acting as middlemen for the black market exchange in foreign currency, sometimes traveling with *sudus* (white people) to the beaches as guides. And Sunil was funny, playful. "Hello, Madam," he would say, as if he'd never seen me before. "You want hotel? Taxi? Smoke?"

"*Nae,*" I'd answer in the little Sinhala I knew. "*Mama tourist-kinek nae*" (I'm not a tourist).

"*Ay-o. Sinhala kata karana pulawan da?*" (Oho! You speak Sinhala?)

"*Tikak pulawan*" (A little), I'd say, and so it would go. Our banter on the streets mocked the usual exchanges between touts and tourists; at the same time, I rehearsed my stance toward local culture: I wasn't a tourist but a student. I wasn't just passing through, I was going to stay for a while. Sunil, on the other hand, despite his mocking attitude, kept the role of tout—ready to please, flatteringly friendly.

My friend Kumar the fruit man once saw me exchange greetings with Sunil in the market and voiced his disapproval. Sunil was bouncing through the halls of the Kandy market, calling out to friends and clerks he knew. "Hi, Lauren!" he called, mispronouncing my name. Kumar would not even look at Sunil; head down, Kumar sliced up a fresh mango for me and said under his breath, in English, "That boy, no good". Sunil wasn't a respectable citizen—I knew that. But I brushed off the local social categories: I could be friends with both these fellows. After all, I knew how to handle myself.

Sunil asked me to tea at the Elephant Café and I went. He seemed different, less cheerful. He pulled his lips tight around his teeth between gulps of smoke. He dumped sugar into his tea, saying, "I like very much sugar. I can't get enough". I asked him where he was from, how old he was, what his family was like. He was eighteen, he said. His dad was Malaysian; he'd gone back home and taken Sunil's mother with him, leaving Sunil alone. Sunil had learned his bit of English—broken yet communicative—simply from talking to tourists. He wouldn't say how he came to be in Kandy. I volunteered a few things about myself; my university studies, my interest in the sources of the ethnic conflict between Sinhalese Buddhists and Tamil Hindus. He shrugged. He could speak some Tamil, he said. He knew plenty of Tamil people in Kandy. He gestured that he would pay, but I refused. Sri Lankan rupees were like play money to me, and the bill came to less than a dollar. Outside the restaurant I took his photo. Looking at it later, I thought the image captured him well: a pretty boy feigning toughness against a backdrop of the streets on which he did business.

In retrospect, it's possible to link the petty hand-to-hand drug trade witnessed in Kandy to larger movements of people and cash and to the civil war itself:

> There . . . have been suggestions that the LTTE raised money through drug running, particularly heroin from Southeast and Southwest Asia. According to a 1995 report . . . the most profitable LTTE activities have been in the form of heroin trafficking. Sri Lankan officials concur, with one senior diplomat asserting that "collection of money from Tamil expatriate sources is insignificant compared to money from narcotics. . . . Certainly, there are extensive profits to be made from the drug trade."[4]

I ran into Sunil and Omal in the market, and they laughingly reported how they had just swindled a fat German tourist, selling him cheap coconut cooking oil as some exotic massage oil. Perhaps they had applied it as well, and left the fat man half naked and choking with expectation of some affection, at least some stroking if he was paying so much. (It was not, they'd suggested, outside their line of work.) I felt weirdly honored that they trusted me enough to tell me about the incident, as if it signaled that they didn't see *me* as an outsider, as if they wouldn't cheat *me* in this way.

In December, rumor had it that the Tamil Tigers were planning to attack a famous Buddhist temple in Kandy. The temple was believed to house a tooth of the Buddha. Government soldiers took up positions outside the vast building with its many corners and crannies; worshippers were frisked, their bags and packages forbidden. Once again, we could not go out after dark. I spent Christmas with two American friends; we laid in supplies— canned food, candles, cash—in anticipation of a siege.

Some weeks later, I was in the market again. I had a bag of fruit on my arm and had finished my errands, but, because I hadn't seen Sunil for a few days, I made an extra turn around the market. Then Mohamet ran up to me: "Hey, you hear about Sunil? The cops got him." The charge was possession of a small amount of heroin. "You his friend, right? You go see him?"

I wasn't sure about that. But it was painful to imagine skinny Sunil in a dark jail cell, pressed in with guys a lot tougher and bigger than him. His parents were far out of touch—in another country. In my flat, I chain-smoked and looked at his photo. From one point of view, it made no sense for a white, credentialed American scholar to go visit a petty drug dealer. But he was also my friend, in a way. And if I did go, what harm would it do, really? *I* hadn't done anything wrong.

I looked for Mohamet in the market, hoping he could show me the way to the remand prison and act as translator, but I couldn't find him. Another tout, Vasanta, offered to guide me. I followed him: though his clothes were neat, he smelled rank and dirty, as if he'd slept in them for days. Outside the remand prison, visitors queued up as if they were at a bus stop. Women with packets of food tried to keep their bored kids in check. A beggar rolled by on a wheeled dolly, muttering to himself in English, "All the world's a stage". Guards pointed at me and snickered. No doubt I stood out: blond, white, well-fed. Finally I was let into a dark hallway; behind bars Sunil was freaking after a few days without heroin. "Help me, Lauren," he said, crying. "The food here is shit. When I'm here I think of you. Bring biscuits, bring cigarettes. Come tomorrow." Sunil held my arms. His tears fell on my cheek. When I came out, Vasanta was waiting.

The next day I did as Sunil asked: got food and biscuits, cigarettes with which to bribe his jailers. At the remand prison, a Tamil cop told me Sunil had been moved to a hospital at another site. He gave me Sunil's full name and case number. Again, I waited in line for hours with women in saris, families huddled together, though this line was more visible to casual passersby. Men in uniform demanded to know which country I was from, why I was there. I know how it looked: I was a druggie too, cheap foreign trash. I didn't want anyone to see me, and yet there I stood in the open. I knew that as a foreign and white visitor in Kandy, I was watched closely; my comings and goings were already a topic of conversation for people I didn't even know. Standing there, not wanting to be seen, but being seen nonetheless: all of this made me quake and stutter, unsure of myself, and doubtful about my own intentions. My presence there—and whatever story was woven around it—could get back to my sponsor, and then how could I explain myself?

Finally they let me see him. Sunil was sitting at a metal table, calm as could be. He held my hand in both of his.

He said, "I'll never smoke again."

I told him not to lie.

"Lauren, please help me. I have no one but you."

Ashamed and mortified, I said, "I don't know why I came here."

"Please, Lauren."

I sighed. "I'll see what I can do."

What he needed was money, of course; money to pay the fine, money to stay out of jail. And I had money—my fellowship gave me more in a month than the "average" Sri Lankan earned in a year. But it wasn't my money, really: it was the US government's money.

Then again, if I didn't help him, what would happen? I'd be a little richer and he'd be in jail, in conditions that were not going to win awards from any human rights groups. Maybe I could help him get some rehab. Surely that was a worthy cause.

But why do it? Why help this one boy out of all the others in Kandy—in Sri Lanka, the world—who needed help? And why help a drug dealer? Because I considered him a friend? Because he asked?

Then again, how did it happen that I was even in this position of privilege? How did it happen that I'd been born white and American? In different circumstances, a guy like Sunil could have been a successful schoolboy, a legitimate businessman. What trick of fate had landed us in these circumstances? And if my privilege and his situation were accidents, helping him had a certain kind of logic. Anyway, my money—government money—was tainted by all the things the US had done to people around the world: I might as well give it to this Sri Lankan who had no other source of help.

As it happened I was about to leave on a research trip to India. Vasanta was willing to help; I left 3000 rupees—about $120—with him, and he promised to go to the upcoming court date and pay what needed to be paid. I gave Vasanta an aerogram with my address abroad so he could let me know how things went. A few weeks later his letter arrived saying that the fine had been more than 3000. He'd had to spend his own money to get Sunil out. "You need to pay me."

"We'll see about that," I thought, relieved at least that Sunil was out. When I got back to Kandy, I soon saw Sunil on the street, and he said the fine hadn't even been 2000. Vasanta had taken the rest. Mohamet laughed: "Vasanta's a rich man now." But Vasanta insisted that I still owed him. He followed me around the market, hissing from behind: "You got to pay more." He knew he had something over me—he knew that I was uncomfortable about my close association with drug dealers, that I wanted to be rid of him, that I was afraid people at the university would hear some gossip.

I began to avoid the market and returned to my long walks in the countryside. One day when I was on one of my long troubled walks, a packed tourist van passed me and then squealed to a stop just ahead: Sunil, in a sarong instead of his usual jeans, jumped out of the van and ran back: "The police got me with ganja." He grabbed my hands. "I'm going home to Galle", he said and rushed back to the van full of impatient travelers.

I stood on the road, both surprised and relieved. So he did have a place to go, some kind of home, after all. He'd lied to me, but that was no surprise.

Walking on, I felt relieved: it would be good to have him gone. At one time I had thought that I might help Sunil get clean, but I'd since learned that Sri Lanka had few resources for this. Kathmandu had a decent place, I was told, but that was many decisions and commitments away. It was better if he was just gone.

From the Colombo newspaper, *The Island*, May 1985:

> More than 30 young drug addicts seeking medical attention at the Angoda Narcotic Ward were refused admission due to lack of staff and accommodation. The Narcotic Unit housed in the top floor of Ward 11 was opened in June 1984. Up to date there has been no instance where a single bed was unoccupied. Health Ministry sources said the present Drug Addicts Ward was opened on the instructions of the Director General of the Health Service although there weren't adequate staff. Drug addicts are now warded along with mental patients at Angoda and sources say there was a possibility of mental patients being addicted to drugs too. There have been instances where drug addicts and mental patients were involved in severe brawls. A mental patient's relations complained to "The Island" that their belongings too have been stolen. Beside the Drug Addict gangs within the ward, staff have been threatened with knives and bombs.[5]

Sunil was gone but Vasanta was still there. Although I no longer dawdled in town, I still had to go to the market for foodstuffs and sundries. There Vasanta trailed me, embarrassing me, hissing behind me: "I need money." He stood in front of me, leaned close, and stared menacingly: "It's not right." I didn't know if he might expose me or even hurt me, but he knew too much. I can still smell him: the stale cigarette smoke, the much-worn clothes. Though he was barely twenty, his face was banged up, the eyes yellow and rheumy. I was jumpy whenever I was in town, not knowing when and where he might appear. I might turn away from a welcome exchange with Kumar and see Vasanta's ugly snarl.

My apartment was outside the city and I'd felt safe there on the quiet hillside until one day my landlady told me that "a Vasanta" had come to see me. She added that she had helpfully pointed out my flat to him. He'd tracked me there through word of mouth, simply by asking after the white lady. I locked my doors and windows. Several nights running I lay in bed, totally enervated; ticks of the clock became footfall on gravel. Acid churned in my gut. Something was there. There was someone outside. Fear took weird shape in the dark; he could threaten me, beat me, knife me, and no one would hear a sound. During the day, I got out of the house; avoiding the market area, I went to the library, I walked in the countryside, I arranged to meet with Peace Corps friends, British Service volunteers, went for tea with acquaintances from the university. Maybe if I filled my days with normal things they would *become* normal again.

I needed other people around—fluent English speakers, white friends; I used them as shields.

Given everything else that was going on in the island, it was a small thing, this fear. But it shook me to the depths. I was afraid of Vasanta, surely, who could make me suffer in body and in reputation. But something else scared me more: I had created this situation because, as I had discovered, I had no solid foundation—no good mechanism for figuring out how to act, how to live. At home, I had the luxury of believing that cultural norms and ethics were relative things; at the same time, I was so deeply enmeshed in prevailing mores and codes that I never really had to work out my own response to complicated ethical situations. In Sri Lanka, though, lost in a kind of radical relativism and sustained only with naive and sporadic good intentions, I didn't how to act or decide. I felt the ground slip away. I could tell myself that I had been trying to help Sunil, but even that wasn't a narrative that I could sustain. I didn't know what I was doing. In Sri Lanka, during a civil war, I faced an ethical conundrum and found there was nothing to stand on but rushing water, that *I* was nothing but rushing water.

During my campaign to create a "normal" life, I had a few friends over for dinner; white friends from California and Cambridgeshire, people my age who'd come to Sri Lanka as volunteers. As we shared liters of beer, I almost forgot to be afraid. My friends filled up the flat's five chairs; their laughter echoed in the under-furnished rooms. And while we were chatting happily there, Vasanta came to the door. He was clearly stoned and mean. He looked in through the open door and said my name: "Laurie." My guests were confused: Vasanta was not the kind of person who fit the paradigm of friend, or even neighbor or servant. I went to the door, and speaking in hushed tones, tried to get him to leave. When he didn't go, Jim, a brash Peace Corps volunteer, sprang up and shooed Vasanta away as if he were a scabby dog. I was impressed with Jim's decisiveness: he had looked at Vasanta, sized up the situation, and acted. He didn't have to think about it; he knew Vasanta was not someone to associate with. After Vasanta left, my guests turned to me for an explanation. What was this guy doing here? How do you know him? I didn't know what to say. I shook my head: I don't know. I tried to pass over the incident, hoping they'd think it was the usual tout harassment.

But now I knew: Vasanta would come, and he wasn't giving up. He came again in the daytime, insisting, "You didn't give me enough. I had to borrow money to get Sunil out". Finally I caved. I no longer cared what the truth was; I just wanted him to leave me alone. I gave him another 3000 rupees: "I'll give you the money and I don't ever want to see you again."

He nodded. "You and I, we both got burned in this", he said. Later I saw the tout named Mohamet. "Yeah, Vasanta cheated you again. He is rich man."

Sri Lanka in 1985 was at the volatile intersection of complex forces. The island became a major transit point for unrefined heroin headed for Europe and the US. Tamil militants trafficked in "brown sugar" to get money for guns and bombs. The government poured more money into fighting the insurgents and ramped up the nationalist rhetoric: Sri Lanka is for the "sons of the soil!"—the Sinhalese, the Buddhists, as Anagarika Dharmapala had said long ago. Civilians, children, soldiers, tourists were starved, blown up. Small time dealers like Sunil and Vasanta got hooked on the heroin that passed through the island. Maybe they, too, were collateral victims.

We knew about some of the complex forces. Some we just lived within.

The civil war, the constant curfews, Vasanta, Sunil: I couldn't wait to leave Sri Lanka and wanted to start again somewhere else. But I was there till July. In May we heard the story: a government-owned bus pulled in the railroad station at the central Sri Lankan city of Anuradhapura, a holy Buddhist city. Four men dressed as soldiers got down from the bus and walked toward the police station, while others collected into two groups around the main square. A man on a motorcycle gave a signal: the men from the bus then fired into the crowd. Later, they tossed a bomb into a tourist van and killed twelve people. Next they went to the site of the sacred bodhi tree, where they shot a monk and four nuns gathered there; they gunned down vendors who sold cold drinks to pilgrims and tourists. Officially, 146 people died in the siege, and more than a hundred were injured.[6]

An American friend and I visited Anuradhapura soon after the massacre: I had put off visiting the holy Buddhist site, but it seemed important to go, even now—*especially* now. Around the sacred tree, other cold drink vendors had taken the place of those who'd been gunned down, their carts well positioned to catch the eyes of visitors. In the business section of town, where shopkeepers offered Chinese thermoses, flashlights, bikes, and food-stuffs, seven shops had been torched. They were picked out of the line of shops and burned, their windows broken: the ones that remained standing were owned by Sinhalese, the burned ones by Tamils.

Ancient stupas dotted the old Buddhist city, now preserved as a World Heritage Site. At the entrance to each stupa rests a typical stone footpad carved in a half-moon shape. In arching bands, the stones are etched with a story about the progress toward Buddhist enlightenment. Flames fill the outermost band: this is the destruction and violence of desire, hatred, delu-sion; this is the world of *samsara*. Next to that, plants tangle in a crazy mess of fecundity; this is the disorder created by clinging and desire, the continuous cycles of birth and death. Moving toward the center, animals and plants become increasingly ordered, tamed by discipline and a search for the truth. Finally, at center, a lotus blooms: only a very few manage to rise out of the disorder of life to realize enlightenment.

I knew this view of the world, but I couldn't accept it as my own. I had embraced the world with its craziness. In any case, all around me in this predominantly Buddhist country, no lesson seemed to have been learned. It felt like there was no beginning or end to the violence; the country was continually in flames. Sinhalese Buddhists killed Tamil Hindus, Tamils killed Sinhalese, and everybody was drawn into the mayhem. Separatists had gunned down Buddhist nuns only days before in that very place, and it all just kept on: people blew up each other—blew themselves up—for the nation, to defend their own people, for the greater glory.

After dinner one evening in Anuradhapura, my friend and I tried to return to our hotel on our rented bikes, but barricades blocked the road, and a crowd had gathered. A truck had run into a state bus full of security forces. As a man standing near us explained, "It was unfortunate that the driver was Tamil". There was more trouble. We turned around to look for another route out of there. Father down the road a man asked us what the problem was. "Not more terrorists?" he asked with both fear and annoyance in his voice.

Not long before I was to leave, I got a letter from Sunil, written from the small village he grew up in outside Galle, a city south of Colombo on the coast. His father, who was not Malaysian after all but Sinhalese, had just returned from working in Saudi Arabia, and he wanted to meet me because I had helped his son. I thought it would be good to see Sunil now that he was out of Kandy and back with his family.

Sunil and I arranged to meet at the bus stand in Galle. He looked good— clear-eyed, cheerful—and wore a clean white shirt and sarong. He said, "Lauren, I must tell you. My name is not Sunil. It is Susantha". We walked to the small hut where his family lived alongside the Indian Ocean and near the beach town of Unawatuna, whose palms and white beaches lured tourists and surfers. His mother made tea; the neighbor women came out from a tangle of shacks to have a look at me. With his parents, I was careful to call him Susantha. His younger sister hopped awkwardly as she helped her mother; she had a severely maimed leg, broken in an accident years before but never properly tended to. The family served rice and fish curry, and treated me like an honored guest. I felt embarrassed. What had I done? When it was time to go, the father took my hands in his, thanking me for my help, saying, "Please take Susantha with you to America". I nodded ambiguously: I wanted him to know that I had heard him, but there was no way.

Susantha/Sunil and I walked along the white sand to Unawatuna. He said he wanted to visit a friend. Broken coconuts littered the beach and no swimmers plied the blue waters; it was the off-season. During tourist season, Bob Marley blasted from every restaurant, and beer and arak flowed freely, but the places were all shut now. Sunil went into a hut and, while I was standing next to him, he bought two tiny packets from a long-haired Sinhalese man in a red sarong. Outside, when I protested, Sunil tried to convince me that what had just happened had not in fact happened. Then he went into a bathroom and didn't return for a long time.

We went back to the bus station. He couldn't come to Kandy to see me off, he said, because of the police, and I was relieved. I gave him a bit of money; I hoped it might get to his family but knew it probably wouldn't. Today he's probably one of those fucked-up older touts whose face has been kicked in many times. Or maybe he's dead.

Sunil had lied about many things: his background, his age, even his name. I lied too, of course, though many of my lies were those of omission—I just didn't tell anyone what was happening. I also violated the terms of my fellowship—to present the US in an upstanding fashion, to spend the funds they gave me responsibly. At one time I had imagined helping Sunil, but my charity was only processed through the drug trade. Sunil and Vasanta got high.

Critics of travel writing have long ago rejected the myth that travelers can create themselves anew in a new place. We've come to accept that we are made by the places we're in, by the people and things we interact with, by the stories that surround us. Most of the time, when travelers are in the middle of things, we can't see how the stories work, how these situations create our possibilities. In writing this, I'm trying to trace some of the threads that make up this web of relations—not to absolve myself, but to think about what happens when we travel—what happened when I traveled to Sri Lanka—and to try to find a way to write about it.

My experience in Sri Lanka was shaped by the effects of living in the midst of a civil war, by the threat of violence, by my status as a privileged white American woman. I've tried to describe what happened to me there, but there were so many ways in which this story was out of my control. And perhaps that's the point. The strings that connect terrorism, addiction, warfare, hate, governments, violence, Sinhalese Buddhism, American ideals, and various forms of nationalism are bigger than me—way bigger than me. And like all the other characters in this tale, I was wrapped up in these forces—or rather, they were wrapped up in us; they shaped who we thought we were, what we did. The war and the call to valor hailed men and women who had few other opportunities. The stinking economy—both a source and the result of the war—helped make Sunil a drug dealer, his father a guest worker. American ideals and privilege created a policy of educational exchange that placed me, their agent, in Kandy in 1984; indeed, American-style ideals shaped my urge to help Sunil, and perhaps even my failure to follow through. And when it comes down to it, I have to wonder if there's some connection between the fear that someone will attack you in the dark, the fear that you will die if you don't get a hit, and the fear that your body will be blown into a million little pieces and blasted into the banana trees. Different though these things may be, they are—all of them—terrifying.

NOTES

1. Jay D. Palmer, "Striking with Deadly Force," *Time* (international ed.), 17 December 1984.
2. For more on the history of Dutugemenu, see K. M. DeSilva, *A History of Sri Lanka* (Delhi: Oxford University Press, 1981), pp. 13–16.
3. Institute of Peace and Conflict Studies, "*Drug-trafficking and Abuse in Sri Lanka*" (22 August 2003) <http://www.ipcs.org/print_article-details. php?recNo=1115> (15 February 2012).

4. Peter Chalk, "Liberation Tigers of Tamil Eelam's (LTTE) International Organization and Operations: A Preliminary Analysis", *Commentary* no. 77 (1999) <www.fas.org/irp/world/para/docs/com77e.htm> (6 March 2009).
5. Nushad Perera, "30 young drug addicts refused admission to narcotics ward," *The Island* (Colombo, Sri Lanka), 23 May 1985.
6. Joseph Treen with Mervyn da Silva, "Days of Fear—And Bloodshed," *Newsweek* (Asian ed.), 27 May 1985.

5 Victor Segalen in the Contact Zone
Exoticism, Ethics, and the Traveler and "Travelee"

Charles Forsdick

Following his premature death at the age of forty-one, the Breton-born doctor, traveler, author, and theorist of the exotic, Victor Segalen (1878–1919), largely disappeared from public attention, a victim of what a number of critics have seen as the radical untimeliness of his literary and theoretical work.[1] Segalen's visibility slowly yet progressively increased, however, as his work was discovered by new generations of readers across the second half of the twentieth century, a process triggered not least by the influential critical engagements with his writings, in the postwar period, by key Francophone postcolonial intellectuals such as the Martinican Édouard Glissant and the Moroccan Abdelkebir Khatibi. Much of Segalen's work appeared (and, indeed, continues to appear) posthumously, since at the time of his death he had published only three books: a poorly received ethnographic novel in which he attempted to recount the "fatal impact" of European colonization of Polynesia from an indigenous perspective, *Les Immémoriaux* (A Lapse of Memory);[2] an elaborately published series of prose poems inspired by the form of Chinese funerary monuments, *Stèles* (Stelae);[3] and a further volume of prose poems, also inspired by Chinese visual culture, *Peintures* (Paintings).[4] All of these works, produced during a period when colonial literature and the exoticist novel were at their height, attempt to produce a narrative perspective that either re-creates that of a non-Western voice or is at least inflected or attenuated by the multiple perspectives that constitute any form of interhuman and intercultural encounter. As such, they contain in embryo elements of the ethical reflections explored in this chapter that underpin Segalen's travel writing as well as his exploration of what he dubs the "aesthetics of diversity" in the fragments of his *Essay on Exoticism* (written 1904–18, but first published in French as "Notes sur l'exotisme" in 1955).[5] The aim of this chapter is to explore the ambiguities of Segalen's engagement with the ethics of travel, and to analyze the extent to which this early twentieth-century literary experimentation may be related in creative terms to contemporary reflections on concepts such as Gayatri Spivak's "teleopoesis", a comparative reading practice that depends on "imagining yourself, really letting yourself be imagined (experience that impossibility) without guarantees, by and in another culture".[6]

Although in the decades following his death several previously unpublished novels, poetry collections and other archaeological writings appeared in print, Segalen's reputation remained restricted to a narrow circle of enlightened or specialized readers, the majority of whom took a particular interest in the geographical regions in which he had spent much of his adult life—namely, Polynesia and China. Part of the challenge for the reader of Segalen, beyond that of the inherent difficulty of a number of his texts, is the marked diversity they represent in terms of genre and disciplinary field. As a literary inventor and experimenter, Segalen operated across a range of genres, most notably poetry, drama, travel writing, the novel, and the essay, but also persistently endeavored to create new generic forms, characterized in particular by a hybridization of French traditions with non-Western models and also by a startlingly modern attention to the instability of the notion of genre itself. As a scholar and practitioner, Segalen's interests are equally varied, tending toward the polymathic and ranging from his professional interest in the medical (he was by trade a naval doctor), passing via art history, archaeology, politics, and philosophy and extending to a personal commitment to the anthropological.

The formal and disciplinary diversity that characterizes Segalen's work may be seen to have served, initially at least, as an impediment to recognition of his importance to the European intellectual culture of the early twentieth century. More particularly, there was a failure to recognize the clear links with explorations—in a context characterized by the still often unquestioned assumptions of colonial expansion—of the relationship between Western self and non-Western other, or in the field of travel, to borrow the terminology of Mary Louise Pratt adopted in the title of this chapter, between "traveler" and "travelee".[7] It was, however, the conceptualization of diversity as guiding principle and federating concept that ensured the recognition of the importance of Segalen in the second half of the twentieth century, as well as his more recent assertion as a key thinker of exoticism and intercultural contact. The reassessment of Segalen's significance occurred in the aftermath of the Second World War, and more particularly in the context of the decolonization of the French-speaking world. A key year in these processes was 1955, four decades following his death, when *Les Immémoriaux* was republished, almost fifty years after its initial appearance, as one of the inaugural titles in Plon's Terre Humaine series. Founded by Jean Malaurie in 1955, this pioneering collection foreshadowed many subsequent debates in anthropology by combining more conventional accounts with first-person, often autoethnographic studies produced by a range of authors from a variety of cultural backgrounds.[8] The collection now comprises over eighty titles, over ten million copies of which have been sold worldwide, with many of these in translation. The most prominent titles remain some of the first published in the series: Malaurie's own *Les Derniers Rois de Thulé* (1955), an account of his life among the Inuit people of Greenland, and Claude Lévi-Strauss's *Tristes Tropiques* (also 1955), a hybrid text combining travel writing with an anthropological account of the indigenous societies of Brazil. Pierre Jakez Hélias's *Cheval d'orgueil: mémoires d'un Breton du pays bigouden* (1975), an autobiographical *Bildungsroman* exploring the transformations of modern Breton society, remains, however, the best-selling title in the collection. Malaurie's editorial project endeavors to federate the activity of a group of writers committed to a renewal of the forms of literary engagement with culture and place, often eschewing objectivity and—in anticipation to a certain extent of the postmodern ethnography outlined by North American figures such as James Clifford and George Marcus in key volumes such as their coedited *Writing Culture*[9]—acknowledging the subjectivity central to those creative processes whereby anthropologists and travelers typically frame their thoughts.[10]

The reemergence of Segalen in postwar France reveals, therefore, a timing that relates these salvaged or republished editions of Segalen's work to such key contemporary texts as Lévi-Strauss's *Tristes Tropiques* or Aimé Césaire's *Discours sur le colonialisme*, both published in 1955, and invites a reading of Segalen's early twentieth-century texts in the light of an increasingly evident anticolonialism as well as of the greater awareness of and even anxiety regarding the European presence beyond Europe with which this is associated. Through the republication of *Les Immémoriaux*, this narrative of the European colonization and religious conversion of Tahiti—a work that had been met with incomprehension, and had even temporarily been yoked to a French colonial literature movement in search of the *Kipling français*—found at last a receptive audience. The readers of Segalen in the new Terre Humaine edition were more willing than their early twentieth-century predecessors to engage in debates about the destructive force of colonial expansion in its many forms. They also began to appreciate a work in which the articulation of subaltern subjectivity, and the inverse exoticism this permitted, were not mere literary conceits but had serious implications for a critique of the new world order—soon to be chronologically postcolonial, yet persistently neocolonial—that was becoming rapidly apparent through the struggle for independence in sub-Saharan Africa and Algeria. Lévi-Strauss, whose own hybrid blend of travelogue, memoir, and philosophical treatise appeared, as has been noted above, at the same time and in the same series, was slowly uncovering the racist assumptions of European universalism while laying the foundations for a structuralism that would permit cross-cultural relativization and a challenge of civilizational hierarchies with roots in Enlightenment thought. At the same time, the dimensions of Lévi-Strauss's work most closely associated with travel writing continued a threnodic indictment of entropy and a lament for the decline of cultural diversity, both of which constitute a clear structure of feeling in European journey narratives, traceable to the early nineteenth century in the work of authors such as François-René Chateaubriand, and apparent in its most developed and articulate form in the negentropic reflections of Segalen himself on the decline of cultural distinctiveness.[11]

In this context, the new edition of *Les Immémoriaux* found a notable readership outside France. The Moroccan sociologist and novelist Abdelkebir Khatibi describes, in his autobiographical text *La Mémoire tatouée*,[12] the way in which he was handed Segalen's work by a teacher seeking to explain not only the dynamics of (de)colonization but also the need to discern a distinctive voice, both individual and collective, in its wake. Also in 1955 appeared a new edition of two of the works published during Segalen's life, *Stèles* and *Peintures*, presented with the first unexpurgated version of the posthumously published Chinese travelogue *Equipée* (Escapades),[13] as well as with excerpts from the unfinished *Essai sur l'exotisme* (Essay on Exoticism). It was this volume that would have a major impact on one of Khatibi's contemporaries, the equally (if not more) influential Édouard Glissant, who was struggling with similar issues of identity and resistance in the context of the recently departmentalized French Caribbean. This postcolonial engagement with texts such as *Equipée* and *Essai sur l'Exotisme* reflects the privileged place they have acquired in discussions regarding exoticism, cultural diversity, and the ethical dimensions of intercultural contact and the interpersonal encounters with which travel is associated. These works are firmly rooted—in terms of their paratexts and their fields of reference—in the context of their production. *Equipée* is, for instance, dedicated to the philosopher of bovarysm, Jules de Gaultier, a thinker whose influence is equally apparent in the fragmented reflections accumulated over fourteen years that constitute the *Essai*. As such, these texts are mired in the French intellectual life of first two decades of twentieth century, and reveal clear connections with the diverse schools and literary milieux of the period, including the *Mercure de France*, "*les Français d'Asie*", and the *littérature coloniale* movement. At the same time, they are the vehicle of a very different, decidedly posthumous Segalen, one feted by Patrick Chamoiseau, Édouard Glissant, and Abdelkebir Khatibi, but at the same time critiqued by Edward Said—a Segalen who, particularly in his writings on exoticism, may be seen as a precursor to the emergence of postcolonialism as a critical discourse, providing a corrective not least to the anglophone biases of such a body of criticism and an indication of the ways in which an awareness of its Francophone roots might permit a way out of the monolingualism of a set of critical practices said to have "ears only for English".[14] It is Segalen's precursory status that is perhaps particularly important here, for while his work has been adopted and widely cited by key Francophone postcolonial intellectuals such as the Martinican *créolistes*, it is linked more firmly to understandings of Western texts such as the travelogue that were subject to the colonial discourse analysis from which, in the academy, much postcolonial criticism emerged. Segalen's writings respond in particular to a questioning of the methodological approaches we might adopt when reading travel literature that avoid the two extremes of reductive aestheticization that denies the wordliness of the text and anthropological representativity that may be seen to overprivilege it. In addition, as I will suggest in this chapter, his work may be seen to outline a precursory contribution of "ethical criticism" to readings of travel literature.

Segalen's travelogues, and most notably a text such as *Equipée*, poses—in its representation of interpersonal encounters in the field between Western travelers and Chinese travelees—clear questions about the ethics of travel, and in particular about the asymmetries of power that such meetings often betoken. By presenting these encounters in terms of a mutually disorientating destabilization of identity, dependent on an understanding of exoticism that is profoundly bilateral and depends ultimately on an imagination of mutual defamiliarization, the traditional solipsism of the European traveler is undermined, and Segalen provides description in his work of sites at which the ethics of travel are at once enacted and (in association with the reflections of the *Essai sur l'exotisme*) theorized. To revisit these early twentieth-century reflections almost a century later is to contribute to a wider, ongoing reflection, both *intercultural* and comparative, on the ways in which texts and ideas travel between historical moments and between intellectual contexts. To read Segalen in terms of contemporary considerations of travel and ethics is not least to ask how this postsymbolist author whose travels were permitted by his status as an agent of empire came to be feted especially in the North American academy, where the translation of the *Essay on Exoticism* was very much presented as an intervention in the field of postcolonialism—that is, as a precursor to postcolonial thought. What does such a process say about the ways in which ideas are transformed as they travel? Is it the responsibility of the scholar always to contextualize such material and risk reductivity, or to what extent does our critical practice permit creative transformations and translations as we read a historical text from the perspective of the present, or perhaps more accurately permit that historical text to play an active role in the formation of a critical paradigm for reading the present? Finally, and in relation to this, what does this say about the genealogy of postcolonialism, one of these perspectives on the present that continues to dominate in the anglophone academy? Does talking about a "postcolonial Segalen" constitute a retrospective recuperation of a would-be precursor, as part of an effort to gain respectability through a sense of a manufactured tradition, or does this permit instead the statement of a genuine if obscured intellectual lineage that connects seemingly disparate texts, moments, and historicocultural niches?

The integration of the reflections and travel practices of Segalen into the reading of travel accounts needs to be understood in the light of the national traditions in which such works are studied. In terms of the critical practices of anglophone and Francophone scholars of travel and its literary manifestations, there is clear evidence of a bifurcation between traditions, although any such crude analysis is of course belied by critical practice. In the anglophone academy, the founding and enduring influence of critics such as Said and Pratt has often meant that travel literature has been read as a form of colonial discourse, and it is clear that a perception of the heavily policed boundaries of the genre and its regular association with a "guild" of travel writers characterized as white, Western, and primarily male have supported such a view.[15] According to such a now well-rehearsed reading, travel narratives have permitted Western cultures to create an archive of elsewhere, the production of which justifies—or even, in certain accounts, enables—the control of that elsewhere. In the Francophone academy, despite a continued unwillingness to engage with postcolonial scholarship and the work of critics such as Said, much imagological research—such as the important work of Jean-Marc Moura on exoticism[16]—has similar aims. However, French-language scholarship on travel literature has traditionally been concerned, on the whole, with poetics—and in particular with questions of narratology, genericity, intertexuality, and literariness—in ways that are only rarely the case among English-language scholars.

Since the late 1990s, anglophone travel scholars have sought a way out of the *impasse* of colonial discourse theory, a critical dead end that Terry Eagleton associates with postcolonial theory and characterizes as the "pretentiously opaque" product of a "gaudy, all-licenced supermarket of the mind";[17] Eagleton proceeds to develop this criticism into a more wide-ranging and acerbic attack on "postmodernism's enduring love-affair with otherness".[18] Claiming that this subject is "not the most fertile of intellectual furrows," he continues, "once you have observed that the other is typically portrayed as lazy, dirty, stupid, crafty, womanly, passive, rebellious, sexually rapacious, childlike, enigmatic and a number of other mutually contradictory epithets, it is hard to know what to do next apart from reaching for yet another textual illustration of the fact".[19] The caricature is a harsh one, and reflects a limited reading of the travelogue whose aim is to prove that colonial propaganda is colonial propaganda—and otherwise to deform, or selectively to read travel narratives, in order to prove preprogrammed conclusions. What Eagleton ignores are more nuanced approaches to the travel narrative suggested in diverse ways by critics such as Graham Huggan,[20] Syed Islam,[21] and Debbie Lisle,[22] all of whom pose alternative sets of questions not necessarily entertainable in a context that assumes the travelogue is a discursive monolith. Such approaches are broadly associated with the political and the ethical, and suggest a clear attenuation of any previous assumption that the travel narrative was automatically and unswervingly conscripted to projects of colonial expansionism. Central to these is the question as to whether travel narratives have become—and even have previously been—less culturally arrogant, or at least less ideologically complicit with established patterns of representation and political orthodoxies, than earlier ethical (and especially postcolonial) critiques have often allowed. By extension, it has become increasingly possible to consider the ways in which travel narratives, far from being inherently conservative, have historically been deployed to elaborate or support oppositional stances or even political radicalism, and—as is the case with the work of an author such as Segalen—may be seen to provide evidence to support claims that the genre has been innovative and experimental, both formally and intellectually. Central to such questioning has been a reopening of debates about how the genre of travel writing has been controlled and for what reasons it has been policed, areas that have permitted, by extension, a reexploration of the relationship between regulatory maneuvers and the perceived right to represent cross-cultural encounters. Finally, such reflection leads to a reassessment of the extent to which the access of the travelee to agency, and ultimately to the means of representation, is genuinely controlled.

A number of these urgent questions are associated directly with an issue central to Segalen's early twentieth-century reflections on travel and the inter-cultural encounters it permits—that is, the relationship between traveler and travelee. In a Saidian reading, the former (i.e., the traveler), through the hallucination or abstract imagination of elsewhere, is said to proceed solipsistically, denying existence to the latter (i.e., to the travelee), or at least reducing her to a lifeless trope. By coining the term *travelee* (in fact only used on three occasions in the main text of *Imperial Eyes*), Pratt attempted to reanimate this passive character who is "traveled over", seeing the traveler and travelee coexisting, and acknowledging what she sees as traces of their copresence:

> the "contact zone" is an attempt to invoke the spatial and temporal copresence of subjects previously separated by geographic and historical disjunctures, and whose trajectories now intersect. By using the term *contact* I aim to foreground the interactive, improvisational dimensions of colonial encounters, so easily ignored or suppressed by diffusionist accounts of conquest and domination. A *contact perspective* emphasizes how subjects are constituted in and by their relations to each other. It treats the relations among colonizers and colonized, or travelers and travelees not in terms of separateness or apartheid but in terms of copresence, interaction, interlocking understandings, and practices, often within radically asymmetrical relations of power.[23]

Instead of the subaltern being denied speech and the critic confirming this denial by seeking evidence of silence, Pratt encouraged a sensitivity to traces of otherness in the travel narrative, and in particular to textual traces of the ways in which Western culture might be seen to have been "transculturated", by which she understood reprocessed and represented in various ways by inhabitants of the periphery to which its travelers journey.

Claire Lindsay, in a recent essay provocatively titled "Beyond *Imperial Eyes*",[24] has explored criticisms of Pratt's work and suggested the ways in which engagement with her 1992 study has enriched and nuanced the concepts central to it. Such criticism has challenged the representativity of the authors that Pratt selected to include in the corpus of primary texts she studies, suggesting that a reliance on published travel narratives can engender a privileging of elite voices—or at least of voices ideologically aligned with those economic and strategic interests with which colonial expansion was associated. At the same time, Lindsay outlines the ways in which the emphasis in *Imperial Eyes* on Manichean and on adversarial structures, and the privileging of the visual evident from the book's title, have been replaced by what she sees as a "phenomenology of colonization". This is a notion explored in particular by Jessica Dubow, who suggests that the aspiration to a "lived reciprocity of subject and space" may be seen as part of a more complex desire on the part of the colonizer to dwell in colonized space.[25] Although limitations have been identified in the definitional development of autoethnography and the spatial dimensions of the contact zone merit continued reflection, Pratt's privileging of the concept of "transculturation" has allowed an overhaul of any assumptions, generated by earlier critical paradigms such as colonial discourse studies, that—in Steve Clark's terms—travel writing is to be read as "one-way traffic".[26] In Pratt's adoption and adaptation of a term first popularized by Fernando Ortiz in his *Cuban Counterpoint*,[27] the travelee's passivity is accordingly transformed into activity, and the indigenous populations denied not only agency but also presence in the terms of Said's "orientalist" paradigm recover a degree of autonomy. On her neologism, Pratt writes,

> This clumsy term is coined on analogy with the term "addressee". As the latter means the person addressed by a speaker, "travelee" means persons traveled to (or on) by a traveler, receptors of travel. A few years ago literary theorists began speaking of "narratees", figures corresponding to narrators on the reception end of narration. Obviously, travel is studied overwhelmingly from the perspective of the traveler, but it is perfectly possible, and extremely interesting to study it from the perspective of those who participate on the receiving end.[28]

Although this initial definition seems to suggest that the travelee's viewpoint may be imagined or seen as a hermeneutic strategy, the passive/active relationship implied by the suffixes deployed—travel-*er*/travel-*ee*—is implicitly and immediately challenged by Pratt's own analyses and by her presentation of copresence as a condition of interaction. The implications of such an understanding are developed in a new direction by the ethnographer James Clifford, whose notion of "traveling cultures" offers the potential to upset further any fixed notions of who has a right to travel and who has a duty to stay still—or, more simply, of who is the traveler and who the travelee. For Clifford,[29] cultures are to be understood in terms of dwelling and traveling, and not in terms of one or the other—that is, by considering "traveling-in-dwelling" and "dwelling-in-traveling", we move away from organicist understandings of culture that depend on a notion of a rooted body that grows, lives, and dies, and see cultures instead as sites of displacement, interference, and interaction. In practical terms, for those studying travel literature, the challenge is to recognize the ways in which the spaces of travel are therefore crossed by countless alternative journeys; the problem, Clifford acknowledges, is finding the means of recovering the narratives, or accounts, or traces, of these "other" journeys, but he persists in stating, "[a]nd if contemporary migrant populations are not to appear as mute, passive straws in the political-economic winds, we need to listen to a wide range of 'travel stories' (not 'travel literature' in the bourgeois sense)".[30]

The critical praxis for what Clifford outlines is provided, I would suggest, by Said. In *Culture and Imperialism*,[31] by developing the notion of counterpoint and contrapuntal reading (a postcolonial comparatism that moves beyond models of center and periphery, and brings together texts in mutually illuminating ways), Said responds to his earlier critics and, to a certain extent, revises his own work and especially its apparent exclusion of indigenous voices. With "travel stories" illuminating "travel literature", assumptions of cultural hierarchies, on which definitions of the latter often depend, become precarious. The results of such maneuvers are multiple, undermining what Johannes Fabian calls the "denial of co-evalness" that characterizes much Western anthropology (and, by extension, much travel writing),[32] and rendering if not redundant at least compromised the string of binaries on which such a concept depends: modern/traditional; writing/ written; observing/observed; mobile/sessile; dynamic/static. As Chris Rojek and John Urry have noted, these binaries are now increasingly eroded: "All cultures get remade as a result of the flows of peoples, objects and images across national borders, whether these involve colonialism, work-based migration, individual travel or mass tourism."[33]

Although Pratt imagines a contact zone in which copresence leads to "interaction, interlocking understandings and practices", and although Said provides an analytic paradigm—counterpoint—that in ways bordering on deconstruction permits the opening of texts to reveal their silences, anxieties, and blind spots, I would suggest that it is only in recent, perhaps more specifically postwar travel narratives that the full implications of what these terms imply for the potential instability of the traveler's identity become apparent. Despite the persistence of imperialist nostalgia and guild mentality, alternative journey accounts have emerged, even within the Western tradition of the genre. The work of Nicolas Bouvier—and in particular perhaps *Le Poisson-Scorpion* (Scorpion Fish)[34]—is characterized, for instance, by what one critic has called "une esthétique de la disparition" (an aesthetics of disappearance),[35] according to which the traveler progressively erases himself from his account in the face of his experience of other cultures. Or François Maspero's *Passagers du Roissy-Express* (Roissy Express: A Journey through the Paris Suburbs), which describes a pair of Parisian travelers whose encounters with others—"des gens qui cheminent vers d'improbables destinations" (people who journey toward improbable destinations)—cause them to relativize their own journey.[36] The subsequent deflation and even trivialization to which this seems to lead invite a new, contrapuntal awareness of competing journeys and underline the implications of such an awareness for conventional understandings of travel literature. Maspero's aim is to operate in a space in which he and his cotraveler Anaïk Frantz are outsiders—or even marginal figures—while allowing to emerge, through both the practice and (textual and photographic) account of their journey, the voices and experiences of those marginal figures they meet. The traveler's autocratic and aristocratic discourse of self-sufficiency is replaced with a more precarious conception of travel literature that invites the reader to pry open conventional definitions of travel.

The identification of these instabilities of identity in the work of contemporary travelers, characterized by postcolonial anxieties and a globalized consciousness, is perhaps not as challenging as their interrogation in earlier narratives. It is with such an exploration that the chapter will conclude, returning to Segalen, the author indicted by Edward Said in one of the catalogs of authors that punctuate *Orientalism*, but cited by other "postcolonial" critics (not least Glissant, who commented on Segalen's work for over fifty years throughout his literary career) as a counterdiscursive figure who challenged yet was ultimately eclipsed by the colonial orthodoxies of the early twentieth century. In the light of some of the terms explored above—most notably, *travelee, contact zone,* and *traveling culture*—I will suggest a rereading of the 1916 travel narrative *Equipée* (published for the first time in 1929),[37] and relate some of the issues it addresses to Segalen's own conceptual reflections in the *Essay on Exoticism*. The travel narrative and essay form a diptych, linked by a shared engagement with the philosophical thought of Jules de Gaultier (and in particular with his concept of bovarysm), and existing perhaps more strikingly in a relationship of theory and practice (an interpretation echoed in the title of Kenneth White's 1979 study of Segalen, *Théorie et pratique du voyage*,[38] written with the *Essai* and *Equipée* in mind).

Unlike many other travel writers and colonial authors of his period, there is a tendency throughout Segalen's work to acknowledge the "traveling"—or mobile—nature of other cultures. The Polynesian or Chinese protagonists of some of his most important fictional works—Térii in *Les Immémoriaux*, or Kouang Siu (Guangxu) in *Le Fils du Ciel*[39]—are themselves travelers, and an important unpublished text of Segalen's, *La Queste à la Licorne* (a manuscript from 1910),[40] is a pastiche of Marco Polo that describes a meeting of medieval travelers, European and Chinese, whose shared experience of contact is one of mutual incomprehension. This understanding of the "traveling" nature of other cultures and of the potential of their inhabitants to be travelers in their own right is radically different from that of the majority of his contemporaries, and is translated via the travelogue *Equipée* into a reflection on the narrator-traveler's relation to, and representation of, the "travelees" and "narratees" he meets.

In *Equipée* there are very few place names, even fewer dates, and only rare references to people other than the narrator himself. The text is an amalgamation of various journeys in China from the years preceding the First World War, and operates primarily as a philosophical treatise that uses "l'épisode périmé d'un voyage" (the faded episode of a journey[41]) to ask the key question, "L'imaginaire déchoit–il ou se renforce quand il se confronte au réel?" (Does the imaginary decline or increase when confronted with the Real?) (p. 11). The clash of worlds that primarily interests Segalen is not that of traveler and travelee but of *réel* and *imaginaire*, and it is this dimension that has primarily interested critics, not least as a result of its relationship with another set of ethical questions linking the traveler to what Percy Adams calls the "travel-liar".[42] The repeated focus on encounter suggests that there is another dimension to the text that merits further investigation. Segalen's narrator is usually (and not unusually for the time) seated on horseback, and—like his creator—seems more interested in statues than humans. He is no participant observer, and the Chinese characters the traveler meets are either anonymous or (ethnographically) generic. In the first category are situated the "trois cent coolies maigres et nus qui piétient" (three hundred weak and naked coolies who shuffle along) (p. 38), the Sampan pilot in whose face a stove explodes and who "se tord au fond du bateau, aveuglé, brûlé, décapé à vif, roussi jusqu'au noir, ne pouvant même pas pleurer" (writhes on the bottom of the boat, blinded, burned, flayed, heavily scorched, unable even to cry) (p. 44); in the second are the character types whom Segalen dubs "L'Homme de Bât" (Man of Burden) and "La Femme au lit du réel" (Woman in the bed of the real). This typology serves as content for the two problematic chapters of *Equipée* in which contact with the indigenous population is discussed and on which a considerable amount has already been written. Segalen's aristocratic and even solipsistic notion of the *exote*—this *voyageur-né* (born traveler) who is distinguished from the majority of tourists—does not allow him to entertain Clifford's suggestion that "a long list of actors" might be considered as travelers, too, who share the space of his journey. What is striking here, apart from the clearly Swiftian irony that causes the reader to be wary of any overly literal reading, is the indictment of French republicanism in whose name the New Imperialist "civilizing mission" (of which Segalen was a clear critic) was being undertaken. Less attention has been paid to two moments of specific contact or encounter with individuals and not types: in describing Chinese interest in the corpse of a dead missionary, murdered on the Tibetan border, the narrator alludes to "ce curieux spectacle d'un squelette d'Européen" (this curious spectacle of a European skeleton) (p. 75), and the sense of an exoticization of elements of the traveler's own culture pervades the text. This first crystallizes in what the narrator later dismisses as "un rêve de marche" (a walking dream), his stumbling across a community that has been without contact with the outside world for three hundred years and who have a profoundly archaic appearance as a result:

> Ils n'ont pas en effet de tresses mandchoues, contemporaines . . . ils ont la coiffure enchignonnée du vieux Ming et les longs vêtements que peignent les porcelaines. Ceci est moins troublant que l'air étrange de leurs yeux; car, pour la première fois, *je suis regardé*, non pas comme un objet étranger qu'on voit peu souvent et dont on s'amuse, mais *comme*

un être qu'on n'a jamais vu. . . . Évidemment, ces gens aperçoivent pour
la première fois au monde, *l'être aberrant que je suis parmi eux. Je me
sens regardé sans rires, dépouillé, je me sens vu et nu. Je me sens deve-
nir objet de mystère.*

Indeed they do not have the contemporary Manchu plaits . . . they
have their hair up in the old Ming style and wear long clothes like those
pictured on pieces of china. This is less troubling than the strange look
in their eyes; as, for the first time, *I am looked at*, not like the foreign
body that is seen very rarely and is a source of amusement, but *as a
being never previously seen. . . .* These people of course catch sight for
the first time in the world of *the abnormal being I represent among
them. I feel myself observed without causing amusement, I feel seen
and naked. I feel myself becoming an object of mystery.* (pp. 98–99,
emphasis added)

What is presented in this passage is what Segalen calls "un grand exotisme
à l'envers" (a great reverse exoticism)—a clear reversal of the imperial gaze
and of the exoticizing strategies on which this customarily depends, a rendering passive and vulnerable of the French traveler ("seen and naked"),
and finally his defamiliarization. There is clearly a need to nuance this
example: the cultural displacement is, of course, supplemented by a historical distance, an aspect made clear by the narrator's dismissive attitude
toward the contemporary Chinese gaze, but I would suggest that this ultimately fantastic text is a preparation for the contemporary encounter in the
following chapter. Having traveled alone for several days, the traveler suddenly finds himself face-to-face with a Chinese girl who blocks his path:

[P]lantée là sur ses jambes fortes, et qui, stupéfaite moins que moi,
regardait passer *l'animal étrange que j'étais*, et qui, par pitié pour
l'inattendue beauté du spectacle, n'osa point se détourner pour la
revoir encore. Car la seconde épreuve eût peut-être été déplorable. Il
n'est pas donné de voir naïvement et innocemment deux fois dans une
étape, un voyage ou la vie, ni de reproduire à volonté le miracle de
deux yeux organisés depuis des jours pour ne saisir que la grande mon-
tagne, versants et cimes, et qui se trouvent tout d'un coup aux prises
avec *l'étonnant spectacle de deux autres yeux répondants.*

[S]tanding there on her strong legs, and, less astounded than me,
watching *the strange animal I was* going past, and out of pity for the
unexpected beauty of the spectacle, not daring to turn round to see it
again. Because the second time would perhaps have been deplorable. You
cannot see naively or innocently twice in the same leg of a journey, or even
of life itself, nor reproduce as required the miraculous experience of a pair
of eyes, accustomed for days to capturing only great mountains, with their
slopes and peaks, that suddenly find themselves faced with *the astonishing
spectacle of two other eyes looking back.* (p. 106, emphasis added)

As elsewhere in the text, the narrator's fellow travelers, European and Chinese, are imagined out of the account, but the indigenous girl who stares at the French traveler produces a troubling moment of contact as the narrator is himself exoticized and, in Pratt's terms, studied "from the perspective of those who participate on the receiving end [of travel]". What Segalen describes here as "the astonishing spectacle of two other eyes looking back" is a glimpsed moment in the contact zone, a moment of—to cite Pratt again—"copresence, interaction, interlocking understandings and practices, often within radically asymmetrical relations of power".

Although the aristocratic, even romantic stances of Segalen's early twentieth-century traveler are undoubtedly connected with the cultural/ethnic hierarchies that underpin the accounts of many contemporary colonial journeys, these stances are at the same time challenged or attenuated by a latent awareness of the ways in which the traveling self might no longer be sovereign and all-seeing, but relativized, destabilized, and exoticized. There is a clear tension, therefore, between Segalen's engagement with contemporary (one might say "colonial") orthodoxies and his undermining of those very orthodoxies. The key to understanding this tension is perhaps suggested by a return to James Clifford—not to *Routes*, but to the earlier work from which much of this subsequent reflection emerged, *The Predicament of Culture*—one of the few works of North American postcolonial criticism, apart from those of Edward Said, to have been translated into French. Clifford sees in Segalen's work one of the first coherent expressions of a "postsymbolist poetics of displacement" focused on "more troubling, less stable encounters with the exotic". In Clifford's terms, "Segalen writes the modern experience of displacement: self and other a sequence of encounters, detours, with the stable identity of each at issue".[43]

What emerges from Segalen's work is a different understanding of exoticism: not the conceit of Voltaire and Montesquieu, whose supposedly external gaze on their own culture ultimately remains a product of the culture it critiques, but something—in Clifford's terms, again—"more troubling, less stable". The *Essai sur l'Exotisme* takes essayism to an extreme by presenting through its unfinished, perhaps even unfinishable fragments sixteen years of reflection on the exotic—or "le Divers" (Diversity). In this work—which is best understood as a laboratory of thought—the reader witnesses Segalen analyzing the transformation (what he sees as the entropic decline) of diversity, and seeking ways of perpetuating gradations of difference in the face of what we might now call globalization. There are two principal movements to his strategy. The first, in his Polynesian and early Chinese texts, is to imagine what Clifford Geertz called the "native point of view",[44]—that is, to produce works in which the travelee was allowed to speak. Segalen writes in the *Essay on Exoticism*, "the familiar 'tu' that will dominate",[45] suggesting an unexpected intimacy between the Western traveler and those he meets that will serve as the basis for a recasting of the poetics of writing travel:

They expressed what they saw, what they felt in the presence of unexpected *things* and people from which and from whom they sought
to experience a shock. Did they reveal what those things and people
themselves thought and what they thought of them? For there is perhaps another shock, from the traveler to the object of his gaze, which
rebounds and makes what he sees vibrate.[46]

The position conveyed in this rhythmic, dense, measured, and
sonnet-like prose cannot be that of the I who feels but, on the contrary,
of the call of the milieu to the traveler, of the exotic to the exote who
penetrates it, attacks it, reawakens it, *and agitates it.* The familiar *"tu"*
will dominate.[47]

Segalen's travels in China led, however, to a recognition of the shortcomings of such an approach, and to an awareness that reversing the poles
in this way, offering a supposedly insider perspective, risked becoming
another form of appropriation—in Glissant's terms, "comprendre" (understanding) contains act of "prendre" (taking).[48] Segalen's later writings—to
which *Equipée* is central—demonstrate instead an early attention to the
mechanisms of intercultural contact, and an early recognition of the troubled copresence on which such contact inevitably depends:

Exoticism is therefore not an adaptation to something; it is not the
perfect comprehension of something outside one's self that one has
managed to embrace fully, but the keen and immediate perception of
an eternal incomprehensibility. Let us proceed from this admission of
impenetrability. Let us not flatter ourselves for assimilating the customs, races, nations and others who differ from us. On the contrary, let
us rejoice in our inability ever to do so.[49]

There remains a considerable distance—historical, cultural and ideological—from the Segalenian concepts of "incomprehensibility" and "impenetrability" to the ethically grounded poetics and politics of cultural opacity
that a thinker such as Glissant has posited in the postcolonial period. There
are nevertheless clear benefits to spanning that distance, and to exploring
the convergences and divergences it contains. Reading Segalen's work as
an untimely reflection on the ethics of travel does not extract it from its
clear complicity with the ideological niche from which it emerged; there is
a need to caution against the postcolonial practice of citing texts selectively
in order to absorb disparate and often contradictory material into what
aims to become a critical orthodoxy. Works such as *Equipée* and the *Essai
sur l'exotisme* nevertheless demonstrate that the critical—even epistemological—shifts that characterize the "postcolonial" turn in humanities and
social sciences scholarship, and have had a considerable impact on ethical readings of the travel narrative, have a complex genealogy that can be
traced back beyond the 1950s and before the period of decolonization from
which postcolonial thought is often said to have emerged.

NOTES

1. For studies of Segalen, see Henry Bouillier, *Victor Segalen* [1961] (Paris: Mercure de France, 1986); Marie Dollé, *Victor Segalen, le voyageur incertain* (Croissy-Beaubourg: Éditions Aden, 2008); Charles Forsdick, *Victor Segalen and the Aesthetics of Diversity: Journeys between Cultures* (Oxford: Oxford University Press, 2000); and Gilles Manceron, *Segalen* (Paris: Lattès, 1992). For a discussion of Segalen's untimeliness, see Kenneth White, "Celtisme et orientalisme", in Eliane Formentelli, ed., *Regard, espaces, signes: Victor Segalen* (Paris: L'Asiathèque, 1979), pp. 211–21.
2. Victor Segalen, *Les Immémoriaux* [A Lapse of Memory] (Paris: Mercure de France, 1907).
3. Victor Segalen, *Stèles* [Stelae] [1912] (Paris: Gallimard, 1973).
4. Victor Segalen, *Peintures* [Paintings] [1916] (Paris: Gallimard, 1983).
5. Victor Segalen, *Essay on Exoticism: An Aesthetics of Diversity*, [1955; first published as *Essai sur l'exotisme*] Yaël Rachel Schlick, trans., (Durham, NC: Duke University Press, 2002).
6. Gayatri Chakravorty Spivak, *Death of a Discipline* (New York: Columbia University Press, 2003), p. 52. For a critical evaluation of the concept in the light of its Derridean origins, see Corinne Scheiner, "Teleiopoiesis, Telepoesis, and the Practice of Comparative Literature", *Comparative Literature* 57, no. 3 (2005): 239–45.
7. Mary Louise Pratt, *Imperial Eyes: Travel Writing and Transculturation* (New York: Routledge, 1992).
8. On the series, see Pierre Aurégan, *Des récits et des hommes—Terre Humaine: un autre regard sur les sciences de l'homme* (Paris: Nathan, 2001).
9. James Clifford and George Marcus, eds., *Writing Culture: The Poetics and Politics of Ethnography* (Berkeley and Los Angeles: University of California Press, 1986).
10. Vincent Debaene, *Adieu au voyage: l'ethnologie française entre science et littérature* (Paris: Gallimard, 2010).
11. Charles Forsdick, *Travel in Twentieth-century French and Francophone Cultures: The Persistence of Diversity* (Oxford: Oxford University Press, 2005).
12. Abdelkebir Khatibi, *La Mémoire tatouée* (Paris: Denoël, 1979).
13. Victor Segalen, *Equipée* [Escapades] [1929] (Paris: Gallimard, 1983).
14. Harish Trivedi, "The Postcolonial or the Transcolonial?", *Interventions* 1, no. 2: (1999): 269–72; see also Charles Forsdick, "Edward Said, Victor Segalen and the Implications of Post-colonial Theory", *Journal of the Institute of Romance Studies* 5 (1997): 323–39; and Charles Forsdick, "Said After Theory: The Limits of Counterpoint", in Martin McQuillan, Graeme Macdonald, Robin Purves, and Stephen Thomson, eds., *Post-Theory: New Directions in Criticism* (Edinburgh: Edinburgh University Press, 1999), pp. 188–99.
15. Charles Sugnet, "Vile Bodies, Vile Places: Traveling with *Granta*", *Transition* 51 (1991): 70–85.
16. Jean-Marc Moura, *Lire l'exotisme* (Paris: Dunod, 1992); Jean-Marc Moura, *La Littérature des lointains: histoire de l'exotisme européen au XXe siècle* (Paris: Champion, 1998).
17. Terry Eagleton, *Figures of Dissent: Reviewing Fish, Spivak, Žižek and Others* (London: Verso, 2002), p. 160.
18. Eagleton, *Figures of Dissent*, p. 1.
19. Eagleton, *Figures of Dissent*, p. 19.
20. Graham Huggan, *Extreme Pursuits: Travel/Writing in an Age of Globalization* (Ann Arbor: University of Michigan Press, 2009).

21. Syed Manzurul Islam, *The Ethics of Travel: From Marco Polo to Kafka* (Manchester: Manchester University Press, 1996).
22. Debbie Lisle, *The Global Politics of Contemporary Travel Writing* (London: Routledge, 2006).
23. Pratt, *Imperial Eyes*, p. 7.
24. Claire Lindsay, "Beyond *Imperial Eyes*", in Justin D. Edwards and Rune Graulund, eds., *Postcolonial Travel Writing: Critical Explorations* (Houndmills: Palgrave Macmillan, 2011), pp. 17–35.
25. Jessica Dubow, "'From a View on the World to a Point of View in It': Rethinking Sight, Space and the Colonial Subject", *Interventions* 2, no. 1 (2000): 87–102.
26. Steve Clark, *Travel Writing and Empire: Postcolonial Theory in Transit* (London: Zed, 1999).
27. Fernando Ortiz, *Cuban Counterpoint*, trans. Harriet de Onis (New York: Knopf, 1947).
28. Pratt, *Imperial Eyes*, p. 253.
29. James Clifford *Routes: Travel and Translation in the Late Twentieth Century* (Cambridge, MA: Harvard University Press, 1997).
30. Clifford, *Routes*, p. 38.
31. Edward Said, *Culture and Imperialism* (New York: Knopf, 1993).
32. Johannes Fabian, *Time and the Other: How Anthropology Makes Its Object* (New York: Columbia University Press, 1983).
33. Chris Rojek and John Urry, eds., *Touring Cultures: Transformations of Travel and Theory* (London: Routledge, 1997), p. 11.
34. Nicolas Bouvier, *Le Poisson-Scorpion* [The Scorpion Fish] (Lausanne: Éditions 24 heures, 1990).
35. Jean-Xavier Ridon, "Pour une poétique du voyage comme disparition", in Christiane Albert, Nadine Laporte, and Jean-Yves Pouilloux, eds., *Autour de Nicolas Bouvier: Résonances* (Geneva: Zoé, 2002), pp. 120–35.
36. François Maspero, *Passagers du Roissy-Express* [Roissy Express: A Journey through the Paris Suburbs] (Paris: Seuil, 1990), p. 45.
37. Victor Segalen, *Equipée* [Escapades] [1929] (Paris: Gallimard, 1983).
38. Kenneth White, *Segalen: théorie et pratique du voyage* (Lausanne: A. Eibel, 1979).
39. Victor Segalen, *Le Fils du Ciel* [The Son of Heaven] (Paris: Flammarion, 1975).
40. Victor Segalen, "La Queste à la Licorne," in Henry Bouillier, ed., *Œuvres complètes* 2 vols. (Paris: Laffont, II.1995).
41. Segalen, *Equipée*, p. 12; hereafter page numbers will be cited parenthetically in the text.
42. Percy G. Adams, *Travelers and Travel Liars, 1660–1800* (Berkeley and Los Angeles: University of California Press, 1962).
43. James Clifford, *The Predicament of Culture: Twentieth-century Ethnography, Literature, and Art* (Cambridge, MA: Harvard University Press, 1988), p. 157.
44. Clifford Geertz, "From the Native's Point of View," in Keith H. Basso and Henry A. Selby, eds., *Meaning in Anthropology* (Albuquerque: University of New Mexico Press, 1976), pp. 221–37.
45. Segalen, *Essay on Exoticism*, 4 October 1908, p. 17, emphasis in the original.
46. Segalen, *Essay on Exoticism*, 9 June 1908, p. 14.
47. Segalen, *Essay on Exoticism*, 4 October 1908, p. 17, emphasis in the original.

48. Édouard Glissant, "Le chaos-monde, l'oral et l'écrit", in Ralph Ludwig, ed., *"Ecrire la parole de nuit": la nouvelle littérature antillaise* (Paris: Gallimard, 1994), pp. 111–29.
49. Segalen, *Essay on Exoticism*, 11 December 1908, p. 21.

6 Ethical Encounters with Animal Others in Travel Writing

Jopi Nyman

INTRODUCTION

While many accounts of the role of ethics in narrative representations of travel emphasize the role of race, class, and gender in carving out images of others (countries, peoples, nations), hitherto scant attention has been paid to the role of animals in travel writing. Historically, travel writing—following the conventions of colonial discourse—has populated unknown lands not only with threatening humans but with monstrous animals such as the *cynocephali* and human-faced sheep.[1] With the advancement of practices such as game hunting in Africa and India, the animal has been objectified, silenced, and transformed into a marginal figure in travel writing and other literary texts. However, as this chapter will show, recent travel writing reveals a different attitude towards animals. This trend stems from the discourses of conservationism and ethics arguing for a renewed relationship with the environment and animals.

It is the aim of this chapter to provide a critical assessment of the changing role of animals in travel writing. Starting with a discussion exploring the notion of the animal other as a part of the ideology of the travel writing genre, I will seek to problematize the animal's allegedly marginal status in travel narratives. By examining different reactions to animals in selected travel narratives, it is my aim to show that our understanding of the role of the other in travel writing is enriched, and has the possibility of becoming truly ethical, when these encounters with nonhuman others, as well as with nature in general, are addressed. In order to be able to show that the animal has a more significant role in travel writing than is generally understood, I have divided my analysis into two parts. First, I will examine texts produced in cultures and periods in which the discourse of colonialism has a role to play: these include Ernest Hemingway's representations of game hunting and conservationist Gerald Durrell's narratives of his animal-catching trips. The second part of the analysis seeks to go beyond the traditional representation of the animal as other by addressing two recent travel narratives, Brian Payton's *In Bear Country: A Global Journey in Vanishing Wilderness* and Linda Spalding's *The*

Follow,[2] which overtly display an ethical attitude toward animals and present a critique of ecocide.

TRAVEL, ANIMALS AND OTHERING

Critics of travel writing have often paid attention to the genre's association with colonialism and nineteenth-century ethnography, emphasizing its tendency to circulate stereotypical images of different others—racial, gendered, and national. While such a generalizing understanding may hold for a particular form of travel writing—that produced in (former) imperial centers—it remains a fact that travel writing produces images of people, landscapes, and sociocultural systems that differ from the writer's own background. This is what Kenneth Iain MacDonald refers to when he suggests that the most central ethical issues that travel writing explores are either related to questions of ideology or concern the effects of the representations it creates.[3] What is overlooked in much of travel writing in this view are "questions of reflectiveness and reflexivity".[4] In other words, while self-reflective postmodern travel writers such as Bruce Chatwin or Amitav Ghosh seek to problematize traditional strategies of representation and classification, many travel writers follow the paths and parameters peculiar to the discourses of Western imperialism and colonialism. According to MacDonald, such writers both follow established patterns and directions of travel and reproduce conventional images of native people encountered and lands traveled through, which shows that travel writing may "explicitly or implicitly prescribe . . . certain modes of behaviour that have material consequences".[5]

Recognizing the role that travel writing and others similar narratives may play in (Western) discourses of domination, critics have examined their denigrating representations of Africans, Asians, and native peoples. In so doing they have often followed the insight of the work of the discourse theorist Michel Foucault and the critique of the Western representation of the Orient as outlined in Edward Said's *Orientalism: Western Conceptions of the Orient*.[6] For Said, travel narratives are a way of constructing an understanding of a foreign culture. The discursive and political power of travel texts can be seen in the fact that together with other narratives (e.g., ethnographies, academic works by linguists and historians, political documents) claiming to present authoritative views on the characteristics and features of the nations and people of the Orient, they carve out images and views considered to be true and real. Yet, owing to their ideological status, such narratives tend to remain one-sided and supportive of views promoting European and Western dominance over the Middle East. As an unknown counterpart of the West, its other, the Orient was to be made manageable by the West. Rather than an ethical encounter, it was a question of confrontation aiming at rule and domination through discourse. To use Said's words:

My contention is that without examining Orientalism as a discourse one cannot possibly understand the enormously systematic discipline by which European culture was able to manage—and even to produce—the Orient politically, sociologically, militarily, ideologically, scientifically, and imaginatively during the post-Enlightenment period.[7]

In this sense the aims of post-Saidian ideological critique of travel writing—exactly like those of postcolonial critics of colonialist literature in general—have been ethical as to their aims of promoting such ideas as equality and humanist principles of the worth of all people. Such interest in questions of representation and their material consequences has been supported and supplemented by the ethical turn in literary studies that occurred in the late 1990s. Writing in his introduction to a special issue of *PMLA*, Lawrence Buell distinguishes between six different strands of ethics in literary study. These range from, but are not limited to, the study of the moral thematics of literary works and an understanding of literature as a parallel form of philosophy (as in the work of Martha Nussbaum) to the renewed understanding of the relationship of ethics and deconstruction and the emergence of postrealist and postcolonial critiques of truth and representation.[8] In Buell's view, while there is no one privileged approach in the field, certain questions are louder in the debate than others, and among them is that "of the role of the socio-political".[9]

An understanding of the role of the animal as a sociopolitical question informs this chapter. This involves thinking about such problems as the presence of the otherness of the animal in travel writing, the links between its representation and questions of dominance and power, and its ways of imagining ethical encounters with nonhuman animals and the environment. For the purposes of this study, a traditional definition of the other as outlined in colonial discourse analysis (as an ethnic or racial other) provides a starting point. Like non-Western people, animals have been imagined as others threatening the colonial order and the maintenance of asymmetrical power relations. In critiquing stereotypical images of others in narrative representations travel writing, critics have, however, tended to focus on human others and left the relationships among humans, animals, and nature unexamined. Yet animal representation is far from neutral, and various cultural texts have used the animal figure to address such questions as animal rights,[10] post-Darwinian evolutionary fears and race,[11] and class.[12] What is important for this study is that studies of colonial discourse suggest that the alterity of the animal is not merely based on its nonhuman status. Rather, the figure of the animal may be articulated with different ideological meanings in different contexts, meanings that may be gendered, racialized, and sexualized, and that may oppose dominant social hierarchies and orders.[13] What colonial discourse analysis shows is that the animal, like the figure of the child studied by Bill Ashcroft,[14] is innocent but potentially vicious, untrained but educable, yet untrustworthy because of its openness to desire and lack of morals. In other words, the other may take various human and nonhuman forms. Consequently, it is important to examine the interplay of human and nonhuman actors and to reflect on their relationship should an account of the ethics of the encounter be aimed at.

As the analyses of selected travel narratives in this chapter aim to show, the relationship between the traveling self and the encountered and narrated others involves human and nonhuman beings. What an understanding of such encounters needs is an account of ethics and ethical encounters that is able to address the human-animal encounter and its specificities and avoid defining the animal as a mere other. While many philosophers have addressed the problem of the animal, ranging from classical attempts to capture the mind of the animal as in Thomas Nagel's famous essay "What It Is Like to Be a Bat?" to Peter Singer's campaigning for animal rights in his *Animal Liberation*, more theoretical perspectives that can be applied to this problem have been provided by such philosophers as Emmanuel Levinas and Jacques Derrida.

What is central to Levinas's thinking is his idea that the relationship between the self and the other is constructed in encounters and forms the basis of ethics.[15] In encounters, the other is recognized as being present through its "face", and the self's responsibility for the other gains emphasis.[16] In applying Levinas's thinking to the encounter between humans and animals, Jones points to its problems, underlining Levinas's stress on interhuman encounters, but argues that Levinas's emphasis on the fact that all encounters are ethical "enable[s] to build accounts of ethical practice not from transcendent universalist positions but from within the practice of encounters".[17] What is important in Jones's view is that all encounters are situated rather than abstract.[18]

A particularly influential view that has problematized the notion of the animal as other has been presented by the French philosopher Jacques Derrida. His essay "The Animal That Therefore I Am (More to Follow)" has opened up new ways of thinking about human-animal relations, both ethically and politically.[19] In Matthew Calarco's view, Derrida's article raises two particularly important issues: first, it tries to deconstruct the binary opposition between humans and animals as "empirically inaccurate",[20] and second, it seeks to promote the view that animals have a role to play in the arenas of the ethical and the political. As sufferers of injustice and objects of violence, "animals confront us with as much, if not more, ethical force than human beings do".[21] A similar view has been presented by another animal studies scholar, Cary Wolfe, who emphasizes that Derrida seeks to show that "the animal difference is, *at this very moment*, not just any difference among others; it is, we might say, the most different difference . . . *particularly* if we pay attention to, as he does . . . to how it has been consistently repressed even by contemporary thinkers as otherwise profound as Levinas and Lacan".[22] In other words, the alleged difference between human and nonhuman animals is for Derrida an extremely important question whose presence is felt everywhere in culture. As Akira Mizuta Lippit writes in his interpretation of Derrida, the animal functions in the manner of the unconscious in language: "The animal brings to language something that is not a part of language and remains within language as a foreign presence."[23] It leaves "traces", to use a term of Derrida's, for everyone and everywhere. In so doing it transforms and problematizes imagined identities and questions the maintenance of traditionally exclusive categories. For Derrida, in fact, the apparently binary categories are deconstructable and mobile:

> I move from "the ends of man", that is the confines of man, to "the crossing of borders" between man and animal. Crossing borders or the ends of man I come or surrender to the animal—to the animal in itself, to the animal in me and the animal at unease with itself.[24]

Derrida's idea is that in the end there is no one single clear demarcation point that would distinguish between the human and the animal: "This abyssal rupture doesn't describe two edges, a unilinear and indivisible line having two edges, Man and Animal in general" (p. 399). Rather, the animal is a word and concept coined by human beings whose anthropocentricity prevents them from understanding animals: "*Animal* is a word that men have given themselves the right to give" (p. 400, emphasis in the original). An attempt to generalize is at the core of the problem, and Derrida argues against the views of many other philosophers from Aristotle to Martin Heidegger and Lacan to Levinas who claim that the animal is categorically different from the human: in their understanding it is without language and thus unable to respond (p. 400). Because of its generalizing character, this "commonplace" use of the phrase *the animal* is lacking in Derrida's view:

> Confined within this catch-all concept, within this vast encampment of the animal, in this general singular, within the strict enclosure of this definite article ("the Animal" and not "animals"), as in a virgin forest, a zoo, a hunting or fishing ground, a paddock or an abattoir, a space of domestication, are all the living things that man does not recognize as his fellows, his neighbors, or his brothers. (p. 402)

Paradoxically, Derrida claims, the only animal not named as an animal is the human (p. 409). The socio-political consequences of Derrida's redefinition of the human-animal problem are clear, demanding ethical treatment of nonhuman beings and new legislation. Matthew Calarco presents Derrida's central argument in a clarifying manner:

> What Derrida seems most interested in developing with these sorts of quasi-subjects and infrastructures is not just a decentering of human subjectivity (as is sometimes supposed), but rather a thought of the same/other relation where the same is not simply a *human* self and

where the other is not simply a *human* other. At bottom, what these infrastructures seek to give for thought is a notion of *finite life as responsivity*, where life is understood not exclusively but broadly and inclusively, ranging from human to animal and beyond. Stated in very bald terms, Derrida's thesis here seems to be that wherever among life forms we find something like an identity, we will invariably also find the play of difference, affect, inheritance, response, and so on, at work. From this perspective, there is no clear separation between human and animal inasmuch as both "kinds" of beings are irreducibly caught up in the "same" network of differential forces that constitute their respective modes of existence.[25]

ANIMALS IN COLONIAL TRAVEL NARRATIVES

A possible way of examining the ethical nature of human-animal relations is to focus on encounters between humans and animals as represented in travel narratives. As Owain Jones mentions, these encounters, occurring in different spaces, display a variety of situations in which ethics has a role to play: "this presents a field of encounters which range from the ethical to the unethical, or from the cruel to the passionate."[26] The examples of encounters to be examined in this section are located in discourses and practices of colonial(ist) writing where the animal figures as an other, the silenced object of the colonial gaze. The role of big game hunting as a means of constructing and maintaining the empire and the "white man's rule" is well-known, and its popular representations have boosted images of the hunter's idealized masculinity in the late Victorian and Edwardian eras in particular. Posing in photographs with his booty, the white hunter's position as being able to rule over the animal world (as well as his superiority over the natives) remains unquestioned. African animals, for example, were then transported to Europe, stuffed, and displayed to European audiences as signs of the empire's ability to rule its colonial lands. To use the words of James R. Ryan:

> These displays not only fabricated and domesticated the animals of distant colonial territories within new public and private spaces "back home", but served as monuments to the big-game hunters who seemed to their contemporaries to wield such mastery over the natural world.[27]

While representations of big game hunting abound in colonialist literature and popular culture, a late example of the performance of such a role can be found in Ernest Hemingway's travel book *Green Hills of Africa*.[28] Telling of a summer's hunting trip to East Africa, Hemingway's first safari in 1934–35, this narrative focuses on its protagonist's (and his friends') desire to hunt a kudu antelope. Relying on tropes of colonialist writing that structure the relations among the protagonist, the African members of his party, the land-scape, and the animals, *Green Hills of Africa* appears to construct its main character as an external observer passing judgment over what he sees in the landscape, including irritating Africans and objectified animals. In this sense Hemingway's text relies on what Mary Louise Pratt has defined as "the-mon-arch-of-all-I-survey mode" typical of colonialist travel narratives: through visualization of the space, the hunter gains "the power if not to possess, at least to evaluate the scene".[29] Hemingway's narrative emphasizes visuality, as it enables, as the quotation below shows, mastery over the space:

> The afternoon of the day we came into the country we walked about four miles from camp along a deep rhino trail that graded through the grassy hills with their abandoned orchard-looking trees, as smoothly and evenly as though an engineer had planned it. The trail was a foot deep in the ground and smoothly worn and we left it where it slanted down through a divide in the hills like a dry irrigation ditch and climbed, sweating, the small, steep hill on the right to sit there with our backs against the hilltop and glass the country. It was a green, pleasant coun-try, with hills below the forest that grew thick on the side of a mountain, and it was cut by the valleys of several watercourses that came down out of the thick timber on the mountain. Fingers of this forest came down onto the heads of some of the slopes and it was there, at the forest edge, that we watched for rhino to come out. If you looked away from the forest and the mountain side you could follow the watercourses and the hilly slope of the land down until the land flattened and the grass was brown and burned and, away, across a long sweep of country, was the brown Rift Valley and the shine of Lake Manyara.[30]

The passage is worth quoting at length. In addition to placing the white pro-tagonist in a central, observing position on the top of a hill from which he is able to look down upon the African landscape, it also shows that his inter-est is in observing the animal, the object of the hunt. Furthermore, the gaze of the colonizer is not one of observing a neutral landscape but one that is represented as a human being, with "fingers" and "heads", which suggests that the gaze belongs to someone mastering the space and its human as well as nonhuman inhabitants. The intertwinement of the gaze, the visual and colonial control over the space of the other is further developed in situa-tions where the controlling gaze is blocked. On such occasions the inability to see equates yielding to the power of the other. This is clear in the follow-ing passage when the party, tracking a wounded buffalo, is forced to enter the thick grass, an unknown and dangerous space where the gaze is useless and is dominated by the wild animal other:

> Finally, it led down from a rocky hillside with the last of the sun on it, down into the stream bed where there was a long, wide patch of the

highest dead reeds that we had seen. These were higher and thicker even than the slough the buff had come out of in the morning and there were several game trails that went into them.[31]

In this representation of big game hunting, the animal is objectified and the encounter involves unethical aspects—in other words, the pleasure to be gained from the encounter is one-sided and results in the death of the other. While waiting for the buffalo to achieve a suitable spot, the narrator expresses his feelings:

> Now, going forward, sure he was in here, I felt the elation, the best ela-tion of all, of certain action to come, action in which you had something to do, in which you can kill and come out of it, doing something you are ignorant about and so not scared, no one to worry about and no respon-sibility except to perform something you feel sure you can perform.[32]

In such narratives the animal other dies to serve the identity formation of a Western hunter. Not only is the hunter photographed with his booty to build up a reputation, but the horns of the dead kudus become symbols of the performance of masculinity. When the narrator hears that the horns that Karl has bagged are bigger than his, his mood changes: "They were the biggest, widest, darkest, longest-curling, heaviest, most unbelievable pair of kudu horns in the world. Suddenly, poisoned with envy, I did not want to see mine again; never, never."[33]

While the general attitude toward the various others seems uniform and supportive of a masculinist identity, colonialist narratives are unable to totally repress their other. Rather, as theorists of the postcolonial encoun-ter such as Homi K. Bhabha have suggested,[34] the various modes of resis-tance such as colonial mimicry show that total domination is not possible. As a sign of this, *Green Hills of Africa* also includes passages in which the native inhabitants of Africa challenge the colonizer. For instance, one of the local hunting guides, nicknamed Garrick by the hunters because of his excessive speaking and posing, irritates the narrator to the extent that he feels the right to silence him physically: "'Shut up, you bastard,' I said. . . . I put the back of my hand against his mouth with some firmness and he closed it in surprise."[35] A similar moment of insecurity and surprise can be found when the animal challenges the hunter by not conforming to his rational plan, as seen when the sable antelopes notice the party and attempt to escape. The narrator's rationality gives way to the moment's excitement that is represented as shameful—and shame is associated with chaos, lack of emotional control, and other qualities inappropriate for a Western big game hunter:

> My eyes, my mind, all inside of me were full of the blackness of that sable bull and the sweep of those horns and I was thanking God I had

the rifle reloaded before he came out. But it was excited shooting, all of it, and I was not proud of it. I had gotten excited and shot at the whole animal instead of the right place and I was ashamed.[36]

Ultimately, in this narrative the problem of the animal other is linked with the more general issue of the colonial other. As the ruptures in the maintenance of masculinity and colonial authority imply, Hemingway's narrative is not entirely monologic but recognizes the presence of various others. In a way that is comparable with the treatment of primitivism in Hemingway's writing,[37] the presence of the animal other reveals the problem of maintaining a masculine identity—while seeking to exclude and dominate its others, it also has to recognize the role the other plays within the self. In other words, big game hunting in Africa is not a mere attempt to institute mastery over the natural but constitutes an encounter where otherness raises its head and challenges the hunter, showing the ambiguity of maintaining colonialist (and masculinist) identity.[38]

Whereas Hemingway's colonial adventure shows animals as colonial others, conservationist and zookeeper Gerald Durrell's animal catching travelogues tell of his encounters with individual animals of various species in different parts of the world. Since the publication of his first travel narrative *The Overloaded Ark,* Durrell's books have provided glimpses into the ways and behavior of the animal other. While deeply embedded in the discourses and values of British colonialism, as I have shown in another context,[39] Durrell's representation of the animal departs significantly from the narrative conventions of colonialist writing such as Hemingway's. While Durrell's images of Africans, for instance, are stereotypical and reveal a sense of Western superiority, the portraits of the animals encountered frequently describe them as individuals and show a sense of cross-species bonding. Although the act of catching and transporting animals from their home habitats to be gazed at and observed in Western zoos can be seen as a colonialist practice, Durrell's narratives also involve ecological aspects and seek acceptance by appealing to the value of knowledge to be gained by a systematic and scientific study of the animals. This can be seen in *The New Noah* (1955):

It is of great value to get to know and study these wild creatures before they are influenced by civilization, for wild animals can be affected just as much by change as people. One of the results of cutting down forests, building towns, damming rivers, and driving roads through jungle, is an interference with their way of life, and they have either to adapt themselves to the new conditions or die out.

It was my intention to find out all I could about the animals of the great forests [in Cameroon] and to bring back as big and varied a collection as possible of its small fauna, the creatures that the African calls in pidgin English, "small beef".[40]

Regardless of the attempt to justify animal hunting and capturing by such reasoning, there is no doubt that animal catching involves causing harm to the animal. For instance, the big Nile monitor caught in Cameroon is first chased by dogs and, when caught with ropes and nets, carried into the main camp "tied to a long pole".[41] However, what emerges in the narratives is that Durrell does not represent his animals as others to humans. Rather, several accounts of his expeditions emphasize an interest in and fascination with the ways of the animals, as also revealed in his book portraying his childhood in Corfu, *My Family and Other Animals*. Furthermore, Durrell's attitude toward the animals emphasizes that his encounters are more with individuals than with generalized and othered animals. Wildness does not necessarily equate danger. This can be seen in the case of the baby red river hog Puff, starving but wary of and resisting the unfamiliar feeding bottle:

> At last I was fortunate enough to get a few drops to trickle down his throat, and waited for him to get the taste of it, which he soon made apparent by stopping to yell and struggle, and by starting to smack his lips and grunt. I dribbled a little more milk into his mouth and he sucked it down greedily, and within a short while he was pulling away at the bottle as though he would never stop, while his tummy grew bigger and bigger. At length, when the last drop had disappeared from the bottle, he heaved a long sigh of satisfaction and fell into a deep sleep on my lap, snoring like a hive full of bees.[42]

By naming it, Durrell, of course, exercises colonial power by imposing an identity—that of a humorous puffer—onto the animal; yet the animal also receives an individual identity that allows for an encounter impossible in narratives animals remain mere objects. This confirms what Jones finds necessary should animals be encountered as individuals rather than as a collective: on such occasions they "are to a degree at least recognized as individually ethically visible".[43] In Durrell's case, care and warmth are part of such encounters.

While seeking to bridge the gap between the human and the animal, Durrell's textual animals remain in the space of the other, exotic and untrustworthy though not necessarily malicious. This may stem from the situatedness of these encounters as they are based on the general premises of colonial discourse. It is the case that, like the native people of Africa and other parts of the globe that Durrell encounters during his travels, animals—and especially those who do not resemble domesticated animals in the manner of the piglet Puff—are exotic and culturally different, and thus, in the end, they are unknowable. In sum, while opening up a space for ethical encounters and promoting the recognition of the animal, Durrell's writing is unable to depart from the constraints of his chosen genre and the expectations of his target audience—after all, he wrote in order to fund his animal collection and his own zoo in Jersey.

SAVING THE SPECIES

Recent years have witnessed a particular type of travel writing in which the travel is conducted in order to document a species on the verge of distinction or a lost form of human-animal relations. In addition to narrating instances of cultural collision and conflict in exotic locations, these texts foreground encounters with little known animals. Whereas Stephen J. Bodio's *Eagle Dreams: Searching for Legends in Wild Mongolia* tries to locate the roots of Kazak and Mongolian eagle hunting,[44] showing a trusting relationship between humans and birds of prey, John Hare's *The Lost Camels of Tartary: A Quest into Forbidden China* sends its conservationist protagonist to the desert of Gobi in search of the last wild Bactrian camels, now threatened by nuclear tests, mining, and the closing of the frontier.[45]

A prime example of a travel narrative combining visits to various parts of the globe with appeals for the preservation of biodiversity is Brian Payton's *In Bear Country: A Global Journey in Vanishing Wilderness*. In this volume Payton conducts eight journeys to different parts of the world, ranging from India and China to Italy and Manitoba, to learn about the current state of eight different types of bears threatened by changes in their habitats, mainly because of human action. In the book's introductory chapter, set in coastal British Columbia, Payton reveals how his interest in the ursine started. Near the mouth of the Khutzeymateen River, in a place where grizzlies gather after their hibernation in what is referred to as "a sleuth of bears",[46] Payton meets bears that have no fear of human beings and are thus unable to behave as other to human. When a big lazy-looking grizzly comes closer and closer to the writer, "whiffing" and "ponderous", the latter feels amazed:

> Then the bear moved closer still. All was silent, save the click and whirr of our cameras. I stopped staring through the viewfinder and slowly rested the camera in my lap. As we sat frozen, mouths agape, it dawned on me that we were in a rare place in our modern world—at the mercy of a large, wild animal.
>
> As it closed the gap between us, I had another of those moments of clarity. My heart was not racing, I felt no panic welling up inside. But I did feel as if the tables had turned, as if I had become the object of curiosity. Ellison [guide] spoke in a soothing voice, informing the bear of our intentions, then quietly suggested that we take a few steps back—which I was happy to do. Choosing to leave us unchallenged and undisturbed, the bear continued past and up an embankment. . . . At the top of the rise, he stopped, took a final look over his shoulder, then lumbered into the woods. (p. 7)

What happens in Payton's encounter with the grizzly is that the animal transforms from the unthinking object of colonial discourse into a subject with intentions and curiosity. While remaining other as a species, and also potentially harmful to humans, it challenges the alleged human mastery over the animal world by looking back (p. 161). In other words, what is revealed to the narrator in the passage is that the bear has a "face", and thus it may be possible to narrow the gap between the human and the animal.

At the core of Payton's book are encounters with bears. Yet in this book encounters are not restricted to his personal experiences but are embedded in the story of contacts between humans and bears since prehistory—one chapter is devoted to a visit to the Chauvet Cave where the oldest man-made paintings of mammals, including bears, can be found (pp. 227–46). Approaching his subject from the perspective of conservationism, and with a political agenda, Payton pays explicit attention to human abuse of bears and the diminishing habitats of the bears. This can be seen, for example, in his account of the maltreatment of farmed moon bears in China, in the report of the Malayan sun bear (sold illegally for culinary or medicinal purposes and threatened by the illegal logging and farming of the rainforest) in Cambodia, and in the state of the Marsican brown bear in Italy, soon to be extinct. Visiting various national parks and rescue centers, Payton provides images of bears suffering from physical and mental abuse to promote a more tolerant attitude. In his report of Chinese bear farming, Payton reveals that many of the bears at the Rescue Centre in Sichuan "are missing parts; paws lost in snares, claws ripped out by farmers, and canines either forcibly extracted or broken from repeatedly biting the bars of their cage" (p. 69). Furthermore, he reports in detail on the medical procedure to be operated on a brown bear called Caesar, formerly a source of bear bile on a bear farm in Tianjin:

> After checking the pulse, the first order of business is the removal of the permanent metal girdle that was affixed to Caesar some nine years ago. The contraption is made of steel rods, bolts, and plates and is held in place by thick canvas straps. It weighs twenty-two pounds and is designed to hold a latex catheter in the gallbladder and to keep the bear from licking or otherwise touching the permanently open sore. It has worn off much of the fur around Caesar's back and shoulders. The veterinarian team refers to it as the Full Metal Jacket. (p. 75)

In addition to abuse, Payton's book pays attention to the question of extinction and focuses on the diminished habitats of many bear species. What is interesting is that this problem is linked with more general societal and cultural changes, especially in the case of the almost nonexistent bears of Lazio and Abruzzo in Italy. According to the book, the Marsican brown bear is on its path to extinction, and in Payton's view the optimism of a local biologist is not justified: "'I hope the bears survive' . . . he's starting to sound like an idealist" (p. 201). Upon visiting the Abruzzo national park and its mountain villages, Payton meets no bears. Rather, his encounters are with old people telling stories of bears "relayed with passion and pride" (p. 208). The old shepherds show respect for the bears, but the government's policies do not prioritize conservationism and former park directors stole the funds; bears appear to be destined to disappear in the manner of the lifestyle of the rural inhabitants. The death of the bear signifies the death of a culture:

> As we travel through the mountains, we meet shepherds in barns, fields, and forests. Virtually all of them are old. It soon becomes clear that I am documenting not only the dying days of an animal unique to this region, but also a way of life that has existed here for hundreds of generations. (p. 207)

This view is supported with a further image of decay and degeneration: the only Marsican bear he sees is held captive in a small zoo. Living in a "tiny enclosure" since 1994, this individual is psychologically damaged and has reverted to nervousness: she "pac[es] back and forth like a mental defective" (p. 218). The relationship between humans and bears, nostalgically described in Payton's book as a natural and respectful one, has disappeared. This is also noticed by one of the shepherds:

> "The bear has something supernatural", he observes. "It is beautiful and gives you a sense of what man is and what nature is. I want to preserve bears, but something in the environment has changed. Something is broken." (pp. 213–14)

In mapping the human-bear relationship, Payton emphasizes that bears have been central to the folklore and mythologies of many cultures, including the Navajo described in the final chapter of the book. This special relationship between the Native American and the bear is in a way recast as a model for future human-bear relationships—or rather, as the above words of the shepherd imply, the relationship must be reconstituted. In this sense the narrator's attempt to perform a purification rite in the final pages of the book, his attempt to ask the bear for forgiveness, is not only personal but also cultural. The gratitude expressed is addressed to all bears, and it emanates, in addition to one writer, from all humans:

> Inside a shallow cave, I light some of the Good Way smoke, which is pungent with sage. Here, I count my blessings. I recognize that I have remained safe throughout these journeys. I thank the bear for all I have experienced, and ask its help in making these stories worthy and true. When the medicine burns down to my fingertips, I step back into the sun. There, I pour the remains into the palm of my hand and offer it up to the wind. (p. 292)

While Payton's book's aims are primarily political, the encounters described in Linda Spalding's *The Follow*, a story of a North American woman's travels to Indonesia in search of a close relationship with orangutans, are explicitly personal. Initially invited to write about the Lithuanian Canadian primatologist Biruté Galdikas and her work of seeking to return to nature domesticated orangutans who do not possess species-based knowledge, Spalding tries to approach this elusive and mysterious disciple of Louis Leakey who repeatedly refuses to talk to the writer—during her three trips to Borneo Spalding sees Galdikas only fleetingly in a boat; the only discussion between the two takes place in Los Angeles before the narrator decides to set off to Indonesia for the first time with her two adult daughters. The story shows her gradual disenchantment with Galdikas, and the scientist emerges in the narrative as an avaricious entrepreneur participating in the orangutan business through ecotourism, lectures, publishing, and film. Through her interviewees Spalding suggests that Galdikas's methods may generate more problems to the apes than previously understood:

> "We counted forty-eight orangutans on her grounds in August," Michelle answered. "All unofficial. No quarantine, no check for hepatitis or GB. More and more come. More and more disappear. There are conflicting answers when you ask what happened to them. She sometimes puts them in the forest within hours of getting them, which endangers the wild, viable population. Lots of them die. Then records disappear, too. So in August the 'volunteers' began to discuss our concerns. (We're volunteers, but she's charging us $1,000 a month for the privilege of helping her 'rescue' orangutans.) Biruté got wind of it and blamed me. She thinks I'm the snake."[47]

In addition to addressing the problems involved in the conservation of orangutans, including deforestation, poaching, environmental pollution, and smuggling, and providing insight into their behavior, *The Follow* explores the relationship between humans and human apes. Rather than seeing the latter as the other of the human, Spalding's narrative discusses such issues as what distinguishes the two from each other and whether the border may be crossed, as suggested by Derrida. Examples of these range from critique of Enlightenment thinkers (p. 156), to commentary on the conceptualizing abilities of the Orangutans ("Orangutans are devious, but it isn't just tricks that they play. Like us, they conceptualize" [p. 156]), to the problem of using language as a criterion of humanness ("If language isn't the thing that separates us, what is?" [p. 189]), and the claim that orangutans have a culture promoting learning:

> Orangutans live in this state of mediation, watching the object of desire, approaching hand over hand, when the moment is ripe. The moment itself is silently teaching the infant who rides on the mother's hip, and the other, the youngster who bounces ahead or follows behind. But it's the mother who teaches them how to touch, how to sniff, how to break

through the skin. It's the mother who hands down this "culture". I use that word because learning is cultural if it occurs in one social group but not in others, if it follows a path of relationships. Among primates, the usual model for a learned behaviour is the mother, which is why Biruté adopts the orphans. Not just to care for them but to teach them. To be orangutans. (pp. 76–77)

To emphasize similarities between humans and orangutans rather than their differences, *The Follow* appears to promote a holistic worldview in which the species difference between the human and the ape is eroded and the border crossing made possible. Such a strategy exemplifies Derrida's suggestion that there are no general criteria to distinguish between the human and the animal. Consequently, encounters become moments when conventional categories are deconstructed. On such occasions the animal is no longer an object and may become a subject whose task it is to lead the humans and teach them new ways of being. To use the words of Derrida, "The animal is there before me, there close to me, there in front of me—I who am (following) after it. And also, therefore, since it is before me, it is behind me. It surrounds me. And from the vantage of this being-there-before-me it can allow itself to be looked at, no doubt, but also . . . it can look at me. It has its own point of view regarding me."[48] This reversal of roles providing a new understanding of the subjectivity of the animal can be seen clearly in the final passage of the book, where the orangutan takes the narrator for a walk:

> I think of the moment Gistok walked up and put his hand around mine. It felt like the baseball glove worn by an older brother every afternoon through childhood, warm, already shaped, already knowing how to grip, pulling me to the trees, leading me away from those who were staring after us. And I felt the reluctance I feel with anyone who is very determined, as if I'd prefer to choose my own time. But I went, and Gistok walked me around the cabin I would live in a few months later and we peered underneath, where there was nothing to see but the bare ground on which he had slept. All of what happened was ahead of me, mine to live in for a time. (p. 315)

However, as the final phrase "to live in for a time" suggests, the conditions enabling such ideal human-animal encounters are temporary and shaded by other factors, including the pollution of the Borneo rivers and the fact that Galdikas's values are, in the end, disappointing to the narrator whose professional integrity as a journalist is repeatedly challenged by restricting her writing and interviewing. In the end the rainforest in contemporary Borneo is no Eden for human beings: "If we *lived* in the garden of Eden, I thought, it wouldn't be like this. . . . We'd sleep in the trees at night in well-constructed nests. . . . We'd learn the plants that create comfort and those that alleviate pain. We'd live in the garden as part of it and teach our children how to survive" (p. 78, emphasis in the original). In addition to separating the human from the space and practices of orangutans, the text becomes a form of cultural critique lamenting the loss of community in the contemporary world. Such a reading is supported by the fact that at one level the journey taken by the narrator together with her two adult daughters aims to reconstruct their harmonious family life by re-creating "a reunion of our original trinity since . . . I had not been alone with them for more than a decade" (p. 7). As the family history is framed in a narrative of idealistic 1960s countercultural values, the striving for lost opportunities gains a more general meaning.

What is problematic for the narrator is the way in which her initial image of Galdikas as a kindred soul sharing her values based on the idealistic principles of the 1960s generation is found lacking, making her idealistic understanding mere wishful thinking and Galdikas an opportunist. In constructing her imaginary Galdikas, the narrator emphasizes their biographical backgrounds: whereas Spalding moved to Hawaii with her former photographer husband at the end of the 1960s, Biruté relocated with her husband to Indonesia at the same time and started orangutan studies in which she often "followed" the animal for days in the jungle in order to find out about its diet, habits, and social networks (p. 7). During the writing of the book Spalding's search for shared values and views with Galdikas transforms from one conducted by an understanding fan to that a critical researcher: "Biruté and I are both children of the magical sixties, formed by the time when everything seemed possible, and the end justified the means. We no longer speak the same language. We chose different ways" (p. 4). What appears to be Spalding's message is that idealism and high ethical values have given way to the realities of a corrupt Indonesia where government officials may also work for logging companies. Similarly, Galdikas's apparently acclaimed position as a leading primatologist runs counter to the realization that her last research permit has expired several years ago and that there are serious flaws in her working practices. These blows at Spalding's high hopes of gaining friendship are in the text represented as her shock reaction to the climate and people in Borneo. As is typical in travel narratives, the space that is initially welcoming soon becomes threatening and unfriendly:

> Under those dark clouds I began to lose my connection to the others, who looked as unlikely in that place as the vegetables piled around them. But even my own hands and feet had begun to look strange. A group of little boys screamed when they saw us, as if we were monsters. The heat was an entirely different substance than it had been in Bali or Java. It was unbearable, oppressive and ovenlike. Solid shapes wavered, melted. I was faint. (p. 50)

While the quest for a "mother", as Spalding's journey is described by her daughter (pp. 249–95), fails, the mother-daughter relationship remains highly important in the text as it is narrated at two levels—human and orangutan. As shown in the description of the first journey taken together by the narrator and her daughters, Spalding seeks to reconstruct the feeling of the 1960s when her daughters were small and refers to her feeling as "something else. Excitement. Nostalgia. There was even a small seductiveness to this" (p. 31). What distinguishes this narrative from other mother-daughter memoirs is the fact that the issue is intertwined with the representation of orangutan mothers and their babies. Not only are orangutan mothers shown with their babies ("A few young orangutans had come swinging down from the trees, some of them with infants clinging to their backs, a tiny head peering out from under an arm or behind a neck" [p. 67]), but at one point the narrator acquires temporarily the role of a mother who cares for an ill orangutan orphan:

> Astra did look sick. If he were human, I'd say looked bleary-eyed, and why not to say the same for an orangutan? He sat in a little heap and shivered. Two tourist children had picked him up and played with him a week before. They had been sick. Now we were invited to pick him up and when I did, a little reluctantly, his small, hot body brought back the memory of holding a feverish human infant, and a particular piece of my past came back—Kristin so sick I was using a cloth to drip water into her mouth—alone, her father somewhere else, but nowhere to be found. This baby had a small, bald head, enormous eyes and tiny, wiry, grasping hands. (p. 70)

By using the trope of memory, this encounter with a sick baby ape forces the initially reluctant narrator to locate similarities between ill human and orangutan infants, which makes this a border crossing moment. Interpreted from the perspective of Derrida criticizing the human-animal boundary, the passage shows that the narrator finds the animal in or at least near herself through the revelation that care and emotions are similar regardless of one's species.

At the same time, however, the passage comes to ponder upon the ethics of Galdikas's policy of allowing close contact with animals and humans; a later part of the passage in fact comments on the dismal conditions at the station. As further signs of increasing unrest are the references to the ways in which Galdikas and her staff do not wish to admit the deaths of several orangutans and the fact that they allow paying tourists to touch and caress orangutans that are for them "photographic collectibles" (p. 75). A German tourist is even mentioned to have slept with them (pp. 298–99). The ethical dimension of such encounters is highly problematic: while showing human desire to approach the animal and cross over, their impact on orangutans remains negative, spreading diseases and generating stress. Subsequently, Galdikas's practices are contrasted with those of other researchers seeking to minimize contact between humans and animals in accordance with "the *new* rehabilitation credo" (p. 188, emphasis in the original). In sum, while Spalding's narrative does not portray the animal as other and shows the opportunities for border crossings, it comes to situate the encounters in a wider framework. In so doing it criticizes the commercialized practices of organized orangutan tourism performed in the name of science to present the politicized question whether what human beings like to do in the name of knowledge or border crossings is good for animals.

CONCLUSION

The different representations of animals in the travel narratives examined in this chapter show a trajectory from a colonialist understanding of the animal as an other to the emergence of a view that undercuts the animal's otherness. When the animal's naturalized role as other is challenged, narratives of animal encounters framed in discourses and practices demanding the animal's total submission show signs of uneasiness. In contrast, encounters embedded in views recognizing the role and identity of the animal allow for making animals noticeable in travel writing and life in general. What this means is that ethical encounters need to be situated rather than based on a generalized view of the animal as other, unable to participate in dialogue. That contemporary travel writing displays this emergent role of the animal shows that the genre is open to new themes and forms, and that it does not have to reproduce colonial and other unequal conventions.

NOTES

1. See Lynn Ramey, "Monstrous Alterity in Early Modern Travel Accounts: Lessons from the Ambiguous Medieval Discourse on Humanness", *L'Esprit Créateur* 48, no. 1 (2008): 86–89.
2. Brian Payton, *In Bear Country: A Global Journey in Vanishing Wilderness* (London: Old Street, 2007); Linda Spalding, *The Follow* (London: Bloomsbury, 1998).
3. Kenneth Iain MacDonald, "Ethics—Issues of", in Jennifer Speake, ed., *Literature of Travel and Exploration: An Encyclopedia*, vol. 1 (New York: Fitzroy Dearborn, 2003), 403.
4. MacDonald, "Ethics—Issues of", p. 403.
5. MacDonald, "Ethics—Issues of", p. 404.
6. Edward W. Said, *Orientalism: Western Conceptions of the Orient* [1978] (London: Penguin, 1995).
7. Said, *Orientalism*, p. 3.
8. Lawrence Buell, "Introduction: In Pursuit of Ethics", *PMLA* 114 (1999): 7–10.
9. Buell, "Introduction: In Pursuit of Ethics", p. 15.
10. See John Simons, *Animal Rights and the Politics of Literary Representation* (Basingstoke: Palgrave, 2002).
11. Susan D. Bernstein, "Ape Anxiety: Sensation Fiction, Evolution and the Genre Question", *Journal of Victorian Culture* 6 (2001): 250–71.

12. Tim Youngs, "White Apes at the Fin de Siècle", in Tim Youngs, ed., *Writing and Race* (London: Longman, 1996), pp. 166–90.
13. See Jopi Nyman, *Postcolonial Animal Tale from Kipling to Coetzee* (New Delhi: Atlantic, 2003).
14. Bill Ashcroft, *On Post-colonial Futures: Transformations of Colonial Culture* (London: Continuum, 2001), pp. 36–40.
15. Emmanuel Levinas, *Is It Righteous to Be? Interviews with Emmanuel Levinas*, ed. Jill Robbins (Stanford, CA: Stanford University Press, 2001), p. 211ff.
16. Levinas, *Is It Righteous to Be?*, pp. 214–16.
17. Owain Jones, "(Un)ethical Geographies of Human-non-human Relations: Encounters, Collectives and Spaces", in Chris Philo and Chris Wilbert, eds., *Animal Spaces, Beastly Places: New Geographies of Human-animal Relations* (London: Routledge, 2000), p. 273. Animals, however, are relevant for Levinas's theory of ethics as shown in his account of Bobby, a dog in Nazi Germany which recognized the Jews as humans. See Emmanuel Levinas, *Difficult Freedom: Essays on Judaism*, trans. S. Hand (Baltimore, MD: Johns Hopkins University Press, 1990) and Bob Plant, "Welcoming Dogs: Levinas and 'the Animal Question'", *Philosophy and Social Criticism* 37 (2011): 49–71.
18. Jones, "(Un)Ethical Geographies", p. 273.
19. Jacques Derrida, "The Animal That Therefore I Am (More to Follow)", trans. David Willis, *Critical Inquiry* 28 (2002): 369–418.
20. Matthew Calarco, "Thinking through Animals: Reflections on the Ethical and Political Stakes of the Question of the Animal in Derrida", *Oxford Literary Review* 29 (2008): 3.
21. Calarco, "Thinking through Animals", 5.
22. Cary Wolfe, *Animal Rites: American Culture, the Discourse of Species, and Posthumanist Theory* (Chicago: University of Chicago Press, 2003), p. 67, emphasis in the original.
23. Akira Mizuta Lippit, "Magnetic Animal: Derrida, Wildlife, Animetaphor", *MLN* 113 (1998): p. 1113.
24. Derrida, "The Animal", p. 372; hereafter page numbers will be cited parenthetically in the text.
25. Calarco, "Thinking through Animals", p. 4, emphasis in the original.
26. Jones, "(Un)Ethical Geographies", p. 268.
27. James R. Ryan, "Hunting with the Camera: Photography, Wildlife and Colonialism in Africa", in Chris Philo and Chris Wilbert, ed., *Animal Spaces, Beastly Places: New Geographies of Human-Animal Relations* (London: Routledge, 2000), p. 203.
28. Ernest Hemingway, *Green Hills of Africa* [1935] (London: Arrow, 1994).
29. Mary Louise Pratt, *Imperial Eyes: Travel Writing and Transculturation* (London: Routledge, 1992), pp. 204–5.
30. Hemingway, *Green Hills of Africa*, p. 36.
31. Hemingway, *Green Hills of Africa*, pp. 82–83.
32. Hemingway, *Green Hills of Africa*, pp. 83–84.
33. Hemingway, *Green Hills of Africa*, p. 208.
34. Homi K. Bhabha, *The Location of Culture* (London: Routledge, 1994).
35. Hemingway, *Green Hills of Africa*, p. 130.
36. Hemingway, *Green Hills of Africa*, p. 187.
37. See Suzanne del Gizzo, "Going Home: Hemingway, Primitivism, and Identity", *Modern Fiction Studies* 49, no. 3 (2003): 496–523.
38. See Jopi Nyman, *Men Alone: Masculinity, Individualism, and Hard-boiled Fiction* (Amsterdam: Rodopi, 1997).

39. See Nyman, *Postcolonial Animal Tale*, pp. 111–27.

40. Gerald Durrell, *The New Noah* [1955] (London: Penguin, 1968), p. 14.

41. Durrell, *New Noah*, p. 22.

42. Durrell, *New Noah*, pp. 40–41.

43. Jones, "(Un)Ethical Geographies", p. 282.

44. Stephen J. Bodio, *Eagle Dreams: Searching for Legends in Wild Mongolia* (Guilford, CT : Lyons, 2003).

45. John Hare, *The Lost Camels of Tartary: A Quest into Forbidden China* [1998] (London: Abacus, 1999).

46. Payton, *In Bear Country*, p. 7; hereafter page numbers will be cited parenthetically in the text.

47. Spalding, *The Follow*, p. 310; hereafter page numbers will be cited parenthetically in the text.

48. Derrida, "The Animal", p. 380.

7 Cultural Sustainability and Postcolonial Island Literatures

Anthony Carrigan

The effects of globalized mass tourism over the last half a century have been both striking and troubling. Many forms of post–World War II tourism exploit uneven distributions of wealth, remapping colonial travel patterns as increasing numbers of citizens from rich nations choose to visit much poorer states. Such rapid industry expansion has clear bearings on issues that are central to postcolonial studies in the era of corporate globalization. Tourism propels environmental transformation, cultural commoditization, and sexual consumption—all processes that are acutely felt in many countries still grappling with the legacies of Western colonialism. At the same time, tourism is consistently welcomed across the postcolonial world as a much-needed source of job creation and foreign exchange, even if the power relations that condition these transactions are distinctly asymmetrical. While such processes highlight the need for ethical considerations to be at the forefront of tourism research and practice, as late as 1999 David Fennell was prompted to observe that "there is a very weak foundation of tourism ethics studies to date".[1] This essay seeks to build on increasing interest in this research area by examining how literary representations of the tourism industry present ethical considerations as central to sustainability debates in postcolonial states.

My geographical focus is on writings from the Caribbean and the South Pacific. These not only represent two of the world's most exoticized sites from a Western touristic perspective but also experience high levels of tourism dependency, even as their islands' bounded topographies and small populations render them distinctly vulnerable to tourism-related change.[2] I am interested in how depictions of tourism by writers from these archipelagos dramatize ethical concerns that emerge when tourism-led commoditization is implicated in what Yorghos Apostolopoulos and Dennis Gayle consider to be "widespread cultural losses and disruptive occupation shifts . . . that threaten the traditional cultural genius" of island communities.[3] This cultural engagement is significant partly because, as Fennell points out, "if we attempt to construct a world view on tourism and ethics at all, we often do so from the perspective of environmental ethics alone".[4] The fact that "[i]slands and island microstates present a special case in development" also makes this a pressing concern; as Apostolopoulos and Gayle observe, "[e]ven where economically and ecologically sustainable development options exist, they may conflict with island cultures".[5] Rather than attempting to reconcile such conflicts, I want to concentrate here on how developing more refined conceptions of *cultural sustainability*—a term that refers in its broadest sense to people's ability to "retain or adapt" elements of their culture while maintaining a sense of distinctive identity— can help complement and extend discussions about environmental ethics in the context of island tourism development.[6]

The need to enhance the cultural dimensions of tourism sustainability in Caribbean and Pacific island contexts connects to how, despite their ongoing industrial transformations and vast cultural, historical, and biogeographi- cal diversity, states in these regions continue to be advertised as unchanged paradises, discursively detached from the forces of capitalist modernity that they contributed centrally to forging.[7] This is linked to assumptions about "timeless natives" and "primitive" cultures that are indebted to construc- tions of islands in Western colonial discourse and were notably reinforced by the empirical writings of early twentieth-century functionalists such as Bronisław Malinowski, Margaret Mead, and Raymond Firth. The influen- tial theories developed by these anthropologists in relation to non-Western cultural systems were rooted in supposed correspondences between the isolated nature of the Pacific islands they visited and their inhabitants' "primitiveness".[8] However, such conflations of bounded topography with cultural closure effaced the circuits of trade, migration, and exchange that more readily characterize archipelagic regional histories worldwide.[9]

More recent academic visitors to the same region, in the form of tourism researchers, have revised cultural understandings in island contexts while also contributing to the increasingly self-reflexive forms of anthropology that emerged in the mid-1980s.[10] This involved a change from interpreting specific cultures and practices as closed systems to understanding them as dynamic, "hybrid, often discontinuous inventive process[es]".[11] Such research has urged a rethinking of tourism's supposedly negative cultural effects, with many ethnographers now insisting, like globalization theorists, on the need to identify how tourism helps produce narratives of "emergence"— including accounts that highlight tourism's role in shaping new cultural practices, formations, and products—as well as the more conventional nar- ratives of "loss".[12] This in turn has created a tension between "progressive" tourism anthropology and "reactionary" cultural tourism practices, which often involve "retelling outmoded stories, reproducing stereotypes, replicat- ing fantasy, or simulating a discarded historical vision".[13] In fact, Edward Bruner goes so far as to describe tourism as "chasing anthropology's dis- carded discourse, presenting cultures as functionally integrated homoge- neous entities outside of time, space, history".[14] Problematically, this friction applies to supposedly "alternative" or "ethical" tourism enterprises as well as to more conventionally reviled mass tourism practices.

Jim Butcher articulates some of the strongest criticisms regarding how recent trends in "ethical tourism" seem to be pandering to a vision of cultural "fragility", particularly in "[p]oorer regions in the Third World", which is detached from ongoing processes in reality. He argues that "the preservation of existing social and economic patterns", seen as "intrinsically desirable" by some ethical tourism programs, has the potential to create "a vicious circle of fragility, or perhaps more accurately, poverty".[15] This process is amplified in small island contexts, where the supposed "fragility" of their diverse ecologies is frequently mapped onto local cultures—a point that corresponds with Michael Cronin's argument in this volume that English-language travel narratives featuring "dying" languages tend to anchor linguistic cultures to specific places and perpetuate the very sociolinguistic devastation that their authors aim to highlight and condemn. Tourism sustainability theory represents an important method of negotiating such assumptions, which according to HwanSuk Choi and Ercan Sirakaya places it at "the center of an ethical debate".[16] This is partly because, despite sustainability's capital-oriented application within economic discourse, it still retains the potential "to offer a moral critique of the development process".[17] In particular, the principle of intergenerational "equity", associated both with sustainability's watershed definition in the 1987 Brundtland Report and in numerous visions for sustainable tourism futures, encodes an imperative for equitability and empowerment that remains essential if global tourism's neocolonial aspects are to be effectively challenged.[18] Adapting this within a postcolonial framework quite clearly requires increased attention to "power in tourism", which leading tourism studies commentators such as C. Michael Hall see as being until recently "a relatively peripheral concern in most [tourism] research".[19] Yet if sustainability suggests ways of harnessing alternative tourism's more positive impulse to respect local cultural practices while rejecting its atavistic and often profoundly negative "preservationist" discourses, the lack of attention to cultural dimensions of tourism ethics means that this theoretical component remains only vaguely defined.

Peter Burns, for instance, sees cultural sustainability as involving "harmonious relationships between host communities . . . tourists, and the supplying tourism business sectors".[20] This is idealistic on a general level as some degree of exploitation is inevitable in all tourism markets. More specifically, in the case of tropical islands, it could also be co-opted into reinforcing rather than problematizing the stereotypes of "harmonious" human-environmental interactions that underwrite paradisal myths. Choi and Sirakaya offer a more nuanced model of "socio-cultural sustainability" that demands "respect for social identity and social capital, for community culture and its assets and for a strengthening of social cohesiveness . . . that will allow community residents to control their own lives". For sustainable tourism practices to be achieved, they argue, "[c]ommunity stakeholders, including governments, tourists, hosts, tour operators and other tourist-related businesses must assume the ethical responsibilities and codes of conduct".[21]

They fall short, however, of clarifying what these "ethical responsibilities" might encompass in relation to a loosely defined concept of "community culture". In this light, the following textual readings aim to elucidate the ethical implications (rather than "responsibilities" as such) that emerge through considering literary depictions of tourism's cultural effects and power relations in island contexts. My examples are taken from two Caribbean and two Pacific authors: V. S. Naipaul (Trinidad), Albert Wendt (Samoa), Epeli Hau'ofa (Tonga), and Jamaica Kincaid (Antigua). Acknowledging the broad distinctions between experiences of widespread cultural fragmentation in the Caribbean and indigenous presence in the Pacific, I compare how different island cultures are portrayed as responding to the similar pressures exerted by globalized tourism development. The following analyses also offer historicized insights into how island tourism sites "are given meaning and are constituted by the narratives that envelop them".[22] These not only *anticipate* the ethical problems raised by rapid tourism expansion but also suggest that the interface of travel, writing, and tourism in postcolonial island literatures represents a key analytical location for cultural sustainability debates. This involves playful and critical subversions of "anthropology's discarded discourse" that highlight possibilities for shifting the object of consumption in cultural tourism practices.

NAIPAUL AND WENDT: TOURISTIFICATION FROM "ABOVE" AND "BELOW"

Published in the year when Trinidad and Tobago elected full independence from the West Indian Federation, V. S. Naipaul's travelogue *The Middle Passage: Impressions of Five Societies* (1962) has since been subject to widespread attack, particularly for its controversial assertion regarding Caribbean culture that "nothing was created in the . . . West Indies".[23] However, the text retains interest partly for its insights into Naipaul's troubled reflections as he returned to the region in his late twenties, following a decade's residence in England. As Tobias Döring points out, the "disdain for Caribbean culture that [Naipaul] articulates" tends to obscure the "anxious self-positioning by which he steers between the different roles of West Indian native-migrant-tourist".[24] The tensions arising from this ambiguous self-positioning feed into the broader ethical and cultural sustainability implications of this text.

In his relatively one-sided analysis of Naipaul's work, Rob Nixon argues that *The Middle Passage* evokes a "peculiar" irony because

> while, on the one hand, [Naipaul] regrets "how strong and ineradicable the wish is, among the bongo islanders, to act up to the tourist image", on the other hand, it is not at all clear what to his mind this process damages, given his dismissiveness toward endemic cultural

forms. As is often the case in Naipaul's travel books, one is left suspended between two categorical negatives, the old and the new, without any positive recommendations.[25]

It is no doubt contentious to imply, as Nixon does here, that readers are entitled to expect "positive recommendations" from the kind of travel writing produced by Naipaul or indeed from travel writing more broadly—as if the genre is somehow obliged to deliver authoritative policy evaluations. Yet in critiquing the text's "categorical negatives" Nixon also raises the question of whether Naipaul provides any means of negotiating these in ways that offer productive insights into Caribbean tourism's cultural dimensions.

One of Naipaul's most revealing passages on tourism and culture features in *The Middle Passage*'s Trinidad chapter. This takes the form of an extended diatribe on the apparent reduction of his native island's diverse cultural practices to tourist performance. He observes how

[f]ew words are used more frequently in Trinidad than "culture". Culture is spoken of as something quite separate from day-to-day existence, separate from advertisements, films and comic strips. . . . Culture is a dance—not the dance that people do when more than three of them get together—but the one put on in native costume on a stage. Culture is music—not the music played by well-known bands and nowadays in the modern way, tape-recorded—but the steel band. Culture is song—not the commercial jingle which . . . has become the folksong of Trinidad . . . but calypso. Culture is, in short, a night-club turn. And nothing pleases Trinidadians so much as to see their culture being applauded by white American tourists in night-clubs.[26]

Two key points arise from this biting critique. First, despite censuring Trinidad's culture of mimicry—claiming elsewhere that the "full meaning of modernity in Trinidad" involves "all races and classes . . . remaking themselves in the image of the Hollywood B-man"[27]—Naipaul nevertheless insists on a broader definition of local culture than is fetishized in tourism marketing. The "night-club turn" is placed in context of a wider cultural milieu where new forms are being created through popular folksongs, impromptu dance, and the indigenization of consumer culture. Second, the passage dramatizes how the manipulation of tourism itself constitutes a form of cultural articulation in a highly performative tourist "borderzone", defined by Bruner as an improvisational "point of conjuncture" where tourists engage in performative interactions with natives that transcend the "localized event" by taking account "of global and international flows".[28] While Naipaul, as a partly deracinated outsider, denounces local people's complicity in this process, he simultaneously sketches, here and elsewhere in the chapter, a vibrant culture of adaptation, based partly on extracting wealth from "white American tourists". If influences like "advertisements, films and comic strips" can become included in Trinidadians' everyday cultural repertoires, then following Naipaul's logic it might be said that tourism here is also being domesticated as part of these.

This section of Naipaul's travelogue preempts aspects of Michel Picard's influential theory of "touristic culture", produced following fieldwork on the Indonesian island Bali. Rather than simply seeing host societies as "victims" of exogenous change, Picard suggests that:

> the touristification of a society . . . proceeds from within by blurring the boundaries . . . between that which belongs to 'culture' and that which pertains to 'tourism' . . . instead of asking whether or not Balinese culture has been able to withstand the impact of tourism, we should ask how tourism has contributed to the shaping of Balinese culture.[29]

The Middle Passage depicts comparable processes of touristification in Trinidad, but rather than seeing these as part of a nascent framework of globalization, Naipaul (understandably, given the time of the writing) evokes colonial models of cross-cultural interaction, characterized by "conditions of coercion, radical inequality and intractable conflict".[30] Moreover, his commentary depends on a functionalist conception of island cultures as structural totalities. This underpins his attempts to account elsewhere for "*the* Trinidadian" personality, a supposedly singular entity produced by the island's "picaroon" society, which must be "re-educated" in order to achieve "political organization"; change, he insists, "must come from the top".[31] Ironically, the narrative's portrayal of community practice contributes simultaneously to the broader cultural sustainability insights I want to advance here. These respond to the interplay between local traditions and adaptive cultural articulations in the context of tourist modernity in ways that challenge how culture is constructed as an object of consumption. Naipaul's work also gestures toward the need for community tourism strategies which emerge from local inventiveness, economic involvement, and conceptions of cultural change rather than from top-down perspectives. This is an imperative that Naipaul's ambivalent "native-migrant-tourist" narrator simultaneously identifies, participates in, and resists.

The creative forms of transformation evident in Naipaul's ethnographic portrayal of Trinidadian tourist modernity suggest a productive counterpoint to the bottom-up perspective on cultural touristification presented in Albert Wendt's epic novel *Leaves of the Banyan Tree* (1979). The link is especially provocative given Wendt's artistic debts to Naipaul: *Leaves of the Banyan Tree* draws on the epic structure, tragicomic trajectory, and familial conflicts that characterize *A House for Mr Biswas* (1961),[32] and both writers unsettle straightforward binaries between insular cultural production and touristic consumption as they revisit their homelands as diasporic writers. The key scene to address in Wendt's "sprawling saga of social change in Samoa" is set just after World War II,[33] and foregrounds similar frictions between cultural continuity and inventiveness to those depicted in *The Middle Passage*, albeit from a deeply ironic, mock-ethnographic perspective. It depicts the attempts of the narrator Pepe and his friend Tagata to persuade a group of American tourists to purchase cultural artefacts from their accomplice Lafoga during an encounter in the Samoan capital, Apia.

Pepe begins by describing how this whole episode is stage-managed by locals who play off discursive tropes of island life, stating that

> before we arranged to meet these Yanks we arranged with friends of ours . . . to put a stall in the market to sell handicrafts and lei and things like that. . . . As we walk there Tagata describes Samoa to the tourists, like it is Hawaii which he has seen in the Hollywood movies.[34]

This establishes an apparent example of counter-exploitation, as tourist-savvy islanders import tropical island stereotypes and manipulate them to their advantage. Yet there are notable ambivalences. The pair begin their routine by confounding the tourists' expectations of primitiveness by speaking a Hollywood-inflected variety of English—causing one woman to exclaim, "I never believed they are as civilised as this."[35] While this seemingly follows Pratt's model of transculturation, which describes "how subordinated or marginal groups select and invent from materials transmitted to them by a dominant . . . culture",[36] the strict power hierarchies that underpin the theory become less assured as the scene unfolds. Whereas in *The Middle Passage* Trinidad's touristic borderzone and its related economic interactions are depicted from Naipaul's "top-down", ethnographic perspective, the scene in *Leaves of the Banyan Tree* presents a grassroots negotiation between tourists and locals in which the manipulation of stereotypes functions—arguably like the novel itself—as a slippery kind of "pidgin" code. In the process, Wendt's portrayal of touristification and indigenization highlights the emergence of a new, collaborative, and strangely intimate cultural practice.

This reading depends on several linked observations. First, although the manipulation of linguistic codes has undertones of mockery (attached to notions of colonial mimicry),[37] it also operates as an inventive form of communication in a collaborative context in which, as in Naipaul's Trinidad, tourism is constitutive of cultural performance. Second, the "real genuine Samoan markit" Pepe describes is not just a "sham", as Robert Chi suggests,[38] but a "real", touristified social phenomenon in its own right. Even as the narrative celebrates the seeming "inauthenticity" of artefacts sold to tourists—supposedly "ancient necklaces" that "Lafoga and Tagata bought . . . for two shillings each from some kids" that are actually "made of tooth-brush handles"[39]—it also highlights how the experience of cultural performance can take precedence over specific products. Moreover, these gain value to both tourists and native vendors through the *stories* that are attributed to them, making them metonymic—like Naipaul's and Wendt's text themselves—for a particular, historically embedded cultural practice. Third, in terms of intimacy, the verb choice in Pepe's claim that "I will never forget one time Tagata showed me how to *make* the tourist dollar"[40] evokes a sexual register that implies a procreative act. This "bringing forth" of the tourist dollar is ambivalently consensual, both counterexploitative *and* creative, with a mutually satisfactory outcome. The tourists acquire "traditional" artefacts, the locals acquire money, and both derive narrative fulfilment from this transaction. While never detached from wider networks of exploitation, this inventive act of cultural articulation shows the touristification of culture to be interwoven with the "indigenization of modernity"—a term Marshall Sahlins uses to describe "attempts to create a differentiated cultural space" within a hegemonizing "World System".[41] At the same time, the scene's contingent power balance puts binary relationships between host and guest, native and tourist, primitive and modern under pressure.

From a sustainability perspective, these points highlight the relative power of local actors to harness processes of cultural commoditization in ways that reinforce economic survival strategies, draw on cultural traditions of trickster role-playing, and contribute to the successful adaptation of this touristified local community. Rather than simply contrasting with Naipaul's top-down critiques, Wendt's playful perspective "from below" reinforces their more productive elements as both texts render preservationist conceptions of culture ethically suspect. Instead, they suggest that cultural sustainability must incorporate the interplay between tourists and locals in performative borderzone encounters, factoring in economic need and market manipulation as key aspects of cultural articulation in contexts where tourism does not always contribute directly to assuaging poverty. Yet the interregional correspondences foregrounded through comparison of Naipaul's and Wendt's texts raise another pressing question: how is local cultural specificity retained if postcolonial islands are not only marketed to tourists but also respond to tourism in culturally similar ways? Is the indigenization of modernity described here in relation to early mass tourism enough to offset the homogenizing effects of spiraling tourist influxes, particularly as tourism promises to become a dominant cultural form? Pepe raises this point just after the market scene:

> Our government, which is run by New Zealand palagi [white people], wants [tourists] to come by the shipload so that Samoa can earn money for . . . "economic development". My country does not need writers like me; it wants tourists; and I am sure that after I die Samoa is going to be like Hawaii and Tahiti and all the other tourist centres which are tropical paradises in posters but which are con-men paradises for stripping tourists naked.[42]

This negative vision of globalized tourism modernity challenges attempts to construct tourism ethics in the context of rampant commoditization.

The passage also has self-reflexive implications as Pepe ironically frames writing as a backward-looking practice, which is not only powerless as a form of resistance to touristic homogenization but is symptomatic of the distinctive cultural productions that are being discarded in favor of more narrowly profitable activities.

This portent of cultural demise is, of course, partly undermined as it contrasts with how the novel's wider engagements with tourist modernity are anything but moribund. Burns notes that the appropriation of culture as a tourism resource means that

> tourism needs to be understood in terms of contested cultures, created by (a) the collision of local realities and globally driven commercialism, and (b) the collusion between state and the tourism sector *to construct social identities and to fuse (and perhaps, muddle) histories*.[43]

Naipaul's and Wendt's texts resist such market-driven constructions of history and identity that can decontextualize local cultural practices in socially destructive ways. Instead, they offer representations of place and social interaction with respect to tourism that disrupt functionalist stereotypes while asserting cultural and historical specificity. The vitality of these very different depictions intersects with Pepe's comments on the future of writing with respect to tourism and "economic development". His self-reflexive commentary on Samoan homogenization buttresses a tacit imperative in Naipaul's text. Both suggest that support for artistic work—and the sustainability of cultural products more generally—must be considered key to ethical tourism initiatives. Along with a broader social commitment to poverty alleviation, reinvestment in this area can help ensure the further generation of "touristified" cultural products like these texts, which in turn play vital roles in critiquing exploitative practices, presenting imaginative strategies for industry negotiation and enhancing the cultural specificity of individual islands.[44]

HAU'OFA AND KINCAID: GLOBALIZATION, CULTURE, AND CREATIVITY

Within these evolving cultural economies, academic research also has a part to play by exploring the productive interactions among tourism, cultural productions such as literary texts, and their ramifications for undermining the more destructive aspects of state and tourism sector "collusion" outlined by Burns. This point is brought into relief through examination of Epeli Hau'ofa's and Jamaica Kincaid's portrayals of tourism and culture. Published a year apart, Hau'ofa's *Kisses in the Nederends* (1987) and Kincaid's *A Small Place* (1988) reflect how mass travel and the neocolonial economies of which it is part have become increasingly prevalent aspects of daily life in many Pacific and Caribbean island states. Hau'ofa's satiri-cal novel is set on the imaginary island of Tipota (a space that is distinct from but bears certain resemblances to Fiji),[45] and shares similar concerns to those examined in Naipaul's and Wendt's texts. These stem partly from Hau'ofa's investment in both the Caribbean and the Pacific: his formal training as an anthropologist was conducted in Trinidad and throughout his career he has "maintained an important conceptual connection between both island regions".[46] There are also stylistic similarities in the way he uses satire to negotiate the tension between attempts "to transcend the binary oppositions upon which much ethnographic, anthropological and colonial discourse has historically been based" and the negative effects of encroach-ing neocolonialism and cultural commoditization.[47]

Interrogating strategies for tackling touristic homogenization, Hau'ofa's novel draws attention to another key ethical consideration on which cul-tural sustainability depends: poverty alleviation. It is notable that, writing in 2007, twenty years after *Kisses in the Nederends*' publication and forty-five years after *The Middle Passage* first appeared, Weibing Zhao and J. R. Brent Ritchie observe that "the relationship between tourism and poverty alleviation largely remains *terra incognita* among tourism academics".[48] Such reticence appears particularly disjunctive when placed alongside the nuanced engagements with tourism's uneven and frequently exploitative economic dimensions displayed in postcolonial island literatures. This is well illustrated in *Kisses in the Nederends*' third chapter, which follows the tourism-related success of unemployed university graduate Amini Sese.

Amini enters the narrative as he attempts to commit suicide by paddling out to sea, an act prompted by his lack of success in securing a job on leav-ing university. Failing even in his attempt to "offer his body and brain to the sharks, since no one else wanted them", he survives after being seren-dipitously washed ashore in "the enormous shell of what must have been a giant turtle".[49] This auspicious event inspires him to reinvent himself as a cultural healer from within the shell. Drawing strategically on indigenous mythologies, he tells local villagers he was taken by "our mighty sea god . . . Toke Moana . . . into the middle of the Pacific Ocean, where the spirit of the great turtle, Sangone, took me into his shell". He proceeds to announce that "Sangone has appointed me his emissary and prophet to spread the good word, to heal the sick, make the blind see . . . the lame to run and the moronic to understand . . . comrades all, spread the good news that tomor-row at noon the Sangone Health Resort will open for business!".[50]

The subsequent success of this enterprise once more sees locals capital-izing on touristic expectations relating to tropical island life, although the economic scale is far greater than in Wendt's novel as Amini embraces a global tourism market via the mass media. It also involves an inevitable (and ironically depicted) degree of cultural commoditization as villagers mass produce miniature shells for tourist consumption. Amini places dis-tinct faith in the cultural and entrepreneurial resources of local inhabitants to adapt to this new phenomenon in ways that will benefit the community. In this sense, his university majors are especially fitting: "Creative Accounting" lends ironic credence to his economic shrewdness, and "Sociology" underwrites his skilled anticipation of local community inventiveness in the face of increased tourism demand.[51] Whereas in *The Middle Passage* Naipaul plays the role of island sociologist "from afar", critiquing mass tourism's extension of dependency cycles, a generation later Amini could be seen as symbolizing how the adaptation of sociological knowledge in island contexts can play a significant role in attracting and manipulating tourist flows. This benefits coastal communities while enhancing the specificity of local traditions in the context of globalized tourist modernity. However, such celebratory readings are destabilized by the fact that Hau'ofa satirically appropriates the redemptive trajectory of local place myths to highlight frictions between economic circumscription and potentiality.

The ethical problem raised by participation in this new market stems partly from Hau'ofa's broader concerns with how "colonialism, Christianity and international capitalism" in the Pacific islands have transformed "hither-to self-sufficient, proudly independent people into wards of rich and powerful countries".[52] While the culturally homogenizing operations of globalized tourism development can—as in Wendt's market scene and (by inference) Naipaul's Trinidad—be productively negotiated, the unlikely turn of events that sees Amini rescued from the oceans is at odds with the more brutal realities underpinning his initial attempt to commit suicide. James Clifford states that, across the insular Pacific, "[p]eople think and act in ambiguous post/neo-colonial situations, in the tension—both contradiction and synergy—of decolonization and globalization."[53] Hau'ofa not only imagines an ironically utopian method of negotiating these pressures but also highlights the dangerous contingencies that lace the intersections between individual lives, the cultures of which they are part, and the more destructive elements of late capitalist modernity.

This tension can be seen in Hau'ofa's serious if humorously negotiated portrayal of how the village of Vonu becomes "both a South Sea tropical paradise and a health centre".[54] A sense of local cultural specificity and adaptation is retained through the marketing of Amini's shell, as processes aligned with cultural commoditization emerge in relation to tourism here which "engender new social relations that operate in *anti*-imperialist interests, empowering the previously dispossessed".[55] However, the less environmentally sustainable aspects of this development, such as the potential pollution caused by increased "flights to Tipota" as well as the "[r]estaurants and coffee houses" that "soon dotted the waterfront of Vonu", is symbolically amplified by rising island arrivals as "the sick and the diseased in body and mind poured in from the richest regions of the world".[56] This new wave of health tourists raises questions about the support structures that exist to prevent the spread of disease, particularly in a novel that consistently satirizes the effectiveness of both Western and indigenous medicine.

Michelle Keown suggests that *Kisses in the Nederends* upholds Fredric Jameson's assertion that "[a]ll satire . . . necessarily carries a utopian frame of reference within itself".[57] At the same time, this chapter shows how such "utopian" frameworks are often shadowed by dystopian counterparts. It self-referentially demonstrates how Tongan storytelling practices, which communicate "criticism of individuals and institutions . . . through humorous stories [that] satirize the target of criticism by means of comic allegory",[58] reveal a nexus of ethical problems regarding the kind of tourism development exhibited in coastal Tipota. These are underscored contextually by histories of human and biotic decimation in the insular Pacific, relating to the introduction of various diseases, and compounded by the toxicity of nuclear testing. In this sense, the text guards against simple valorizations of the relationship between tourism and cultural production even when islanders are able to negotiate the globalized industry advantageously; it uses Amini's suicidal counternarrative and the ironies attached to welcoming legions of "sick and . . . diseased" tourists to highlight how such developments can exact a severe toll on local populations. The chapter also alludes to how the object of consumption involved in cultural tourism in the Pacific (as distinct from health tourism) continues to inherit the region's destructive colonial histories—with the potential for significant loss as well as emergence to occur within "the tension . . . of decolonization and globalization".[59] This is not due to supposed cultural "fragility" but because poverty and invasive over-development remain constant dangers to how island communities retain control over their environments and everyday practices. The tragic or dystopian counternarrative built into Hau'ofa's text highlights an ethical requirement to ground forms of cultural articulation in a diverse array of social and economic formations while exposing the pitfalls of over-reliance on tourism. Simultaneously, the chapter's utopian element suggests that more affirmative tourist industry manipulations by local communities can be produced through annexing the cultural resources attached to local mythologies. The creative appropriation and rearticulation of these through indigenous narrative practices, reflected in Hau'ofa's indigenization of the satirical novel, offers one way of asserting island specificity which is bound up with the wider touristification of culture. Hau'ofa's negotiation of the utopian/dystopian binary that frequently characterizes discursive constructions of islands in this sense represents an inventive means of remoulding these tropes for the purpose of humorous commentary and cultural critique.

Kincaid's polemical text *A Small Place* brings tensions regarding globalized island tourism, cultural sustainability and poverty alleviation into yet sharper focus. Also taking the form of a stylized travelogue, numerous critics have read its interrogation of postcolonial Antigua's culture and economy as indebted to Naipaul's *The Middle Passage*.[60] These critiques tend to efface both the differences and points of consonance between the texts where intimations of more positive futures might be found. Writing from an environmental viewpoint, Nixon argues that Kincaid's text can be read as an attempt to return her supposedly paradisal homeland "to a transnational ethics of place", allowing Antigua to be viewed, "like Naipaul's Trinidad, as a shadow island, a corrective to the spatial amnesia of a self-contained, regenerative English pastoral" that underpins certain aspects of tourist marketing.[61] Such parallels shed light on *A Small Place*'s more progressive aspects—especially its negotiation of both tourist and local perspectives and their ramifications for sustaining cultural products specifically.

There are notable correlations between Hau'ofa's and Kincaid's explorations of how cultural sustainability is undermined by systemic poverty and Pepe's prophecy in *Leaves of the Banyan Tree* that tourism will become "the new missionary trade", with "the Bible . . . the Yankee dollar . . . the priests . . . tourist owners, and the altar of sacrifice is to be our people".[62] Although the missionary analogy is more relevant to Pacific than Caribbean contexts, *A Small Place* implicates tourists and locals in similar circuits of circumscription to those which see local people as sacrificial objects and tourists as victims of co-optation, "owned" by tourism entrepreneurs. Crucially, Kincaid's text responds to what Mick Smith and Rosaleen Duffy call "[t]he key problem of ethics" in tourism—"understanding the Other"[63]—by reconfiguring the "native-migrant-tourist" subject position adopted by Naipaul.

Kincaid's narrator draws on structural oppositions between tourists and natives in order to expose their limitations, challenging the marketing of cultural "otherness" prevalent in brochure discourse. It is this "otherness" that the "sort of tourist" described in the narrative associates hermeneutically with the people and cultures that this tourist observes in islands such as Antigua.[64] In so doing, the tourist transforms from a resident American or European "to being a person marvelling at the harmony (ordinarily, what you would say is the backwardness) and the union these other people (and they are other people) have with nature" and "the things they can do with a piece of ordinary cloth".[65] The parenthetical comments highlight how cultural differences between tourists and natives constructed on the basis of the latter group's "otherness" are put under erasure by the groups' shared similarities as *people*. Suzanne Gauch argues that the confrontation of "otherness" and its replacement with what she terms Antigua's "ordinariness" as a dwelling place is crucial to *A Small Place*'s destabilization of exoticist island tropes and "levels many of the distinctions upon which self and other are predicated".[66]

It is therefore provocative that, in discussing contemporary Antiguans, Kincaid's narrator mimics the primitivist stereotypes of early island ethnographers that are embedded in tourist brochure fetishizations of native cultures.[67] According to Kincaid's narrator, most Antiguans lack the ability to see the interconnections between tourism and neocolonial exploitation that the text foregrounds. She thus frames them as equally blinkered "primitives", asserting that "[t]o the people of a small place, the division of Time into the Past, the Present, and the Future does not exist".[68] Along with the description of Antiguans as "an exquisite combination" of "children", "artists", and "lunatics", such sentiments appear "suspiciously like condescension" to some critics.[69] However, this notion is partly undercut by the contrapuntal description of the tourist-reader as "a nice blob just sitting like a boob in your amniotic sac of the modern experience".[70] This prenatal simile situates tourists and their experiences of modernity in a timeless zone: the primordial sleep of the fetus. Clichéd stereotypes of the timeless native are hereby refashioned and applied to touristic participants in Western modernity (with an ironic suggestion that some tourists "don't know they're born").

This equivalence emphasizes how both tourists and locals seem hopelessly manipulated by their respective experiences of modernity, remaining similarly alienated and distinguished primarily by economic rather than cultural factors. At the same time, a strong incentive remains for local communities to inhabit cultural stereotypes as, despite their reductive and often exploitative dimensions, they nevertheless allow access to tourism's vast economic flows. This consideration is expressed in *A Small Place*'s conclusion when Kincaid's narrator suggests that at times it seems as if the beauty of the island were "a prison, and as if everything and everybody that is not inside it were locked out".[71] This chimes with one of the more troubling implications of Picard's work on touristification in Bali as he claims that "the Balinese are now prisoners of a cultural image promoted by the marketers of Bali as a tourist paradise. In as much as they are expected to display evidence of their Balineseness, the Balinese run the risk of becoming signs of themselves."[72] Yet, rather than seeing cultural commoditization as a universally homogenizing process, wherein both tourists and natives are exploited (albeit unevenly) and local cultural specificity is lost as island destinations coalesce into a "hundred Havanas and mini-Miamis", as Derek Walcott puts it,[73] *A Small Place* positions itself as a kind of caustic antidote. Nadine Dolby suggests that:

> Kincaid's critique of tourist practices, her relentless insistence that the tourist is not free, that self and other are not separate, and that the world is locked together in one relationship, furnishes a model of how to reframe ethnographic practice into a vital exploration of the ties that bind us together, with the promise—however distant—of remaking those ties anew.[74]

While Dolby's commitment to revising models of intercultural relations is laudable, the stasis implied by mutual imprisonment within a problematically singular version of modernity is destabilized in Kincaid's text by the movements not only of tourists but also of migrants (such as Kincaid herself) and commodities across the island's borders. This process is reinforced by *A Small Place*'s status as a touristified cultural production in its own right, highlighting how Antigua's import culture and implication in global travel flows buttress continued articulations of diasporic cultural identities.

A Small Place reflects the other tourism representations addressed in the present chapter by putting pressure on the cultural objects fetishized by island tourism, suggesting the need for (and implicitly acting as) alternative cultural engagements that give access to the often partial and contested histories of specific island states. Together, these texts articulate points of conjuncture between the economic imperative of sustaining tourism and the need to create conditions in which cultural negotiations of tradition and adaptation can be positively enhanced. As such, their representations of tourism and culture self-reflexively characterize the cultural terrain wherein, as Stuart Hall has it (drawing on Antonio Gramsci), ideological change is articulated and disarticulated, and the ethical questions raised by touristification can be analyzed in nuanced depth.[75] This places a different slant on Walcott's 1970 criticism of how Caribbean "folk arts" in particular have been reduced to emblems of an "accommodating culture . . . adjunct to tourism".[76] Rather than becoming annexed to tourism, texts by both Pacific and Caribbean writers constitute forms of ambivalent "accommodation" that recognize the industry's economic potency and potential for productive cultural intercessions but destabilize its atavistic desires. This is foregrounded through a process of creative exchange that frustrates simple insider/outsider subject positions while also reflecting the ambiguous import/export status of tourism, with texts often being reimported after being produced beyond their island subjects' geographical bounds.

The link between tourists and locals that is figured in terms of collaborative intimacy in Wendt's text and which Kincaid's narrative presents as crucial to addressing economic dependency also has important bearing on how these texts contribute to *creative processes* of industry negotiation. This is interesting in light of Greg Richards and Julie Wilson's work on "creative tourism", which they define as "an extension of or a reaction to cultural tourism" that "offers visitors the opportunity to develop their creative potential through active participation in . . . learning experiences which are characteristic of the holiday destination where they are undertaken".[77] Part of creative tourism's aim is to reinforce cultural specificity in a context in which increasing numbers of states "compete in (re)producing and promoting themselves for tourism . . . [by] employing the same formulaic mechanisms", arguably reducing "their ability to create 'uniqueness'".[78] One way of envisaging cultural tourism's productive reconfiguration in this context is to follow Kincaid's rejection of "otherness" as a neocolonial component of "anthropology's discarded discourse" and explore instead ways of ensuring that tourism promotes the kind of cultural innovation that will maintain destinations' distinctiveness.

The imprisoning dimensions of cultural commoditization foreground the difficulty of reconfiguring paradisal island tourism's market-oriented motivations within an ethical framework. Nonetheless, the insights produced in this essay can be aligned with fiscal imperatives if considered in the terms set out by cultural economists such as David Throsby, who emphasizes the importance of cultural "diversity" for increasing particular localities' "cultural capital" and, by extension, attractiveness to tourists.[79] While Throsby's capital-oriented idiom jars with culture's unquantifiable dimensions, it speaks to sustainability's economic rationale by asserting that failure to "maintain and increase the stock of both tangible and intangible cultural capital" places "cultural systems in jeopardy and may cause them to break down, with consequent loss of welfare and economic output".[80] Creative tourism has the potential to militate against some of these risks. It not only provides an important model for adapting mainstream approaches to cultural commoditization but can also play a role in ensuring that the richness of specific cultures—which is often disproportionate to postcolonial communities' experiences of economic poverty—is maintained. This is essential if creative tourism is to achieve its ethically oriented promise to help "revers[e] the usual power relationships of the host–guest encounter", "develop innovatory new cultural products", and even "nourish the cultural economy".[81]

The depictions of tourism and culture addressed here form part of such "cultural economies" and are also constitutive of regional cultural heritage, not least in terms of how they negotiate multiple experiences of tourist modernity in the context of globalized power relations. By drawing tourists into island storytelling traditions, they show how "the narratives of place [and culture] created and sold by tourism professionals" are not simply endpoints but also initiate, as Kevin Meethan argues, "a form of interaction between people and place" that foregrounds tourism's role in creative "processes of transformation".[82] This unsettles any "fixed, static model that sees producers as in control, natives as exploited, and tourists as dupes"[83] while also highlighting the patterns of exploitation that produce further inequalities and cultural pressures. The different examples addressed in the present chapter indicate how one long-standing and mutually beneficial implication of touristic collaboration involves finding ways to sustain the conditions for active cultural production. They also suggest an ethical basis for how cultural tourism practices can be partly transformed in relation to the imaginative contract that readers—also "consumers" of sorts—share with island literatures and other cultural texts. These disrupt the serial reproduction of culture and place, challenge notions of homogenization and cultural "fragility", and agitate for culturally attentive economic redistribution without which the everyday practices on which tourism depends are rendered unnecessarily vulnerable.

COMPARATIVISM AND THE ETHICS OF CULTURAL TOURISM RESEARCH

Part of the purpose of this chapter has been to highlight an imperative for mainstream tourism researchers to engage more seriously with aesthetic perspectives on tourism as part of the ethical project that sustainability in its more progressive manifestations encodes. The instances of commensurability among all four depictions of tourism addressed here present a collective rationale for cross-regional comparison, particularly in terms of mass tourism's participation in the exoticist logic of globalized cultural consumption. They also draw attention to a notable silence in cultural tourism theory that is implicated in the revision of tourism ethics and approaches to cultural sustainability in postcolonial island contexts. That is, while tourism researchers have keenly retraced Western colonial anthropologists' steps in the insular Pacific, resulting in much groundbreaking ethnographic work, little of this has been applied to the world's most tourism-dependent region, the Caribbean. The archipelago has received much sociological attention, inspiring challenging and insightful work on sex tourism especially.[84] Yet those analyses that do address tourism and culture in the Caribbean fail to engage fully with the recent theoretical trends outlined in this chapter. To offer a few examples, Polly Pattullo acknowledges that "there are now significant points at which the interaction between tourism and Caribbean culture has created a new dynamic",[85] but does not explore this in detail, relying instead on the dualistically determined logic of authenticity and cultural integrity. Likewise, Ian Gregory Strachan's book *Paradise and Plantation: Tourism and Culture in the Anglophone Caribbean* (2002) makes virtually no reference to interdisciplinary tourism theory, continually criticizing tourism's negative "impact" on "authentic" cultural forms without setting this in context of recent cultural tourism studies debates. And although David Duval's essay "Cultural Tourism in Postcolonial Environments", which features in the empirical collection *Tourism and Postcolonialism* (2004), displays admirable sensitivity to conflicts regarding "the authentic", the fact that his case study is based on the history and experiences of St Vincent's indigenous Carib population indicates how tourism's effects on diasporic Caribbean cultures continue to be bypassed.[86]

Such observations raise a worrying concern: might cultural tourism theorists' overwhelming preference for focusing on Pacific islands reflect, at some level, the long history of assumptions regarding the Caribbean's supposed *lack* of distinctive cultural traditions? This is not to suggest that tourism researchers have paid less attention to tourism's effects on Caribbean island cultures because they subscribe to notions of the region as "cultureless". However, as most revisions of theories regarding commoditization, authenticity, and tradition have been derived from case studies in the indigenous Pacific, it is important to ask whether this trend relates to how these regions are marketed touristically. This is a serious point, for if such beliefs are being reinscribed—unwittingly or not—at the level of academic inquiry, what hope is there of confronting the kind of mental colonization exhibited by the *Guardian*'s travel editor, Andy Pietrask, in 2001 when he asserted that "[t]he Caribbean is, after all, about indulging the senses: eating, sleeping and, of course, snorkelling. You don't exactly go there for culture?"[87] The complementary readings in this essay suggest that representations of tourism and culture in Caribbean and Pacific island literatures, which speak to a shared sense of postcoloniality in the face of globalization and neocolonialism, are self-reflexively implicated in cultural tourism debates. As such they present a responsibility to tourism researchers in both regions to build these considerations into future study agendas. Such comparativism is critical to enhancing tourism sustainability frameworks that account for cultural as well as environmental specificity and incorporate both into future industry transformations.

NOTES

1. David A. Fennell, *Ecotourism: An Introduction* (London: Routledge, 1999), p. 254.
2. Rapid industrial change has transformed the Caribbean into "the most tourism-dependent region of the world"; Stefan Gössling, "Tourism and Development in Tropical Islands: Political Ecology Perspectives", in Stefan Gössling, ed., *Tourism and Development in Tropical Islands: Political Ecology Perspectives* (Cheltenham: Edward Elgar, 2003), p. 4. Meanwhile, many small island states in the Pacific appear to be moving from MIRAB (migration, remittances, aid, and bureaucracy) to TOURAB economies; see Yorghos Apostolopoulos and Dennis Gayle, "From MIRAB to TOURAB? Searching for Sustainable Development in the Maritime Caribbean, Pacific, and Mediterranean", in Yiorgos Apostolopoulos and Dennis John Gayle, eds., *Island Tourism and Sustainable Development: Caribbean, Pacific, and Mediterranean Experiences* (Westport, CT: Praeger, 2002), pp. 3–14.
3. Apostolopoulos and Gayle, "From MIRAB to TOURAB?", p. 6.
4. Fennell, *Ecotourism*, p. 12.
5. Apostolopoulos and Gayle, "From MIRAB to TOURAB?", p. 7.
6. Martin Mowforth and Ian Munt, *Tourism and Sustainability: Development and New Tourism in the Third World*, 2nd ed. (London: Routledge, 2003), p. 99. This approach also intersects with recent developments in postcolonial ecocriticism that have emphasized the importance of "factoring . . . cultural difference into . . . ecological and bioethical debates". Graham Huggan and Helen Tiffin, "Green Postcolonialism", *Interventions* 9, no. 1 (2007): p. 9. For further discussion of the insights postcolonial ecocriticism can shed on tourism sustainability in the Caribbean, see Anthony Carrigan, "'Hotels are Squatting on My Metaphors': Tourism, Sustainability, and Sacred Space in the Caribbean", *Journal of Commonwealth and Postcolonial Studies* 13, no. 2 and 14, no. 1 (2006–7): 59–82; and Anthony Carrigan, "Preening with Privilege, Bubbling Bilge: Representations of Cruise Tourism in Paule Marshall's *Praisesong for the Widow* and Derek Walcott's *Omeros*", *ISLE: Interdisciplinary Studies in Literature and Environment* 14, no. 1 (2007): 143–59.
7. Elizabeth M. DeLoughrey, *Routes and Roots: Navigating Caribbean and Pacific Island Literatures* (Honolulu: University of Hawaii Press, 2007), p. 4.
8. For further elaboration, see James Clifford, *The Predicament of Culture: Twentieth-century Ethnography, Literature, and Art* (Cambridge, MA: Harvard University Press, 1988), pp. 29–32; Rod Edmond and Vanessa Smith, "Editors' Introduction", in Rod Edmond and Vanessa Smith, eds., *Islands in History and Representation* (London: Routledge, 2003), pp. 2–3; and Godfrey Baldacchino, "Islands, Island Studies, Island Studies Journal", *Island Studies Journal* 1, no. 1 (2006): p. 4. Rod Edmond, *Representing the South*

Pacific: Colonial Discourse from Cook to Gauguin (Cambridge: Cambridge University Press, 1997), provides a historical overview of concerns that help shape twentieth- and twenty-first century constructions of the Pacific.

9. DeLoughrey, *Routes and Roots*, pp. 15–16.
10. See, for instance, Ruth Behar and Deborah A. Gordon, eds., *Women Writing Culture* (Berkeley and Los Angeles: University of California Press, 1995) for a feminist revision of this official history.
11. Clifford, *Predicament*, p. 10. David Harrison and Martin Price state that "[s]ome Western critics of tourism, especially in island communities, have focused almost entirely on its allegedly destructive effects on local culture", often "ignor[ing] attitudes of islanders themselves"; David Harrison and Martin Price, "Fragile Environments, Fragile Communities? An Introduction", in Martin F. Price, ed., *People and Tourism in Fragile Environments* (Chichester: Wiley, 1996), p. 6. Such research dovetailed with increasing concerns regarding globalization's homogenizing effects, engendering numerous investigations into the ways in which "traditional" cultures were either being "corrupted" by tourism or presenting versions of "staged authenticity" to tourist audiences that did not correspond with their "real" activities "offstage". See Dean MacCannell, *The Tourist: A New Theory of the Leisure Class* [1976] (Berkeley and Los Angeles: University of California Press, 1999), chap. 5.
12. MacCannell, *The Tourist*, p. 19. See also Shinji Yamashita, *Bali and Beyond: Explorations in the Anthropology of Tourism* (New York: Berghahn, 2003), p. 10.
13. Edward M. Bruner, *Culture on Tour: Ethnographies of Travel* (Chicago: University of Chicago Press, 2005), p. 21.
14. Bruner, *Culture on Tour*, p. 4.
15. Jim Butcher, *The Moralisation of Tourism: Sun, Sand . . . and Saving the World?* (London: Routledge, 2003), p. 56.
16. HwanSuk Chris Choi and Ercan Sirakaya, "Sustainability Indicators for Managing Community Tourism", *Tourism Management* 27, no. 6 (2006): p. 1277.
17. William Mark Adams, *Green Development: Environment and Sustainability in a Developing World*, 3rd ed. (London: Routledge, 2008), p. 198.
18. See Anthony Carrigan, *Postcolonial Tourism: Literature, Culture, and Environment* (London: Routledge, 2011), pp. 5–8, for further discussion of tourism and sustainability discourse.
19. C. Michael Hall, "Power in Tourism: Tourism in Power", in Donald V. L. Macleod and James G. Carrier, eds., *Tourism, Power and Culture: Anthropological Insights* (Bristol: Channel View, 2010), p. 199.
20. Peter M. Burns, "Social Identities and the Cultural Politics of Tourism", in Peter M. Burns and Marina Novelli, eds., *Tourism and Social Identities: Global Frameworks and Local Realities* (Oxford: Elsevier, 2006), p. 13.
21. Choi and Sirakaya, "Sustainability Indicators", pp. 1275–76.
22. Bruner, *Culture on Tour*, p. 12.
23. V. S. Naipaul, *The Middle Passage: Impressions of Five Societies* [1962] (London: Picador, 2001), p. 19. For a summary of attacks on Naipaul, see Ian Gregory Strachan, *Paradise and Plantation: Tourism and Culture in the Anglophone Caribbean* (Charlottesville: University of Virginia Press, 2002), p. 153.
24. Tobias Döring, *Caribbean-English Passages: Intertextuality in a Postcolonial Tradition* (London: Routledge, 2002), p. 21.
25. Rob Nixon, *London Calling: V. S. Naipaul, Postcolonial Mandarin* (New York: Oxford University Press, 1992), pp. 64–65.
26. Naipaul, *The Middle Passage*, p. 67.

27. Naipaul, *The Middle Passage*, p. 57.
28. Bruner, *Culture on Tour*, p. 15.
29. Michel Picard, "Cultural Tourism, Nation-building, and Regional Culture: The Making of a Balinese Identity", in Michel Picard and Robert Everett Wood, eds., *Tourism, Ethnicity, and the State in Asian and Pacific Societies* (Honolulu: University of Hawaii Press, 1997), p. 183.
30. Mary Louise Pratt, *Imperial Eyes: Travel Writing and Transculturation* (London: Routledge, 1992), p. 6.
31. Naipaul, *The Middle Passage*, p. 74, emphasis added; pp. 70–71.
32. *A House for Mr Biswas* is mentioned directly in Wendt's text, and Wendt's protagonist, Tauilopepe, is described as "'one of the 'mimic men', as one writer has put it so aptly". *Leaves of the Banyan Tree* (Auckland: Longman, 1979), pp. 366, 368. Paul Sharrad also relates Naipaul to Wendt in his monograph, *Albert Wendt and Pacific Literature: Circling the Void* (Manchester: Manchester University Press, 2003), p. 141.
33. Sharrad, *Albert Wendt*, p. 123.
34. Wendt, *Banyan Tree*, p. 188.
35. Wendt, *Banyan Tree*, p. 188.
36. Pratt, *Imperial Eyes*, p. 7.
37. See Homi K. Bhabha, *The Location of Culture* [1994] (London: Routledge, 2004), pp. 121–31.
38. Robert Chi, "Toward a New Tourism: Albert Wendt and Becoming Attractions", *Cultural Critique* 37 (1997): p. 79.
39. Wendt, *Banyan Tree*, p. 188.
40. Wendt, *Banyan Tree*, p. 187, emphasis added.
41. Marshall Sahlins, "Goodbye to Tristes Tropes: Ethnography in the Context of Modern World History", *Journal of Modern History* 65, no. 1 (1993): p. 20.
42. Wendt, *Banyan Tree*, p. 189.
43. Burns, "Social Identities", p. 18, emphasis added.
44. This is an important point given the difficulties of measuring cultural sustainability in a holistic manner. Examining how community members and commentators interpret the quality and diversity of cultural products is one way of approaching a tangible (if still by no means straightforward) understanding of cultural sustainability more generally.
45. For more on the relationship between Tipota and Fiji, see Michelle Keown, *Postcolonial Pacific Writing: Representations of the Body* (London: Routledge, 2005), p. 205.
46. DeLoughrey, *Routes and Roots*, p. 25.
47. Keown, *Postcolonial Pacific Writing*, p. 68.
48. Weibing Zhao and J. R. Brent Ritchie, "Tourism and Poverty Alleviation: An Integrative Research Framework", in Colin Michael Hall, ed., *Pro-poor Tourism: Who Benefits? Perspectives on Tourism and Poverty Reduction* (Clevedon: Channel View, 2007), p. 10.
49. Epeli Hau'ofa, *Kisses in the Nederends* (Auckland: Penguin, 1987), p. 47.
50. Hau'ofa, *Kisses in the Nederends*, p. 49.
51. Hau'ofa, *Kisses in the Nederends*, p. 47.
52. Keown, *Postcolonial Pacific Writing*, p. 62.
53. James Clifford, "Traditional Futures", in Mark Phillips and Gordon J. Schochet, eds., *Questions of Tradition* (Toronto: University of Toronto Press, 2004), p. 157.
54. Hau'ofa, *Kisses in the Nederends*, p. 50.
55. Graham Huggan, *The Postcolonial Exotic: Marketing the Margins* (London: Routledge, 2001), p. 12, emphasis in the original.

56. Hau'ofa, *Kisses in the Nederends*, p. 50.
57. Fredric Jameson, quoted in Keown, *Postcolonial Pacific Writing*, p. 82.
58. Keown, *Postcolonial Pacific Writing*, p. 62.
59. Clifford, "Traditional Futures", p. 157.
60. See, for instance, Jane King, "A Small Place Writes Back", *Callaloo* 25, no. 3 (2002): 885–909 (at p. 907); and Strachan, *Paradise and Plantation*, p. 225.
61. Rob Nixon, "Environmentalism and Postcolonialism", in Ania Loomba, Suvir Kaul, Matti Bunzl, Antoinette Burton, and Jed Esty, eds., *Postcolonial Studies and Beyond* (Durham, NC: Duke University Press, 2005), p. 241.
62. Wendt, *Banyan Tree*, pp. 189–90.
63. Mick Smith and Rosaleen Duffy, *The Ethics of Tourism Development* (London: Routledge, 2003), p. 166.
64. Jamaica Kincaid, *A Small Place* (London: Virago, 1988), p. 3.
65. Kincaid, *A Small Place*, p. 16.
66. Suzanne Gauch, "A Small Place: Some Perspectives on the Ordinary", *Callaloo* 25, no. 3 (2002): p. 910.
67. See also Alison Donnell, "She Ties Her Tongue: The Problems of Cultural Paralysis in Postcolonial Criticism", *Ariel* 26, no. 1 (1995): p. 114.
68. Kincaid, *A Small Place*, p. 54.
69. Patrick Holland and Graham Huggan, *Tourists with Typewriters: Critical Reflections on Contemporary Travel Writing* (Ann Arbor: University of Michigan Press, 1998), p. 52. Holland and Huggan proceed to argue that while "deeply committed to the drive for social change", in drawing on travel narrative conventions, *A Small Place* "remain[s] complicit with the tourism [it] denounce[s]", p. 52.
70. Kincaid, *A Small Place*, p. 16.
71. Kincaid, *A Small Place*, p. 79.
72. Michel Picard, "Cultural Heritage and Tourist Capital: Cultural Tourism in Bali", in Marie-Françoise Lanfant, John B. Allcock, and Edward M. Bruner, eds., *International Tourism: Identity and Change* (London: Sage, 1995), p. 61.
73. Derek Walcott, "What the Twilight Says", in *What the Twilight Says: Essays* [1970] (New York: Farrar, Straus and Giroux, 1998), p. 24.
74. Nadine Dolby, "A Small Place: Jamaica Kincaid and a Methodology of Connection", *Qualitative Inquiry* 9, no. 1 (2003): pp. 58–59.
75. Stuart Hall, "Gramsci's Relevance for the Study of Race and Ethnicity", *Journal of Communication Inquiry* 10, no. 2 (1986): p. 23.
76. Walcott, "What the Twilight Says", p. 7.
77. Greg Richards and Julie Wilson, "Developing Creativity in Tourist Experiences: A Solution to the Serial Reproduction of Culture?", *Tourism Management* 27, no. 6 (2006): p. 1215.
78. Richards and Wilson, "Developing Creativity in Tourist Experiences", p. 1210.
79. David Throsby, *Economics and Culture* (Cambridge: Cambridge University Press, 2001), p. 57.
80. Throsby, *Economics and Culture*, pp. 57–58.
81. Richards and Wilson, "Developing Creativity in Tourist Experiences", pp. 1221, 1215.
82. Kevin Meethan, "Introduction: Narratives of Place and Self", in Kevin Meethan, Alison Anderson, and Steve Miles, eds., *Tourism Consumption and Representation: Narratives of Place and Self* (Wallingford: CABI, 2006), p. 9.
83. Bruner, *Culture on Tour*, p. 12.
84. See, for instance, Kamala Kempadoo, ed., *Sun, Sex, and Gold: Tourism and Sex Work in the Caribbean* (Lanham, MD: Rowman and Littlefield, 1999);

Kamala Kempadoo, *Sexing the Caribbean: Gender, Race, and Sexual Labor* (London: Routledge, 2004); and Amalia L. Cabezas, *Economies of Desire: Sex Tourism in Cuba and the Dominican Republic* (Philadelphia: Temple University Press, 2009). For more on the conjunction of sex, tourism and embodied experience in postcolonial island contexts see also Carrigan, *Postcolonial Tourism*, chaps. 6 and 7.

85. Polly Pattullo, *Last Resorts: The Cost of Tourism in the Caribbean* (London: Cassell, 1996), p. 179.

86. David Timothy Duval, "Cultural Tourism in Postcolonial Environments: Negotiating Histories, Ethnicities and Authenticities in St Vincent, Eastern Caribbean", in Colin Michael Hall and Hazel Tucker, eds., *Tourism and Postcolonialism: Contested Discourses, Identities and Representations* (London: Routledge, 2004), pp. 57–75.

87. Cited in Mimi Sheller, *Consuming the Caribbean: From Arawaks to Zombies* (London: Routledge, 2003), p. 122.

8   Gourdes and Dollars
How Travel Writers Spend Money

Alasdair Pettinger

> I remember that sonofabitch Robert Redford. He comes in here, doesn't say hello, shuffles around. So impolite. Then he says: "How much for this painting?" I say: "Ten." He says: "$10?" and gets out his wallet. I say: "I don't think so, buddy. $10,000."
>
> —Haitian art collector and gallery owner Issa El-Saieh,
> quoted in Julia Llewellyn Smith,
> *Travels Without My Aunt: In the Footsteps of Graham Greene*[1]

RICH AND POOR

When travelers write about places where the language or dialect spoken is different from that of their assumed readers, they make use of a range of devices for representing their communications (or attempts to communicate) with the people they meet. As Michael Cronin has shown, the result often simplifies the complex negotiations of the encounter to the extent that both traveler and travelee appear to occupy the same homogenous, monolingual space.[2]

This essay explores a parallel phenomenon. For travel writers must find ways of negotiating economic as well as linguistic differences. Given that many of them offer accounts of journeys from rich countries to poor (to use a common shorthand), it is surprising that their treatment of the daily rituals of buying and selling, giving and receiving have not been studied more closely. Often widely perceived as immensely wealthy, they may yet find spending money as difficult as speaking a language they do not know. Their transactions are as liable to confusion and misunderstanding as their conversations. The question I wish to explore is, how do these confusions and misunderstandings figure in their narratives?

One's immediate impulse, perhaps, is to reply: hardly at all. It is normally only in—the comparatively rare—accounts of journeys where the protagonist faces financial hardship that her economic circumstances are likely to be worthy of note. They figure most prominently in those—typically more circumscribed—journeys that require their authors to leave their wallets at home and experience life on the other side of the tracks in order to publish a damning exposé of atrocious working and living conditions.[3]

None of the examples I draw on here—all taken from recent travel writings about Haiti—neatly falls into either of these categories, but all of them point to another possible reason for them to dwell on monetary and other forms of exchange a little more than is usually the case.

Since the fall of Jean-Claude Duvalier in 1986, the most popular travel books about Haiti have been preoccupied with the changing political land-scape that saw Jean-Bertrand Aristide win a landslide election victory in 1990, only to be forced out a few months after taking office, and not restored until after US military intervention in 1994. They include works by journalists Amy Wilentz, Bob Shacochis, and Kathy Klarreich, who cov-ered events for North American news media. Another reporter, Herbert Gold, writes of this period too, although his account ranges more widely to include his visits from the early 1950s as a "bohemian floater".[4] An alterna-tive perspective is provided by Stan Goff, a senior noncommisioned officer (NCO) in a special forces unit of the US Army.[5] Less directly concerned with the struggles for power going on around them are the more conventional travelogues of Ian Thomson and Eric Sarner, who use their visits to explore the history of the country from the struggle against colonial slavery to the dark years of the Duvalier dictatorship.[6] Finally, there have been anthropo-logical studies based on extensive fieldwork in Haiti, focusing on subjects as various as *vodou* (Karen McCarthy Brown), AIDS (Paul Farmer), and the lives of street children in the capital (J. Christopher Kovats-Bernat).[7]

This brief summary may suggest a certain shift in the thematic preoc-cupations of European and North Americans who write about Haiti. For a long time—certainly since the 1850s—the country has been known abroad primarily through the prism of *voodoo*, a term that condensed a whole lexicon of stereotypes (which, in Jan Morris's succinct formulation, define it as "religiously fantastic, politically grotesque, artistically explosive, sexu-ally wild"[8]) that would both attract and repel outsiders in equal measure. While there is still a sense of ambivalent attraction to a place deemed exotic and dangerous (but unlike other such places in Africa and South East Asia only a short flight from Miami)—and voodoo (or, as is increasingly the case, the more ethnographically sensitive *vodou*) continues to flavor their accounts—it may be that Haiti is no longer captured by an exotic word.

But if the horizons of visitors have broadened, there is a danger that another obsession may have begun to take hold, one indicated not by a single word but by a rather pedestrian phrase: "the poorest country in the Western Hemisphere". As Joel Dreyfuss points out in an exasperated article, this formula routinely appears in almost every international news report about his country. "Even when I don't put it in," one (unnamed) journalist told him, "the editors add it to the story."[9] But it is also invoked in most of the travel books I have mentioned, and not only those written by journalists, implying that it is not just a convenient short cut to inform a casual reader of the country's socioeconomic status, nor only (as it is often contrasted with the stupendous wealth it generated in colonial times) an abbreviated fable of postcolonial failure, but also rather a useful superlative that endows their choice of destination with intrinsic interest and importance.[10]

The—dare I say—currency of this expression suggests that while none of the authors of the travel accounts I have mentioned seem to have suffered significant economic hardship, they are likely to have at least a heightened awareness of their status as relatively wealthy visitors. Consider, for example, this scene of arrival:

> [T]he sun-baked border crossing at Jimani clogged with legions of harried reporters, photographers, cameramen, technical crews, fixers, and producers, their gear measured by the ton and fought over by bands of screaming porters, the road gridlocked with convoys of vans and flatbed trucks hauling satellite dishes, generators, warehouseloads of foot-lockers packed with electronics, lighting and sound equipment and videotape and bottled water, everybody slick with sweat, pissed off and verbalizing in half-dozen languages, peeling hundred-dollar bills off their bankrolls—ten grand in hard cash, minimum, if you were working for a major news organization.[11]

Bob Shacochis's description of the motley media personnel making their way from Santo Domingo to Port-au-Prince in September 1994 awkwardly both includes and excludes himself. As such, it might serve, provisionally at least, as a vivid illustration of the position in which most elite travelers to Haiti find themselves and the troubling discrepancy between visitor and host that haunts their accounts, as we shall see.

STRUGGLING TO PAY

Under these circumstances, it is not entirely surprising that the opening scene in Ian Thomson's book, *Bonjour Blanc* (1992) involves an encounter with a beggar.

> "*Eh blanc*, gimme a dollar." It was the spindle-shanked old man brandishing as usual an empty bottle of rum.
> "Not today, Papa Noir," I said. "Not today."
> Every morning in Port-au-Prince the old man was there, busking for alms outside the National Palace. Often he sat crouched over a pannier piled with rotted breadfruit, mischievously hooking any ankles in reach of his stick. I never knew his name; people called him *Papa Noir*. He was half-blind, Black Daddy, with cataracts, the elderly face worn and crumpled. A great moustache like a housepainter's brush lent him an air of dignity, but he looked a sight swaddled in shapeless gunny-sacking, his sandals fashioned from a used tyre. One day the old man appeared in a new T-shirt. It bore the sad injunction: "Shop Till You Drop."

"Life lasts too long sometimes," he said sourly, "even for a white man." Then he spat—*tfui!*—and added with a faint derisive smile: "But you will not last very long in Haiti. Nobody does."[12]

Words are exchanged, though money is not, yet the linguistic and the economic gap between traveler and travelee are both evident—if only schematically—in this passage. Written almost wholly in English, the passage hints that it reports a conversation taking place in another language, with those words in italics. That Thomson refers to the slogan on Papa Noir's T-shirt as "sad" suggests its wearer does not understand English and flags up a certain dramatic irony, but it is not clear if the conversation took place in French or Kreyòl, French being the official language of Haiti but spoken only by the educated elite (and rapidly losing ground to English), while Kreyòl—with its largely French-derived vocabulary but distinctively Afro-Caribbean grammar—is universally spoken and understood. "*Eh blanc*" sounds the same in either language; though Thomson renders it here in French orthography. It is likely that a city-center beggar would speak a few words of French, but it is also not out of the question that Thomson would have mastered enough Kreyòl to get him through.

None of these linguistic complexities—and their potential for misunderstandings—is addressed here (or elsewhere in the text), and there is a similar flattening of the economic register of the encounter. The narrator is asked for money; he refuses—or at least postpones—a gift. He doesn't tell us why, though the reference to the empty bottle takes us dangerously close to one rather conventional image of the beggar as feckless drunk, while the last words given him in the closing paragraph draws on another, that of the blind seer.

By describing the scene in this way, Thomson avoids confronting his specific position as an elite traveler. Although it opens with him being addressed as a generic *blanc*—anticipated by the title of the book itself—which offers a glimpse of how Haitians might view him (as hugely rich), this perspective is quickly reversed, but not symmetrically. The rest of the encounter is staged so as to convert Papa Blanc into not a generic *noir* (which would at least have kept in view some of the peculiarities of the situation) but a generic beggar, fixed in the apparently static codes of almsgiving through the ages.

In guidebooks, the difficulties associated with language and money are addressed much more directly. After all, they usually contain a few pages of useful words and phrases, and offer abundant guidance on what prices to expect for key goods and services, such as meals, drinks, rooms, and journeys via public transportation.

But sometimes even guidebooks don't help much. Consider this, from Amy Wilentz's *The Rainy Season* (1989):

"You think I can find a Pepsi?" I asked her, in my Frenchified Creole.
The day was still hot.

"Mimette," she said to one of her daughters who had brought in the
water. "Help the blanc to find a Pepsi, over at Bòs Jean-Jacques's."

. . .

"I'm looking for a Pepsi," I said. Mimette stood next to me, unsnarl-
ing the string of her kite. Another of Madame's daughters was doing
laundry with a washboard and a stone, singing to herself. The smell of
sawdust rose up from the nearby coffin workers.

Madame Jean-Jacques did not reply. The first daughter kept braid-
ing. Mimette said something in Creole that I could not understand.
Madame Jean-Jacques sat stonily.

"I think she wants money first," Mimette said, speaking slowly.
"They are afraid they will not have so much money now. Give her
some money."

I reached into my pocket and pulled out a dollar.

"More," Mimette said.

I pulled out another two.

"Good," she said. "I'll give it to them." She took the money and
hopped over to the girl, who put out her hand, and I saw two dollars
go into her hand and one dollar into the little front pocket of Mimette's
white dress.

Madame Jean-Jacques's daughter motioned to me and turned
brusquely, guiding me into a small cement house behind the board-
ed-up borlette. It was dark and hot inside; the cement holds the heat. In
the back room stood an old-fashioned icebox, which the girl opened.
There was one Pepsi, and seven or eight Sekola Oranges, a sweet, sticky
Haitian drink. She looked up at me questioningly.

"Pepsi," I said. She opened it.[13]

This is a rare passage where we glimpse something of the complex drama
behind an ordinary transaction. Though framed by a command ("Pepsi")
that in other circumstances might signal a rather stereotypical touristic
transaction, Wilentz is otherwise at the mercy of others, who tell *her* what
to do ("Give her some money. . . . More"). The scene, set against a background of labor she has no part in (making coffins, doing the laundry), the
narrator does not know how to pay for her drink or how much, and goes
with the flow, follows instructions, and observes what happens to the notes
she hands over. It shows that not only is the seller due money for the drink,
but also the girl who took her there (though she in fact slips the dollar
back to her mother when she returns). Just as the language difficulties are
gently foregrounded here (the "Frenchified Creole" that prevents her from
understanding everything that is said), so too are those of exchange. To this
extent, the discrepancies within both the economic and linguistic registers
are more pronounced than in Thomson's account.

In Haiti, just as there are several languages, there are a number of ways of expressing prices. The official unit of currency is the gourde; but you will also hear of the Haitian dollar, which has no official existence but is a colloquial way of referring to five gourdes (as the value of the gourde was for many years tied to the US dollar at this rate of exchange); the US dollar itself is also widely accepted. Wilentz makes no comment on the amount she pays, although if the dollars in question were US rather than Haitian dollars, this would no doubt be classed as excessive by the authors of the Lonely Planet guide, who warn us that

> Haiti can be a perplexing country when it comes to the cost of things. Surviving in Haiti can be extremely cheap, but there is the feeling that it is easier for a foreigner to pass through the eye of a needle than to find a bargain. The true price of everything, if there is one, is one of the best-kept secrets in the country. You will rarely be over-charged for hotels, street food or public transport, but taxis, guides and sellers of souvenirs will undoubtedly try it on.[14]

By "true price" they mean, of course, the price locals pay. The assumption that if visitors pay more they are being "overcharged"—as if, moreover, they are victims of a malicious conspiracy—is a commonplace of travelers' "common sense", and indeed part of the rhetorical armor that allows them to distinguish themselves from "gullible" tourists.[15] That the notion of a "true price" is unexpectedly qualified here ("if there is one") suggests that it may reward further scrutiny, and I will return to this below. But there is little doubt that this received wisdom is reinforced by first-person travel narratives that betray a certain unexamined disturbance whenever there is a possibility of money changing hands or some other economic exchange, as if the going rate for tourists must be avoided at all costs.[16] Travel writers rarely seem to simply pay for something or give anything away; they do so only against a background of calculation and intimidation.

"I bought a carton of cigarettes to hand out to the boys at the barricades," remarks Wilentz, casually, but makes clear that this is to buy their assistance.[17] In an echo of his opening scene, Thomson writes:

> "Eh blanc!" He moved aggressively toward me. "Donnez-moi un smoke, blanc!" Often I could spend a whole afternoon dispensing Comme il Fauts.[18]

Later he talks of haggling "violently" over the fee demanded by a guide.[19] And Wilentz refers in passing to the "many approaches" she uses "to get around . . . aggressive salesmen".[20]

This sense of the transaction as a struggle or a contest is a common theme. It is as if it is important to avoid paying the tourist "rate" at any cost, either by spending as little as possible ("Not today") or being overly generous (spending whole afternoons giving away cigarettes). That the latter involves an assertion of power as much as the former is perhaps best illustrated by the cruelty in the charity shown by US soldiers, as observed by Bob Shacochis. He tells us of the reservist who "was in the habit of winging bonbons at children as we drove down the roads", occasioning fights between those who got and those who didn't, and of the fantasy of the NCO who was "keeping count of beggars, planning to grab beggar number 1,000 and pull him into the Humvee and say, *Friend, today's your lucky day, you're king of Haiti*, give him an MRE, give him a dollar, and take him wherever he wanted to go".[21]

The latent or open hostility in travel writers' attempts to escape the tourist economy seems an inevitable consequence of being a wealthy visitor. Perhaps it is born of the frustration that becoming a "local" is strictly impossible. "Pretending I was invisible: the ultimate delusion for a white man in Haiti," acknowledges Shacochis ruefully.[22] Although there may be moments of solitude when one can entertain the fantasy, they can only highlight encounters with others as a kind of return to combat. As Goff writes:

> I confiscated time to disappear almost every day to Fort Dauphin, especially around sundown, where I would smoke and drink a Presidente and wish I could turn into a Haitian for a while, so no one would interrupt my glorious sunset with a request for food or a crowd of stares. My white skin and my uniform had become a beggar's magnet.[23]

THE DANCE OF RECIPROCITY

Goff implies that his relationships with Haitians were mainly with strangers, and his account bears this out. Even though he spends several months in one small town, there is little sense that he got to know any of its inhabitants very well. But he does make some interesting observations on Magda, the woman hired by his team as a housekeeper and cook, and there is a glimpse here of her point of view in the economic (and sexual) relationships between her and his military colleagues.[24]

And this is what we would expect. Once travel writers begin to get to know the people they meet—and write about them—their exchanges are less likely to be marked by that narrow instrumental struggle to pay the "true price", and more likely to prompt more considered reflections on the broader context of their relationship. Shacochis, for instance, recalls looking for his interpreter, Gary Metellus, in a neighborhood in Port-au-Prince, so he can hire him for a new assignment, and he notices that "the mood of the street brightened, because Gary's paychecks helped finance life in the neighborhood".[25]

Some journalists become more involved than their profession usually requires. While Herbert Gold reported on the events of the 1980s and '90s for the *San Francisco Chronicle* and the *Los Angeles Times*, he had visited Haiti many times over the previous four decades. An anecdote recounted toward the end of his memoir concerns "an unusually pesky street zazou" and ends with them "giving each other high fives"; Gold's ability to pleasingly disrupt the expectations of his readers here reinforces the way he feels more at home in the country than most of his journalist colleagues.[26] Kathie Klarreich went one step further and married a Haitian. Her remarks on a rookie human rights researcher carelessly peeling off large-denomination notes to pay for small street items similarly serves to underline her transition from foreign reporter to local resident.[27]

But even a long acquaintance with a place does not guarantee any extended insights into the ways travelers spend money. The snapshots of economic transactions I have just cited remain weakly contextualized. Anthropologists, on the other hand, might be expected to have more to say on the matter—not so much because they typically spend more time in the "field" than the average literary traveler but because their training would tend to make them reflect more on the relationships with their informants. It is true that for a long time their linguistic and economic exchanges were not considered a proper subject for the published monograph in which the author usually only appeared in person in the opening chapter and the intricacies of day-to-day contact surfaced only in diaries or separately published autobiographical writings. Nowadays, however, ethnographies frequently foreground the fieldwork experience itself.[28]

J. Christopher Kovats-Bernat's *Sleeping Rough in Port-au-Prince* (2006), based on interviews and conversations with street children over a ten-year period, is a carefully documented work of social science, but if the introduction, conventionally enough, remarks on the techniques used to gather and filter information (and how dangerous this could be), there are personal touches in the main body of the text that remind the reader of the day-to-day circumstances in which the author's research was conducted. For instance, we learn that after lunch at the Plaza Hotel on one occasion, he asks the waiter to wrap the uneaten portion, which he does only when Kovats-Bernat promises not to give it to street children.[29] In another passage, he explains how he often paid the children (for their help) by discreetly slipping cash into the bags he gives them soft drinks in.[30]

There are intimate moments, too, in the brief portraits of five boys and one girl that are placed between the main numbered chapters that carry the academic argument. The style here is perhaps more akin to "travel writing" as traditionally understood, and allows the author to appear as a character as well as a narrative voice:

> I do like Michel, and so I sit with him for a while and chat. He tells me that he is hungry. I reach into my pocket and give him a handful of gourde notes, enough for him to eat a few modest meals, though I am sure that at least some of the money will be used to buy more glue.

> Michel asks me for a cigarette and I give him several. He thanks me and lights one, and I do the same. We smoke in silence.[31]

Kovats-Bernat gives us a sense of more complex layers of giving and receiving than we see in the work of the more conventional—literary or journalistic—travel writers. He shows it is not just a one-on-one relationship between him and his informant, but modulated by third parties (the local business who discriminate against the street children, the other children who may resent the relationship, or intend to steal the gifts for themselves). Furthermore, even on a purely interpersonal level, the exchange takes place against a background of previous transactions that help to define what each expects of the other (one says he is hungry, the other gives him money; one asks for a cigarette, the other provides him with one). There is a certain predictability and ease about the transaction—suggested by (and making possible) the first-person plural that ends the quotation above, a "we" that is missing from writers like Thomson and Wilentz.

Nevertheless, the layers, while made visible, are not discussed, let alone theorized, in depth. Kovats-Bernat's main focus is on the culture of the street children as it exists independently of himself (a culture that predates his visit and will persist essentially unchanged after his departure), not on the interpersonal transactions that make his knowledge of this culture possible.

In another anthropological study, however, the ethics of giving and taking, buying and selling receive more sustained attention. *Mama Lola* (1991) by Karen McCarthy Brown is based on the author's long acquaintance with Alourdes Margaux, a *Vodou Priestess in Brooklyn* as the subtitle has it. In fact, it is not just a biography and a study of *vodou* but also the record of the friendship between the author and her informant.

One section of the book gives an account of their journey to Haiti—paid for by Brown—and their visit to Alourdes's relatives in the north of the country. As she is about to leave one village, the bus waiting outside, Brown hurries in to her host's house to pick up her things:

> As I opened the door, Marie Thérèse froze. My duffle bag was open on her bed, and she had my bottle of Ammens Medicated Powder in her hand. She had been shaking its contents into a small round box with a fluffy purple powder puff, an incongruous object in this spare setting. Her matchstick arm stopped in mid-air, and powder dribbled from the half-open holes in the lid. Her whole body communicated shame at being caught in this act of pilfering.
>
> Discussing logistics is sometimes helpful in awkward moments. "You have to open it all the way," I said in a matter-of-fact tone. I took the bottle from her, twisted the cap open, and poured half its contents into her powder box. (I held some back because Ammens Powder is one of the few things I find essential when traveling in Haiti. It eases insect bites and, in a pinch, is a reasonable substitute for a bath.)

Marie Thérèse responded to my half-gift with embarrassingly genuine gratitude. "Don't tell Alourdes," she whispered like a child. I gave her money, a skirt, and a purple T-shirt. Then I ran.[32]

If familiarity can bring a certain ease to transactions ("We smoke in silence"), this is clearly not always the case. The break between the paragraphs here separates a still image of an embarrassed Marie Thérèse, caught in the gaze of the narrator, and a sequence of rapid, assured actions on the part of Brown.

But the assurance does not last. Reflecting on the incident later, she realizes it was just one more piece in a puzzle that she was struggling to understand. She begins to realize that her gift of the powder was not the generous resolution she imagined at the time. "Charity breeds thievery," she writes, "and both are deeply flawed human exchanges because both lack reciprocity", something Marie Thérèse reminds her of by calling her, "a woman of her own age", *manman*.[33]

She also reflects on the conduct of her companion during the trip. Alourdes—herself a relatively wealthy visitor from New York (if not as wealthy as Brown)—too dispenses gifts, but in a more practiced, measured way, rarely giving into requests immediately and encouraging her relatives to scale down their demands. Moreover, she takes care to avail herself of all the benefits of hospitality that she can—ostentatiously allowing herself to be washed simultaneously by four children, for example—which give her hosts an opportunity to repay her gifts in kind. Of her own behavior, on the other hand, Brown recalls, "I cheerfully attended to my own luggage and amiably turned aside Marie Thérèse's inquiries about favorite foods and the way I like things cooked", thus demonstrating her ignorance of what she calls "the dance of reciprocity", which Alourdes has, by contrast, mastered.[34]

Brown's text would seem to confirm the insight of Marcel Mauss, who, in his celebrated essay on the topic, asserted that the exchange of gifts—so prevalent and fundamental in precapitalist societies, compared to "our own"—are never "voluntary, disinterested and spontaneous" but governed by complex obligations: the obligations to give, to receive, and to repay.[35]

Mauss inspired a wide range of anthropological, sociological, and philosophical investigations that sought to determine what, if anything, distinguishes gifts from other exchanges. For some, gifts are just like any other exchanges, but don't look like it because of the time lag between giving and receiving or because what is exchanged is not so much material as symbolic wealth: their logic is explained in terms of status and power (cementing alliances, containing conflict, and establishing relations of dominance and subordination).[36]

But Brown might also indicate a certain blind spot in this literature, which tends to focus on the distinction between "traditional" and "modern" societies, or the transition from one to the other (necessarily incomplete and hence the "persistence" of the "gift" category in "our" societies).

A consequence of this emphasis is that the conventions that establish what counts as an acceptable and appropriate gift and countergift are assumed to be fairly unproblematic. The ethical dimension to giving is assumed to revolve around the (rather rarefied) question of whether the—strictly impossible—ideal of the "pure" gift is a notion worth holding on to.

In the case of personal encounters at the points where the different "systems" of exchange collide, however—precisely the concern in the passage of *Mama Lola* under discussion—the rules on giving and taking are often radically uncertain. When a traveler from a rich country visits a poor country, and strays from the touristic zones where the prices of goods and services are relatively fixed—where even "gratuities" come with their own set of rules—gift economies emerge across the gap between guest and host. Once the traveler strikes up more personal relationships with strangers, the guidebook—like a compass in the vicinity of magnetic rocks—becomes useless. The buying and selling of objects may be mixed up with the exchange of less clearly defined services or more symbolic goods such as status or dignity. To give and receive something may produce unexpected modulations in prevailing relations of power and authority unless a reciprocal act neutralizes it. But when to respond and with what? When asked for something, does one give, decline, or negotiate? Brown remarks that "Alourdes works hard to keep her relations with family in the arena of reciprocity" and doesn't always find it easy "to achieve even the appearance of balance". How much harder for the narrator, who has not had the same practice.[37]

What this calls for is a form of ethical reflection that considers the right course of action less by deduction from relatively fixed rules or principles than by the close scrutiny of particular circumstances. It will necessarily involve careful deliberation and a certain rhetorical skill in managing potentially explosive confrontations through face-saving compromises that reconcile opposing interests and points of view.[38]

The adversarial character of encounters between elite travelers and locals—evident in the "sour" and "derisive" tone Thomson attributes to Papa Noir and the confrontational flavor of Lonely Planet's remarks on prices—may be a sign that a traveler is persisting in a narrowly economic interpretation of a transaction. Indeed, aggression on the part of locals may be not simply a means to solicit a gift or higher price but also a way of negotiating the relation of power involved in the exchange if successful. The pressure allows the donee to position himself less as the passive recipient of a benevolent, charitable act and more as a participant in a "dance of reciprocity".

The Pepsi scene recounted by Wilentz is free of aggression, but there is a tactical game being played out nonetheless. The narrator is not just paying for an item (a fizzy drink) but paying for a range of services that justify the higher price: the transaction, as it turns out, allows locals to play the role not only of vendor but also of guide, interpreter, and even—by opening the bottle for her—waiter.

Whether Thomson or Wilentz intend their scenes to illustrate these points is doubtful, since the dynamics of exchange feature only obliquely in their texts as a whole. But once alerted to these dynamics—as we are by Brown's account—the difficulties posed by "charity" and the measures required to make a transaction more reciprocal become clearer, even if not explicitly articulated, in the first two. Because this articulation is not explicit, it seems reasonable to argue that Thomson and Wilentz sustain Lonely Planet's commonplace that assumes that touristic transactions ideally take place against a background of a single, clearly-defined market exchange rather than a terrain of competing systems of values that demand sophisticated negotiation.

Haiti is only "the poorest country in the Western Hemisphere" in a particular statistical scenario in which measures of national product or income are compared after converting them to a common currency—typically the US dollar, which continues to be the lingua franca of the international finance community.[39] Expressing, say, average income in Haiti in US dollars tells us little about what that income can buy locally. As a template on which to forge personal relations between visitor and local this phrase is worse than misleading, for it cannot compute the wealth of care and expertise and sacrifice that the "poor" give back to the "rich" who so often patronize them.

Contemporary works of travel literature are often marketed in tandem with tourist guidebooks; usually shelved alongside them in bookstores, and offered as "recommended reading" as a way of further preparing the traveler for her trip, or inspiring the trip in the first place. To this extent they act as "conduct books" as much as their more practical counterparts, setting a horizon of expectations that govern the day-to-day behavior of elite travelers in exotic countries.[40] For this reason, I think, (imaginative, literary) travel writers have a certain ethical responsibility to be more reflective on their own circumstances and privilege. Not in order to succumb to a paralyzing guilt or despair, nor to offer recipes for radical social change in the global economic order, but simply to acquaint those readers who will follow in their wake with the micropolitics of the personal interactions they are likely to engage in. How travel writers spend money—or rather, what they tell us about how they spend money—is of more than theoretical interest.

NOTES

1. Julia Llewellyn Smith, *Travels Without My Aunt: In the Footsteps of Graham Greene* (London: Penguin, 2001), p. 247.
2. Michael Cronin, *Across the Lines: Travel, Language and Translation* (Cork: Cork University Press, 2000).
3. Seminal texts in this tradition include Jack London's *The People of the* Abyss (1903) on London's East End, George Orwell's *Down and Out in Paris and London* (1933), and *The Road to Wigan Pier* (1937). For more recent examples see Gunter Wallraff, *Lowest of the Low*, trans. Martin Chalmers (London:

Methuen, 1988); and Barbara Ehrenreich, *Nickel and Dimed: Undercover in Low-wage USA* (London: Granta, 2002). More conventional travel books that draw attention to their authors' limited means include Nicolas Bouvier's account of his epic journey across Asia in the mid-1950s, *The Way of the World*, trans. Robyn Marsack (Marlboro VT: Marlboro, 1992). Funded by the odd jobs Bouvier and his companion could find along the way—as artists, writers, tutors, lecturers—the forward thrust of the narrative regularly stalls as they carefully count the pennies, waiting to earn enough to cover the cost of the next leg of the journey. The question of money is also predictably at the fore in the accounts of Ernesto "Che" Guevara and Alberto Granado of their circuit of South America as cash-strapped students during the same decade; see Ernesto Guevara, *The Motorcycle Diaries*, trans. Ann Wright (London: Verso, 1995); and Alberto Granado, *Traveling with Che Guevara: The Making of a Revolutionary*, trans. Luciá Álvarez de Toledo (New York: Newmarket Press, 2004).

4. Amy Wilentz, *The Rainy Season: Haiti since Duvalier* (New York: Simon and Schuster, 1989); Bob Shacochis, *The Immaculate Invasion* (London: Bloomsbury, 1999); Kathie Klarreich, *Madame Dread: A Tale of Love, Vodou and Civil Strife in Haiti* (New York: Nation, 2005); Herbert Gold, *Best Nightmare on Earth: A Life in Haiti* (London: Flamingo, 1994).

5. Stan Goff, *Hideous Dream: A Soldier's Memoir of the US Invasion of Haiti* (New York: Soft Skull, 2000).

6. Ian Thomson, *Bonjour Blanc: A Journey through Haiti* (London: Hutchinson 1992); Eric Sarner, *La Passe du Vent: Une Histoire Haïtienne* (Paris: Payot, 1994).

7. Karen McCarthy Brown, *Mama Lola: A Voodoo Priestess in Brooklyn* (Berkeley and Los Angeles: University of California Press, 1991); Paul Farmer, *AIDS and Accusation: Haiti and the Geography of Blame* (Berkeley and Los Angeles: University of California Press, 1992); J. Christopher Kovats-Bernat, *Sleeping Rough in Port-au-Prince: An Ethnography of Street Children and Violence in Haiti* (Gainesville: University Press of Florida, 2006).

8. Jan Morris, "Introduction", in Gold, *Best Nightmare on Earth*, p. 9.

9. Quoted in Joel Dreyfuss, "A Cage of Words", in Edwige Danticat, ed., *The Butterfly's Way: Voices from the Haitian Dyaspora in the United States* (New York: Soho, 2001), p. 57.

10. The phrase was alive and well in February 2004 when it was pressed into service to report the second enforced departure of Aristide following several months of violent unrest. And it is capable of considerable variation, such as Klarreich's reference to Cité Soleil in Port-au-Prince as "the largest slum in the Western hemisphere" (*Madame Dread*, p. 147) and US President Bill Clinton's description of the dictatorship of Joseph Raoul Cédras (1991–94) as "the most violent regime in our hemisphere" (address to the nation, Washington DC, 15 September 1994); sometimes it comes with a satirical shift of focus, most notably perhaps by Goff, who speaks of the "most misunderstood nation in the Western hemisphere" (*Hideous Dream*, p. 1) and the "first independent black nation in the Western hemisphere" (*Hideous Dream*, p. 42).

11. Shacochis, *Immaculate Invasion*, p. 83.

12. Thomson, *Bonjour Blanc*, p. 9, emphasis in the original.

13. Wilentz, *Rainy Season*, pp. 58–59.

14. Scott Doggett and Joyce Connolly, *Dominican Republic and Haiti* (Melbourne: Lonely Planet, 2002), pp. 329.

15. Anthony Bourdain writes how in Cambodia he asks a British expat how much to tip his moto driver. He suggests three dollars. Bourdain gives him five.

"What the hell? Two extra dollars, right? He needed it more than I did."
"What are you doing?," complained Tim. "You'll ruin it for everybody."
Anthony Bourdain, *A Cook's Tour: In Search of the Perfect Meal* (London: Bloomsbury, 2002), p. 169.

16. "Tourists who want to 'meet the locals' express the greatest of pleasure at encounters which do not involve money"; Polly Pattullo, *Last Resorts: The Cost of Tourism in the Caribbean* (London: Cassell, 1996), p. 146.

17. Wilentz, *Rainy Season*, p. 99.

18. Thomson, *Bonjour Blanc*, p. 99; Comme il Faut is a popular brand of cigarette in Haiti.

19. Thomson, *Bonjour Blanc*, p. 29.

20. Wilentz, *Rainy Season*, p. 71.

21. Shacochis, *Immaculate Invasion*, pp. 337, 338, emphasis in the original. For a particularly aggressive response to the attentions of would-be guides and the amounts charged for meals, accommodation and car rental see the chapter on Haiti in Brian Thacker, *The Naked Man Festival and Other Excuses to Fly around the World* (Sydney: Allen and Unwin, 2004), pp. 193–230.

22. Thacker, *The Naked Man Festival*, p. 225.

23. Goff, *Hideous Dream*, p. 402.

24. Goff, *Hideous Dream*, pp. 445–46.

25. Shacochis, *Immaculate Invasion*, p. 237.

26. Gold, *Best Nightmare*, p. 300.

27. Klarreich, *Madame Dread*, pp. 249–50.

28. Farmer's *AIDS and Accusation*, a study of the impact of AIDS in a Haitian village, is an exception. Farmer, the fieldworker, barely features in his own account at all. On the changing conventions of the deployment of the first-person narrative in the ethnographic monograph see James Clifford, "On Ethnographic Authority", in James Clifford, *The Predicament of Culture: Twentieth-century Ethnography, Literature, and Art* (Cambridge, MA: Harvard University Press, 1988), pp. 21–54; Mary Louise Pratt, "Fieldwork in Common Places", in James Clifford and George E. Marcus, eds., *Writing Culture: The Poetics and Politics of Ethnography* (Berkeley and Los Angeles: University of California Press, 1986), pp. 27–50. For personal testimonies by fieldworkers on the role of money in their research see Stefan Senders and Allison Truitt, eds., *Money: Ethnographic Encounters* (Oxford: Berg, 2007).

29. Kovats-Bernat, *Sleeping Rough*, p. 53.

30. Kovats-Bernat, *Sleeping Rough*, pp. 55–56.

31. Kovats-Bernat, *Sleeping Rough*, p. 107.

32. Brown, *Mama Lola*, p. 178.

33. Brown, *Mama Lola*, p. 179.

34. Brown, *Mama Lola*, pp. 178–79. "The dance of reciprocity" is the title of this section (pp. 177–82).

35. Marcel Mauss, *The Gift: Forms and Functions of Exchange in Archaic Societies*, trans. Ian Cunnison [1925] (London: Routledge and Kegan Paul, 1969), p. 1.

36. See, for example, Arjun Appadurai, ed., *The Social Life of Things: Commodities in Cultural Perspective* (Cambridge: Cambridge University Press, 1986); Jonathan Parry and Maurice Bloch, eds., *Money and the Morality of Exchange* (Cambridge: Cambridge University Press, 1989); Jacques Derrida, *Given Time: 1. Counterfeit Money* [1991], trans. Peggy Kamuf (Chicago: University of Chicago Press, 1992); Alan D. Schrift, ed., *The Logic of the Gift: Toward an Ethic of Generosity* (London: Routledge, 1997); Judith Still, *Feminine Economies: Thinking against the Market in the Enlightenment and the Late Twentieth Century* (Manchester: Manchester University

Press, 1997). For two model explorations of these themes by literary scholars, see David Murray, *Indian Giving: Economies of Power in Indian-white Exchanges* (Amherst: University of Massachusetts Press, 2000); and Mireille Rosello, *Postcolonial Hospitality: The Immigrant as Guest* (Stanford, CA: Stanford University Press, 2001).

37. Brown, *Mama Lola*, p. 179.
38. For robust arguments in favor of such forms of practical ethical reflection (and their recent reemergence) see Jeffrey Minson, *Questions of Conduct: Sexual Harassment, Citizenship, Government* (Basingstoke: Macmillan, 1993), esp. pp. 1–40; and Richard B. Miller, *Casuistry and Modern Ethics: A Poetics of Practical Reasoning* (Chicago: University of Chicago Press, 1996).
39. The absurdity of this dominance is illustrated well (but unremarked upon) by Tom Fremantle, who tries to convey the significance of a cash amount in Niger by first converting it to sterling and then weighing its value by setting it against the average income, which he expresses in US dollars, even though this is neither the local currency nor the currency most familiar to the author or his British readers. See Tom Fremantle, *The Road to Timbuktu* (London: Robinson, 2005), p. 256.
40. For an excellent discussion of guidebooks from this perspective, see Rudy Koshar, *German Travel Cultures* (Oxford: Berg, 2000), esp. pp. 1–18, 203–12.

9 Writing across the Native/Foreign Divide

The Case of Kapka Kassabova's *Street Without a Name*

Ludmilla Kostova

The writing of migrants has been attracting considerable critical attention over the last fifty years or so, and this is symptomatic of the high level of geographical mobility and the resultant "topology of fluidity" characterizing the world in the aftermath of the Second World War.[1] For the purposes of the present chapter, *migrant writing* is defined as work by writers who are positioned between cultures and, in Mads Rosendahl Thomsen's apt phrasing, "navigate between languages".[2] The output of migrant writers raises questions about the varying relationships between *foreign* and *native* and, at present, *global* and *local*. While a lot of notice has been taken of migrant writers' contributions to "high" literature, as exemplified by the novel, relatively little has been written about non- or semifictional travel and/or (auto) biographical accounts by such writers. Moreover, the approach to individual migrant writers has been selective, with a lot of critical evaluations focusing either on canonized literary figures within modernism and (early) postmodernism, such as Vladimir Nabokov and Samuel Beckett, or on writers whose familial roots could be traced back to former Western colonies, such as Salman Rushdie. Writers with Eastern European antecedents, whose migrancy was the outcome of considerably recent events like the fall of communism in 1989 and into the 1990s and the subsequent opening up of the former Eastern Bloc,[3] have received comparatively little critical attention so far, but there are distinct signs, such as academic conferences and volumes of proceedings, that this is changing—for some of them, at least.[4]

Bulgarian-born Kapka Kassabova, who writes in English and whose memoir-cum-travelogue *Street Without a Name: Childhood and Other Misadventures in Bulgaria* is the object of analysis in this chapter,[5] has been rather lucky in this respect. Academic interest in her work is steadily growing,[6] and reviews of her books have appeared in prestigious publications such as the *Guardian*, the *Independent*, the *Financial Times*, the *Sunday Times*, the *Scottish Review of Books*, the *Edinburgh Review*, and *Poetry Review*.[7] In addition, the writer herself has been rather active on the conference circuit.[8]

Born in 1973, Kassabova left Bulgaria for Britain at the age of seventeen, briefly returned, and then moved with her family to New Zealand, where she attended two universities and worked until 2004. She is currently based in Edinburgh where, according to her bio on the website of Bloodaxe Books, she "writes travel guides".[9] Such an occupation seems fitting for an author whose work is largely informed by the related themes of mobility, flux, and displacement. Kassabova "refers to her family as *economic migrants*" and accepts the label *migrant* for herself, claiming that "being displaced serves as a motivating factor in her creativity".[10] It is important to bear in mind, however, that the adult members of the writer's family were not refugees or some other kind of "coerced migrants" at the time of their displacement but "free-willing . . . subjects",[11] aware of the economically convertible professional skills and other cultural capital that they possessed and hoping to make the best possible use of them away from the country of their birth. Kassabova's family's exodus was part of what is known in that country as "the Bulgarian brain drain", as well-educated, highly qualified professionals chose to leave, as soon as they could, in search of more adequate pay and better living conditions in the West. Significantly, the displacement of such professionals and their offspring has led to the emergence of a distinctive *postnational* migrant middle-class identity that, to the best of my knowledge, has not been the object of serious study yet.

Street Without a Name is (arguably) Kassabova's most highly acclaimed book to date. It was short-listed for the Authors' Club Dolman Best Travel Book Award (2009) and the European Book Award (2009), reviewed in the *Guardian* by Misha Glenny,[12] and selected by Jan Morris as her book of the year for the *Financial Times* (2008). Eminent travel writer and essayist Pico Iyer pronounced it to have "the force of revelation": "it leads us into a country most of us have hardly read about with . . . a heart-rending precision that can make you see the world quite differently".[13] Significantly, *Street* has been praised by Western readers but a number of Bulgarian reactions to it and its author have been far from favorable. Aspects of the book's reception will be examined in this chapter's second section, "The Book, Its Readers and the Author", and an attempt will be made to contextualize and compare different attitudes to it. Attention will likewise be paid to Kassabova's own response to her book's reception as revealed in her 2010 article "From Bulgaria with Love and Hate: the Anxiety of the Distorting Mirror (A Writer's Perspective)" and some interviews. The interaction between the writer and (some of) her Bulgarian readers poses certain ethical problems that will be dwelled upon.

This chapter will first consider aspects of the book's production and preparation for successful marketing, and particularly, the guiding role played by the publisher in the process. Having next examined *Street*'s reception, it will dwell on the persona, which Kassabova fashions for herself in her poetry and the book, while also taking into account the image she projects in select interviews. Both will be linked to the emergent type of middle-class identity mentioned above and will be analyzed within the context of present-day ideas of cosmopolitanism. Throughout, the chapter will investigate the writer's claim that "Bulgaria is a country without a face" as far as the "Western mind" is concerned and the representational strategies she employs in order to lift the country out of its "obscurity". What makes *Street* particularly relevant to the purposes of this volume is that it problematizes "the logic of identity/difference" on which, according to Debbie Lisle, the travel genre is based,[14] and this has distinct ethico-political implications. In my exploration of those I will not be guided by any universal principles of judgment but will instead pose a number of specific questions, some of which will touch upon Kassabova's interaction with her chosen medium of expression, the anglophone travelogue with its imperialist legacy and present-day cosmopolitan orientation,[15] and the presence/absence of "political reflexivity and critical thought" in her text.[16]

ENGENDERING A BOOK ABOUT A LITTLE-KNOWN LAND

In an interview Kassabova explains how her book came into existence. She was approached by the British publisher Portobello Books and told that "they . . . wanted a book about Bulgaria because there aren't any. . . . Bulgaria is such an obscure place in the Western mind".[17] Her "Bulgarianness" was evidently perceived as the kind of "cultural capital" that would give the book "distinctiveness", a quality highly valued by publishers.[18] She was thus assigned the role of a cultural guide and commissioned to guide Western anglophone readers through an "obscure" country, nonetheless situated on the map of the "old" continent and holding membership in the European Union. Kassabova was likewise chosen for her task of intercultural mediation because of her familiarity with such readers and her ability to represent Bulgaria in a comprehensible way to them. This familiarity could be seen as the outcome of her own successful *cultural (self-)translation* into *le monde anglophone*, borne out by her education and previous experience as a writer.

Kassabova further adds that the publisher wanted "a personal story", a "travel book that also had a memoir feel to it".[19] She explains that "once I started writing about my childhood, it sort of shaped up as part memoir, part travelogue".[20] The story Kassabova recounts in the interview cited above is of a pact between publisher and writer that must of necessity shape a lot of travel writing in the present. On the basis of what she says we can even outline a scenario of the market-dominated relationship between the two parties. In it the publisher thinks in terms of marketability: the perceived absence of books about Bulgaria is an empty niche that must be filled insofar as the market, like nature in the well-known Latin saying, *abhorret a vacuo*. A competent writer with a "hyphenated" identity is chosen for the purpose. The writer complies with the publisher's wishes and finds that her compliance does not sap her creative energy: the text "*sort of shape[s] up* as part memoir, part travelogue"[21]—that is, (to use another cliché) it seems to take on a life of its own. The final outcome is a *generic hybrid* portraying the narrator's early life and family history as well as her later visits to Bulgaria.

The first part of *Street* links it to a number of books in English that portray the complexities of latter-day transcultural subjecthood by recounting earlier pre-migration family histories. Zadie Smith's *White Teeth* (2000) is perhaps the most famous of such narratives and may be said to have provided a formula that has been successfully employed by a variety of writers ranging from other "postcolonials" to second-generation Eastern European migrants like Marina Lewycka.[22] Following her publisher's guidance, Kassabova utilizes the formula and this further contributes to her book's marketability. Her anglophone audience should be able to approach her book through analogies with earlier migration-related narratives while also taking into account its novelty: it is, after all, about life in and migration out of *a little known land*.

THE BOOK, ITS READERS AND THE AUTHOR

Street is evidently targeted at a community of readers with a taste for experimental plotting. The book does not represent the narrator's experiences in a neat, chronological way. There are a number of discontinuities in the narrative, the most striking one being the absence of any account of Kassabova's life in New Zealand or elsewhere in the West. One Western reviewer has found the narrative's discontinuous structure "disorienting" and would have apparently welcomed a text that provided more autobiographical details:

> Halfway through, the book stops being a memoir of life under communism and turns into a travelogue, a report of her [Kassabova's] trip back to Bulgaria after living in New Zealand and Scotland. This is disorienting at first; deliberately so, I think, for we hear nothing about her life elsewhere, yet suspect that something has happened in the interim. And I suspect that that something is not too much more than leaving Bulgaria.[23]

Other specialized readers of the book, however, have found its experimental structure an asset rather than a drawback. For Jan Morris *Street* is "an *unusual* and *genre-bending* book".[24] Glenny is not confused by the plot's structural discontinuities either. Taking into account the book's mixing up of memories and later travel experiences, he pronounces it to be an "autobiographical travelogue".[25] For literary critic Claudia Duppé, "discontinuity is the linchpin of *Street Without a Name*" insofar as it functions as a sign of the narrator's displaced condition and her inability to reconcile her past and present.[26]

Significantly, the readers considered above mostly show interest in the first part of the book, "Childhood", and as a result tend to read the text as a memoir, thus practically negating its hybridity. For instance, Duppé's article is titled "Tourist in Her Native Country: Kapka Kassabova's *Street Without a Name*", but it only deals with the "tourist" part of the narrative, which constitutes almost two-thirds of the whole text, in a series of comparatively short comments on a limited number of episodes. Nicholas Lezard, from whose review I quoted above, also concentrates on the first part and discusses the narrator's "other misadventures" in Bulgaria in a single paragraph.[27] The title of Glenny's review, "'Mum, Why Is Everything So Ugly?'" is a quote from the first part of the book; it is a question that the young narrator asks her mother as she looks at the gray and grim state-socialist cityscape that surrounds them. The focus of these three specialized readers is symptomatic of Westerners' continuing fascination with life behind what used to be known as the Iron Curtain.

Kassabova appears well aware of the Western preoccupation with life under communism. In the closing paragraph of "From Bulgaria with Love and Hate" she remarks that "much of [Bulgaria's] fascination on the outside . . . of the [distorting] mirror [in the West] comes from the communist experience".[28] Her account of her childhood and adolescence aims at dispelling stereotypes about that experience. Like other writers from the former Eastern Bloc, Kassabova stresses the *ordinariness* of her own and her family's life under communism,[29] and aims at acquainting Western readers with what it felt like to grow up in a politically repressive, one-party system and experience perpetual shortages of consumer goods and restrictions upon the geographical mobility of ordinary citizens. She further recounts how she became aware, at an early age, of the discrepancy between "the commonplaces of individual life" and "[ideology-inspired] national dreams".[30] Her narrative is punctuated with pre-1989 Bulgarian political jokes and distinctive phrases (e.g., she states that she is the child of "poor engineers") that are instances of what Michael Billig has identified as "rebellious humour", a form of "innocuous revenge" on the system by ordinary people living under totalitarian regimes.[31] For all of Kassabova's resentment of communism, of which she has spoken and written many times,[32] "Childhood" is above all about adjustment and survival. The narrator makes relatively few references to violations of human rights, such as the forced renaming of ethnic Turks and the outlawing of the use of the Turkish language in public,[33] and mostly stresses the ability of the adults in her family to make "cakes without ingredients" and perform other feats of domestic prowess.[34] In that context, the West emerges above all as a consumer paradise replete with "glossy objects",[35] not as a stronghold of democracy and freedom.

The use of humor in "Childhood" enables Kassabova to steer clear of sentimentality. Nevertheless Duppé and Glenny have adopted sentimentalizing approaches to this part of her book. Thus, Duppé maintains that the narrator resorts to humor in it in order to "cover *her very personal bereavement for a childhood that never was*".[36] The critic applauds Bulgaria's post-1989 adoption of "Western lifestyles" because in the new circumstances children are more likely to get playgrounds and adults may acquire "room for living as individual human beings rather than citizens of a state apparatus".[37]

While Duppé commiserates with Kassabova over her "dysfunctional" childhood in Bulgaria, Glenny dwells on the sad story of her early encounter with the "real" West as a teenager. He remarks that "Britons don't face too much grief when travelling abroad".[38] They generally have an easy time outside their own country because "everyone has heard of Britain", "'English is almost ubiquitous", and they can always make use of their credit cards or have recourse to their travel insurance, if "a real crisis" occurs.[39] Kassabova, on the other hand, became the victim of Bulgaria's "obscurity" when her family first moved to Britain, and had to learn the hard way that "her Bulgarian heritage bred not interest among her classmates but contempt".[40] There can be no doubt that the difficulties the future writer experienced in the process of her resettlement and adjustment to life elsewhere were real enough (Kassabova herself decries Westerners' insensitive denigration of Bulgaria and Bulgarians[41]) but I cannot help quibbling about the way in which Glenny has chosen to present her predicament. The contrast that he builds between the Eastern European teenager who is mocked by her classmates on account of her "cheap canvas sports shoes" and British credit card holders who "don't face too much grief when travelling abroad" does not stimulate understanding of the reasons behind the rudeness of some first world adolescents or, for that matter, behind privileged travelers' scarcity of grief, but seems to demonstrate Western superiority above all. Mixed with that is pity for anyone who has not had the good fortune to belong by birth to a nation that "everyone has heard of".[42]

As has been mentioned, *Street* was not initially targeted at a Bulgarian reading public but was intended for British and other anglophone readers outside the country. However, it was translated into Bulgarian in 2008 and thus made available to readers in Bulgaria. Needless to say, a number of expatriates and other anglophone Bulgarians read it in English. To my mind, "native" Bulgarian and Bulgarian expatriate readers may be grouped into four categories. The first category comprises "(n)ostalgists" with a markedly positive vision of life under state socialism. Such readers tend to regard Kassabova's representation of her childhood as "inauthentic".[43] The second category includes less hostile readers of the writer's own generation who claim to have had happy and carefree childhoods despite the chronic shortages of consumer goods and the hidden inequalities and general unfairness of the state socialist system that she portrays.[44] Readers of both kinds are likewise critical of the writer's portrayal of present-day Bulgaria, with some commentators in forums going so far as to seek denying her the right to speak about the country of her birth on account of her status as an "emigrant".[45] The third category includes Bulgarian journalists whose comments are mostly positive. However, such commentators do not so much analyze *Street* as focus on Kassabova's career as a writer and her success in the West. They make a point of meticulously listing the literary prizes that she has been awarded,[46] and thus suggest that somehow "we" (all Bulgarians!) collectively take credit for her achievements. The fourth category includes expatriates, who, according to the writer, have found her object and strategies of representation highly congenial.[47]

On the whole, Kassabova distinguishes between the empathetic responses of Bulgarian expatriates and the hostile reactions of some of "those who stayed behind and didn't emigrate".[48] For the latter, in her view, "the sufferings of the past are overridden by the difficulties of the present" and for this reason "[t]here is no space in [their] lives to safely explore the recent past".[49] This statement points to a tendency on the writer's part to privilege Bulgarian expatriates who may be said to constitute her own in-group. In her article she represents them as less prone to nationalist excesses and more resistant to a "collective breakdown" caused by the Bulgarian nation's "painfully insecure self-perception as a European country".[50] Their experience of life elsewhere has evidently helped them to "see the world from perspectives remote from the outlook in which [they were] brought up" and that may be defined as one of the necessary conditions for "cosmopolitan openness".[51]

Kassabova occasionally adopts a more balanced perspective on the differences between expatriates and "natives". For instance, in one of her Bulgarian interviews she speaks of the relative "blindness" that each group suffers from: "those Bulgarians, who have never left their country for longer periods of time", are "blind" to certain things, and those, who left it long ago and return to it only occasionally, are "blind" to others.[53] This reasoning partly echoes the view expressed in the disclaimer with which *Street* opens. In it Kassabova stresses the "highly personal" nature of her portrayal of Bulgaria.[53] She also adds that this makes her observations "highly unreliable" and, presumably, open to debate and contestation.[54] Nevertheless, when she is challenged by "those who stayed behind and didn't emigrate", the writer grows impatient and attributes their reactions to her book to "a two-fold conflict . . . in the national psyche" comprising, on the one hand, "*the broad Balkan inability* to separate the individual from the national tribe" and, on the other, "the tortured relationship all Bulgarians over the age of thirty have with the recent communist past".[55] Kassabova's "diagnosis" of a "broad Balkan inability" is an example of rather crude stereotyping. The writer favors, in principle, greater openness to the outside world and the kind of cultural self-translation that would enable Bulgarians to "live amongst nationalities" in happy acceptance of "cultural mongrel[lism]" rather than be tormented by the "mirroring effect of pride and shame, love and hate, self-denial and self-obsession" (pp. 75, 77). Literal and/or metaphorical translocation could provide a way of achieving those goals. However, the writer appears to deny this to "Bulgarians of certain generations—the generations who spent longer under communism than on top of it" (p. 77). For them "the boundary between national self-perception and individual self-image is blurred like the reflection in a distorted, foggy mirror" (p. 77). The mirror, Kassabova maintains, is "*our* collective unconscious" and in it she glimpses "anxiety, anger and apocalyptic thinking" (p. 77, emphasis added).

In "From Bulgaria with Love and Hate" Kassabova begins her analysis of her book's reception by condemning intolerance as expressed, for instance, in the comments of Bulgarian readers who deny her the right to speak on account of her "emigrant" status, but then goes on to adopt a rather hegemonic view of the difference between her own in-group and readers who contest her representations of Bulgaria's recent history and the country's contemporary life. She seems to view such readers as a hostile out-group. The writer speaks of that out-group's inability to accept "cultural representations [coming from] abroad" (p. 77), and attributes this to historically, nationally, and even *regionally* determined limitations (cf. her reference to "the broad *Balkan* inability", above). Significantly, Kassabova does not take issue with the largely complimentary comments of the *Western* readers considered above.

The author's interaction with her Bulgarian readers may be linked to wider concerns among practitioners and theorists of the travel genre over readerly perceptions of the travel writer (see William Dalrymple's comments, cited in the introduction to this volume, and Alexander Drace-Francis's Chapter 10, this volume). To my mind, travel writers should not so much make pleas for *acceptance* by readers and critics as they should view differences of opinion and readerly resistance to their representations as a means of initiating and conducting productive *dialogues*. The present example shows how difficult it is for a writer and her readers to become engaged in such a dialogue, despite the facility of interpersonal communications in the amazingly "small" world that we all inhabit at present and the writer's avowed cosmopolitanism. An examination of the persona that Kassabova has fashioned for herself in her poetry and *Street* as well as aspects of the self-image she has projected in select interviews may shed more light on the difficulties and contradictions involved in the process of representing others.

BEING A TOURIST WITH A "GLOBAL SOUL"

According to Lisle, the travel writer "must be fashioned over and against a series of others who are denied the power of representing themselves".[56] This implies ethical responsibility on his/her part. The critic further envisions the contemporary travel writer as "a site of struggle between a masculine, imperial subjectivity . . . and a liberal, cosmopolitan subjectivity that actively resists the colonising and patronising aspects of cultural encounter".[57] Predictably, Kassabova is strongly attracted by the liberal, cosmopolitan element in contemporary anglophone travel writing. It remains to be seen, however, whether her cosmopolitan orientation has completely neutralized the imperialist legacy the inertia of her chosen medium has preserved. That orientation manifests itself in, among other things, a skeptical attitude to the traditional conception of *home* as a defining point of origin and as a powerful influence upon the self's subsequent development.

The absence of an identifiable home is part of the psychological makeup of the poetic speaker in Kassabova's collection of poetry *Geography for the Lost* (2007).[58] One of the collection's most memorable poems is significantly titled "I Want to Be a Tourist". The poem may be read as an ironic commentary on Claude Lévi-Strauss's famous lament in *Tristes Tropiques* (1955) over "the end of journeying" in the age of mass tourism.[59] The speaker unashamedly voices the tourist's stereotypical wish of "find[ing] things for the first time" while strolling around in tourist "uniform" ("shorts and baseball hat").[60] She is very much an urban tourist, and "the city of [her] life" is "in the third world, or the second" rather than in the privileged "*First* world".[61] In addition, the speaker is something of a rebel who shies away from "that which has been discovered by entrepreneurship and prepared for [tourists] by the arts of mass publicity".[62] Instead she yearns for "open sewers . . . stunted dreams . . . ruins . . . lepers, [stray] dogs" and "signs in a funny language that I never have to learn".[63] In a non-metaphorical journey, the hunt for such unsavory aspects of reality might blur the distinction between tourism and the "genuine" travel experience, which, in Paul Theroux's words, affirms that "the world is still large and strange".[64] The speaker, however, never adopts the (quasi)heroic stance that one would associate with a valiant traveler and (despite discomforts) appears content with the modest position of a tourist who accepts the "unoriginal" form of her mobility. As has already been noted, the distinction between *home* and *away*, which is among the manifestations of "the logic of identity/difference" theorized by Lisle, is absent from Kassabova's poem: we are never told where the *home* of her tourist persona might be.

The poetic speaker's disavowal of an identifiable home is paralleled by statements that Kassabova has made in interviews. In one of them she describes herself as a "mongrel" and remarks on the difficulty she encounters every time she is asked where she comes from.[65] She regrets the fact that despite the increasing "mongrellism" of the world at large, "people still like to be able to pigeonhole you" and goes on to point out that "we are not necessarily the place we come from",[66] thus rejecting cultural rootedness in any shape or form.

The narrative persona that Kassabova fashions for herself in *Street* decidedly favors continual flux and mobility. As has been mentioned, a considerable part of the book is about the narrator's childhood and adolescence in communist Bulgaria, which is also the country in which some of Kassabova's relatives live. Yet Bulgaria is not a point of origin in any traditional sense. Notably, in her narrative Kassabova also experiences the country as a *visitor* and a *tourist*. In other words, her book is largely shaped by the condition of a particular kind of migrancy. A migrant's narrative, it would seem, *has* to violate what is (arguably) the most enduring convention of traditional representations of travel and tourism: "a narrative progression which includes *departure, transit and return*".[67] The middle stage of *transit* is where the migrant's experience is situated.

Kassabova stresses that aspect of the migrant condition in an account of the beginning of one of her "return" journeys to Bulgaria:

> Where do nations begin? In airport lounges, of course. You see them arriving soul by soul, in pre-activation mode. They step into no man's land, with only their passports to hold onto, and follow the signs of the departure gate. There, among the impersonal plastic chairs and despite themselves, they coalesce into the murky Rorschach stain of nationhood.[68]

The airport lounge is a liminal space ("no man's land"), but it is also a space in which identities are constructed, judged, and even policed. Therefore "holding onto" one's passport as a conventional emblem of national belonging is essential. The airport lounge may foster dreams of transnationalism and a borderless existence, but it also sets limits to such dreams. The narrator appears well aware of this contradiction. In the episodes following the above quotation, Kassabova uses the liminal space of the lounge at Frankfurt Airport as a setting for the performance of different kinds of "Europeanness" and migrancy.

The narrator identifies a number of fellow migrants, mostly Bulgarian-born *Gastarbeiter*, and engages one of them in a brief conversation.[69] Like her, the man left Bulgaria years ago, but whereas Kassabova acquired education and the sophistication of "a global soul" in the meantime,[70] he is said to present a picture of defeat and resignation. The *Gastarbeiter* is one of a group of patiently waiting people identified as Bulgarian (and *Balkan*) through stereotypical physical characteristics such as "wide, lived-in faces and rounded shoulders".[71] They are contrasted with "a small cluster" of Germans, who are similarly portrayed through stereotypical traits ("ruddy faces" and "blondness") but also, through signs of opulence ("gold-plated watches").[72] Unlike the Bulgarian *Gastarbeiter*, the Germans resent being made to wait in the lounge and are eager to continue their journey.

Despite their shared "Europeanness", the two groups differ markedly. One is made up of confident people who appear secure in their identity and social privileges whereas the other group comprises "poor cousins", a description that the narrator applies to herself and her family under communism as she becomes aware of significant differences between the Eastern and Western lifestyles.[73] In the airport lounge the narrator occupies an uneasy position between the two groups. She claims some kinship with the *Gastarbeiter* but also acknowledges the fact that this kinship is engendered by the resentment that the opulent, confident Germans fill her with. When the narrator experiences these conflicting emotions, she realizes that she has become part, yet again, of "the murky Rorschach stain of nationhood",[74] and that her Bulgarianness has not been completely erased by her extensive experience of global mobility and replaced by her acquired cosmopolitanism.

The narrator's position exemplifies some of the contradictions typical of the *postnational* migrant middle-class identity that has been brought into existence by the fall of communism and the subsequent dislocations of members of Eastern Europe's intellectual and technocratic elites. Using an instructive parallel with the postcolonial situation, we can argue that those elites were among "the major beneficiaries" of postcommunist change by virtue of the economic and cultural benefits that they were able to acquire through their education and other convertible skills.[75] I prefer to describe their identity as *postnational* rather than as *transnational* because of the links they retain with the cultures of their birth, despite their claims to "rootlessness" and cosmopolitanism. As we saw earlier, such links could function as cultural capital and be successfully utilized for economic ends.

Reflecting upon the position of postcolonial elites, Simon Gikandi is reminded of Ulf Hannerz's statement that the "willingness to become involved with the Other" is among the conditions of cosmopolitanism.[76] Kassabova's narrator is moved to *pity* the *Gastarbeiter* as she compares them with the representatives of the affluent West in the airport lounge. In combination with her resentment of the latter, pity does not signify adequate involvement with the less privileged migrants whom she observes. It deprives them of their *subjecthood* and turns them into *objects* largely defined by the narrator's superior, cosmopolitan gaze. As has already been indicated, she perceives them as a *group* and fails to register any individualizing differences among them.

Significantly, the narrator imagines herself as part of that group in a fantasy expressing anxiety over Bulgaria's marginal "Europeanness" only to realize that the "we" of identification is, in her case, a "borrowed" one;[77] she is separated from the *Gastarbeiter*—and, presumably, the Bulgarians who "stayed behind and didn't emigrate"—by her experience of displacement, which has turned her into "a cosmopolitan, a connoisseur of modern cultural goods" not easily accessible to them.[78] Her admission that she differs from those two groups suggests that she cannot speak for them. This distinguishes her *ethical* stance from the stances of certain members of the postcolonial elites, studied by Gikandi, who claim to speak for others and thus erase significant differences between their own group and less privileged migrants.[79]

However, such respect for difference does not always characterize the narrator's position in the text. She adopts a patronizing stance further on as she is confronted with the experience of people whom she knows personally. In a chapter of her book titled "Balkan Blues", the narrator recounts a visit to some elderly members of her family and tells the story of Vera, a young Bulgarian woman, who briefly emigrated to Germany in the hope of changing her life for the better but instead came very close to becoming a victim of sex trafficking.[80] She was saved from forced prostitution by her own quick wits and resourcefulness, and especially by her knowledge of Turkish, which she had acquired from living in an ethnically mixed community all her life. Vera was also helped by an anonymous Turk in Frankfurt who chose not to ignore her desperate plight and called the police. As a result her would-be pimps were arrested, taken to court, and sentenced to imprisonment.

The narrator is unimpressed by this happy ending, though, despite the fact that it reflects an aspect of Bulgarian life and culture for which she professes great admiration elsewhere in her text: Bulgaria's legacy of ethnic hybridity and relatively high level of cultural and religious tolerance (p. 160–61). This legacy is part of the cultural conditioning that made it possible for Vera to mix with Turks and become bilingual. In addition, the narrator does not recognize any part of the young woman's story as being similar to her own family's quest for a better life outside Bulgaria. For her, Vera is doomed: with 'no father, no education, no prospects' (p. 209), she is only too likely to become, yet again, a victim of her "provincial innocence" (p. 211). The narrator hints, rather broadly, that the young woman might next be sold into prostitution by her own Turkish boyfriend (p. 211). She therefore tells Vera's mother, "in a pitiful last attempt at being helpful", to send her to the neighboring town of Veliko Turnovo, "not [to] Germany again" (p. 212).

It is possible to read the narrator's rendition of Vera's story in terms of concern over the young woman's vulnerability. Indeed, earlier in the book, she presents another story of sex trafficking that does not end happily:

> We hear about a Bulgarian girl who was sex-trafficked in provincial Greece. When she managed to escape and drag herself to the police, the five policemen on duty gang-raped her. They will be sacked but not prosecuted. The Bulgarian ambassador in Greece makes a po-faced statement about trafficking being under control and working closely with the Greek police. After all, she was only a whore, runs the text between the lines (p. 188).

This could also be Vera's story, but that is only one of a number of possibilities. One could imagine a different scenario in which she would achieve moderate material prosperity in Germany, her Turkish boyfriend would not become her pimp, and the two of them would be helped by first- and/or second-generation migrants from the Balkan region. The mass migration of the needy in today's world has resulted in ethnic "localities [being] produced and reproduced in . . . metropolitan centres".[81] Relations within such localities need not be seen only in terms of the resurgence of religious fundamentalisms and the import of "primitive" customs from the migrants' "old" countries. The production and reproduction of localities may also result in the forging of various forms of solidarity and mutual help between their members.

The fact that the narrator does not envision a positive scenario for Vera reveals the limits (and the limitations) of her cosmopolitan outlook. In the context of *Street*, successful displacement to the West appears to be only possible for those who are already in the possession of certain privileges, such as education and proficiency in languages in international circulation like English, French, or German rather than regional ones like Bulgarian and Turkish. Vera and her kind are assigned the status of passive victims doomed to failure, not the role of active agents whose life choices have to be treated with respect. This may likewise be read as a sign of the ethical limitations of the new migrant middle-class elite, whose attitude to members of their out-group is likely to be patronizing.

LIFTING BULGARIA OUT OF ITS OBSCURITY

In her article Kassabova speaks of the Western tendency to approach Bulgaria through an "imaginative compendium of clichés" that would also fit a number of other postcommunist countries.[82] By way of an example she cites a tongue-in-cheek Australian-published travel guide focusing on the imaginary Eastern European republic of Molvania, humorously identified as *A Land Untouched by Modern Dentistry*.[83] Apart from being portrayed as a postcommunist *Anonymiana*, Bulgaria is increasingly seen, especially in Britain, as "a cheap and nasty place, mostly associated with cheap beer, cheap skiing, cheap sea-side resorts, cheap property and cheap sex".[84] The new set of clichés may be less humorous that the ones that make up Molvania but they are equally denigrating.

Kassabova remarks that cultural clichés are not conducive to "emotions or experiences that the reader can identify with".[85] Her own strategies of representation therefore invite readerly identification. Most of her narrative persona's journeys through Bulgaria and neighboring Macedonia, where one of her grandmothers was born, follow what may be described as a *familial* route as she visits relatives and close friends of her family. *Street* also presents a number of conventional tourist sites but they are either linked to childhood memories (the town of Balchik) or to personal encounters with local people.[86] Through such encounters the narrator manages to deconstruct privileged sites of officially sanctioned collective memory, such as the Monument to the Creators of the Bulgarian State, "built to commemorate 1,300 years of Bulgarian statehood".[87]

Throughout her account of the country of her birth, Kassabova stresses its multilayered history and the legacy of ethnic and religious hybridity and relative tolerance of others that it left in its wake. The positive valorization of that legacy was touched upon earlier in this chapter. The narrator contrasts the country's heritage of interethnic conviviality (Bulgarians, Turks, Jews, and other groups living side by side) with politically engineered eruptions of ethnocentricity and nationalism in the nineteenth century as well as in the more recent past. She specifically dwells on the forced renaming of ethnic Turks under communism, which was tacitly accepted by the overwhelming majority of Bulgarians at the time,[88] and on its traumatic consequences for the victimized minority.[89] The narrator provides glimpses of her own progress away from the state-sponsored nationalist myths of her childhood, which stressed medieval clashes between Islam and Christianity, to a liberal cosmopolitan vision of Bulgarian and Balkan history as marked by "marriage[s] of civilizations" no less than by violent conflicts.[90] Her encounters and conversations with ethnic Turks in the course of her journeys may also be approached in the light of atonement for the silence of her fellow Bulgarians and their unwillingness to recognize, in the forced renaming of the country's largest ethno-religious minority, an element of the political repression that they themselves had to endure under communism.

The narrator likewise remarks on the resettlement to Bulgaria of migrants and property owners out of Britain as well as on the arrival of Western, Russian, and other entrepreneurs bent upon securing substantial profits out of their investments in local industries and tourist ventures. On the whole, Bulgaria's opening up to the world is represented as a controversial process reflecting the contradictory character of global mobilities and economic changes.

CONCLUSION

Written in today's global language, Kassabova's autobiographical travelogue aims at filling a gap in Europe's compendium of images of ethnocultural terrains by representing Bulgaria's changing face. Her book embodies some of the ethico-political ambiguities of a genre that is moving away from its imperialist legacy towards rearticulations of cosmopolitanism and wider recognition of the claims of the other. The narrative persona that Kassabova fashions in her text exemplifies some of the dilemmas that a new generation of Bulgarian expatriates faces as it struggles to find its bearings across political, cultural, and psychological boundaries and to come to terms with different kinds of global politics. Such expatriates are among the new voices in contemporary writing in English.[91] While we should not celebrate the visions of Kassabova and other Bulgarian expatriate writers uncritically or turn a blind eye to the contradictions in their work, we should certainly acknowledge the seriousness of their engagement with the interpretation of cultural difference, undertaken as it is from a position that cuts across the native/foreign divide.

NOTES

1. John Law and Annemarie Mol, "Situating Technoscience: An Inquiry into Spatialities", quoted in Michael Cronin, *Translation and Identity* (London: Routledge, 2006), p. 28.
2. Mads Rosendahl Thomsen, *Mapping World Literature: International Canonization and Transnational Literature* (London: Continuum, 2008), p. 62.

3. Political terms such as *communist*, *state-socialist*, *postcommunist*, *postsocialist*, *totalitarian*, and their cognate nouns are often used in ambiguous and/or partisan ways. Throughout this chapter, *communism* and *communist* will be used interchangeably with *state socialism* and *state socialist* to refer to the repressive political and economically dysfunctional regimes of the former Eastern Bloc. *Postcommunist* and *postcommunism* will refer to developments in Eastern and Central Europe following the 1989 collapse of such regimes. The terms *totalitarian* and *totalitarianism* have come in for a lot of criticism over the last ten or fifteen years. For an informed commentary on the emergence and subsequent history of the concepts designated by them, see Alex Delfini and Paul Piccone, "Modernity, Libertarianism and Critical Theory: Reply to Pellicani", *Telos* 112 (1998): 23–47. Despite skepticism among Western scholars and social scientists, I will retain the use of *totalitarianism* and *totalitarian*, and will follow a well-established precedent in applying them to the pre-1989 political regimes of Eastern and Central Europe.
4. See, for instance, Barbara Korte, Eva Ulrike Pirker, and Sissy Helff, eds., *Facing the East in the West: Images of Eastern Europe in British Literature, Film and Culture* (Amsterdam: Rodopi, 2010). The volume is the outcome of an earlier academic conference.
5. Kapka Kassabova, *Street Without a Name: Childhood and Other Misadventures in Bulgaria* (London: Portobello, 2008).
6. See Kapka Kassabova, "Interview and Poems: 'Refugees', 'Coming to Paradise', 'Immigrant Architectures', 'My Life in Two Parts', 'In the Shadow of the Bridge'", in Michael Hanne, ed., *Creativity in Exile* (Amsterdam: Rodopi Publishers, 2004), pp. 135–41; and Claudia Duppé, "Tourist in Her Native Country: Kapka Kassabova's *Street without a Name*", in Korte, Pirker, and Helff, eds., *Facing the East in the West*, pp. 423–36.
7. I discuss some of the reviews of *Street without a Name* later in this chapter.
8. See Kassabova, "From Bulgaria with Love and Hate: The Anxiety of the Distorting Mirror, A Writer's Perspective", in Korte, Pirker, and Helff, eds., *Facing the East in the West*, pp. 67–78; which was originally presented as a conference paper; and Kassabova, "Interview and Poems".
9. Kapka Kassabova, "Bloodaxe Books, author webpage", <http://www.bloodaxebooks.com/personpage.asp?author=Kapka+Kassabova> (12 December 2009).
10. Kassabova, "Interview and Poems", p. 135, emphasis in the original.
11. On the distinction between "coerced migrants" and "free-willing . . . subjects", see Simon Gikandi, "Between Roots and Routes: Cosmopolitanism and the Claims of Locality", in Janet Wilson, Cristina Sandru, and Sarah Lawson Welsh, eds., *Rerouting the Postcolonial: New Directions for the New Millennium* (London: Routledge, 2010), p. 28.
12. Misha Glenny, "'Mum, Why Is Everything So Ugly?'", *Guardian* 5 July 2008, p. 6.
13. Pico Iyer, quoted at "Kapka Kassabova author webpage", <http://www.kapka-kassabova.com/street.html> (20 February 2013).
14. Debbie Lisle, *The Global Politics of Contemporary Travel Writing* (Cambridge: Cambridge University Press, 2006), p. 269.
15. For a critical commentary on the imperialist legacy of the travel genre, see Carl Thompson, *Travel Writing* (London: Routledge, 2011), pp. 153–55.
16. On the significance of political reflexivity and critical thought in travel writing, see Lisle, *Global Politics of Contemporary Travel Writing*, pp. 265–66.
17. Kapka Kassabova, "Poet Kapka Kassabova on *Talk Talk*", <http://www.youtube.com/watch?v=ZDQ95KHN4a4> (12 December 2009).

18. Doris Lechner, "Eastern European Memories? The Novels of Marina Lewycka", in Korte, Pirker, and Helff, eds., *Facing the East in the West*, pp. 437–50, discusses the significance of "distinctiveness" for the book market.

19. Kasabova, "Poet Kapka Kassabova on *Talk Talk*".

20. Kasabova, "Poet Kapka Kassabova on *Talk Talk*".

21. Kasabova, "Poet Kapka Kassabova on *Talk Talk*", emphasis added.

22. On the formula's relevance to marketability and on its employment by Lewycka, see Lechner, "Eastern European Memories?" p. 438.

23. Nicholas Lezard, "Danube Blues", (13 February 2009) <http://www.guardian. co.uk/books/2009/feb/14/street-without-name-kapka-kassabova> (15 December 2009).

24. Kapka Kassabova, "Author webpage, books", <http://www.kapka-kassabova.com/books.shtml> (12 December 2009), emphasis added.

25. Glenny, "'Mum, Why Is Everything So Ugly?'", p. 6.

26. Duppé, "Tourist in Her Native Country", p. 433.

27. Lezard, "Danube Blues".

28. Kassabova, "From Bulgaria with Love and Hate", p. 78.

29. See, among others, Svetlana Boym, *Common Places: Mythologies of Everyday Life in Russia* (Cambridge, MA: Harvard University Press, 1994).

30. Svetlana Boym, *Common Places: Mythologies of Everyday Life in Russia* (Cambridge, MA: Harvard University Press, 1995); Kindle edition, p. 321.

31. Michael Billig, *Laughter and Ridicule: Towards a Social Critique of Humour* (London: Sage, 2010), pp. 207–17.

32. See Kassabova, "From Bulgaria with Love and Hate"; and Kassabova, "Poet Kapka Kassabova on *Talk Talk*".

33. Kassabova, *Street Without a Name*, p. 113.

34. Kassabova, *Street Without a Name*, p. 66.

35. Kassabova, *Street Without a Name*, p. 64.

36. Duppé, "Tourist in Her Native Country", p. 429, emphasis added.

37. Duppé, "Tourist in Her Native Country".

38. Glenny, "'Mum, Why Is Everything So Ugly?'", p. 6.

39. Glenny, "'Mum, Why Is Everything So Ugly?'", p. 6.

40. Glenny, "'Mum, Why Is Everything So Ugly?'", p. 6.

41. Kassabova, "From Bulgaria with Love and Hate", p. 67.

42. Kassabova, *Street Without a Name*, p. 125; Glenny, "'Mum, Why Is Everything So Ugly?'", p. 6.

43. See, for instance, *Pisatelkata emigrantka Kapka Kassabova: Balgariya ne e geografskomyastosprznikashtizaanglichanite* [Emigrant Writer Kapka Kassabova: Bulgaria is not merely a geographical space with empty houses for English buyers] <http://novinar.bg/news/pisatelkata-emigrantka-kapka-kasabova-balgariia-ne-e-geografsko-miasto-s-prazni-kashti-za-anglichanite_MjczMjs3OQ==.html> (12 December 2009).

44. See "*'Ulitsa bez ime' ot Kapka Kassabova*" [*Street without a Name* by Kapka Kassabova] <http://kambanka.wordpress.com> (2 March 2012).

45. See *Pisatelkata emigrantka Kapka* Kassabova <http://novinar.bg/news/pisatelkata-emigrantka-kapka-kasabova-balgariia-ne-e-ge> (12 December 2009).

46. See, among others, "Pisatelkata emigrantka Kapka Kassabova," accessed 12 December 2009 at http://tinyurl.com/pge2rjp; and Olya Stoyanova, "Kapka Kassabova i vyatarat na promenite" [Kapka Kassabova and the Wind of Change], Dnevnik, 11 September 2008; accessed 12 December 2009 at www.dnevnik.bg/razvlechenie/2008/09/11/548878_kapka_kasabova_i_viaturut_na_promenite/

47. See Kassabova, "From Bulgaria with Love and Hate", p. 73.
48. Kassabova, "From Bulgaria with Love and Hate", p. 75.
49. Kassabova, "From Bulgaria with Love and Hate", p. 75.
50. Kassabova, "From Bulgaria with Love and Hate", p. 69.
51. Kwame Anthony Appiah, *Cosmopolitanism: Ethics in a World of Strangers* (London: Allen Lane, 2006), p. 5.
52. Kapka Kassabova, *Knigi adres: 'Ulica bez ime'* [Books that address you: Street without a Name], *Kapital* (28 August 2008) <http://www.capital.bg/light/revju/knigi/2008/08/28/543314_adres_ulica_bez_ime/> (12 December 2009).
53. Kassabova, *Street Without a Name*, p. i.
54. Kassabova, *Street Without a Name*, p. i.
55. Kassabova, "From Bulgaria with Love and Hate", p. 77, emphasis added; hereafter page numbers will be cited parenthetically in the text.
56. Lisle, *Global Politics of Contemporary Travel Writing*, p. 69.
57. Lisle, *Global Politics of Contemporary Travel Writing*, p. 69.
58. Kapka Kassabova, *Geography for the Lost* (Highgreen: Bloodaxe, 2007), p. 11.
59. The distinctions between travel/journeying and tourism have received a lot of critical attention. For a lucid commentary on some of the contradictions implicit in the stereotyping of the two activities and on Lévi-Strauss's lament, see James Buzard, *The Beaten Track: European Tourism, Literature, and the Ways to "Culture": 1800–1918* (Oxford: Clarendon, 1993), pp. 1–17.
60. Kassabova, *Geography*, p. 11.
61. Kassabova, *Geography*, p. 11.
62. Kassia Boddy, "The European Journey in Postwar American Fiction and Film", in Jas Elsner and Joan-Pau Rubies, eds., *Voyages and Visions: Toward a Cultural History of Travel* (London: Reaktion, 1999), p. 237.
63. Kassabova, *Geography*, p. 11.
64. Paul Theroux, *The Great Railway Bazaar* (London: Penguin, 1975), p. 135.
65. See, for instance, Kassabova, "Poet Kapka Kassabova on *Talk Talk*".
66. Kassabova, "Poet Kapka Kassabova on *Talk Talk*".
67. Vita Fortunati, Rita Monticelli, and Maurizio Ascari, "Foreword", in *Travel Writing and the Female Imaginary* (Bologna: Patron Editore, 2001), p. 5, emphasis added.
68. Kassabove, *Street Without a Name*, p. 5.
69. Kassabove, *Street Without a Name*, p. 6.
70. Kassabove, *Street Without a Name*, p. 7.
71. Kassabove, *Street Without a Name*, p. 6. For a commentary on stereotypical physical signs of "Balkanness", see Alexander Kiossev, "The Dark Intimacy: Maps, Identities, Acts of Identification", in Dusan Bjelić and Obrad Savić, eds., *Balkan as Metaphor: Between Globalization and Fragmentation* (Cambridge, MA: MIT Press, 2002), pp. 165–90.
72. Kassabova, *Street Without a Name*, p. 6.
73. Kassabova, *Street Without a Name*, p. 60.
74. Kassabova, *Street Without a Name*, p. 5.
75. On postcolonial elites as "beneficiaries", see Gikandi, "Between Roots and Routes", p. 29.
76. Gikandi, "Between Roots and Routes", p. 24.
77. Kassabova, *Street Without a Name*, p. 7.
78. Gikandi, "Between Roots and Routes", p. 23.
79. Gikandi, "Between Roots and Routes", p. 34.

80. Kassabova, *Street Without a Name*, pp. 209–11; hereafter page numbers will be cited parenthetically in the text.
81. Gikandi, "Between Roots and Routes", p. 33.
82. Kassabova, "From Bulgaria with Love and Hate", p. 68.
83. Kassabova, "From Bulgaria with Love and Hate", p. 67.
84. Kassabova, "From Bulgaria with Love and Hate", p. 68.
85. Kassabova, "From Bulgaria with Love and Hate", p. 68.
86. Kassabova, *Street Without a Name*, pp. 291–92.
87. Kassabova, *Street Without a Name*, pp. 275, 276. See also Duppé's reading of this part of *Street* in "Tourist in Her Native Country", pp. 433–34.
88. Kassabova, *Street Without a Name*, p. 113.
89. Kassabova, *Street Without a Name*, pp. 226, 227, 231.
90. Kassabova, *Street Without a Name*, p. 231.
91. For an overview of contemporary anglophone texts about Bulgaria by expatriates and other writers, see the program of the recent international conference "Re-inventing Eastern Europe", Vienna, 17–19 May 2012, esp. panel 7, "Representations of Eastern Europe in Anglophone Literatures"; accessed 20 May 2012 at http://euroacademia.eu/conference/international-conference-re-inventing-eastern-europe/.

10 "Like a Member of a Free Nation, He Wrote Without Shame"

Foreign Travelers as a Trope in Romanian Cultural Tradition[1]

Alexander Drace-Francis

In October 2004 the prominent Romanian writer Horia-Roman Patapievici—perhaps the archetypal representative of Bucharest's current metropolitan intelligentsia—launched a literary-intellectual review titled *Ideas in Dialogue*. The title of the review indicated a programmatic intention to supply a forum for a type of cultural discussion perceived to be lacking in Romania. Patapievici took up this theme in an essay introducing the first issue, which begins:

> If a foreign traveler were to undertake a sojourn in Romanian cultural life of recent decades, he would be struck by the fact that there is no intellectual debate here, original books fail to provoke discussion, while schools of thought are, in reality, borrowed trends or interest groups whose coherence is maintained by force of profitable convictions. Although not exactly a cultural desert, Romania is a field where people shout, prattle or titter, but where there is little listening, still less understanding, and the calm sound of discussion is rarely heard.
>
> Modern Romanian culture was created in the nineteenth century, growing around the nucleus of the model of general education. And general education, in its turn, was built around *belles-lettres*. You could be considered cultured, if you knew the names of a few canonical authors, if you were up on the literature which circulated, if you listened to a certain music and you proved yourself capable, either orally or in writing, of handling in an assured fashion the classic locutions of the pink pages of Larousse. In short, to be cultured meant to have read high literature.[2]

How should we interpret this opening gambit? A "domestic" writer, attacking the sterility and superficiality of contemporary Romanian intellectual life, calls upon the testimony of "a foreign traveler". No explanation is required: his readers are assumed to be aware of the importance—and, it is implied, accuracy—of the putative foreigner's putative verdict. The trope of the foreign traveler is therefore, it seems, a "classic locution", to cite the phrase Patapievici uses to denote widely detained cultural knowledge. But what, precisely is the nature and role of this "foreign traveler"? How did he acquire such symbolic authority?

Scholars—mainly in Romania—have enumerated, translated, and ana-lyzed the relatively large number of foreign accounts of Romanian life and culture that were produced from the sixteenth to the twentieth centu-ries.[3] Critiques have appeared in English, largely pursuing a neo-Saidian approach, showing how "Westerners" elaborated a superficial and deroga-tory discourse about small, "Balkan" or "Ruritanian" cultures.[4] At more or less the same time, scholars in Romania and elsewhere in Eastern Europe were starting to take a more scholarly and critical look at the evolution of discourses of national identity, and precisely identifying a reaction to foreign writings about them as being a central trope in this ideology.[5] For instance, it was posited that the paradigm of East European alterity imposed itself "not only as an ambivalent and necessary ingredient of west European identity, but also as an essential element of the self-identification processes of local elites".[6]

A further notable assumption often made by analysts of Romanian iden-tity issues is that the description of Romanian lands by foreign travelers, as an act of cultural hegemonization, will tend to produce as a symptom a split, stigmatized identity or "inauthenticity complex" among the people constituted as objects of travel description.[7] This has sometimes involved the transposition of the thesis of "incompleteness" or ambivalence that was elaborated by Homi Bhabha to denote a state engendered in colonial sub-jects as a result of mimicry or fixation on the colonizer's discourse.[8] I have already attempted to question this diagnosis in an earlier article dedicated to Dinicu Golescu, the author of the first Romanian travel book and a figure considered paradigmatic for the national tradition of "occidentalism".[9]

In this chapter, I propose to continue this debate with reference to some sources that enable a more precise focus, not just in relation to generalized Romanian discourses about foreigners at the beginning of the modern age, but specifically with reference to Romanian discourses about foreign travel-ers. In doing so, I seek to raise questions concerning not just the status of Western travelers as imputed ethical arbiters but also some of the problems and dilemmas raised by the presence and function of this trope in a variety of forms within an allegedly "minor" culture.

More specifically, I will analyze a series of texts, composed between 1702 and 1858, in which Romanian authors either describe British and French travelers, or respond to their writings about their country or people. I identify various modes of treating the theme, which range from relative indifference at an early stage, to high indignation, through to a later phase in which anger is displaced by the use of irony and literary distancing to perhaps indicate that the theme has crystallized and can become the object of humor. Without wishing to make these examples bear too much inter-pretive weight, I propose that this roughly corresponds to the establishment of the "foreign traveler" as not merely an occasional object of remark but as a motif of cultural significance as used by Patapievici in the early years of the twenty-first century. It bears some relation to tropes of "writing back" against occidental misrepresentations—but the attitudes evinced are in themselves complex and contrasting, for some identify with the traveler as a source of authority while others explicitly polemicize against him, questioning his legitimacy.

In the wider scholarly discussion, some attention has been paid to the role and influences of Western practices of topographical representations on "peripheral" self-identities. Mary Louise Pratt has coined the term "travelees" to denote the inhabitants of the described lands. She did so by making an analogy with "addressee", meaning "persons traveled to (or on) by a traveler, receptors of travel".[10] The term is, I argue, a useful way of drawing attention to the function of travel descriptions in casting certain actors in positions of passivity or objectivization. However, the category encompasses quite diverse potential roles, involving greater or lesser degrees of contact and more or less active or passive relationships with travelers. Furthermore, despite the morphological homology, there is also a semantic opposition between travelee and addressee, in that travelees are often specifically excluded from the group of recipients of the message. Whether they are excluded from speaking, Pratt doesn't say. The Romanian travelees I am referring to here are relatively independent commentators on travelers, who neither appear to be taken into account by the authors of travel accounts, nor necessarily address their commentary to the traveler's cultural milieu, although they use both vernacular and metropolitan languages. In conclusion, I argue that part of the importance of these Romanian texts lies in the way in which, through responding to foreign (not necessarily Western) discourses, they reorganize the relationship between traveler/travelee and addresser/addressee. Sometimes this involves not just writing back *at* foreign travelers but finding ways of re-presenting them, either by ironizing their persona or simply using it as a mask to speak to domestic agendas.

GRECEANU ON PAGET

In a number of standard accounts of Romanian (or, more broadly, "Balkan") occidentalism, a fascination with Western culture and society, often mediated through travelers, is seen as a new development appearing at the end of the eighteenth century or during the course of the early nineteenth.[11] But Romanian observations on foreign travelers can be found as early as the late seventeenth century, when quite extensive historiographical chronicles began to be composed and disseminated both in Moldavia and in Wallachia. While these sources may not be classic instances of "reverse gaze" literature such as is furnished by say, Arab views of the Crusaders, or Native American responses to European *conquistadores*, they merit more attention than they have received, particularly in terms of what they tell us about cultural attitudes to outsiders. Most of these early texts of encounter involve descriptions not of "Westerners" but of neighboring peoples, Poles, Swedes, Russians, Tartars, Germans, Magyars, Serbs, Bulgarians, Albanians, Greeks, or Turks, brought into view by the accidents of war and politics.[12] A rare, but detailed and significant, example of a description of an English traveler through the Romanian lands can be found in Wallachian chronicler Radu Greceanu's *History of the Reign of Prince Constantin Brancoveanu*.[13] Like many early Romanian chronicles, Greceanu's work is centered on the deeds of the prince, on the principle that "truly the virtues and deeds of man are to be praised, and held in greater honour than his wealth or possessions".[14] These "deeds" frequently involve reaction to external events, as at the turn of the eighteenth century Wallachia found itself caught between the rival designs of Habsburg, Ottoman, and Russian strategy. Representatives of all three of these powers, or intermediary forces like the ones mentioned above, are frequently sent into Wallachia, or, conversely, summon the prince to send envoys to resolve issues of military requisitioning, territorial delimitation, or appointment of officials. About halfway through this episodic "history", Chapter 55 offers an elaborate description of the visit to Bucharest in 1702 of Lord Paget, the British ambassador to the Ottoman Empire, and his entourage.[15] Paget, "a great, honourable and wise man" according to the chronicler, had acted "entirely in the Porte's favour" in the recent negotiations at the Treaty of Karlowitz, and therefore merited special hospitality in his route through Wallachia toward England.[16] On his arrival at Tutrakan on the south bank of the Danube, "two great boyars with princely carriages, marquees and all equipage, with a few equerries such as were worthy of performing office" received Paget "with all possible honours, and with great pomp brought him to the princely seat at Bucharest". The next day, Brâncoveanu sent two of his sons and three great boyars to greet Paget at Văcăreşti, to the south of Bucharest, whence he was brought with great ceremony to the Prince's lodgings. Official dinners were accompanied by the firing of cannon and other guns, and toasts were offered:

> with great merriment, so that not only he [Paget] but also his entourage, became drunk (although they hadn't been forced to by anyone). And when they got up from table, His Majesty the prince dressed him in a robe with sable lining, and sent him to his lodgings to rest.[17]

Aside from this early signaling of a British propensity to inebriation when on continental travels, Greceanu's account is on the whole more concerned with detailing the ceremonies of the Wallachian court than with developing a symbolic discourse around this Western traveler, who features here as just one aspect of the political calendar requiring the attention of a chronicler.

Some useful comparative light on Paget's visit to Bucharest, and on its perception, can be obtained by considering the account composed by a member of Paget's entourage, Edmund Chishull, chaplain of the English factory at Smyrna.[18] In his posthumously published *Travels in Turkey and Back to England*, Chishull makes some incidental observations on his way through Wallachia, which he describes as "luxuriantly rich, but desolate for want of culture and inhabitants". By way of example, "a miserable collection of cottages, scarcely deserving the name of a village" is juxtaposed to "a pleasant wood, enriched with lily of the valley, and other flowers".[19] On the whole, however, he gives a comparatively favorable account of the local culture and conditions: his lodgings, for example, are reckoned:

> fair and gentile, built of stone and covered agreeably to the custom of this place with wooden tiles; and being furnished with apartments after the Christian fashion, may be esteemed magnificent when compared with the barbarous edifices of the neighbouring Turks.[20]

After a similar description of courtly ceremonies, and visits to the printing presses of Bucharest—where he was able to witness the production of some of the earliest printed Arabic books, being prepared by the Patriarch of Jerusalem for the Orthodox Christians of the Middle East—Chishull described Ambassador Paget as taking leave of Bucharest "with a deep sense of the generous, honourable and affectionate treatment he had received in this court".[21]

In conclusion, the reciprocal images produced by early English and Romanian chroniclers were relatively even-handed; colorful and critical notes are included, but there is no sign of them metastasizing into grosser stereotypes. Scholars have used this and other material to posit—rightly or wrongly—that in the premodern period, Romanians stood in a complex-free relationship with Europe, which they referred to as "our Europe".[22]

CARRA AND HIS CRITICS

Before the second half of the eighteenth century, information in Western languages on the Romanian lands tended to be confined to these kinds of incidental observations by scholars, traders, or diplomats usually on their way between larger centers such as Vienna, Istanbul, Warsaw, or St. Petersburg. And in the context of a relatively reduced reading public, and limited commercial or communicational networks between the Romanian lands and the West, it is unlikely either that Chishull's book was read in Bucharest, or that Greceanu's chronicle was taken note of in London.[23] The possibility of comparing notes, or even of offering conflicting reactions to reciprocal encounters, increased during the course of the eighteenth century as the circulation of both people and books grew more rapid and frequent.

A particular stimulus for interest in the area was the renewed conflict between Russia and the Ottomans which broke out in 1768 and was often cast as part of the broader question of the revival of Greece.[24] In the absence of any designated territory of Greece during this period, the status of Moldavia and Wallachia as lands governed semiautonomously by "Phanariot" princes appointed from Istanbul, as well as their location in the path of the Russian armies on their way south, rendered them the focus of "European" attention.[25] In this context, it is understandable that foreign debates over the status and quality of the region have been labeled by modern literary historians as "the polemic of Ottoman Greece".[26] However, the label "Greece" hides not only the localized nature of a number of these polemics but also the fact that local actors engaged in them from a relatively early stage. In the following section I will examine some polemics of Ottoman Moldavia and Wallachia, which clearly show the impassioned responses of travelees to travel writing concerning their countries.

The first monographic work on these lands appeared in French in 1777 under the title *Histoire de la Moldavie et de la Valachie: avec une dissertation sur l'état actuel de ces deux provinces*, with the author's name only hinted at by the designation "M[onsieur] C". Scholars have long since identified "C" as Jean-Louis Carra (1742–93), an erratic and somewhat tempestuous citizen of the Republic of Letters, who spent the early part of his career writing political and diplomatic memoranda and attempting to find patronage; the middle part espousing the fashionable subjects of electricity and mesmerism;[27] and the final part as a Jacobin instigator, which activities led to his death on the Parisian scaffold in 1793.

Carra's *Histoire*, a pretentious compilation of geography, history, travel, and cultural analysis, takes a bold stance on questions of the political economy of knowledge:

> It is not at all the business of these barbarian, ignorant peoples to get to know us first; on the contrary, it is for us, whom the favorable influence of a temperate climate and the fortunate advantage of the exact sciences have raised so far above the other peoples of the globe, in courage, in industry and in enlightenment, to discern the character, the genius, and even the physiognomy of the modern peoples, placed on this earth as if subject to our observations and criticisms. It is, in the end, for us to know these very peoples, before these peoples may know themselves and, in their turn, seek to know us.[28]

And at the end of his book, he sees fit to draw some "philosophical" conclusions, using his findings to question Jean-Jacques Rousseau's praise for the simple life: "After all this, if M. Rousseau would fain tell us once more that the barbarous and lawless peoples are worth more than the civilized ones, I would entreat him to go and live for a year in the forests of Moldavia."[29] While Carra's book was favorably received in some quarters—the *Journal Encyclopédique* described it as containing "precise and judicious observations"—it was also reckoned to include "certain rather frivolous remarks [*plaisanteries*] that the Moldavian nation may well deserve, but constitute something of a digression from history".[30] In other circles, it attracted criticism, being adjudged "so confused and poorly digested that it would be hard to extract any element capable or arousing the curiosity of our readers".[31] Furthermore, later scholarship has shown that Carra recycled a fair amount of the historical information that he used from the previously published accounts of the indigenous historian Prince Demetrius Cantemir.[32]

Despite these scholarly exposures of Carra's work as a superciliously negligent compilation, and some attention from the newer Orientalism-derived critiques,[33] what is less well known outside a small group of specialists is that it was the object of a counterblast that was published as early as 1779, and to which Carra responded.

The piece in question, entitled *Letter to the Authors of the Bouillon Journal* [i.e. the *Journal encyclopédique*] *on their Review of a Book Entitled 'Histoire de la Moldavie, et de la Valachie'* appeared as a pamphlet in Vienna in 1779, and offered a searing critique of Carra's text.[34] The author—whose identity I will discuss shortly—describes himself as having "hastened to acquire this history" being persuaded that "as regards knowledge of those countries that we Europeans visit least, and of their inhabitants, as well as of their customs, practices, laws and politics, we are ordinarily much deceived by travelers' reports, be they ignorant, credulous or composed in bad faith". However, perusal soon led him to "surprise" and "deflated expectations" when, on closer examination, he found the work to be "nothing but an assemblage of gross errors for which one would not even excuse a schoolboy".[35] The critique focuses initially on matters of classical history and historical geography, particularly the false localization of certain places or their inaccurate correlation to classical ones; then goes on to mock Carra's treatment of more recent political history, apparently "nothing but a series of anachronisms, absurdities and puerilities".[36] His allegation that the Princess of Moldavia was unable to read or write was labeled "most impolite and coarse"; his speculations on the Balkan policy of the courts of Vienna and Berlin showed him to be a "charlatan"; while his critique of the Austrian administration of the Banat of Temesvar apparently proved that "Mr. Carra has never seen the Banat".[37] His observations on the princely court were "calumnious and misplaced platitudes".[38]

The following month, the editors of the *Journal* wrote that

> we were going to review this brochure, when we received the reply which M. Carra saw fit to give, of which we publish an extract. It seems to us excessively crude in many respects, even if he had been attacked in too harsh a fashion.[39]

Carra's response is addressed largely in the second person to a "seigneur Saul", who has been identified as Gheorghe Saul, a Moldavian courtier whose erudition Carra had himself praised in his *Histoire*.[40] However, another contemporary author, the Swiss German Franz Josef Sulzer, indicated a different source, attributing the pamphlet to a certain "Bosniak" designated by the initial *R.*, who in turn has been identified as Ignaz Stefan Raicevich, a Dalmatian who acted first as secretary to the Prince of Wallachia, Alexandru Ipsilanti, then as Austrian agent in Wallachia, and himself was to publish an important book on the principalities in 1788.[41] The author of the pamphlet defines himself as being one of "us Europeans" for whom "these countries" are "among those we frequent the least",[42] and as being of Western dress: "they have as much right to mock our curled wigs, our small hats, our justaucorps, as we do to laugh at them, e.g. at their beards, turban and their long shorts".[43] However, he also seeks to defend the prince and indeed the Sublime Porte's policy as a whole, which makes it likely that he had some links with the local courts, and possible that his work was commissioned therefrom.[44] We have evidence that the Bishop of Râmnic in Wallachia read Carra's book, finding that "it contains many errors" and suggested to the person who sent it to him "that it would be good to print another book to correct those errors".[45] There was also, apparently, a second reply, a *Réponse au libelle diffamatoire*, which Sulzer attributed to "a friend of his" but may well have been his own.[46]

None of this information enables us to solve definitively the mystery of this pamphlet's authorship. What is perhaps interesting from our point of view is that, irrespective of the true identity of the participants in this polemic, it presents itself not as a case of powerful Western authors lambasting wretched and mute Romanians, but as a many-sided skirmish in which provincial French, Swiss German, Dalmatian, and possibly Greco-Albanian authors all jostle and position themselves as the detainers of truer information concerning the state of the principalities. The modern Western-language historiography of Moldavia and Wallachia is thus imprinted at its origins with the mark of polemic and denunciation.

GOLESCU ON THORNTON

From the 1770s to the 1820s, interest in Western countries and cultures grew steadily in the principalities. However, for the kind of direct engagement by a native with a Western travel text, we have to wait until after the outbreak of the Greek Revolution, which led not only to "Europe fixing its eyes upon us" but an increased attentiveness by locals to foreign publications about them. In 1826, the Wallachian boyar Dinicu Golescu published the first account in Romania of a journey to "Europe", in his case Hungary, Austria, Bavaria, Switzerland, and Northern Italy. In describing his urge to publish he wrote the following:

[Europe] makes her nations happy through the communication of goodness gathered through the travels made by some nations in the lands of others, and through publishing them in books.

Europe is full, as of other things, so of such books. There is no corner of the Earth so overlooked, no country, no city, no village unknown to a single European, so long as he knows how to read. But we, in order to know our country well, have to obtain this knowledge by reading some book written by a European. There are a great number of histories of the Romanian Land in Europe, written in her languages, and in the Romanian language, but still by foreigners; while there is no mention of one made by a native of this land.[47]

His own book was not a history of his native land but an account of his personal confrontation with what he insistently asserted to be the superiority of "European" institutions. He encouraged his compatriots to take seriously the critiques of foreign travelers:

[W]e have come to be ridiculed in the world's opinion, and foreign pens have painted us accordingly. But what good will it do us if we want to keep such things hidden amongst ourselves, and we make believe that they are not known, when all nations read them, as they are written by people who wish us ill? It is better for us to know them, to acknowledge them, and make a determined decision to rectify ourselves.[48]

In the same year, 1826, there appeared a Romanian translation of Thomas Thornton's well-known book on the Ottoman Empire, *The Present State of Turkey*.[49] On account of Golescu's clearly expressed views on the need to pay attention to foreign writers' assessments, early scholars naturally attributed the authorship of the translation to him.[50] While this opinion is no longer upheld by modern literary historians, it remains likely that somebody from Golescu's circle carried out the work, possibly at his instigation or under his patronage.[51] The anonymous author of the preface emphasized the shame of the Wallachians that their country appeared in the eyes of European travelers to be so badly governed; but justified the publication of his work by arguing that the European evaluation was correct:

[S]ome would reproach me and, I think rather would defame and curse me, saying: that I thought it was clever to bring to light and publish slanders against an entire nation. If I were to hear people saying this, or were they to ask me, I would reply that they have no reason to get upset or angry at me; for everybody reading it should realise that, that Englishman being a foreigner, and having no personal quarrel with any of the locals, wrote nothing false about the deeds and customs practised in Wallachia and Moldavia; nor did he pass over or ignore the excellent natural resources or the wretchedness of the poor inhabitants of those Principalities; but he wrote about the good things with sweetness and a humble heart; and like a member of a free nation, he wrote without shame and listed with his pen for ridicule those things worthy of defamation and jeering. When I read and saw these things, the quickness of shame overtook me, disgust at the wretchedness of my nation penetrated me, their shameful deeds, their slanderous things, idiocies, wretched habits, idlenesses, lazinesses, false expectations, sleepiness, deceit, blunder, theft, rape, punishment, torture and failure to attend to the beneficial, enlightening teachings and crafts. Seeing all these things told and written and printed in all the languages of Europe; and most of the libraries and most of the houses of the Europeans full of such books, and the people laughing while reading them and poking fun at us, just like we Romanians do for Gypsies . . . tell me, dear reader, without feigning and with a clean heart, whether I am guilty because I translated this rather short description into the language of the Fatherland?[52]

In other words, at this important time of reform and institutional transformations, local authors were no longer attempting to rebut foreign travelers' denigratory depictions of barbarism but to concur with their evaluations, indeed using them as a tool with which to promote the cause of modernization.

MOLDAVIAN WRITERS DEVELOP AND CONSECRATE THE THEME, 1837–58

In the first half of the nineteenth century, Romanian secular literature and national history developed to an unprecedented extent. In some aspects this involved emancipation from the tyranny of being known and written about from afar. Some historiographers analyzed or rejected the information and opinions offered by foreign (not necessarily Western) writers. The Transylvanian Romanian scholar Petru Maior, for instance, railed angrily at foreign historians, accusing them of:

pouring the vomit of their pens on the Romanian people . . . seizing any opportunity to make things up without the slightest evidence, even telling barefaced lies about the Romanians, even imagining that everybody ought to believe their delirious fantasies. Furthermore, for some time now, like donkeys scratching themselves against other donkeys, they pick up slanders from one another, without bothering to search for the truth, putting them into print one more time.[53]

In Transylvania this discourse was bound up with rivalry between the different nations of that province or of the Habsburg monarchy more broadly: Romanian scholars identified "enemies of the people" among neighboring nations, rather than among Westerners in particular.[54] One argued that it was because "our neighbors [*vecini*] blackened us first" that "people of other lands [*străini*], who knew us only from what our neighbors had to say", then "filled the world with books in which we were painted in such humiliating and disgraceful colours that they came to believe their own inventions".[55]

In Moldavia and Wallachia, more explicit blame was placed on foreigners, and not just any foreigners: travelers and historians in particular were singled out for critique. In 1837, for instance, the young Moldavian nobleman Mihail Kogălniceanu, who studied in Berlin and was the first Romanian to publish a synthetic history of his homeland—significantly in French, in other words addressed at a foreign audience—wrote home to his father about his motives. "I do not write to speak ill, but well, against the lies that foreign travelers write about Moldavia."[56] This tradition, in which Romanian scholars continued the efforts to maintain the national dignity allegedly tarnished by the superficial observations of foreigners, was to endure in the modern period. It can often be found alive and well in the twenty-first century, as Romanian academics continue to question the image of their country presented in foreign publications.[57]

Mihail Kogălniceanu was part of a group of younger writers, known collectively as the *bonjuriști*, on account of their French education and modern sociability (*bonjour!*). In the 1830s and '40s, the *bonjuriști* began publishing travel sketches, autobiographical fragments, pastiches, and novellas in a series of reviews published in Iași, the province's capital before Moldavia was absorbed into the new state of Romania after 1859. They developed a perhaps more complex approach to negotiating self-identity in the face of foreign frames, scripts, and stereotypes. For instance, in an unpublished sketch from 1839, essayist and memoirist Alecu Russo described how reading foreign travel descriptions of his homeland actually relieved the melancholy that reflecting on his fatherland's sad situation had induced in him:

> If by chance there appeared at Iași a brochure printed in Paris or even in Czernowitz, titled *Tour en Moldavie, Voyage en Moldavie, Esquisse* or any other similar title, in which the author would use grand and high-flown phrases to say more or less the following: "In a country ignored by Europe, or at least scarcely known, I have found a people both good and naive, poetic in their unaltered traditions and also in their savage ignorance. . . ." Then, as though awoken from a dream, we would find even our own land bearable.[58]

For Russo, being described as "good", "naive", and "poetic" was somehow better than not being described at all. Specifically, he used this trope to try and persuade local writers to avoid producing artificial adaptations of "your scenes from Italy, your Parisian *soirées*, your German fantasies" or imitation comedies and novellas, and concentrate on the "suave melancholy" and the "primitive *je ne sais quoi*" of the Moldavian landscape. At the same time, there is more than a hint of irony in his portrayal of the foreign travel text, as Western travelers' recourse to "grand and high flown" phraseology, and implicitly presumptuous titles, is gently mocked, as is their claim to have personally achieved some unique ethnographic discovery ("I have found") of domestic realities that, for the inhabitants themselves, bore no hint of the exotic or unfamiliar.[59]

A few years later, in 1848, *bonjurist* writer Vasile Alecsandri, notable author of poems, plays, essays, memoir pieces, and travel accounts, published a sketch titled "Balta Albă" [The White Lake] in a calendar issued by the local official newspaper.[60] The sketch uses the classic figure of the foreign visitor to a domestic setting, in the form of a Frenchman traveling in Wallachia, in order to satirize local mores. Because of the provinces' discursive position on the borderline between barbarism and civilization, the satire actually draws on two, usually separate, French fictional traditions. The first is that of the fictional Oriental traveler to a "civilized" country, who is nevertheless able to discern certain shortcomings.[61] The second is that of the Westerner who travels to an exotic location to paint an idyllic, innocent scene.[62] In Alecsandri's text, these two traditions are effectively merged, as the hero, a French traveler in search of the picturesque, finds *both* the exotic scenes he had set off to look for *and* the shortcomings to which Alecsandri's domestic audience would have been all too alert.

The sketch opens with the narrator identifying himself as one of a group of friends "assembled, and all stretched out on *divans*, after the Oriental custom, and armed with long *chibouks* [pipes], whose output of smoke produced an effect worthy of a Pasha's *selamlik*". Among the group is a young French painter, who, having embarked on an Oriental journey, found himself diverted to Wallachia, of whose existence he had no idea. "But," he says:

> I shouldn't complain at all, since, like a new Columbus, I had the pleasure of discovering for myself these beautiful parts of the world and assuring myself that, far from being inhabited by cannibals, they contain a most agreeable society. . . .

—an opinion that causes one of the group to express reservations.[63] The rest of the sketch consists of the painter's narration of his journey and arrival in Wallachia. His attention had initially been drawn during his passage along the Danube, by "the wild beauty of the banks of this river between the Banat and Serbia".[64] This constituted the boundary between the Habsburg and Ottoman Empires, and Alecsandri's fictional traveler's description of it is contemporary with the classic one of A. W. Kinglake in *Eothen*, who was likewise thrilled to have arrived at "the end of this wheel-going Europe" and to see "the Splendour and Havoc of the East".[65]

In faux-naive fashion, Alecsandri's (unnamed) fictional French artist finds himself "overcome by a boundless urge to knowledge, and decided to make a detailed study of this country unknown to me, and of that—to me—completely new race of men".[66] Most of the piece then centers on the comedy of such an enterprise. Descending at Brăila on the left bank of the lower Danube, he is greeted by the French consul, who directs him toward "a miracle-working lake" of recent discovery, where thousands gather in search of cures for their illnesses. Hiring a carriage, our painter is astonished to find it drawn by "four small horses, all skin and bones, deeply marked by the whip", wielded by 'a wild, bearded, ragged man armed with a six-foot long flail!" After an alarmingly noisy and bumpy journey, interrupted by losses of both wheel and horse, and finally abandoning the carriage to make the final part of the journey on foot, through a pack of hungry dogs. The whole experience causes him to "completely lose my train of thought" on account of the "diverse and contradictory sensations I underwent in the space of a few hours".[67] Arriving finally at the lake, he was astonished at the European characters, equipages, and toilettes:

> I couldn't believe I was not dreaming, and reckoned myself in the presence of some unfathomable phantasmagoria: one that was all the more curious for displaying so many kinds of contrasts: Viennese balloons, with vehicles totally unknown to us; French hats and Oriental *işliks*; morning coats and *anteris*; Parisian *toilettes* with bizarre foreign costumes.[68]

Despite further hazards and alarms, the sketch ends with the description of "a delightful ball", which is presented as evidence of "a completely European society", "civilized manners", and "agreeable dress". In conclusion, the Frenchman declares Wallachia to be "a land of wonders" and leaves his assembled audience of boyars to judge the question of whether they are "a part of the civilized world, or a barbarous province".[69] Perhaps more important than the boyars' answer to this question is the narrative frame of the sketch: for once—if only in a fictional world—the foreign traveler is made to address his question directly *to* the travelees, the members of the described society, instead of talking *about* them to his compatriots.

A third and (for the purposes of this chapter) final example of Moldavian reaction to, and subversion of, foreign travelers' discourses on their domestic culture can be found in the work of Moldavian essayist and travel writer Dimitrie Rallet, who deployed a similar tone when writing about his own oriental journey in 1858. His book *Recollections and Impressions of Travel* is mainly dedicated to his experiences of Bulgaria, Istanbul, and European Turkey, which he traversed on a diplomatic mission in connection with the political union of Moldavia and Wallachia after the Crimean War. But he insisted to his readers that "Before I leave Iaşi, you should know something about it". And his remarks on the city are situated explicitly against the deficiencies of foreign accounts:

> Travelers who never visited it make it a city ravaged by fires, with streets paved with planks, with oriental customs which, in Malte-Brun's geography of 1839, we find them cited from Wolf, who wrote in 1798, so if

you were to take him as your guide, you would expect to find turbans and *mehterhané* [Oriental percussion music], tambourines and slippers, or even mosques; despite this, nothing of the kind exists.[70]

In his turn, Rallet responds with a list of what he considers important cultural knowledge about his home city, assuring readers that:

–the remains of the blazes and the Janissaries can no longer be seen;
–that fires are rare and the firemen excellent;
–that the main street is paved with stone and the people walking down it have no recollection of it having been paved with planks of wood;
–that the music is completely European, and while it might make you dizzy, it won't deafen you;
–that the courts, despite retaining the name divan, nevertheless—just like those in other civilized countries—offer few facilities and many formalities for their clients;
–that light hats have replaced the heavy round *işlik*;
–that [female] heads have been divested of the burden of those oriental veils that, while stifling the path of thought, furnished nonetheless an air of stability and gravity;
–that the small Parisian boots look wonderful in place of the Oriental slippers that forced one to walk with a balanced gait for fear they might fall off;
–that French is spoken naturally, and with a rapidity that can only be compared *en sens inverse* with the sluggishness with which the quadrille is danced;
–that, just as in Paris, visiting cards are used, often as a way of avoiding finding us at home;
–that, as elsewhere, I might invite you to dinner, not so that you may eat, but for you to forget your hunger by waiting;
–that servants are no longer summoned by clapping one's hands, rather, a bell is rung;
–that without opera glasses, you can't see anyone;
–that nobody can live without frequenting distant spa resorts and amassing unpaid debts, or without a great number of accessories—expensive but fashionable, unnecessary, but brought from afar;
–in short, that we are civilized![71]

It is notable that Rallet, while adopting the traditional strategy of a "domestic" writer indignant at the dated and erroneous impressions of foreign authorities, uses this counterblast mode to foreground what *he*—an insider—sees as the deficiencies of the elite of his own society: modishness, extravagance, social snobbery. Effectively, he takes the foreign traveler's presumed unique right to emit judgments and reorganizes both the framework of traveler/travelee and addresser/addressee and the subject matter of the topography—the things to be considered noteworthy. The foreign traveler's authority is thus somehow both domesticated and ironized, at the same time as it offers a licence to criticize. According to a much later article by Alecsandri on Rallet, this work—which appeared in Paris in Romanian—was also translated into French, so apparently its author sought to address it at least in part to a metropolitan audience, although no trace of the translation survives, and even to nineteenth-century Romanians it was "very little known".[72]

CONCLUSIONS

In the space of a century and a half, the perception of the Western traveler in the Romanian countries grew from a state of relatively indifferent curiosity, to one of fierce indignation, and was then transmuted through the use of irony and fiction into a bearable—not least because sometimes comical—figure, who can constitute the object of satire as well as the source of reproach. A discourse of ethical outrage or remorse at "foreign pens" gave way to an approach using the classic tropes of fiction: irony, dialogue, free indirect speech, embedded narratives, and so on.[73] This led partly to its ossification, into the kind of "classic locution" referred to by Patapievici in the essay quoted at the beginning of this chapter. Further investigations could trace the later history of this image in Romanian culture, through both fictional allegories and polemical essays, to understand how foreigners were adduced, adopted, adapted, or rejected as generators of ethical authority at Europe's edge. Different cases will provide disparate evidence of both agency and dependency in individual authors' moral self-postitionings vis-à-vis the imagined West(erner). Ultimately, however, it is not a discourse of (conscious or diagnosed) psychological fragmentation, and in many cases the foreigners are rendered as baffled or distraught by their inability to interpret "Moldo-Wallachian" realities as the natives. Romanian travelees, then, ceased portraying themselves as helpless victims of a hegemonic discourse foisted on them from outside but instead as *re addressers* of that discourse to different audiences, for different purposes, while maintaining some commonalities of subject matter.

NOTES

1. Versions of this chapter were presented in May 2010 to the Long Nineteenth Century Seminar, Faculty of Modern History, Oxford University, and to the Doctoral School, Faculty of Letters, University of Bucharest. Thanks to David Hopkin, Christina de Bellaigue, and Mircea Anghelescu for affording me these opportunities; to both audiences for their questions and observations; and to Wendy Bracewell and Ludmilla Kostova for comments on a revised draft. All translations herein are mine unless otherwise indicated.

2. Horia-Roman Patapievici, "Calmul discuţiei, seninatatea valorilor", *Idei in dialog* 1 (2004), reprinted in a slightly different form in his book *Despre idei si blocaje* (Bucharest: Humanitas, 2007), chap. 1. In his autobiographical memoir *Zbor în bătaia săgeţii* (1995), Patapievici describes himself as having cultivated this immersion in high culture during the Ceauşescu period, within a context of resistance to the dominant ideology. See Patapievici, *Flying against the Arrow: An Intellectual in Ceauşescu's Romania*, trans. Mirela Adăscăliţei (Budapest: CEU Press, 2003).

3. See the compendium *Călători străini despre ţările române*, 10 vols. (Bucharest: Romanian Academy, 1968–2001); new series, 6 vols. (Bucharest, 2004–10). Over three hundred accounts for the period 1700–1850 are to be found in vols. 8–10 of the old series and 1–5 of the new.

4. Larry Wolff, *Inventing Eastern Europe* (Stanford, CA: Stanford University Press, 1994); Maria Todorova, *Imagining the Balkans* (New York: Oxford University Press, 1997); Ludmilla Kostova, *Tales of the Periphery* (Veliko Tŭrnovo: St. Cyril and Methodius University Press, 1997); Vesna Goldsworthy, *Inventing Ruritania* (New Haven, CT: Yale University Press, 1998); Božidar Jezernik, *Wild Europe* (London: SAQI, 2004); Andrew Hammond, *The Debated Lands* (Cardiff: University of Wales Press, 2007). While all these authors touch on Romania, many texts still await systematic treatment in English. I made a brief survey in Alex Drace-Francis, *The Making of Modern Romanian Culture* (London: I. B. Tauris, 2006), pp. 27–39; and a review of some recent Romanian-language scholarship in Alex Drace-Francis, "Review", *Colloquia: Journal of Central European History* 12, nos. 1–2 (2005): 269–71.

5. Alexandru Zub, "Political Attitudes and Literary Expressions Illustrative of the Romanians' Fight for National Dignity", *Synthesis* 4 (1977), 17–33; Katherine Verdery, "Moments in the Rise of the Discourse on National Identity, Seventeenth through Nineteenth Centuries", in A. I. Cuza, ed., *Românii în istoria universală* (Iaşi: Universitatea A. I. Cuza, 1988), pp. 25–60; Sorin Mitu, *National Identity of the Transylvanian Romanians*, trans. Sorana Corneanu (Budapest: CEU Press, 2001), pp. 15–53. Some relevant primary texts are now accessible in English; see, for example, Balázs Trencsényi and Michal Kopeček, eds., *Discourses of Collective Identity in Central and Southeast Europe*, 4 vols. (Budapest: CEU Press, 2006–10); and Wendy Bracewell, ed., *Orientations: An Anthology of East European Travel Writing* (Budapest: CEU Press, 2009).

6. Sorin Antohi, *Imaginaire culturel et réalité politique dans la Roumanie moderne*, trans. Claude Karnoouh and Moni Antohi (Paris: L'Harmattan, 1999), p. 269.

7. Verdery, "Moments", pp. 58–59, speaks of an "interstitial subject"; Antohi, *Imaginaire*, of the constitution of a "stigmatic social identity"; Sorin Alexandrescu, *Identitate în ruptură* (Bucharest: Univers, 2000), of "identity fragmentation"; cf. Denise Roman, *Fragmented Identities* (Lanham, MD: Lexington, 2003).

8. According to Bhabha, "the ambivalence of mimicry" produces "an uncertainty which fixed the colonial subjects as 'partial' presence"—i.e. "both 'incomplete' and 'virtual'". Homi K. Bhabha, *The Location of Culture* (London: Routledge, 1994), p. 86.

9. Alex Drace-Francis, "Constantin 'Dinicu' Golescu and His *Account of My Travels*: Eurotopia as Manifesto", *Journeys, The International Journal of Travel and Travel Writing* 6, nos. 1–2 (2005): 24–53. See also the critique of a related diagnosis, that of Romanian "passivity", made in Dennis Deletant, *Romania Observed* (Bucharest: Encyclopedic, 1998), pp. 333–51.

10. See Mary Louise Pratt, *Imperial Eyes: Travel Writing and Transcultura-tion* (London: Routledge, 1992), p. 242n42.
11. See, for example, George Călinescu, *History of Romanian Literature*, trans. Leon Levițchi (Milan: NAGARD, 1982), chap. 2; Vlad Georgescu, *Political Ideas and the Enlightenment in the Romanian Principalities*, trans. Mary Lăzărescu (Boulder, CO: East European Monographs, 1971); Adrian Marino, *Littérature roumaine—littératures occidentales*, trans. Annie Bentoiu (Bucharest: Ştiinţifică şi Enciclopedică, 1981), pp. 10–48; Barbara Jelavich, *History of the Balkans*, 2 vols. (Cambridge: Cambridge University Press, 1983), vol. 1, pp. 185–86; Dan Berindei, *Românii şi Europa* (Bucharest: Museion, 1991); Paul E. Michelson, "Romanians and the West", in Kurt Treptow, ed., *Romania and Western Civilization* (Iaşi: Center for Romanian Studies, 1997), pp. 11–24; Harald Heppner, "Introduction", in Treptow, ed., *Romania and Western Civilization*; Harald Heppner, ed., *Die Rumänen und Europa* (Vienna: Böhlau, 1997), p. 16; Alexandru Zub, "Europa in der rumänischen Kultur", in Heppner, ed., *Die Rumänen und Europa*, p. 275; and George Cipăianu, "Opţiunea occidentală a românilor", in Nicolae Bocşan and Ioan Bolovan, ed., *Călători români în Occident* (Cluj, Romania: Presa Universitară, 2004), pp. 37–45.
12. Mihai Berza, "Turcs, Empire Ottoman et relations roumano-turques dans l'historiographie moldave des XVe–XVIIe siècles", *Revue des etudes sud-est européennes* 10, no. 3 (1972): 595–627; Leon Volovici, "Polonii şi Ţara Leşească în literatura romană", *Anuar de lingvistică şi istorie literară* 28 (1981–82): 57–64; Veniamin Ciobanu, "Imagini ale străinului în cronici din Moldova şi Ţara Românească (secolul XVIII)", in Alexandru Zub, ed., *Identitate/alteritate în spaţiul românesc* (Iaşi: Universitatea A. I. Cuza, 1996); and Florea Ioncioaia, "Veneticul, păgînul şi apostatul. Reprezentarea străinului în Principatele Române (secolele XVIII–XIX)", in Zub, ed., *Identitate/alteritate în spaţiul românesc*; Dan Horia Mazilu, *Noi şi ceilalţi* (Iaşi: Polirom, 1999).
13. The full title is *Începătura istorii vieţii luminatului şi preacreştinului domnului Ţării Rumâneşti, Io Constantin Brîncoveanu Bassarab Voievod, dă cînd Dumzezeu cu domnia l'au încoronat, pentru vremile şi întîmplările ce în pămîntul acesta, în zilele Măriei-sale s-au întîmplat* [Outline of the history of the life of the enlightened and most Christian prince of Wallachia, Constantin Brincoveanu Bassarab Voevod, from the time of his coronation by the Lord, recounting the times and events which took place in this land in the days of His Majesty]. See the latest critical edition in *Cronicari munteni*, ed. D. H. Mazilu (Bucharest: Univers Enciclopedic, 2004), pp. 403–671.
14. Mazilu, "Preface", in Greceanu, *Cronicari munteni*, p. 7.
15. Greceanu, "Începătura istorii vieţii", in *Cronicari munteni*, pp. 517–21. There are no translations into Western languages, but Nicolae Iorga, *Histoire des relations anglo-roumaines* (Iaşi: Neamul Românesc, 1917), pp. 40–48, gives a longer précis.
16. On Paget, see Colin Heywood, "Paget, William, Seventh Baron Paget (1637–1713)", *Oxford Dictionary of National Biography*, new ed., 60 vols. (Oxford: Oxford University Press, 2004), vol. 42, pp. 383–84. For a Latin ms account of the journey from the British archives, see E. D. Tappe, "Documents Concerning Rumania in the Paget Papers", *Slavonic and East European Review* 33, no. 80 (1954): 201–11,; for further details from the Romanian side, such as the costs of entertaining Paget borne by the Wallachian court, see Paul Cernovodeanu, "Contributions to Lord Paget's Journey in Wallachia and Transylvania", *Revue des etudes sud-est européennes* 11, no. 2 (1973): 275–85.
17. Greceanu, "Începătura istorii", in *Cronicari munteni*, p. 520.

18. On Edmund Chishull, see William Gibson, "Chishull, Edmund (1671–1733)", *Oxford Dictionary of National Biography*, vol. 11, pp. 493–94; and David Constantine, *Early Greek Travelers and the Hellenic Ideal* (Cambridge: Cambridge University Press, 1984), pp. 34–52.

19. Edmund Chishull, *Travels in Turkey and Back to England* (London, 1747), p. 77.

20. Chishull, *Travels in Turkey and Back to England*, p. 78.

21. Chishull, *Travels in Turkey and Back to England*, p. 80.

22. Vlad Georgescu, *The Romanians: A History*, trans. Alexandra Bley Vroman [1984] (London: I. B. Tauris, 1991), pp. 106–7; Andrei Pippidi, "Pouvoir et culture sous Constantin Brancovan", *Revue des études sud-est européennes* 26, no. 4 (1988): 285–94; Antohi, *Imaginaire culturel*, p. 232; Michelson, "Romanians and the West", p. 12. A different, longer view is in Verdery, "Moments", p. 31. See also Adrian Marino, "Vechi complexe românești", *Observator cultural* 76 (6–13 August 2001); and Dennis Deletant, "Romanians", in Manfred Beller and Joep Leerssen, eds., *Imagology: The Cultural Construction and Literary Representation of National Characters* (New York and Amsterdam: Rodopi, 2007), pp. 223–26.

23. Chishull's text (with a translation by Caterina Pitești eanu) was presented to the Romanian Academy in March 1921 as "unknown" by Ion Bianu, "Un călător englez necunoscut în România la 1702", *Buletinul Societăţii Regale Române de geografie* 41 (1922). However, it had previously been signaled by Marcu Beza, "Early English Travelers in Roumania", *English Historical Review* 32, no. 126 (1917): 280–81; and Iorga, *Histoire des relations anglo-roumaines*, p. 45. When considering the phenomenon of "writing back", it is worth remembering how some texts are subjected as much to oblivion as to indignation.

24. Constantine, *Early Greek Travelers*, pp. 168–87; Olga Augustinos, *French Odysseys: Greece in French Travel Literature from the Renaissance to the Romantic Era* (Baltimore: Johns Hopkins University Press, 1994), pp. 131–73.

25. See Georgescu, *The Romanians*, pp. 73–80; and Hugh Ragsdale, "Evaluating the Traditions of Russian Aggression: Catherine II and the Greek Project", *Slavonic and East European Review* 66, no. 1 (1988): 91–117.

26. Nigel Leask, "Byron and the Eastern Mediterranean: *Childe Harold II* and the 'Polemic of Ottoman Greece'" in Drummond Bone, ed., *The Cambridge Companion to Byron* (Cambridge: Cambridge University Press, 2004), pp. 99–117; Ludmilla Kostova, "Degeneration, Regeneration and the Moral Parameters of Greekness in Thomas Hope's *Anastasius*", *Comparative Critical Studies* 4, no. 2 (2007): 177–92. Both these studies cover much wider ground than their titles suggest.

27. Carra features as a minor character in Robert Darnton's classic work of cultural history, *Mesmerism and the End of the Enlightenment in France* (Princeton, NJ: Princeton University Press, 1968). There is now a comprehensive scholarly biography: Stefan Lemny, *Jean-Louis Carra (1742–1793). Parcours d'un révolutionnaire* (Paris: L'Harmattan, 2000).

28. Jean-Louis Carra, *Histoire* (Jassy: Société Typographique des Deux-Ponts, 1777), pp. xvi–xvii.

29. Carra, *Histoire*, p. 197.

30. "*Journal encyclopédique*, 15 July 1778"; "*Journal de Paris*, 22 September 1778", cited in Lemny, *Jean-Louis Carra*, pp. 85–86. Lemny has the first of these sources as 15 June, but 15 July is correct.

31. "*Affiches, annonces et avis divers*, 21 October 1778", cited in Lemny, *Jean-Louis Carra*, p. 86.

32. See especially Maria Holban, "Autour de l'*Histoire de la Moldavie et de la Valachie* de Carra", *Revue historique du sud-est européen* 21 (1944):

155–230; and Maria Holban, "Jean-Louis Carra", in *Călători străini*, 10-i, pp. 234–42. Cf. Frederick Kellogg, *A History of Romanian Historical Writing* (Bakersfield, CA: C. Schlacks, 1990), p. 89.

33. Wolff, *Inventing Eastern Europe*, pp. 291–92; Drace-Francis, *Making of Modern Romanian Culture* , p. 27.

34. *Lettre à Messieurs les auteurs du* Journal de Bouillon *sur le compte qu'ils ont rendu d"un livre intitulé* Histoire de la Moldavie (Vienna, 1779); cited in Alexandru Ciorănescu, "Le Serdar Gheorghe Saul et sa polémique avec J. L. Carra", *Societas Academica Daco-Romana. Acta historica* 5 (1966): 33–71.

35. Ciorănescu, "Le Serdar Gheorghe Saul et sa polémique avec J. L. Carra", p. 50.

36. Ciorănescu, "Le Serdar Gheorghe Saul et sa polémique avec J. L. Carra", p. 57.

37. Ciorănescu, "Le Serdar Gheorghe Saul et sa polémique avec J. L. Carra", pp. 57–58.

38. Ciorănescu, "Le Serdar Gheorghe Saul et sa polémique avec J. L. Carra", p. 60.

39. Ciorănescu, "Le Serdar Gheorghe Saul et sa polémique avec J. L. Carra", p. 61.

40. Cioranescu, "Le Serdar Gheorghe Saul", attributes the *Lettre* to Saul on the basis of Carra's response. Lemny, *Jean-Louis Carra*, p. 87, considers this probable, without committing himself fully.

41. Holban ("Jean-Louis Carra", p. 239, defending her earlier attribution in "Autour", pp. 173–75) contests Cioranescu's attribution, on the grounds that Sulzer "designates Raicevich fairly clearly". What Sulzer actually said in his *Geschichte des Transalpinen Daciens*, 3 vols. (Vienna: Rudolph Gräffer, 1781–82) is inconsistent; in 1:12, he mentions the pamphlet derisively but is coy about giving any names; in 2:92, he mentions the "gedungene Verfasser des ehrenruhrigen Briefes an die Journalisten von Bouillon"; in 3:142 he mentions "Herr R". as being the one who called Carra a "Kalumnianter", which is at odds with 3:76, where he speaks of two authors flinging their "Bosnian fists" at "the poor Swiss". (He might be using "Bosnian" as a catch-all pejorative term to refer to Raicevich, a Dalmatian, and/or Saul, who had an Albanian/Greek background.) In 1779 Raicevich was still in the secretarial service of Prince Ipsilanti. In general Sulzer is very rude about him, calling him "a fehlgeschlagener Arzt und starker Cholerikus" (3:142; cf. 3:49, 53) and well disposed toward Saul ("den beruhmten und gelehrten Doktor und Gros-Serdar", 3:160, and "mein hochzuverehrende Freund", 3:542); from whose letters in French about the bishopric of Milcov he quotes large extracts (3:569–70). On Raicevich, see Francesco Guida, "Un libro «italiano» sui paesi romeni alla fine del settecento", in *Italia e Romania*, ed. Sante Graciotti (Florence: L. S. Olschki, 1998), pp. 344–65, although Guida misses numerous contemporaries' piquant characterizations of him: "Jeremy Bentham to William Eaton, 8 January 1786", in Jeremy Bentham, *Correspondence*, ed. I. R. Christie (London: Athlone Press, 1971), 3:437 called Raicevich "a Man of industry and extensive knowledge" but added that "his good qualities are tinctured by a certain hauteur which might be spared". Neapolitan envoy Constantine Ludolf, quoted in Mircea Popescu, "La vendetta dell'abate", *Societas Academica Dacoromana. Acta historica* 1 (1959): 281–90, believed him to be "of Ragusan origin", a "man of great spirit and most learned, but ruined by an excess of vanity". Patrick Griffin, "Fathers and Sons in Nineteenth-Century Romania", PhD diss., University of Southern California, 1969, 41n43, has him down as a mere "Serb pig dealer".

42. *Lettre à Messieurs les auteurs*, p. 50.

43. *Lettre à Messieurs les auteurs*, p. 61.

44. Cioranescu, "Le Serdar Gheorghe Saul", pp. 50, 61.

45. Bishop Chesarie of Râmnic to Hermannstadt merchant Hagi Constantin Pop, October 1778, in Nicolae Iorga, "Contribuții la istoria literaturii române în veacul al 18-lea si al 19-lea. Scriitori bisericești", Analele Academiei Române. Memoriile secțiunii literare, 2nd. ser., 28 (1905–6), p. 196; cf. Lemny, *Jean-Louis Carra*, p. 87. Saul spent some time in Hermannstadt at the end of the 1770s and early 1780s. Nicolae Iorga, *Istoria literaturii românești în secolul al XVIII-lea*, 2 vols. (Bucharest: Ed. Didactică și Pedagogică, 1969), vol 2, p. 107, citing an Austrian diplomatic letter of 1785.

46. Regarding the *Réponse au libelle diffamatoire* (Warsaw 1779—which has not been found, and for the existence of which he is in fact the only source), Sulzer says it is written by an "ungenannte" (1:126), "einer von meinen Freunden" (2:93), and that it contains information concerning his own maltreatment at the Wallachian court. Cf. L. Baidaff, "Note marginale la 'Istoria' lui Carra 1777–1779", *Universul literar* 43, no. 2 (1927), pp. 21–23.

47. Dinicu Golescu, *Însemnare a călătorii mele* [1826], cited in Golescu, *Scrieri*, ed. Mircea Anghelescu (Bucharest: Minerva, 1990), preface. See also my translation in Bracewell, ed., *Orientations*, pp. 101–2.

48. Golescu, *Însemnare*, p. 29.

49. Thomas Thornton, *The Present State of Turkey*, 2 vols. (London: Joseph Mawman, 1807). This was not the first Western text about the principalities to be translated locally. In 1789, General F. W. Bawr's memoir on Wallachia, *Mémoires historiques et géographiques sur la Valachie* (Frankfurt, 1778) had been translated into Greek (then the language of the elite in the Principalities) and printed in Bucharest as Περιγραφη της Βλαχιας (Bucharest, 1789).

50. Petre V. Haneș, *Un călător englez despre Români. O scriere englezească despre Principatele Românetradusă în românește de Constantin Golescu* (Bucharest: L. Alcalay, 1920).

51. See Mircea Anghelescu, "Dinicu Golescu în vremea sa", introduction to Golescu, *Scrieri*, pp. l–lii.

52. Anonymous translator's preface to Thomas Thornton, *Starea de acum din oblăduirea geograficească, orășenească și politicească a Principatelor Valahiei și Moldaviei* (Buda: Royal University Press, 1826), reprinted in *Bibliografia românească veche*, ed. Ioan Bianu, Nerva Hodoș, 4 vols. (Bucharest: SOCEC, 1903–44), vol 3, pp. 519–20.

53. Petru Maior, "Preface", in *Istoria pentru începutul românilor in Dachiia* (1812), cited in Zub, "Political Attitudes", p. 18, and Mitu, *National identity*, p. 15; I have amended the translation in conformity with the original.

54. See the comments of Gheorghe Șincai and Ioan Budai-Deleanu, cited in Major, "Preface" p. 21.

55. Timotei Cipariu, "Notița literară" [unpublished, c. 1846], cited in Major, "Preface", p. 23.

56. Mihail Kogălniceanu to his father, in Mihail Kogălniceanu, *Scrisori din vremea studiilor*, ed. P. Haneș (Bucharest: Tipografiile Române Unite, 1934), p. 126.

57. See, for example, Vintilă Mihăilescu, "Orientalism după Orientalism", *Dilema veche* 5, no. 221 (2008); in English as "Neo-Western Supremacism", trans. Monica Voiculescu, *Plural* 32, no. 2 (2008) <http://www.icr.ro/bucuresti/bucharest-the-forbidding-city-32–2008/neo-western-supremacism.html> (3 March 2013). Mihăilescu finds "a dose of well-orchestrated hypocrisy" in the way in which Romania is presented in an English tourist brochure as an "exotic . . . land of contrasts".

58. Alecu Russo, "La pierre du tilleul", in Alecu Russo, *Scrieri* (Bucharest: Minerva, 1908), p. 208. See my translation of (and Wendy Bracewell's introduction

to) an extract from this work in Bracewell, ed. *Orientations*, pp. 130–31. See also Russo's "Jassy et ses habitants en 1840", in Russo, *Scrieri*, pp. 237–38, for an ironic aside about the "fleeting and inaccurate accounts" of foreign travelers, among whom he mentions Baron De Tott, Domenico Sestini, William Wilkinson, and Andreas Wolf.

59. Pompiliu Eliade, *Histoire de l'esprit publique en Roumanie*, 2 vols. (Paris: Hachette, 1905–14), vol. 2, pp. vii–xiii, shows how the Western image of *La Roumanie inconnue* became increasingly absurd as the number of repeinted texts increased.

60. Vasile Alecsandri, "Balta Albă", in *Calendarul Albinei* (1848), reprinted in Vasile Alecsandri, *Proza*, ed. George C. Nicolescu (Bucharest: Literatură, 1966), pp. 172–87.

61. On the history of this literary figure, see Donna Isaacs Dalnekoff, "A Familiar Stranger: The Outsider of Eighteenth-century Satire", *Neophilologus* 57 (1973): 121–34; Syrine Chafic Hout, *Viewing Europe from the Outside: Cultural Encounters and Critiques in the Eighteenth-century Pseudo-oriental Travelogue and the Nineteenth-century "Voyage en Orient"* (New York: Peter Lang, 1997); and Perry Anderson, "Persian Letters", in *The Novel*, ed. Franco Moretti, 2 vols. (Princeton, NJ: Princeton University Press, 2006), vol. 2, pp. 161–72. I thank my colleague Kate Marsh for drawing the first of these references to my attention.

62. This tradition is typified by Bernardin de Saint-Pierre's *La chaumière indienne* (1791), which was translated into many European languages; in Moldavia a version appeared in 1821.

63. Alecsandri, "Balta Albă", p. 172. Cf. Goldsworthy's use of the Columbus trope to describe Byron's discovery of the Balkans at the outset of the nineteenth century; Goldsworthy, *Inventing*, p. 3.

64. Alecsandri, "Balta Albă", p. 173.

65. Alecsandri is unlikely to have read Kinglake—his pastiche is modeled rather on French authors such as Lamartine, or Saint-Marc Girardin. On the importance of French travel literature on the Orient for the development of the Romanian tradition, see Florin Faifer, *Semnele lui Hermes* (Bucharest: Minerva, 1990), pp. 75–90.

66. Alecsandri, "Balta Albă", p. 173.

67. Alecsandri, "Balta Albă", p. 181.

68. Alecsandri, "Balta Albă", pp. 185–86. This signaling of conflicting "European" and "Oriental" fashions was a classic trope of foreign descriptions of the principalities; see Neagu Djuvara, *Le pays roumain entre Orient et Occident* (Paris: Publications Orientalistes de France, 1989); and Wolff, *Inventing*, p. 22.

69. Alecsandri, "Balta Albă", p. 187.

70. Dimitrie Rallet, *Suvenire și impresii de călătorie* (Paris, 1858), cited in the critical edition, ed. Mircea Anghelescu (Bucharest: Minerva, 1979), p. 4. Rallet refers to Conrad Malte-Brun, Danish-French geographer and author of *Précis de la géographie universelle* (Paris, 1810–39); and Andreas Wolf, Transylvanian-Saxon medic, author of *Beiträge zu einer statistisch-historischen Beschreibung des Fürstenthums Moldau* (Sibiu, 1805).

71. Rallet, *Suvenire și impresii de călătorie*, pp. 4–5.

72. Alecsandri, "Dimitrie Ralet" [1882], in *Proză*, p. 464.

73. For closer identification of specific procedures, see Mihaela Mancaș, "Structura narației în perioada romantică", in *Structuri tematice și retorico-stilistice în romantismul românesc* (Bucharest: Romanian Academy, 1976), pp. 212–13; and Liliana Ionescu-Ruxăndoiu, *Narațiune și dialog* (Bucharest: Romanian Academy, 1991).

11 Traveling the Times of Empire

Syed Manzurul Islam

One of the claims about our present world is that it has gone thoroughly global. Michael Hardt and Antonio Negri, two of the most influential theorists of this supposed phenomenon, call it "Empire".[1] They claim that: "[w]ith boundaries and differences suppressed or set aside, the Empire is a kind of smooth space where subjectivities glide without substantial resistance or conflict".[2] Since, according to them, there is no outside to the "smooth space" of the Empire, which entirely encompasses planet Earth, there is no room for other locations or subject positions within it. In other words, differences that hitherto divided the world have given way to a radical form of singularity, where each place and each subject resemble each other. From now on wherever one goes—irrespective of previous cultural, racial, or political differences—one will meet those who are like oneself. My purpose in this chapter is not to scrutinize or critique the conceptual framework on which Hardt and Negri have built their idea of empire, nor do I intend to draw out its detailed political implications, but I want to take it as symptomatic of dominant thinking on globalization, and to explore its implications for the experience of travel and transcultural ethics.

From an ontological point of view it is fair to say that difference is the precondition of travel's possibility; in the absence of difference—real or imagined—it is not possible to partake in the experience of travel, let alone to recount its significance. Difference also provides the possibility for ethical response. Just as there can be no travel (which always amounts to a movement to elsewhere) without other places, so there can be no ethics (which involves responding to others) without the awareness that in the world there are other kinds of beings beside oneself. If the world has become thoroughly flattened into a "smooth space", inhabited only by one kind of subject, how is it possible to address the question of travel and ethics, especially transcultural ethics? I explore this question by means of a number of contemporary travel narratives. First, however, I wish to clarify what I mean by travel and ethics in this essay.

Historically, difference—as the ontological presupposition of travel—is realized though a number of binaries: geographical proximity and distance; territorial (dis)continuity of power and sovereignties; and racial and cultural (dis)similarity. In their various configurations, these differences caused borders and boundaries to carve up the land into territories. By traversing these points the experience of travel was made possible. The ethical question is, how does one negotiate difference? One of the best ways of exploring this question is by means of Emmanuel Levinas. In *Totality and Infinity*, Levinas mentions in passing Martin Buber's "I and thou" relationship, which his own ethical ideas appear to resemble. However, Levinas suggests that Buber's relationship falls short of the ethical genre. Apart from drawing attention to the "formalism" of Buber's dyad, Levinas also points out that this mode of relationship "does not enable us to account for . . . life other than friendship: economy, the search of happiness, the representational relation with things".[3]

Levinas claims that he does not wish to correct Buber, but to reconsider his ideas on relationship to encompass "the idea of the Infinite".[4] Cursory though these comments mightbe, they have a crucial bearing on the discussion of travel and ethics since they suggest the very precondition of the ethical genre. What is wrong with the model of friendship presumed in the "I and thou" dyad? For Levinas, this circuit does not allow the intrusion of the foreign and the stranger. Behind the dyad of friendship lie the dialectics of reciprocity and the recognition of mutual egos. Such processes can only take place within the boundary of an intimate community where each subject knows each other, feels bound by the same set of cultural rules and values, and knows each other's worth. In other words, friendship of this type is possible among subjects who share the same immanent condition. But Levinas contends that ethics demands the other to come before me with the attributes of the *infinite*. The infinite always brings to me a stranger who not only fails to recognize me but also eludes my attempt to know him. It is by stubbornly remaining outside the parameters of my knowledge and recognition that the infinite allows an unconditional response to the other. Only then can there be a sense of obligation, a sense that lies at the crux of the ethical genre. If we are searching for friendship on ethical terms, then, we must allow the would-be friend to call on us in his absolute strangeness; not as the other self of whom I might have foreknowledge, but simply the vacant eyes and blank skin that solicit a response from me. Levinas writes, "It is my responsibility before a face looking at me as absolutely foreign (and the epiphany of the face coincides with these two moments) that constitute the original fact of fraternity."[5]

Yet how is it possible to have a friendship with a stranger if the stranger remains a stranger? Does the very recognition of the strangeness of the stranger not shed light on that very stranger's being? This dilemma is shared by travel writing and ethics alike. The point is best illustrated by a passage from Edith Wyschogrod's *An Ethics of Remembering* (1998).[6] In the course of presenting her meditation on the ethics of historical memory, Wyschogrod provides a personal anecdote that resembles the encounter between same and other that is usually found in a travel narrative. The encounter takes place on a street in New York. As she guards a van for someone in the process of moving, Edith Wyschogrod meets "an old, homeless African-American man" with a swollen left foot.[7] Moved by his plight and feeling obliged to help this seemingly destitute and afflicted man, she offers to accompany him to a nearby hospital. However, he refuses. To her surprise, his only demand is that she remembers his name: Billie Joe. Sensing that this request places her in a new kind of ethical terrain, Wyschogrod poses a series of questions. I cite them here as fully as possible because they present the dilemmas faced by any ethically-orientated traveler:

> Was the injunction to remember his name a means of informing me that he was one of the forgotten, that a transpersonal history was locked into the name Billie Joe, that he was a particular, as it were, that exhibited a universal meaning, that of destitution? Or was he pointing to himself proudly as the unique individual, a singularity, designated by this name? Was his history the inalienable property of a people and a culture upon which an outsider had no purchase? Yet, if I, such an outsider, am prohibited from inquiring into the history of the other, is this constraint not tantamount to an endorsement of historical solipsism? If, per contra, I enter into the other's history, recount it, have I not created in his name a particular constellation of verbal or gestural instances having practical import, one that imposes a language of dominance and alien historical identity? Would I come to remember this incident through the screen of later literary encounter, perhaps through the celebrated words of Toni Morrison's *Beloved*, who pleads in a moment of sexual desire. . . . Or, more insidious, was my offer and is the present telling of it not gesture of narcissism, the self-congratulatory display of good intentions on the part of the relatively privileged?[8]

Wyschogrod does not provide an immediate and direct answer to these questions yet they reverberate throughout her text, which seeks to resolve the tension between being a historian who validates the veracity of historical events on one hand and testifying to memories that are not hers on the other. This is precisely the dilemma faced by an ethical traveler. Aside from the dilemma inherent in the manner and terms in which knowledge of the other is to be conveyed in writing, the very event of such knowledge-gathering makes any ethical approach seem highly precarious. Even before Wyschogrod faces the dilemma as to the terms in which she should remember the name of Billie Joe or the ethical implications of such remembering, her gesture of lending a hand to the stranger compromises his strangeness. She already knows that he is "an old, homeless African-American man". Her gesture is grounded in the knowledge of the man's historical location. Moreover, such preknowledge is unavoidable. Billie Joe is a stranger to Wyschogrod only in so far as not being an acquaintance or a friend before they met in the street. Their separately classed and raced positions, as well as their contrasting experiences of privileges and health, also make them mutual strangers upon the historical stage where they appear. But the sentiment that moves Wyschogrod to offer her care to Billie Joe does not materialize in view of an unknown other. The very invocation—"an old, homeless African-American man"—conjures up a long and terrible story of destitution, which then moves a cognizant and benevolent soul into her role as a carer. Yet Levinas disallows such preknowledge from any act of ethical friendship. We might thus ask instead, is it possible to feel an obligation to care for someone or something of which one possesses no foreknowledge? If it is difficult to imagine such an event ever taking place, then it is impossible to narrate or write about or make sense of it. There is no language fit for such a task.

Levinas is aware of the impossible demands he makes of ethical conduct. In a late work, he writes, "The correlation of the saying and the said, that is, the subordination of the saying to the said, to the linguistic system and to ontology, is the price that manifestation demands. In language *qua said* everything is conveyed before us, be it at the price of a betrayal, language is ancillary and thus indispensable."[9] The mode of ethical response to the strange other, which Levinas terms as *saying*, cannot really be expressed without the signifying language—the *said*—which forecloses the possibility of encountering the strange other by introducing historical recognition. Yet, since the signifying language is the only way that the strange other can be borne in testimony, the ethical gesture will always be compromised. In other words, it would be impossible to maintain an unconditional stance. Ethics must therefore proceed with a paradox. The task is to bring an ethical perspective to bear on knowledge production: to find space in the travel narrative to bear witness to the predicament of the other.

More, not less, intercultural knowledge is required when narrating the travel encounter. In particular, it requires more of that which Clifford Geertz has called "thick description", although "thicker" and more precise knowledge does not secure the feeling of unconditional obligation demanded by the ethical relation. One way forward is the "as if" mode. Since ethics is a vocative genre, it is the "as if" mode that secures a feeling of "otherwiseness" in the addressee. In order to guarantee that one feels unconditionally obliged toward the other, one has to relate to the other *as if* one knows nothing about him. Knowing about Billie Joe is unavoidable. Yet one must know his history and understand his location as accurately as possible, ensuring that he is not presented as a "type". This does not negate the historical memories that his ancestors have endured and whose legacy still determines his place in the world. Despite this, he has a particular way of being. One who gathers knowledge of others, if that knowledge has an ethical pretension, has to pay attention to these peculiarities. Moreover, the account of Billie Jo and his world must consider the way he expresses meaning about the world in which he dwells. Having gathered such knowledge, however, and learning to see things from his interpretative viewpoint does not secure the feeling of obligation that moves one to take care of him. For that it is necessary to respond to his elemental presence, or *the face*, as Levinas calls it, as though he were a stranger. A sense of unconditionality, albeit virtual, cannot otherwise be secured. Ethics loses its core condition of existence if any gesture of care has particular preconditions, such as the desire to be charitable to Billie Jo because his ancestors have suffered so much. The impulse that prompted this gesture of care would in that case proceed from a sense of guilt, which has little to do with ethics. Besides, without the feelings of unconditional care, gaining knowledge of others cannot be conducted with an ethical sensibility.

To summarize, in *any* narrative, one can never hope to find uncompromised testimony to strangers. In tune with its generic orientation, travel writing is charged with the task of producing knowledge about other people and places. Consequently, the task of an ethicist is not to seek a pure ethical language, which is impossible, but to find a way of finding room for ethical expression in the language of representation. This may take two forms. First, knowledge production and communication need to alter their perspective: instead of seeing the world from the vantage point of the writer, precedence should be given to the point of view of the travellee. Second, the narrative subject must find a way of articulating a sense of care for the other, who is a neighbor, a brother, or a sister and yet also a stranger. Despite the likely failings of such an approach, ethics has no avenue other than these.

But if there are no longer strangers in this world, if difference has disappeared, then ethical language becomes redundant, no matter how it is formulated. One can respond to this in two ways. Despite globalization's homogenizing tendencies, cultural, regional, religious, and class differences among the inhabitants of the world persist. A traveler still encounters these differences as she goes around the world. Moreover, the ethical imperative is not invalidated because of radical changes in state sovereignty or the economic order. As we have seen, ethical responsibility is conducted on the premise that the other face that looks at me ought to be regarded as that of a stranger regardless of whether I have an intimate familiarity with her world.

No one has been as fervent as Pico Iyer in championing the notion that hybridity has homogenized former differences across the globe. Almost every page of his *The Global Soul* (2000) is made to bear the weight of this presumption.[10] For a contemporary soul, it is impossible to discriminate between here and elsewhere because, as he writes, "Everywhere is so much made up of everywhere else" (p. 11). This makes travel virtually impossible. When he visits the far-flung outposts of the globalized world, he finds in them not only similar styles, fashions, shopping malls and consumer desires but also hybrid cosmopolitans residing as though in their natural habitat. The citizens of cities in the Western world mirror those who live elsewhere due to immigration from the peripheries.

As Iyer knows, the globalization of trade, exchange and even production is nothing new and it particularly flourished under colonial rule. Iyer argues that, recently, the "speed" of this process has drastically altered our common sensibilities, or "global souls". A self-confessed "global soul", he writes, "The notion of home is foreign to me" (p. 24). Despite his assertion that the world has left its differences behind, a claim that is reiterated on almost every page of his book, the self-proclaimed standard bearer of the "global soul" cannot help but stumble on the divisions that persist in the world. When traveling through Haiti he passes a billboard announcing "Tomorrow Belongs to Haiti". Iyer observes that his view this billboard was "obscured by mountains of trash" (p. 26). In Manila he found children "piled up like rags on the pedestrian overpass" (p. 27). Even in Japan, a supposed example par excellence of new globality, Iyer finds himself "inside another country" that hangs onto its old ways (p. 273). These old ways hearken back to a time when one's mode of existence was relatively localized.

The ongoing disparities between the have-gots and the have-nots, which reflects to a large extent the old division between the West and the rest, suggests that difference has not disappeared from the world. Iyer himself contradicts his insistence on global sameness when he comes to acknowledge that "the world is more divided than ever" (p. 30). Hence, in one's encounter with people of different circumstances of life—in one's own city or in a distant place—the imperative to respond with a sense of obligation remains. Despite the accelerated movements of people in a globalized world, travel and its narrativization is still a prerogative of Western subjects. If in the past much cross-cultural and interterritorial information has been channeled though the genre of travel writing for all kinds of practical and epistemological reasons, in contemporary times it is almost entirely given over to the care and pleasure of the self. In this pursuit, the journey elsewhere becomes an occasion for consuming experiential value or aesthetic charm. One of the strangest things in reading Alain De Botton's *The Art of Travel* (2003) is the singular absence of people in it.[11] Somewhere between a personal travel account and metacriticism of the genre, De Botton's text erases most traces of people and the messy texture of quotidian life. Seen thus, place offers an untrammeled site for aesthetic experience. Enticed by a brochure of "Winter Sun" and armed with the classical Greek concept of *eudaimonia*, he goes off to Barbados, where the presence of the "yellow and the green logo of British Petroleum" or a "bureau of change" makes it "harder to *see* the Barbados I had come to find".[12] Staging the difference between Barbados and England only in terms of "the radical discontinuity in the landscape and climate",[13] Barbados is distilled of its cultural, historical, and demographic impurities so that he can be gaze upon it as a pure "aesthetic object". Strangely the place appears so empty of habitation that it parallels the *terra nullius* of the conquistadores' imagination that led to the extermination of the Caribs, the Arawaks, and the Tainos alongside other *indígenas*. This is an extreme exercise of erasing the world of difference by primarily drawing attention to the variation of aesthetic objects.

For travelers like the Swiss explorer Isabelle Eberhardt, a hundred years ago, the desert was a densely packed site of cultural and spiritual difference that offered a means of radical self-transformation. For De Botton, however, the desert represents an emptiness that prompts him to pursue the sublime object of his quest. Musing on the romantic take on the concept of the sublime, he travels to the Sinai Peninsula in Egypt. He does not tell the reader what he sees there, but muses, "Sublime landscapes do not therefore introduce us to our inadequacy. Rather, to touch on the crux of their appeal, they allow us to conceive of the familiar inadequacy in a new and more helpful way."[14] Even in aesthetic terms, the disorientating power of the sublime à la Immanuel Kant is transformed into a beautiful object that nourishes the self-possessed style of the aesthete. It no wonder that De Botton enthusiastically celebrates Joris-Karl Huysmans's Duc des Esseintes's refusal to travel so that he doesn't have to face "the ugliness and stupidity of others".[15] Freed from the messy difference of the world and protected from its possible contaminating effects on the self, De Botton—like his hero Duc des Esseintes—can enjoy the beautiful world. In this singular aestheticization of the world, the disappearance of others prematurely forecloses the possibility of an ethical position.

In contrast to Iyer and De Botton, backpackers are desperately seeking difference. Yet, they also travel in a globalized world where familiar cultural traits seem to follow them wherever they go. Rolf Potts's recent self-conscious narrative has come to capture this dilemma more energetically and amusingly than any others. Potts's signature text, *Marco Polo Didn't Go There* (2008),[16] narrates the adventures of a self-reflective backpacker from an account of his attempt to break into the film set of *The Beach* in Thailand to offering himself as an object of curiosity in northwestern Cambodia, where he traveled without a phrasebook. With the rare exception of his journeys through northwestern Cambodia and remote parts of Vietnam, Potts narrates his experiences of lurching from one Western backpacking milieu to another. In his narrative, backpackers hang out with each other, fall in and out of love, and amuse each other with travel anecdotes. Even the seeming exceptions express the backpackers' desire to be singular and exceptional. Of his travel to Vietnam, Potts writes, "I had come to a remote corner of Vietnam with no sense of the language and culture—with no host or guide, and no specific ideas about what to find there. The decision that brought me there was not a savvy act of independent travel, but an insipid act of negation—a ritual of avoiding other travellers, as if in itself was somehow significant" (p. 124).[17]

At one level Potts's narrative differs little from that of Iyer. Like Iyer, Potts charts the wandering of globalized cosmopolitans, and the presence of Western culture is all-pervasive. Even the remoteness of northwestern Cambodia does not allow him to escape such pervasion. In a supposedly pristine zone of otherness, he writes of "One man [who] pulls out a faded colour photograph of a middle-aged Cambodian couple decked out in 1980s American casual-wear. The back of the photo reads: 'Apple Valley, California'" (p. 273). One by one, Potts visits Western backpacking enclaves in search of rare experiences and adventures in seemingly unfamiliar places that have yet to be consumed. His journey across these globalized landscapes undoes the conceit of such an undertaking. This impression is accomplished by foregrounding the play of irony and parody in his text in ways that are recognizably "postmodern". The effect is to denaturalize his narrative, revealing his hand by showing the selectivity, omission, invention, exaggeration, and other deliberate shaping that went into producing it. He also comes clean on his motivation to write, which comes down to various commissions born of marketability. Meanwhile, he parodies his traveling and writing self. It is unclear whether these gestures are meant to undermine his narrative authority or to enhance it. I suspect that it is the latter. Let me explain. In a world where the Western reading public for which he writes has become sceptical of claims to truth, cynical of enlightened and ethical values, Potts adopts a paradoxical strategy to gain the approval of such a readership. The downright phoniness of his narrative and his deliberate display of inauthenticity combine with his confession that he writes for narrow materialistic gains to make him a more credible writer than any straitlaced purveyor of authenticity. By purposely presenting his narrative persona as given to narrow self-interest, the narrative's playful humor counters expectations of ethical and epistemological seriousness, thereby presenting Potts as truthful and authentic.

Between self-reflexivity and self-parody, and the paradoxical narrative authority that he gains by theses means, Potts deconstructs some conceits of contemporary travel. About the supposed distinction between tourists and travelers, he writes:

> I use the word "tourism" intentionally, since it defines how people travel in the twenty-first century. Sure, we all try to convince ourselves that we're "travellers" instead of "tourists", but this distinction is merely a self-conscious parlour game. . . . Regardless of how far we try to wander off the tourist trail (and no matter how long we try and stay off it) we are still outsiders and dilettantes, itinerant consumers of distant lands. (p. 15)

He amusingly parodies this distinction with an anecdote about when he was employed as a "traveler" extra on *The Beach* movie set. He writes:

> That is, if you had dreads or wore a sarong or sported tattoos or clutched a set of bongos, you were grouped together with the "travellers". If you kept your hair short or wore nice clothes or had a reasonably neat appearance, you spent on-camera time as a "tourist". Though my suntan was lacking at the time, I made the cut as a "traveller" on

the basis of my hair (which was longish) and clothing (which, while not
suitably ethnic, was a bit tattered). (p. 25)

He also deconstructs ecotourism, about which he writes that it "seeks
'unspoiled' places that have not been categorized or prepared for tourist consumption, yet ecotourism itself is a form of categorization and consumption.
Ecotourism promises an escape from the trappings of affluence and information society, yet by attracting affluent tourists to isolated points around the
globe, ecotourism spreads the gospel of information society" (p. 43).

While these passages deconstruct the travel genre, they do not amount
to an ethical position. Such gestures belong squarely to the epistemological
genre, exposing the self-fashioning of travelers as so many illusions and
falsehoods. It is true that the likes of Rolf Potts do not offer an idealized
model of travel narrative and traveler subjectivity except those of self-
conscious ironists. Although the ironists, as we have seen, are effective at
deconstruction, they easily slide into cynicism, one of the most unethical of
all responses. It amounts to saying, well, I know what the conceits, traps,
and illusions of the genre are, but what else can I do other than what everyone else is doing? Potts is simply content with self-deprecation, irony, and
parody. For a traveler to adopt an ethical position he needs to have a sense
of obligation for those who dwell in the places he has come to consume.
This is not present in Potts's text.

On the other hand, Brad Newsham's *Take Me with You* (2002) keeps
the ethical anguish of the traveler alive.[18] Newsham, a San Francisco taxi
driver, travels the world looking for someone to invite to the US. Like Potts
he is aware that he cannot counter his desire to consume places and people,
despite his noble intentions. He writes, *"The being needs travel—new sights,
new people, new experience*—I was a collector" (p. 153, emphasis in the
original). Moreover, witnessing the desperate plight of the others, he comments, "I'd come here not to get *them* fixed, but myself" (p. 30). The very
notion of choosing someone worthy of his gift smacks of benevolent arro-
gance from the affluent West. Much of his narrative takes the familiar form
of the traveler's self-fashioning of the reporting of strange tales from other
places. Yet despite traveling a world filled with the signs of globalization,
Newsham's encounters with zones of difference prompt ethical disquiet.

In Manila he meets a fellow taxi driver whom he wishes to regard as a
brother. Soon, though, he realizes that their income levels differ so much
that they are "not brothers, not even cousins" (p. 17). He goes on to say,
"In American terms I was the classic financial dud—the ne'er-do-well uncle
or brother-in-law—but by these people's standards I was a millionaire" (p.
21). Despite the saturation of global signs and the accelerated movement
of capital, the world has not flattened into a "smooth space" of uniform
sameness. It is a bumpy and uneven place with huge disparities of wealth,
life chances, and living conditions. Newsham travels with the burden of
this awareness. In India he ponders, "Everyday, I walked miles through

Calcutta's slums and parks and plazas, held my breath down alleys knee-deep in garbage, dodged cows, streetcars, and the ranks of cripples and beggars and men pissing against walls, and thought: *Thank God I'm not him. Thank God I'm not her. Oh, geezus, look at that—thank God that's not me*" (p. 79, emphasis in the original).

This narrative of Calcutta, no doubt, repeats the old clichés about third world misery that allowed the West to feel smug about itself. Yet forgetting the disparity and difference that exist between it and others amounts to closing the door on ethical obligation. The Western subject remains hugely privileged while multitudes of others have nothing. Newsham travels with this anguish in his soul and invites one among this multitude to the United States, hoping that his people will make the man "feel welcomed, honoured" (p. 282). This gesture is full of naive sentimentality, yet without being moved by the plights of the others in a divided world there is no possibility of ethics. This world is still very much with us.

I want to end this chapter by reflecting on an episode from Alfonso Lingis's *The Community of Those Who Have Nothing in Common* (1994),[19] in which Lingis, a philosopher-traveler from the United States, describes an encounter with a travellee in Mahabalipuram in the south of India. After being cooped up in a hut for weeks, seriously ill and alone, Lingis stumbles out into the dark believing that he is dying. A man, who is also a stranger to India, comes to his aid. All we get to know about this stranger from Lingis's narrative is that he is a destitute Nepalese who goes about almost naked and who speaks to Lingis in a language unintelligible to him. Upon finding Lingis paralysed and seemingly at death's door, the Nepalese stranger puts him in an outrigger canoe and paddles for sixty-five miles, disembarks at a fishing port, and carries him on a rickshaw before taking him by bus to a hospital in Madras (Chennai). Leaving Lingis in the care of the hospital staff, the stranger disappears without a word or a backward glance. For Lingis, this travel encounter embodies the fundamentals of an ethical relation, which involves imagining a community with those with whom one shares nothing in common, rather than a community founded on "family resemblance" in recognition of kinship and common discourse that is given to a normative obligation, a sense of duty sanctioned by law and inculcated by tradition so that the people of the "same" can look after each other. In opposition to this kind of community, Lingis's encounter with the destitute Nepalese man leads him to propose a community of those who have nothing in common. "Nothing in common" does not signify absolute difference, however, but the relative difference between the inhabitants of planet Earth to be encountered in travels far from one's own home, however defined, and sometimes at the margins of that home. For Lingis, then, "nothing in common" denotes the relative difference between the parties in encounter where "no racial kinship, no language, no religion, no economic interests" tie them into a relationship of normative obligation.[20] How then can the feeling of obligation with the absolute stranger that Levinas demands, and which Lingis carries in his head as he travels the world, be secured?

Let me address this question by citing a passage from *The Community of Those Who Have Nothing in Common*. The passage comes just before Lingis's encounter with the destitute Nepalese man. He writes:

> To catch sight, beyond kinship, of this *community in death*, we should have to find ourselves, or put ourselves through imagination, in a situation at the farthest limits of kinship—in a situation in which one finds oneself in a country with which one's own is at war, among foreigners bound in a religion that one cannot believe or which excludes one, with whom one is engaged in no kind of productive or commercial dealings, who owe one nothing.[21]

For the purpose of this essay, I want to focus on two ideas from the passage above, namely "community of death" and "imagination". Difference, as we have seen, can only be experienced in a relative sense, in terms of the presence/absence binary. In this context, the idea of a "community of death" is a useful way of relating to the idea of absolute difference and unconditional obligation that nonnormative ethics demand. Following Martin Heidegger, Lingis points out that death is a singular experience: no one can die for another. Death, in this sense, is a marker of absolute difference. Yet everyone will die: it is a universal predicament. Hence, death simultaneously suggests commonalty and absolute difference. The imperative to be there for the other who is dying or who will die secures an absolute sense of obligation while at the same time allowing one to imagine a community with the others because death is also one's own experience. Given the singularity of the other's death and the virtuality of one's own death, it can only be imagined as an "as if" moment. As we have seen, "as if" moments are the only way ethics can proceed.

The relative differences that divide the world have not disappeared; hence, the question of travel and ethics is very much alive. Even if some of the familiar markers of difference have disappeared, the ontological difference announced by the singularity of death will always be there. One will always be obligated to travel toward the other, and to be there for the other's death.

NOTES

1. Michael Hardt and Antonio Negri, *Empire* (Cambridge, MA: Harvard University Press, 2000).
2. Hardt and Negri, *Empire*, p. 198.
3. Emmanuel Levinas, *Totality and Infinity*, trans. Alfonso Lingis (Pittsburgh: Duquesne University Press, 1969), pp. 68–69.
4. Levinas, *Totality and Infinity*, p. 69.
5. Levinas, *Totality and Infinity*, p. 214.
6. Edith Wyschogrod, *An Ethics of Remembering* (Chicago: University of Chicago Press, 1998).

7. Wyschogrod, *An Ethics of Remembering*, p. 4–5.
8. Wyschogrod, *An Ethics of Remembering*, p. 5.
9. Emmanuel Levinas, *Otherwise than Being or Beyond Essence*, trans. Alphonso Lingis (The Hague: Martinus, 1981), p. 42, emphasis in the original.
10. Pico Iyer, *The Global Soul* (London: Bloomsbury, 2000); hereafter page numbers will be cited parenthetically in the text.
11. Alain De Botton, *The Art of Travel* (London: Penguin, 2003).
12. De Botton, *The Art of Travel*, p. 13, emphasis in the original.
13. De Botton, *The Art of Travel*, p. 22.
14. De Botton, *The Art of Travel*, p. 169.
15. De Botton, *The Art of Travel*, p. 10.
16. Rolf Potts, *Marco Polo Didn't Go There* (Palo Alto, CA: Traveler's Tales, 2008); hereafter page numbers will be cited parenthetically in the text.
17. Potts, *Marco Polo Didn't Go There*, p. 124.
18. Brad Newsham, *Take Me with You* (London: Bantam Books, 2002); hereafter page numbers will be cited parenthetically in the text.
19. Alphonso Lingis, *The Community of Those Who Have Nothing In Common* (Bloomington: Indiana University Press, 1994).
20. Lingis, *Community of Those Who Have Nothing In Common*, p. 10.
21. Lingis, *Community of Those Who Have Nothing In Common*, p. 157.

12 The Rhetorics of Arctic Discourse
Reading Gretel Ehrlich's *This Cold Heaven* in Class

Jan Borm

Ethics, according to Albert Schweitzer, designate "our responsibility, extended to the infinite, for anything that lives".[1] May this idea serve here as a general reference point for the teaching and reading of travel writing. If one agrees at least in some respects with what Schweitzer has stated in absolute terms, the notion of "responsibility" appears central and even challenging when it comes to representing one's encounters with others on the road. Claude Lévi-Strauss's famous outburst—"I hate travelling and explorers"—at the opening of his seminal *Tristes Tropiques* (1955) set the agenda in many ways for postcolonial debate.[2] The history of colonial encounters seemed indeed to reflect a sad story of imperial enterprise leading to colonial domination and exploitation. Lévi-Strauss saw the urgent need in the immediate years after the Second World War to engage in a critique of colonial encounters and discourse, a critique that would extend to his own profession and the practice of ethnography. At this moment, more or less reflexive anthropology based on participant observation together with access to the language of the culture under study had become a standard requirement in methodological terms, as is clear in key texts such as Bronislaw Malinowski's *Argonauts of the Western Pacific* and Michel Leiris's *L'Afrique Fantôme*. But Lévi-Strauss's work also drew on Jean-Jacques Rousseau's precept that one should "say it all" (*tout dire*) if one intends to relate one's experience.[3]

Such a statement of intent is only useful if one agrees with Clifford Geertz's claims that ethnographic data "are really our own constructions of other people's constructions of what they and their compatriots are up to".[4] The writing of ethnography should reflect this complex interaction between observer and "observee", and their respective narratives, if the aim consists to say as much as may seem feasible. But there is not only the writing. The ethnographer's stance as observer also has to come under scrutiny, as Clifford Geertz pointed out when he examined the ethical dilemma of fieldwork: "Most social scientific research involves direct, intimate and more or less disturbing encounters with the immediate details of contemporary life, encounters of a sort which can hardly help but affect the sensibilities of the persons who practice it."[5] This leads to active engagement with the concerns of the people and societies observed, although one may often feel limited in one's capacity for meaningful solidarity with such issues. Geertz defines this predicament as "anthropological irony": "[t]he first indications, having to do with blunt demands for material help and personal services . . . are fairly easily adjusted to. . . . Much more difficult to come to terms with, however, is another very closely related sort of collision. . . . I represent an exemplification, a walking display case, of the sort of life-chances they themselves will soon have, or if not themselves, then surely their children" (pp. 30–31). It is the moral problem, Geertz adds, "of the bourgeois informing the poor to be patient" (p. 31). Be that as it may, thinking is seen here as a social act for which one is responsible (p. 21). As to observation, anthropology should attempt "to see human behavior in terms of the forces which animate it" (p. 40). The prime objective consists in understanding what one sees, or trying to do so at least. "To judge without understanding," Geertz concludes, "constitutes an offense against morality" (p. 40).

Claude Lévi-Strauss's *Tristes Tropiques* was first published by the French anthropo-geographer Jean Malaurie in the Terre Humaine series he founded in 1955. The other title to appear that same year was Malaurie's own *The Last Kings of Thule*, a narrative that has become one of the classics of twentieth-century Arctic travel literature, translated into more than twenty languages including English.[6] Arctic travel literature is to be taken here in a broad, elastic sense as narratives whose main subject is the Arctic: explorer and travel accounts, ethnography, memoirs and autobiography, reportage as well as fiction (including, therefore, Jack London's Arctic works, for instance), and poetry. Malaurie dedicated the first edition to Knud Rasmussen, the Danish explorer partly of Inuit origin who was the first to engage in a circumpolar enterprise, the so-called Fifth Thule Expedition, which led to the publication of some ten volumes that have become standard works of reference in the field of Arctic studies. Gretel Ehrlich's account of several journeys to Greenland titled *This Cold Heaven: Seven Seasons in Greenland* refers repeatedly to the works of Rasmussen and Malaurie.[7] She discusses Arctic issues in relation to ethics, clearly one of her chief concerns, as her recent volume *In the Empire of Ice* also reveals.[8] Although Ehrlich's approach and writing are not, from an epistemological point of view, predominantly anthropological. Her work is based on (more or less sustained) participant observation, though she does not always seem to have direct access to the language of the societies she is writing about. Geertz's reflections on the ethnographer's predicament appear to be applicable nonetheless in a more general sense to any traveler who observes cultures at any length. At least, the reflections that follow are based on this premise.

This Cold Heaven was the set text of a third-year optional course on travel writing I taught for several years in the undergraduate English program at the University of Versailles Saint-Quentin-en-Yvelines, France. The choice of this work for the academic year 2006–7 is to be explained for a number of reasons, which I now detail in accordance with the principle of "saying it all".[9] Given that the purpose of this chapter is to focus on questions of ethics and pedagogy, what follows relates to direct experience of teaching travelogues. The reader is therefore asked to kindly bear with the more personal tone of what follows. Having taught a variety of courses on contemporary British travel writing, including set books by Bruce Chatwin, Robyn Davidson, Redmond O'Hanlon, Jonathan Raban, and Wilfred Thesiger, I was looking for an Arctic text while preparing the international conference "Arctic Problems: Environment, Societies, and Heritage", organized with Jean Malaurie in March 2007 in Paris, one of the first French events of the most recent International Polar Year (2007–9). Ehrlich's narrative seemed particularly suited as to what for almost all of the students in the group of some twenty-five turned out to be an introduction to the Arctic and Arctic Studies. The intertextual dimension of the work allowed her account to be put into perspective by comparing it with some of the major works in the field that students could thus become familiar with, including a major French author some of the students had possibly heard of but probably not read (though some of their parents were likely to be familiar with his name and works). Questions of gender would be raised. While Ehrlich's encounters also provided the opportunity to address environmental issues, one of the manifest rhetorical purposes of her narrative is to alert her readership to possible threats to Greenland's environment and society. Finally, an American author drawing on Greenlandic-Danish and French work called for intercultural readings of her representation of Inuit culture, little of which turned out to be known by students. The choice of the set text therefore also aimed at contributing to a comparative study of the history of ideas and cultures while hopefully offering an enjoyable read—adhering, as I do, to Horace's precept that texts (and teaching ideally too) should be both instructive and delightful (or at least pleasurable). The reader may judge the success of such an approach by considering the evidence presented below.

As far as the structure of the course was concerned, the module contained a general introduction to the Arctic, Arctic Studies, and Arctic travel writing. Students read a number of passages from seminal texts in several tutorials, while a total of twelve hours was spent working on close readings of excerpts from Ehrlich's text in class. One of the students offered to screen a documentary on the Arctic that was shown on French television during the semester, a suggestion that met with general approval. The students were required to read the set text and produce a reader's report outside of the class, as well as a written commentary in class for the end-of-term exam (in accordance with university exam regulations). Three of these reports are presented below with the students' permission.

In order to allow the reader a fuller view of the case study, some of the major issues raised by Ehrlich in her text need to be addressed. From what follows, and bearing in mind Geertz's comments quoted above, it will hopefully become evident that ethics are necessarily at the core of Arctic Studies, both from a historical point of view and as far as contemporary economic development is concerned. More generally, the notion of responsibility is one of the key questions to be addressed when it comes to studying travel writing in its historical context.

THE FREEZE ON ARCTIC ISSUES

Gretel Ehrlich had visited Greenland on a number of occasions before she set out to write *This Cold Heaven*. The account therefore relies on first-hand experience based on prolonged contact with the local Inuit population, some of whom the author refers to as friends. The title is indicative of one of her major rhetorical aims: to persuade the reader of the distinguished or noble and even sacred character of the Inuit civilization that reaches back thousands of years, an effect enhanced by the sacred number of seven featured in the subtitle—a figure that is not only to be read in referential terms.[10] A particular way of looking at Greenland is therefore announced from the outset, suggesting strong emotional engagement, even though the immersion is not total since English remains the principal mode of communication throughout. The point needs to be underlined, since issues of translation play a chief role in travel writing studies. Many of the people met with are anglophone, however, allowing a degree of privileged access to interior, Greenlandic points of view. The text is documented throughout and therefore invites intertextual comparison (Robert Edwin Peary, Knud Rasmussen, Peter Freuchen, Jean Malaurie, and Rockwell Kent, among others). The time frame corresponds to the author's journeys to Greenland between 1995 and 1999, with an epilogue dated 2001. Several chapters refer to previous moments in history, providing useful introductions to those not familiar with writings about Greenland or the Arctic at large.

Since close readings of Gretel Ehrlich's text are not the main purpose here, it suffices to focus on some of her themes in relation to ethics. Like any travel book, the principal narrative thread relates the experience by way of a quest. To illustrate this briefly, the narrator affirms at one point, "I tried to do less and less every day, tried weeding out the mind."[11] Facing icebergs, she notes, "I felt small, lost and happy" (p. 100). The aim consists in searching to create an inner void in order to experience a kind of rebirth, a well-known trope in Arctic discourse: "We camped for a night, then finally headed for home, crossing the wide monochrome monastery of ice. The Arctic functioned like a monk's cell, without need for walls. The ice floor and the ice mountains invited inward liberation and deterred escape and frivolity" (p. 335)—hence the religious illusions in the title. Elevation of the mind allows for heightened perception, as one can deduce from the words Ehrlich reports from one of the Greenlandic hunters: "At this time of the year, the ice comes to teach us how to see" (p. 351). A more immediate awareness of humanity's reduced place in the environment, let alone the universe, is also the theme of the epigraph taken from Ralph Waldo Emerson: "I am nothing. I see all". Perceiving the invisible or, rather, seeing further than anyone else is after all one of the chief traits lent to the shaman, the community's vital link between the visible and invisible world.

The dogsled trips related in Ehrlich's account are just one of a series of narrations about her own experience in Greenland which give rise to reflections on gender. Among these, one can refer to some standard topoi of Inuit ethnography, such as the trading of wives and what she terms "merely a non-chalance about matters having to do with the body" (p. 177). Another aspect of traditional Inuit life on whose decline authors have repeatedly commented is the natives' communalism, discussed here by quoting the anthropologist and archaeologist Torben Diklev: "The tradition of sharing is what is left of ceremonial life here. When a whale is caught everyone who was on the hunt shares the meat. Widows are given food, the less able hunters always get a share, equipment and dogs are traded around, huts are used by everyone. No one owns land here" (p. 340). Such comments may lead the reader to contemplate "the Inuit alternative",[12] the prospect of becoming an expatriate in the far north like the Japanese Ikuo Oshima, who came to northwest Greenland on an expedition in 1972 and has lived in Qaanaaq ever since.

Qaannaaq is, together with Siorapaluk, one of the northernmost places inhabited by humans. It is the village that the Inuit of Thule were forced to leave at the shortest of notices and under threat when the US Air Force established one of its major air bases close by in the early 1950s. Malaurie witnessed the arrival of the Americans and decided to write *The Last Kings of Thule* to pay homage to his Inuit friends in the northwest. The photograph of his closest companion Kutsikitsoq features on the cover of the French edition. Malaurie interrupted his doctoral research to alert readers across the world to his narrative about this forced displacement, itself such a traumatic experience for the Inuit given their intimate relation with lived space and the spirits of their ancestors believed to roam about their former places of residence on earth. Aqqaluk Lynge, a well-known leader of the Inuit Circumpolar Council from Greenland, has written on the epic battle of the Inuit of Qaannaaq for reparation in a book titled *The Right to Return: Fifty Years of Struggle by Relocated Inughuit in Greenland*.[13] This is how he presents their case: "The Inughuit population is among the smallest in the indigenous world, and their current home to which they were exiled in 1953 cannot support them as before. The number of animals within reasonable hunting distances are simply insufficient."[14] Ehrlich does not refer to Lynge's book, but is aware of the multiple difficulties the subsistence hunters from Qaannaaq have to face, including dramatic effects of climate change in the region, a theme she returns to at length in her latest book.

The threats of climate change and global warming to subsistence hunting in northern Greenland are also a subject Ehrlich has frequently discussed with Olejorgen Hammeken of Ummannaq, a Greenlandic friend whom she introduces as follows in the book: "Olejorgen was surprised that I knew about Rasmussen. Dark-skinned and almond-eyed, he had a slow, soft voice and enough Danish blood mixed into what he called his Eskimo genes to make him tall. Those genes linked him by blood to Rasmussen through one of Greenland's most famous families" (p. 6). It so happens that I met Olejorgen in France before and during the conference mentioned above. He recommended Ehrlich's book as an accurate-enough account of some major aspects of Greenland today, including climate change—comments that were naturally passed on to students at the time. Olejorgen's family is related to Hans Egede, one of the first Danish missionaries to have reached Greenland in 1721. Egede and his family, as well as the Moravian Brothers from Herrnhut in Germany, played a major role in converting Greenlanders to Protestantism, notably establishing the first schools in the country; Ehrlich also refers to these events in her book. Once again, it appears interesting to read her comments, some years after the teaching of the course, in parallel with Lynge's introduction to the journal of Hans Egede's grandson Hans Egede Saabye, edited by Lynge in 2009: "Given the context of the time, we Greenlanders must also forgive Saabye as an individual, 'for he knew not what he did'. . . . Saabye often risked his life in helping others. He also acknowledged his own moral anguish when disagreeing with his superiors back in Denmark."[15] Reading these remarks in relation to Albert Schweitzer's sense of "responsibility" allows us to enhance the importance of comparing competing views of Greenlandic society and its history whenever possible. Point of view was necessarily one of our chief concerns when studying Ehrlich's text in class, trying to read passages on the history of Greenland and the Arctic in context. A striking example of contextualization is Heinz Israel's monograph on cultural change of the Greenlandic Eskimo in the eighteenth century, which one may be permitted to mention here in passing even if Israel's study was not part of the course's reading list at the time.[16] In a slightly different vein, Michael Harbsmeier's anthology of voices from the extreme north published in 2001 offers Greenlanders' views of Europe—another German-language publication not consulted at the time, but important to mention to insist on the necessity of comparing interior and exterior views whenever possible in the name of reflexivity.[17]

Two more subjects dealt with at length in class need to be mentioned here: global warming and the protection of the environment. Our starting point was Barry Lopez's widely-acclaimed book *Arctic Dreams*, in which the author engages systematically with environmental issues, launching a powerful call: "It seemed clear to me that we need tolerance in our lives for the worth of different sorts of perception, of which the contrasting *Umwelten* of the animals on the island are a reminder. And we need a tolerance for the unmanipulated and unpossessed landscape. But what I came to see, too, was that we need to understand the relationship between tolerance and different sorts of wealth."[18] No matter how powerful the voice of Lopez and those of others may have been, global warming has accelerated ever since in the far north. Numerous publications on the subject have appeared.[19] One should mention at least briefly that Lopez has been studied within the context of nature writing and ecocriticism, but to do so here would lead us too far astray. More important to our purpose is the fact that contemporary travel writing is also concerned with environmental debates. Once again, we can refer to Ehrlich's latest book, but also Sara Wheeler's *The Magnetic North*,[20] not to forget the work of Malaurie himself, who has been alerting public opinion about the threats to Arctic societies and the environment since the 1950s. In his preface to the English translation of the second volume of his autobiography *Hummocks*, Malaurie recently observed, "In the Far North, the clash of civilizations has been particularly brutal, and the West never more cynical. Today, the world's three largest fortunes represent more wealth than that of all the less-developed countries (LDC) with their combined population of 600 million. For the Inuit, the clash has been as dramatic as the military defeats suffered by the American Indians."[21] Malaurie has remained faithful to the convictions of the angry young man he was in the 1950s, and his writings set the tone for a number of debates in class.

STUDENT FEEDBACK

Having outlined the conceptual framework and the major themes of the course, a discussion of student feedback allows an understanding of how ethical issues were received in class. Three students allowed me to quote here from their readers' reports, a part of the course assessment for an option that represents three ECTS (European Credit Transfer System) credits out of a total of thirty they have to validate per semester for their BA degree. The report was an experiment I introduced: students were encouraged to write as personal a report as they wished, an unusual exercise in their curriculum, but one with which a number complied voluntarily. This yielded refreshing responses from the students, three of which I focus on here.[22]

Mélanie Septier's summary of Ehrlich's book allows us to see to what extent she chose to foreground some of the themes mentioned above:

> Throughout the book one can feel that Gretel Ehrlich wants to understand this Arctic territory, its inhabitants and their frame of mind. She progressively discovers by living their way that the Eskimos are closely linked to their environment. She goes on trips on dogsleds, and witnesses the life of a subsistence hunter from the inside. She even feels the pang of hunger, which is inherent to traditional life in the Arctic. In this harsh environment, the only way is to adapt oneself. And the Inuit people's versatility is wonderful. As the ice is constantly moving and metamorphoses according to the seasons, the Inuit were traditionally always moving, following herds of reindeers or looking for seals and

walrus. Gretel Ehrlich shows that their hunting skills are essential for them to survive. In many of the stories Rasmussen told in his notes, there are tragedies of people who starved to death because they could not find animals to hunt.[23]

Accurate description is not the object of our attention here, though I was satisfied with the manifest effort of careful reading reflected in all three reports. Mélanie was also interested in the legends of the Inuit, the stories they like to tell, and their community life, an aspect we return to below.

Sabrina Arab also focused on the author's way of relating to the people and the environment:

> Ehrlich's travel in the Arctic is a spiritual quest. . . . In fact, at the beginning of the book, she explains that when she arrived in Greenland she was not used to the cold and the seasons. However, she manages to adopt the Eskimos' way of life. In this place, she discovered things about herself that she did not know before, that is why she falls in love with this wonderful place and the Greenlanders. Ehrlich is therefore an amazing woman as she travels alone in this "land of desolation" and she does not know the Inuit language.

Ehrlich's personal engagement, understood here as courage, is highlighted, and so is the evocation of what Sabrina calls a "wonderful place", a remark which responds to the wondrous tales told by Ehrlich and pictures that Sabrina may have formed in her own mind.

Emilie Al Saleh sums up her reading in general terms: "What is interesting I guess," she states in her report, "is to go beyond the reading, to focus on what I have been taught, what I have discovered and what I have felt, how it changed me since reading sometimes if not usually changes me". She moves on to her commentary by reflecting on her awareness of hybrid generic functioning of the text, a subject also dealt with in class: "*This Cold Heaven* is not a novel, a historical or geographical review, an autobiography or a lyrical ballad, it's the mixing of all these genres which was quite new for me as I had never read a book constructed in this way. I found it complete, informative and lyrical, pleasant to read". She also refers to some of the challenges encountered when reading the travelogue: "The difficulty to get accustomed to Inuit words made me remember that when one wants to understand a concept, a culture or a person, he has first to get used to sounds and to accept to change his own habits, his own perception of things". Language and intercultural adaptation are once again highlighted, Emilie insisting on the personal engagement of the reader with the culture represented in the text.

This is a theme with which Mélanie and Sabrina also dealt. Here is Mélanie's response:

The Inuit people traditionally live in communities. It is very interesting to compare their way of life with ours. In our individualistic societies, many people are depressed. For the Inuit, someone who is alone is thought to be sad. It is even considered a "failure" to be on one's own. To them, the group is more than the individual. Gretel Ehrlich explains that this frame of mind has developed for five thousand years of a harsh struggle for life. The wisdom of the Inuit is very precious in our societies where so many people are alone.

Once again, the interest of looking at these observations does not consist of evaluating their degree of accuracy compared to Ehrlich's text, nor of understanding them from an anthropological point of view, but to illustrate our main point of ethics being at the core both of contemporary Arctic discourse and its reception by readers, as the student feedback seems to show. As Sabrina notes on Ehrlich's discussion of communalism,

The Inuit do not own land; the only thing they own is their house. . . . This means that there are no problems of property. We can also draw a parallel between the Eskimos' life, Rousseau's myth of the noble savage and Daniel Defoe's *Robinson Crusoe*: the fact that there is no private property in Greenland suggests that man is good and he is different from Europeans who are corrupted. Jean Malaurie also emphasises this fact.[24]

Emilie's appreciation of Inuit life is expressed in this comment on a particular phrase:

"Great joie de vivre" [p. 349]. This sentence made me shiver. People over there are happy to be alive, happy to go hunting and to catch a narwhal, happy to feel warm. What matters most is to be alive. In Western countries, the average people have never experienced great cold, starvation or survival in extreme conditions—except during times of war, thus they take life for granted and complicate things trying to find a sense to existence, a reason to live.

These passages reflect the "Inuit alternative" theme. To what extent the students and readers of the present work appreciate this perspective is a question not to be considered here. The point I wish to underline is the will to respond to Ehrlich's rhetorics of a "friendly Arctic", a well-known trope for readers familiar with Arctic discourse.[25]

All three students sympathize with the Greenlanders' culture while voicing concern about the preservation of the Arctic societies' culture and their environment. This is how Sabrina reflects on the issue:

Ehrlich denounces how a culture can be annihilated by touching the spiritual way of life of people. The sentence which justifies the importance of culture for the Inuit is the following: "Being an Eskimo is not just race and nationality, it's also how you live" (p. 266). Another factor threatens the Eskimos' way of life and culture: pollution. . . . Ehrlich brought an important testimony about the Greenlanders' future. She asked Uutaap, an Eskimo, about the survival of the Inuit culture. He claimed that everything is changing. Effectively, animals are disappearing because of the climate. Maybe in the future there will be no more ice because of the warmth of the planet. The Inuit and their land are therefore threatened. However, according to Ehrlich the Inuit are going to survive as they are fighting to preserve their traditional culture.

Olejorgen Hammeken's return from Denmark and his choice to acquire skills in dogsled riding and hunting is one illustration of the will that Ehrlich comments on in her book: "He had made a pact with the memory of the long-gone Rasmussen, who had also abandoned a European education for the life of an Eskimo. 'Give me winter, give me dogs, you can have the rest,' Rasmussen had said. Soon Olejorgen would learn the art of driving dogs, reading the ice, surviving storms and cold" (p. 9). This way of reaffirming Inuit culture is also promoted by Olejorgen and his wife Ann, a Faroe Islander, in the school she runs in Ummannaq for neglected children, trying to make them feel proud of their own culture by taking them on dogsled tours. What Aviaaja Lynge calls "mental decolonisation" is a major subject in current Greenlandic debates on education.[26] As to Aqqalak Lynge, he looks further ahead: "As Greenlanders today move with healthy optimism into tomorrow, we take with us the knowledge of our past, including our angakkoks and illisiitsoqs, our colonial history, our old religion and our new one. . . . I believe, however, that despite the attempts of missionaries, our society was not turned upside down."[27]

Mélanie also comments on the clash:

> Gretel Ehrlich expresses her feeling of a constant duality in Greenland. First there is the duality of this world and ours, or the two sides of the looking glass. Our world seems very materialistic compared with the world of the Eskimos. We often pay much more attention to the objects we own than to our relationships with the others. In general our God has become money, and to get money, some people can go very far, they can kill for that. The Inuit people traditionally did not use money. They got everything they needed from their environment. Their only concern was the preservation of life and not its destruction. They cared about essentials, whereas we often lose sight of them and only look for non-essentials.

The degree of purpose might be too absolute for some, but her concern with ethics is manifest and her remarks once more evidence prolonged engagement with Ehrlich's text. So does Emilie's:

I would like to experience Greenlanders' freedom: their communion with Nature, and the absence of the unnecessary. The reading of *This Cold Heaven* made me feel somehow sad and jealous. I wish I could content myself with basic things and get rid of all the required compulsory surplus. I wish I had fewer possessions so that I could feel really alive. Again I will quote Ikuo page 164 in *Qanaaq, 1997* (my favourite chapter) because his reply to Gretel when she asks him if he wants her to send him something special, is what I consider to be real success: "Everything I need . . . it's out there . . . no it's better if I get everything myself. Needing things, that leads to unhappiness. And all the time I need less and less." What a marvellous sentence!

The exclamation mark retrospectively expresses the reader's emotional engagement.

What conclusions did the three students draw? Sabrina's is perhaps the least emotional, but definitely concerned with questions of responsibility: "I found this book very interesting because Ehrlich describes a wonderful and unique world. She studies the culture and traditions of these people. I think that people should help them to preserve their culture instead of destroying it. *This Cold Heaven* is a very nice book because it makes us dream". Mélanie's outlook into the future comes at the end of a paragraph on contemporary life:

In our "modern" societies, humans are detached from nature precisely because we think we are the only beings to have souls. Our frame of mind leads us to neglect our environment, whereas the Inuit people take care of it. The problem is that they are the first to suffer from the consequences of our lack of respect toward nature. I found that Gretel Ehrlich addresses environmental issues a little but not too much, so that her book did not depress me. It even gave me many reasons to be hopeful, which is necessary to react to challenges of today's world.

Emilie reflects on her own reactions to Ehrlich's book:

Without doubt I have been both delighted with my reading and disturbed: proximity with nature, freedom, independence blended with communalism, purity and beauty are things I feel like experiencing at least once in my life, however, coldness, hunger, life in a hostile environment where you have to watch every step that you take on ice for fear of confusing it with water and never come back truly frightens me. Many of us feel like experiencing the unknown and venturing themselves in a remote country, maybe to discover themselves or to measure their capacity, to have a new insight of life, to get rid of the superfluous, meanwhile we are few to toe the line, to accept our desires and not put them aside like mere silly whims.

All three students chose to engage thoroughly with the set text, as the above-quoted passages illustrate. Admittedly, their remarks focused less on some subjects I had anticipated, such as gender or colonialism. Though their comments do not read as militant statements in political terms, it is easy to see their ethical involvement and sincere effort of reflecting on the issues raised by Ehrlich. Specific classes on such topics might have lead to further comment, though I generally did not stray beyond the terrain of literary analysis. The course was designed as an introduction to the study of travel writing within the framework of anglophone literature rather than a research seminar in which ideological aspects of the text are necessarily of more immediate concern from an epistemological and ethical point of view. Still, all three allowed themselves to be unsettled by the text.

FROSTBITE

Whether the choice of Gretel Ehrlich's text was fortunate is a question the reader can appreciate in the light of the evidence provided. As to the structuring of the course and student assessment, the choice of a reader's report was meant to allow for maximum leeway, not imposing a particular passage or a theme for an essay, which some students arguably might have preferred. It is conceivable at least that some readers are not comfortable with expressing themselves in a more personal mode, at least in a French university, although this was obviously not the case with the reports I have quoted from here. The potential emotional impact of such travel writing is clear. Narratives of travel may move and even perturb readers up to a certain degree, as some of the quotes above illustrate. That Gretel Ehrlich's book was thought-provoking to the degree witnessed here is a happy outcome, even if it cannot always be assured. Intellectual engagement with the ethical dimension of Ehrlich's narrative was also strong, giving rise to stimulating class discussion. I have tried to account for ethical questions that occurred in designing and teaching the course. The subject concerned the Arctic, but what has been pointed out about Arctic discourse also appears applicable more generally when it comes to teaching travel writing, at least as far as my own experience is concerned.

The hermeneutics of travel writing invariably call for reflections on ethics. The form's links with colonial discourse are an obvious case in hand. Gender studies are another, and so are environmental issues, to name but three. Global warming has caused considerable change in the Arctic, opening up new perspectives and destroying others. Greenlanders are currently engaged in major debates about economic development and its corresponding impact on the ecological and social environment. As can be seen above, a more balanced approach to the country's history is needed, as one of Greenland's indigenous leaders suggests, inviting reflection on a range of competing views. Discussion in class should strive to reflect this by considering both prominent voices and those less often heard. It is equally important to read texts in parallel with others, allowing particular remarks to be contextualized while paying attention to the form's generic hybridity. Texts can also be examined from various disciplinary angles such as anthropology, cultural studies, history, language, and literary studies, as well as, among others, philosophy.

In her latest work, Ehrlich voices a concern shared by many today: "Biological and cultural diversity is of the utmost importance. It enables land- and ice-based ecosystems to work. It ignites empathy and the power of the human imagination and functions as a survival tactic: If one language or one crop of berries fails, there are others to choose from."[28] At the risk of appearing polemical, it can only be hoped that those who make decisions regarding language policies and foreign language programs at universities are aware of what is at stake. Be that as it may, the numerous problems Arctic societies have to deal with today involve to a large extent the question of responsibility, notably in cultural, economic, environmental, historical, political, and social terms. "The Arctic will be a new world", Alun Anderson observes, only to add, "An Arctic that freezes over and melts again each year is a completely different place for the creatures and people that live there now. If change happens that fast, it will be the most unimaginable, wrenching challenge for the Arctic's animals, ecosystems, and people."[29] The idea of a new world certainly rings a bell. "History repeats itself" is the maxim we were taught at school. One can only hope that this is not true as far as the Arctic is concerned. Contemporary travel writers on the far north purport to contribute to a heightened awareness of Arctic problems, alerting international readerships like some well-known authors have done in the past. Studies in travel writing certainly have to reflect such ethical concerns to be representative. Arctic studies bring us into contact with worldviews that are not based on anthropocentrism but on a different sense of the relationship between humans and the environment, a different "practice of the wild", to borrow the title of one of Gary Snyder's books. "Nature is not a place to visit", Synder writes, "it is *home*—and within that home territory there are more familiar and less familiar places. Often there are areas that are difficult and remote, but all are *known* and even named."[30]

Every place has a name and its history. Some histories are told more often than others. It is one of travel writing's eminent functions to contribute to a more general understanding, or at least familiarity, with the societies that have remained or been deliberately kept on the margins of world history. The Inuit, like other first nations, invite us to shift our mental maps to more nature-centered views. Ethics is a question of responsibility, as we have seen above; the same is true of writing about travel—and the teaching thereof.

NOTES

1. Albert Schweitzer, *Humanisme et mystique*, selected and presented by Jean-Paul Sorg (Paris: Albin Michel, 1995), p. 470: "L'éthique, c'est la

reconnaissance de notre responsabilité, élargi à l'infini, envers tout ce qui vit."

2. Claude Lévi-Strauss, *Tristes Tropiques* (Paris: Plon, 1955). English translation by John Russell under the same title (New York: Atheneum, 1963).

3. See Jean-Jacques Rousseau's preliminary remarks to *The Confessions* (London: Wordsworth), p. 1.

4. Clifford Geertz, *The Interpretation of Culture* (New York: Basic Books, 1973), p. 9.

5. Clifford Geertz, *Available Light: Anthropological Reflections on Philosophical Topics* (Princeton, NJ: Princeton University Press, 2000), pp. 22–23; hereafter page numbers will be cited parenthetically in the text.

6. Jean Malaurie, *Les Derniers Rois de Thulé: Avec les Esquimaux Polaires face à leur destin* [1955] (Paris: Plon, 1989). English translations: *The Last Kings of Thule: A Year among the Polar Eskimos of Greenland*, trans. Gwendoline Freeman (London: Allen and Unwin, 1956); and *The Last Kings of Thule: With the Polar Eskimos, as They Face Their Destiny*, trans. Adrienne Foulke (London: Jonathan Cape, 1982).

7. Gretel Ehrlich, *This Cold Heaven: Seven Seasons in Greenland* [2001] (New York: Vintage, 2003).

8. Gretel Ehrlich, *In the Empire of Ice: Encounters in a Changing Landscape* (Washington, DC: National Geographic, 2010).

9. On the illusion of trying to write a full or exhaustive account of a field experience, see Walker Evans and James Agee, *Let Us Now Praise Famous Men* (1939). French edition: *Louons maintenant les grands hommes*, trans. Jean Queval [1972] (Paris: Plon, 1993).

10. Since this volume focuses on ethics, my chapter does not devote much attention to the poetics of travel writing, though it is related to ethical issues in certain respects. It may suffice to point out that some epistemological reflections on travel writing and the study thereof were part of the course, though far from being the main focus, since the course was designed as optional, offering students an introduction to the form of travel writing, rather than focusing on literary theory, a domain difficult to approach at length during a BA program in foreign languages, at least from the author's point of view, and dealt with in more depth in my Masters seminar. It was, however, pointed out to students that it is prudent to distinguish between the author and her narrative voice in the account for the purposes of literary analysis.

11. Ehrlich, *This Cold Heaven*, p. 37; hereafter page numbers will be cited parenthetically in the text.

12. An allusion to an essay by Bruce Chatwin titled "The Nomadic Alternative", printed in his posthumous collection *Anatomy of Restlessness* (London: Jonathan Cape, 1996).

13. Aqqaluk Lynge, *The Right to Return: Fifty Years of Struggle by Relocated Inughuit in Greenland* (Nuuk: Forlaget Atuagkat, 2002).

14. Lynge, *The Right to Return*, pp. 9–10.

15. Aqqaluk Lynge, "Introduction", in Hans Egede Saabye, *Journal in Greenland 1770–1778* (Hanover, NH: International Polar Institute Press, 2009), p. 16.

16. Heinz Israel, *Kulturwandel grönländischer Eskimo im 18. Jahrhundert*, Abhandlungen und Berichte des Staatlichen Museums für Völkerkunde Dresden 29 (East Berlin: Akademie-Verlag, 1969).

17. Michael Harbsmeier, ed., *Stimmen aus dem äussersten Norden: Wie die Grönländer Europa für sich entdeckten* (Stuttgart: Jan Thorbeke Verlag, 2001).

18. Barry Lopez, *Arctic Dreams: Imagination and Desire in a Northern Land-scape* [1986] (London: Harvill, 1999).
19. For a comprehensive overview of Arctic problems today, see Alun Anderson, *After the Ice: Life, Death and Politics in the New Arctic* (London: Virgin, 2009).
20. Sara Wheeler, *The Magnetic North: Notes from the Arctic Circle* (London: Jonathan Cape, 2009).
21. Jean Malaurie, *Hummocks: Journeys and Inquiries among the Canadian Inuit*, trans. Peter Feldstein [1999] (Montreal: McGill-Queen's University Press, 2007), p. xi.
22. All three of the students were within the top echelon of the class, and all three have since completed both their BA and MA degrees. Emilie and Sabrina enrolled in our doctoral school; Emilie is working on the voyages of Captain James Cook, Sabrina on representations of the Arabian Peninsula in British travel writing. Mélanie decided to take the French schoolteachers' examination after her MA on the travel writing of Robert Louis Stevenson. I am very grateful to all three students for giving me permission to quote from their work in this chapter.
23. The term *Eskimo* and its potentially problematic use were discussed in class. As we have seen, Jean Malaurie uses it in the preface quoted above. Olejorgen Hammeken has confirmed to me that he personally does not object to the word, but other Inuit take a different stance. As a general guideline, the term *Inuit* appears irreproachable.
24. Idealizing first nations is of course an old theme in literature, a point raised in class. It is not without interest to remember that the only book recommended for reading in Rousseau's *Emile* is Daniel Defoe's *Robinson Crusoe*.
25. *The Friendly Arctic* is one of Vilhjalmur Stefansson's most famous works, published in 1922. In her magnificent monograph *Canada and the Idea of North* (Montreal: McGill-Queen's University Press, 2007), p. 29, Sherrill E. Grace notes about Stefansson's book, "Even in this text, which at times might sound like a monologic rant, Stefansson is *extremely* sensitive to other voices, some of which are quoted directly, some of which are re-presented intertextually and reaccentuated. The final effect of *The Friendly Arctic* is not unlike that of a debate in which the reader is left to listen and decide for himself". Stefansson's Arctic expeditions and his relations with his Inuit "wife" Fanny Pannigabluk have, of course, been the subject of extended debate. For the latter subject, see Gisli Palsson's edition of Stefansson's notebooks *Writing on Ice* (Hanover, NH: University Press of New England, 2001).
26. Aviaaja Lynge, "Mental Decolonization in Greenland", *Inter-Nord* 21 (2011): 273–76.
27. Lynge, "Introduction", pp. 21–22.
28. Gretel Ehrlich, *In the Empire of Ice*, p. 13.
29. Anderson, *After the Ice*, p. 97.
30. Gary Snyder, *The Practice of the Wild* (Emeryville, CA: Shoemaker and Hoard, 1990), p. 7, emphasis in the original.

13 Hauntings
W. G. Sebald as Travel Writer

*Graham Huggan**

Cultural criticism, it has been suggested, is currently going through a "Gothic" period, characterized by an outpouring of often densely theoretical work on trauma, mourning, and various aspects of contemporary late-capitalist "wound culture".[1] "Spectrality", particularly in connection with Jacques Derrida's radically revisionist study *Specters of Marx: The State of the Debt, the Work of Mourning, and the New International* (1994), has become a key term within this Gothicized cultural-critical vocabulary. As Derrida speculates in *Specters of Marx*:

> If there is something like spectrality, there are reasons to doubt . . . the border between the present, the actual or present reality of the present, and everything that can be opposed to it: absence, non-presence, non-effectivity, inactuality, virtuality, or even the simulacrum in general.[2]

Spectrality posits a challenge to an entire metaphysical tradition, belonging to what Derrida punningly calls a surreptitious counterphilosophy of "hauntology".[3] As Bill Spanos, glossing Derrida, puts it, "haunting is fundamentally an ontological condition. Haunting derives from the forgetting of a domain of being . . . which the thinking and the language of the Western tradition, as it is developed in the present technological moment, has obliterated by way of reifying the unsayable."[4] At a less rarefied level, spectrality may be more immediately associated with the ubiquitous figure of the ghost or specter. Ghosts, argues Derrida, are characterized above all by their untimeliness. The anxiety they cause is a function, not just of their general capacity to unsettle us, but also of the temporal uncertainty surrounding their appearance; for if they probably belong to the past, who is to say that they do not belong to the future? As "figures of a lost past", ghosts can easily become vehicles for acute nostalgia; but they are also disconcerting manifestations of the in-between.[5] Neither quite dead nor fully alive, they straddle worlds, simultaneously occupying nominally separate time zones or inhabiting ontologically indeterminate shadow spaces. Ghosts continue to haunt us despite the reparative work of mourning. In this last sense, they can be seen as anticommemorative; for whereas mourning domesticates the past with a view toward eventually exorcising it, ghosts move freely between the past and the present, confronting us against our will.

This chapter asks what role ghosts might have to play in contemporary travel writing. More specifically, it looks at the work of one of the best, and surely one of the strangest, of late twentieth-century travel writers, the German expatriate W. G. Sebald. Sebald's work, combining elements of fiction, (auto)biography, memoir, real and imaginary travel, photography, and history, makes a virtue of its own unclassifiability. Whether it is travel writing or not is moot, but—rather like the work of Sebald's contemporary, Bruce Chatwin—it certainly counts as a contemplative exploration of the *poetics* of travel: a sustained inquiry into the "metaphysics of restlessness" and its motivating influences,[6] as well as an experiment in linked digression and the synchronic dimensions of "spatial form".[7] This poetics is underpinned by a debilitating nostalgia, an at times almost unbearable apprehension of the weight of the past upon the present; and by a hypersensitivity, as well, to the ethical responsibilities attached to a freewheeling textual/intellectual practice marked by fluid movement across a large number of seemingly parallel ontological spaces.

Sebald's writing is haunted in several senses, not just in the most obvious sense that it restlessly shuttles between the realms of the dead and the living, but also insofar as it articulates the anxieties of a traumatic aftermath that contains within it the memory of not one but multiple disintegrated worlds. The Shoah looms large here, particularly in the expansive fictional biography *Austerlitz*, and the intricately structured post-Holocaust requiem *The Emigrants*;[8] but for Sebald, "aftermath" is not so much a reckoning with the specific legacies of historical catastrophe as part of his general vision of a world poised between the calamities of the past and the apocalypse to come.[9] This vision involves the negotiation of a double residue: one through which catastrophe survivors, in recollecting their own painful experiences, also bear witness to friends and family long gone, but whose haunting presence still powerfully remains. In negotiating between these two residues, Sebald takes upon himself, in an elaborate transferential process, both the differentiated traumas of the living and the accumulated burden of the dead. Sebald's entire oeuvre can be seen, in fact, as a deeply poignant, and highly unusual, ghost story: a story in which past and present coalesce, each intruding on the other's consciousness, and in which the writing process may be likened at once to an agonized rehearsal of the memories of the living and to an imaginary communion—at times deliberate, at others involuntary—with the massed ranks of the dead. Sebald's work constitutes, in this sense, a variation on uncanny travel writing, in which the narrating consciousness—who both is and is not the author—roams, with tormented uncertainty, through a half-lit Gothic landscape of ephemeral images, macabre dream visions, eerily duplicated resemblances, and disquieting shadow selves.[10]

Travel, in this context, is perhaps best seen as an unfulfillable penance, in which the traveler-writer, suffering from an incurable condition of "originary displacement",[11] joins himself to a confraternity of lost and restless souls.[12] Travel-as-penance, needless to say, provides rich opportunity for melancholic self-reflection, triggering memories that, together, constitute a vast litany of suffering and loss. Physical travel, under these oppressive conditions, is often excruciatingly slow moving, and runs the risk at times of turning into its own opposite, almost total immobility or paralysis.[13] But it also provides the impetus for astonishing feats of imaginative divagation, so that the boundaries among actual, remembered, and imagined journeys are continually blurred.

Probably the best illustration of this is in Sebald's third book *The Rings of Saturn* (1998, originally published in German in 1995), a characteristically heady blend of fiction, travel, and history loosely based on the author's convalescent wanderings through Suffolk in the late summer of 1992. Two epigraphs to the text, an excerpt from a letter by Joseph Conrad and a dictionary definition of the rings of Saturn, place the book within the context of a latter-day pilgrimage circling around its melancholic subject. Melancholia, indeed, provides the theme and tone for the mental and physical circumnavigations that follow, which involve—as to some extent in Sebald's other books—the unremittingly lugubrious traveler's concerted efforts to surround himself with the places, objects, and people that most resemble himself.[14]

Melancholia, like nostalgia, on which it often draws, is perhaps best seen as a "disease of the afflicted imagination",[15] in which memory becomes, overpoweringly, "a source of unhappiness and perturbed consciousness" and a "burden of remorse".[16] Melancholia is always incomplete and unfulfilled; it is a kind of "eternalization of pensiveness" that feeds incessantly on its own accumulated sorrows.[17] The work of the melancholic text, similarly, is never finished, embodying a strand of "exiled modern thought which, having no [other] option, is continually propelled forward, never ceasing its mulling over of things".[18] According to the literary theorist Ross Chambers, the melancholy condition is almost always physically debilitating; but it may also be imaginatively stimulating, since melancholy points both to the capacity of memory to hang heavy on the conscience, inducing physical torpor, and to the fertility of associative memory, its uncanny ability to create an imaginary kinship between seemingly disparate things.[19] This ability points to the protean character of melancholy, captured in Julia Kristeva's felicitous phrase "melancholic jouissance".[20] Max Pensky, likewise, in his book on the German philosopher-critic Walter Benjamin— one of several literary ghosts to (re)appear in Sebald's pages[21]—sketches out the lineaments of Benjamin's melancholy dialectics, its availability as a "source of critical reflection that . . . empowers the subject with a mode of insight into the structure of the real at the same time as it consigns the subject to mournfulness, misery, and despair".[22] Melancholic reflection thus becomes, as Pensky claims for his exemplary subject Benjamin, both a potential route to secret knowledge and a perpetual reminder of "the impossibility of recovering what was lost".[23]

The Rings of Saturn serves as an excellent example of the workings of melancholy dialectics. The narrator's wanderings are underpinned by a dark, distinctly Borgesian, premonition that the "real" world is dying, to be replaced inexorably by the secondary and tertiary worlds of the imagination.[24] Similarly, the present is receding, revealing beneath its fading colours the much more extravagant—often extravagantly violent—narratives and images of the past. These competing narratives and images merge with dreams and elaborate flights of fancy, attesting to melancholic writing's combination of physical lassitude and imaginative excess. Both qualities are projected in the text onto a succession of forlorn, if hardly empty, East Anglian land- and seascapes, creating a marked contrast between the "waning splendour" (p. 37) of modern England and its hyperanimated past. As in other Sebald works, an atmosphere of gloominess and "encroaching misery" is created through linked images of dereliction (p. 42), and by the author's spectrally indistinctive photographs, which back up the apocalyptic foreboding—again taken from Jorge Luis Borges—that "life is no more than the fading reflection of an event beyond recall", and that "time [itself] has run its course" (p. 154). The narrator's feeling of alienation is only increased by the affinities he nurtures with his past and present interlocutors. These belong to a wider pattern of Baudelairean *correspondances* in Sebald's fiction, which often creates disconcerting parallels between the life of the narrator and his imagined precursors (pp. 182, 187). In particular, the narrator's ventriloquistic "conversations" with his eclectic band of literary forebears—Sir Thomas Browne, Joseph Conrad, François-René Chateaubriand, Algernon Charles Swinburne, and several others—create the unnerving impression that, in willingly absorbing his own experience into the lives of others, he is performing a "colloquy with the dead" (p. 200).

The phantom presences of others, allied to a series of uncanny experiences of "ghostly repetition" (p. 187), contribute to a feeling of bewilderment and insubstantiality, as if the narrator himself belonged to a different time and space; as if he himself were a ghost speaking from somewhere beyond the grave (p. 255). This pattern is repeated, with the insistence of an idée fixe, in Sebald's other fictions, particularly in the early travelogue-cum-psychoanalytic-case-study-cum-metaphysical detective story *Vertigo* (1999, first published in German in 1990). *Vertigo*, like *The Rings of Saturn*, plays skilfully between memory and imagination, making it clear that each serves the other, but sometimes in ways that produce "a vertiginous sense of confusion" by which the traveler-writer risks becoming "undone".[25] Also as in *The Rings of Saturn*, memory mediates between real and imaginary worlds to create a cross-hatched narrative of suffering—a martyrology of sorts, in which the traveler-writer allows or, perhaps better, invites himself to be haunted by the various places he has visited, the books he has read, and the people he has met. Many of these people appear alarmingly to share his own afflictions: melancholia, depression, pathological nostalgia, and a creeping anxiety that sometimes escalates into full-blown paranoia and panic attack. Travel, in this context, becomes an outlet for the mass projections of neurosis, as even holiday revelers in Italy, absurdly likened to zombies, are made to appear inconsolably morose (p. 93).

Uncanny travel writing, meanwhile, is taken to its own preposterous limits, with multiply duplicated journeys, a succession of ominous doppel-gängers and impostors, and a wide range of other Gothic motifs supporting the narrator's (and the world's) imagined path to "gradual destruction" (p. 63). All roads appear to lead to death, and the traveler imagines his whole life to have been predestined, his every journey to be cursed. In this manner, the text establishes a semiosis of the haunted imagination, suffused with conspiratorial portents of impending disaster, in which travel becomes but the interregnum between one calamity and another, and the traveler-writer is propelled toward the apocalyptic conclusion that "history is now nearing its close" (p. 133). Religious (leit)motifs freely scattered throughout the text—exterminating angels, martyred saints, devil figures, all taken from a grotesquely overexercised Catholic imaginary—provide further warnings of this rapidly approaching apocalypse, convincing the fearful traveler-writer of the catastrophe that awaits him, and of "the torments and travails that await us all" (p. 224). A hallucinatory vocabulary thus builds up, culminating in a vivid dream vision, brought on by reading Samuel Pepys's diary, of the Great Fire of London: a calamity to end all calamities, and a foreshadowing, perhaps, of "the end of time" itself (p. 262).

To a greater extent than *The Rings of Saturn*, *Vertigo* parodies the conventions of the Gothic, producing an operatic vision of the past that is frequently appalling, but just as frequently absurd (p. 212). Childhood fears and phobias, magnified over time, conjure up a rogue's gallery of dangerous assassins and vaguely threatening spectral figures, while places—Vienna, Venice, Padua, Verona, Sebald's own home village in southern Germany—take on the aura of almost interchangeable ghost towns, inflected and infected by the narrator's all-consuming fantasies and fears. The narrator is haunted, likewise, by the specters of European literature, who operate throughout as "ghostly shadow[s] of his own restlessness" (p. 152). In one way or another, these literary figures—Stendhal, Flaubert, Grillparzer, Kafka—all come across as being afflicted, either by a degenerative condition of extreme melancholy and depression or by a hyperactive imagination acutely given over to representations of suffering and distress. The portrayal of Kafka ("Dr. K"), in particular, gives credence to Svetlana Boym's wry historical observation that nostalgia, at least in the minds of many of those who believed they suffered it, often "shared some symptoms with melancholia and hypochondria".[26] This neuralgic combination, while it sometimes provided a stimulus to artistic creativity, often proved to be incurable.[27] Certainly, Dr. K, like several other doctor-figures, real and imaginary, in Sebald's work, proves ineptly unable to heal himself; while in a further recurring pattern, the place of convalescence metamorphoses into a place of death, another of Sebald's ubiquitous mortuary sites.

The deeper structure embedded in the text, and within the greater body of Sebald's work, belongs to the topography of elegy. "Lieux de mémoire"[28]—churchyards, battlefields, dilapidated houses and hotels, ghost towns—double as "lieux de mort", offering plangent reminders of the inevitability not just of death but of prolonged earthly suffering. This pattern is at its most apparent in what is probably Sebald's best-known work, *The Emigrants* (1997, first published in German in 1992). In it, the narrator imaginatively retraces the journeys of four German Jews in exile. These journeys create a densely cross-referenced emigrants' trail that winds its way across Europe, the Middle East, and North America, with touchstone locations in the decayed cities of Manchester and Jerusalem, the one presented as a now hollow "miracle [industrial] city",[29] the other as a crumbling sacred site. These places, and others like them, create a haunting atmosphere of semiruin that corresponds to, while always threatening to unravel, the narrator's affectionate reassemblage of the fragments of his subjects' largely forgotten lives. These subjects—a doctor, a teacher, a painter, and the narrator's own great-uncle—are all, like the narrator himself, highly gifted but inconsolably melancholic misfits whose lives are touched with sadness and over whom the shadow of death is described as hovering "like a bird in flight".[30] These figures function, to some extent, as the narrator's intimately imagined travel companions; they are also his physical/spiritual guides, conducting him through a variety of uncannily familiar landscapes, allowing him to reinhabit and be reinhabited by the haunting spirit of place.

Travel, in this context, becomes both a reminder of the condition of originary displacement and a desire for death as an entry point into other, partly or wholly imaginary, spaces.[31] In both cases, memory is the vehicle through which the dead are brought into concert with the living, and through which an imaginative geography that combines the intersecting worlds of the past, present, and future can be explored. Memory, however, as elsewhere in Sebald's work, is as likely to prove debilitating as enabling. As the narrator muses at one point:

> Memory . . . often strikes me as a kind of dumbness. It makes one's head heavy and giddy, as if one were not looking back down the receding perspective of time but rather down from the earth from a great height, from one of those towers whose tops are lost to view in the clouds.[32]

At times like these, memory provides a source of momentary disorientation. At others, it is a source of lasting pain, as when the narrator, in rehearsing the recollected thoughts and writings of others, creates the pathological conditions under which the pain of separation, intensifying over time, conveys an impression of repeated or multiplied loss.

Sebald's (partly) Proustian deliberation into the uncanny effect of time on place and the transpositional effects of involuntary memory is informed by two main conceptions of temporality. The first of these is open-ended time, in which there is no clear dividing line between past, present, and future;[33] the second is apocalyptic time, in which an accretion of past and present experience apparently confirms a process of inexorable decline.[34] Both of these conceptions underscore a general apprehension of untimeliness, further reinforced by shared nostalgia and by the distinctly anachronistic language of the narrator, whose contemplations and dream visions are expressed in elegantly circuitous, archaically gentlemanly prose.[35] Illustrations and photographs, meanwhile, establish a visual counterpart to untimeliness, either by creating an uncanny geography in which topographical images, dispersed across time, carry the burden of resemblance, or by accumulating images of decay (disused factories, semiderelict hotels, abandoned gardens, etc.) in what amounts to an iconography of desolation and despair. The individual memories these images evoke overpower and paralyze the senses, confirming the painter Max Ferber's darkly melodramatic view of time itself as "nothing but a disquiet of the soul".[36] Collective memories, similarly, contribute to a mood of paralyzing anguish, in which the active desire to remember is overshadowed by the countervailing need to extinguish the pain of memory—to forget.[37]

By verbal and visual means such as these, Sebald's book works toward establishing an open-ended genealogy of representations that creates the impression of a merging of different consciousnesses, of voices drifting over time. The operating principle, as elsewhere in his work, is one of cumulative haunting. The "spectrality" of the text is an effect of a superimposition of ghostly representations: its pictorial equivalent is Ferber's palimpsestic portraits which, obsessively reworked, contain within them the memories of previous creations, each portrait in itself a gallery of "ancestral faces".[38] Ferber himself is something of a ghost: an indeterminate presence hidden in the shadows of his gloomy studio or, "walk[ing] about amidst [Manchester's] immense and time-blackened nineteenth-century buildings", a shadowy descendant of Benjamin's quintessentially melancholic flâneur.[39]

Meanwhile, Ferber is haunted, in turn, by his memories of Germany, a country "frozen in the past, destroyed, a curiously extraterritorial place, inhabited by people whose faces are both lovely and dreadful".[40] As one might expect from an expatriate with an at best ambivalent relation to the country from which he fled, and to which he returns with obvious trepidation, the unquiet ghosts of the German past are everywhere in Sebald's fiction: in translated Holocaust testimony (*Austerlitz*); in grisly photographic histories of war and transferred visual/verbal metaphors of the concentration camps (*The Rings of Saturn*); in neglected memorial sites such as the overgrown Jewish cemetery in Kissingen (*The Emigrants*); in abundant family archives—letters, diaries, journals, photo albums—that recall better days but always carry within them the hint of future destruction (*The Emigrants*); and in Sebald's sleepy home village of "W.", in which childhood memories become entangled with hallucinatory visions of apocalypse, producing a surreal "chronicle of calamities" in which history merges imperceptibly with myth and legend, and the narrator's obsessive cataloging of death and human suffering hovers somewhere between the unbearably poignant and the patently absurd (*Vertigo*).[41]

These oppressive recollections, far from demonstrating the allegedly healing power of mourning, contribute to a melancholic's heightened awareness of his own entrapment within a self-perpetuating cycle of sorrow, pain, and failure. As Chambers suggests, referring to the "melancholic writing" of the French Symbolist poet Charles Baudelaire:

> Memory is . . . a double or even triple source of painful self-consciousness, since the remembrance of lack and loss is accompanied by the burden of an obsessive sense of irreparable failure, as well as by a lightness of being, a sense of fragmentation and dispersion of identity, that makes one feel like a living residue.[42]

Chambers's diagnosis of Baudelaire's writing also fits Sebald's very well: from its identification of the repeated suffering caused by memory, to the melancholic's paralyzing sense of failure, to the dizzyingly fractured identity of the narrating consciousness, scattered and split between a host of real/imaginary surrogate selves. Above all, Sebald's writing is characterized by its intense, though at times also playful, contemplation of a series of linked residual states operating under the sign of the spectral. The writing "travels" between these already volatile states, moving back and forth not so much between as among the multiply intersecting worlds of the present and the past, the living and the dead.

Travel can be considered, in this last sense, as an exploration of extreme states of ontological confusion; it creates an irresolvable uncertainty about who one is, where one belongs, or even whether one is "in the land of the living or already another place".[43] At the same time, travel expresses the desire for a release from the eternal repetitions (what Derrida might call the "frequentations") of the spectral.[44] This desire is perhaps best captured in a characteristically cryptic Kafka parable that (re)appears as a leitmotif in *Vertigo*. In the tale, Gracchus the huntsman falls one day to his death, but is subsequently unable to complete the "journey beyond" that might lay his soul to rest. As a consequence, he turns into a ghost who "has been voyaging the seas ever since, without respite . . . attempting now here now there to make land".[45] According to the narrator, "the meaning of Gracchus the huntsman's ceaseless journey lies in a penitence for a longing for love . . . precisely at the point where there is seemingly, and in the natural and lawful order of things, nothing to be enjoyed".[46] This unsubstantiated longing—call it nostalgia—appears to be the greatest impulse behind the narrator's own tormented travels in *Vertigo*; and perhaps, by a risky corollary, we might conclude that it is the main impulse behind Sebald's melancholic travel texts. Nostalgia is the afflictive condition of the restless soul, "possessed by a mania of longing".[47] Travel, Sebald suggests, merely confirms the shared pain of worldly entrapment; while nostalgia, signaling the desire for travel to "other" worlds, ultimately registers a longing for the journey to end all journeys, the "journey beyond". A strange kind of travel writing, this, that is always looking to eradicate the conditions of its own existence. But such is the geography of desire in Sebald's haunted fictions. If haunting can be seen as an iterative function of the unfinished work of mourning,[48] Sebald's travel writing articulates a desire to have that process end, to find a time (out of time) and a place (beyond place) where the haunting might cease. Yet this desire is acknowledged, at the same time, as being essentially unfulfillable. Hence the narrator's melancholia, his contrary desire for further haunting;[49] and hence his aching, inevitably unanswered, question: "And how are we to fend off the fate of being unable to depart this life?"[50]

NOTES

* This chapter is reprinted with permissions. Graham Huggan, *Extreme Pursuits: Travel/Writing in an Age of Globalization* (The University of Michigan Press: Ann Arbor, 2009, pp. 137–47).
1. Gail Jones, "Mourning, Australian Culture, and the Stolen Generation", in Judith Ryan and Chris Wallace-Crabbe, eds., *Imagining Australia* (Cambridge, MA: Harvard University Press, 2004), pp. 159–71. See also Dominick LaCapra, *Representing the Holocaust: History, Theory, Trauma* (Ithaca, NY: Cornell University Press, 1994).
2. Jacques Derrida, *Specters of Marx: The State of Debt, the Work of Mourning, and the New International*, trans. Peggy Kamuf (New York: Routledge, 1994), p. 39.
3. Derrida, *Specters of Marx*; see also Michael Sprinker, ed., *Ghostly Demarcations: A Symposium on Jacques Derrida's Specters of Marx* (London: Verso, 1999).
4. William Spanos, "Bill Spanos in Conversation", with Robert Kroetsch and Dawn McCance, *Mosaic* 34, no. 4 (2001): 1–19.
5. Derrida, *Specters of Marx*; Julia Briggs, *Night Visitors: The Rise and Fall of the English Ghost Story* (London: Faber, 1997).
6. Bruce Chatwin, quoted in Patrick Holland and Graham Huggan, *Tourists with Typewriters: Critical Reflections on Contemporary Travel Writing* (Ann Arbor: University of Michigan Press, 1998).
7. See Joseph Frank, *The Widening Gyre: Crisis and Mastery in Modern Literature* (New Brunswick, NJ: Rutgers University Press, 1963). In this famous 1963 essay, Frank notes that the spatialization of form in the modern novel creates the impression of synchronicity, of "simultaneous activity occurring in different places" (p. 17). Synchronicity is a common feature of Chatwin's and Sebald's work, often being allied, particularly in Sebald's, to an uncanny chain of coincidences (see, especially, *Vertigo*). Synchronicity is counterbalanced, however, by an equally strong awareness of untimeliness. Probably the most startling apprehension of untimeliness in Sebald's work is in the following lengthy passage in *Austerlitz*: "It does not seem to me . . . that we understand the laws governing the return of the past, but I feel more and more as if time did not exist at all, only various spaces interlocking according to the rules of a higher form of stereometry, between which the living and the dead can move back and forth as they like, and the longer I think about it the more it seems to me that we who are still alive are unreal in the eyes of the

dead, that only occasionally, in certain lights and atmospheric conditions, do we appear in their field of vision. As far as I can remember . . . I have always felt as if I had no place in reality, as if I were not there at all." W. G. Sebald, *Austerlitz*, trans. Anthea Bell [1999] (New York: Random House, 2001), p. 261. Other interesting parallels between Chatwin's and Sebald's work include their exoticist fascination with arcane knowledge, etymology, the history of art, and the social life of museum/antiquarian relics; their exploration of the metaphysical dimensions, as well as material conditions, of expatriation and exile; their romantic sympathy with the underdog and their attempt to rehabilitate the lives of the unjustly forgotten, the self-acknowledged failures, the oppressed; their highly developed sense of the "literariness" of travel and the tradition of the *voyage imaginaire*; and their use of modernist (not postmodernist) techniques of symbolic association. This is not to deny the many obvious differences between these two highly gifted, and undoubtedly idiosyncratic, writers, neither of whom would have been likely to call himself a "travel writer". It is rather to stress that both are working within well-known conventions of travel writing—especially the conventions attached to the "literary traveler"—that make their work possibly less original than it might appear at first sight.

8. W. G. Sebald, *The Emigrants*, trans. Michael Hulse [1992] (London: Harvill, 1997).

9. W. G. Sebald, *The Rings of Saturn*, trans. Michael Hulse [1995] (London: Harvill, 1998). W. G. Sebald, *Vertigo*, trans. Michael Hulse [1990] (London: Harvill Press, 1999).

10. Much of Sebald's work resonates with Sigmund Freud's, particularly the well-known essay "Mourning and Melancholia", in *The Standard Edition of the Complete Psychological Works of Sigmund Freud*, vol. 14, ed. and trans. James Strachey [1915] (London: Hogarth, 1957), pp. 243–58; and "The Uncanny", in *The Standard Edition of the Complete Psychological Works of Sigmund Freud* [1919], vol. 17, ed. and trans. James Strachey (London: Hogarth, 1955), pp. 217–52. Sebald's associative style also draws on Freudian techniques—e.g., those used in *The Interpretation of Dreams*—and it is certainly tempting to see works like *Vertigo* and *The Rings of Saturn*, in which the narrator's neuroses are writ large, as extended case studies. Sebald stops short, however, of deploying a full-blown Freudian vocabulary, and it is often his deliberately anachronistic (pre-Freudian) treatment of mental illness that comes to the fore.

11. Dennis Porter, *Haunted Journeys: Desire and Transgression in European Travel Writing* (Princeton, NJ: Princeton University Press, 1991).

12. Sebald, *The Emigrants*, p. 67. For a more detailed analysis of "originary displacement", and its connection to the phenomenon of the "haunted journey", see Porter, *Haunted Journeys*, especially the chapter on Naipaul.

13. See, for example, Sebald, *The Rings of Saturn*, p. 3; Sebald, *The Emigrants*, p. 115.

14. Sebald's landscape and architectural photographs, in particular, are a sustained exercise in the objective correlative, the romantic melancholics's attempt to find Baudelaire's "un paysage qui [lui] ressemble".

15. Svetlana Boym, *The Future of Nostalgia* (New York: Basic Books, 2001), p. 4.

16. Ross Chambers, *The Writing of Melancholy: Modes of Opposition in Early French Modernism*, trans. Mary Seidman Trouville (Chicago: University of Chicago Press, 1987), p. 31. For a distinction between "private" melancholia and "public" nostalgia, see also Boym, *The Future of Nostalgia*, p. xvi.

17. Chambers, *The Writing of Melancholy*, p. 169.

18. Chambers, *The Writing of Melancholy*, p. 173.
19. Chambers, *The Writing of Melancholy*, pp. 166–69.
20. Julia Kristeva, *Black Sun: Depression and Melancholia* (New York: Columbia University Press, 1989).
21. Sebald, *Austerlitz*, pp. 59–60.
22. Max Pensky, *Melancholy Dialectics: Walter Benjamin and the Play of Mourning* (Amherst: University of Massachusets Press, 1993).
23. Pensky, *Melancholy Dialectics*, p. 19.
24. Sebald, *Saturn*, pp. 68–71; hereafter page numbers will be cited parenthetically in the text.
25. Sebald, *Vertigo*, 17, 15; hereafter page numbers will be cited parenthetically in the text.
26. Boym, *Future of Nostalgia*, 5.
27. Boym, *Future of Nostalgia*, pp. 5–6.
28. Pierre Nora, "Between Memory and History: Les Lieux de Mémoire", *Representations* 26 (1989): 7–25.
29. Sebald, *The Emigrants*, p. 151.
30. Sebald, *The Emigrants*, p. 63.
31. Sebald, *The Emigrants*, p. 46.
32. Sebald, *The Emigrants*, p. 145.
33. Sebald, *The Emigrants*, p. 207.
34. Sebald, *The Emigrants*, p. 137. Sebald's indebtedness to Marcel Proust is obvious, although the great French writer, perhaps surprisingly, is not given a cameo appearance in Sebald's pages. Analogies can certainly be made between Proust's and Sebald's sinuous syntax, their carefully managed detours and divagations, and between both authors' enormously wide-ranging efforts to investigate, through the multiple transpositions of memory, the uncanny effect of time on place. A crucial distinction, however, is between Proust's "optimistic" conception of time as, in the critic Malcolm Bowie's words, "a connection-making and irrepressible potentiality" (Malcolm Bowie, *Proust among the Stars*, New York: Columbia University Press, 1998, p. 64), and Sebald's "pessimistic" view of irreversibly degenerative historical processes and his apparently unredemptive foreshadowing of the apocalyptic "end of time" itself.
35. It is worth noting that all of Sebald's works were originally written in German, nominally his native language, even though his literary reputation seems to be notably higher in the English-speaking world than it is in the country he left behind several decades ago. Michael Hulse's superb translations not only capture the anachronism of Sebald's mannered language but also the atmosphere of untimeliness he wishes to create, which, despite his work's wealth of historical references, is curiously unanchored from any specific time or place.
36. Sebald, *The Emigrants*, p. 181.
37. Sebald, *The Emigrants*, p. 114. On the connections between memory and amnesia, see Andreas Huyssen, *Twilight Memories: Marking Time in a Culture of Amnesia* (London: Routledge, 1995); see also LaCapra, *Representing the Holocaust*.
38. Sebald, *The Emigrants*, p. 161.
39. Sebald, *The Emigrants*, p. 156. See also Rob Shields, "Fancy Footwork: Walter Benjamin's Notes on Flânerie", in *The Flâneur,* ed. Keith Tester (London: Routledge, 1994), pp. 61–80.
40. Sebald, *The Emigrants*, p. 181.
41. Sebald, *Vertigo*, p. 240.
42. Chambers, *The Writing of Melancholy*, p. 32.
43. Sebald, *Vertigo*, p. 15.

44. As Derrida points out, ghosts cause anxiety, not only because they appear to watch us (like the sawn-off portraits in *Vertigo*, some reduced to eyes which implacably stare down the viewer) but, because they do so repeatedly. The spectral, in fact, is an effect of repetition: an effect well captured in Sebald's work, where ghostly figures, sometimes linked in groups, either drift in and out of or semipermanently hover behind the text. Some of these figures are actively conjured by the narrator, others intrude against his will. The "spectrality" of Sebald's work arguably consists, however, less in the frequency with which ghosts appear or the specific conditions governing their appearance than in the general uncertainty they raise over the passage, or even the nature, of time (as in the narrator's perception of himself as a ghost).
45. Sebald, *Vertigo*, p. 165.
46. Sebald, *Vertigo*, p. 165.
47. Boym, *Future of Nostalgia*, p. 4.
48. Derrida, *Specters*, p. 94.
49. Michael Ignatieff, "The Metaphysics of Restlessness," *Granta* 21 (1987): pp. 23–37.
50. Sebald, *Vertigo*, p. 167.

Bibliography

Abley, Mark. *Spoken Here: Travels among Threatened Languages*. London: Heinemann, 2001.

Adams, Percy G. *Travelers and Travel Liars, 1660–1800*. Berkeley and Los Angeles: University of California Press, 1962.

Adams, William Mark. *Green Development: Environment and Sustainability in a Developing World*. 3rd ed. London: Routledge, 2008.

Alecsandri, Vasile. "Balta Albă". In *Calendarul Albinei* (1848). Cited in Vasile Alecsandri, *Proza*, edited by George C. Nicolescu. Bucharest: Literatură, 1966.

Alexandrescu, Sorin. *Identitate în ruptură*. Bucharest: Univers, 2000.

Anderson, Alun. *After the Ice: Life, Death and Politics in the New Arctic*. London: Virgin, 2009.

Anderson, Perry. "Persian Letters". In *The Novel*, edited by Franco Moretti. Princeton, NJ: Princeton University Press, 2006, vol. 2, pp. 161–72.

Antohi, Sorin. *Imaginaire culturel et réalité politique dans la Roumanie moderne*. Trans. Claude Karnoouh and Moni Antohi. Paris: L'Harmattan, 1999.

Apostolopoulos, Yorghos, and Dennis Gayle. "From MIRAB to TOURAB? Searching for Sustainable Development in the Maritime Caribbean, Pacific, and Mediterranean". In *Island Tourism and Sustainable Development: Caribbean, Pacific, and Mediterranean Experiences*, edited by Yiorgos Apostolopoulos and Dennis John Gayle. Westport, CT: Praeger, 2002, pp. 3–14.

Appadurai, Arjun, ed. *The Social Life of Things: Commodities in Cultural Perspective*. Cambridge: Cambridge University Press, 1986.

Appiah, Kwame Anthony. *Cosmopolitanism: Ethics in a World of Strangers*. London: Allen Lane, 2006.

Arrington, Melvin. "Untitled review of *They Built Utopia*, by Frederick J. Reiter". *Hispania* 80, no. 1 (1997): 71–72.

Ashcroft, Bill. *On Post-colonial Futures: Transformations of Colonial Culture*. London: Continuum, 2001.

Augustinos, Olga. *French Odysseys: Greece in French Travel Literature from the Renaissance to the Romantic Era*. Baltimore: Johns Hopkins University Press, 1994.

Aurégan, Pierre. *Des récits et des hommes—Terre Humaine: un autre regard sur les sciences de l'homme*. Paris: Nathan, 2001.

Baidaff, L. "Note marginale la 'Istoria' lui Carra 1777–1779". *Universul literar* 43, no. 2 (1927): 21–23.

Baldacchino, Godfrey. "Islands, Island Studies, Island Studies Journal". *Island Studies Journal* 1, no. 1 (2006): 3–18.

Barker, Francis, Peter Hulme, Margaret Iversen, and Diana Loxley, eds. *The Politics of Theory: Proceedings of the Essex Sociology of Literature Conference*. Colchester: University of Essex, 1982.

Baudrillard, Jean. *America*. [1986] Trans. Chris Turner. London: Verso, 1988.
Baudrillard, Jean. *Baudrillard Live: Selected Interviews*, edited by Mike Gane. London: Routledge, 1993.
Baudrillard, Jean. *The Evil Demon of Images*. Trans. Paul Patton. Sydney: Power Institute, 1987.
Baudrillard, Jean. *Fatal Strategies: Revenge of the Crystal*. Trans. Philip Beitchman and W.G.J. Niesluchowski. New York: Semiotext(e), 1990.
Baudrillard, Jean. *The Gulf War Did Not Take Place*. Trans. Paul Patton. Bloomington: Indiana University Press, 1995.
Baudrillard, Jean. *The Illusion of the End*. Trans. Chris Turner. London: Polity, 1995.
Baudrillard, Jean. *The Perfect Crime*. Trans. Chris Turner. New York: Verso, 1999.
Baudrillard, Jean. *Symbolic Exchange and Death*. Trans. Iain Hamilton Grant. London: Sage, 1993.
Baudrillard, Jean. *The Vital Illusion*. Ed. Julia Witwer. New York: Columbia University Press, 2000.
Baudrillard, Jean, and Sylvère Lotringer. "Forgetting Baudrillard" (interview). *Social Text* 15 (1986): 140–41.
Bauman, Zygmunt. *Legislators and Interpreters: On Modernity, Post-modernity and Intellectuals*. Cambridge: Polity, 1987.
Bawr, General. *Mémoires historiques et géographiques sur la Valachie*. Frankfurt, 1778.
Behar, Ruth, and Deborah A. Gordon, eds. *Women Writing Culture*. Berkeley and Los Angeles: University of California Press, 1995.
Bellaigue, Christopher de. *Rebel Land: Unraveling the Riddle of History in a Turkish Town*. London: Penguin, 2011.
Bentham, Jeremy. "Letter to William Eaton, 8 January 1786". In *Correspondence*, edited by I. R. Christie. London: Athlone Press, 1971, vol. 3, p. 437.
Berindei, Da. *Românii şi Europa*. Bucharest: Museion, 1991.
Bernstein, Susan D. "Ape Anxiety: Sensation Fiction, Evolution and the Genre Question". *Journal of Victorian Culture* 6 (2001): 250–71.
Berza, Mihai. "Turcs, Empire Ottoman et relations roumano-turques dans l'historiographie moldave des XV–XVII siècles". *Revue des etudes sud-est européennes* 10, no. 3 (1972): 595–627.
Bhabha, Homi K. *The Location of Culture*. [1994] London: Routledge, 2010.
Billig, Michael. *Laughter and Ridicule: Towards a Social Critique of Humour*. London: Sage, 2010.
Boddy, Kassia. "The European Journey in Postwar American Fiction and Film". In *Voyages and Visions: Toward a Cultural History of Travel*, edited by Jas Elsner and Joan-Pau Rubies. London: Reaktion, 1999, pp. 237–51.
Bodio, Stephen J. *Eagle Dreams: Searching for Legends in Wild Mongolia*. Guilford: Lyons, 2003.
Bongie, Chris. *Exotic Memories: Literature, Colonialism and the Fin de Siècle*. Stanford, CA: Stanford University Press, 1991.
Bouillier, Henry. *Victor Segalen*. [1961] Paris: Mercure de France, 1986.
Bourdain, Anthony. *A Cook's Tour: In Search of the Perfect Meal*. London: Bloomsbury, 2002.
Bouvier, Nicolas. *Le Poisson-Scorpion*. Lausanne: Éditions 24 heures, 1990.
Bouvier, Nicolas. *L'Usage du Monde*. Paris: Payot, 1992.
Bouvier, Nicolas. *The Way of the World*. Marlboro, VT: Marlboro, 1992.
Bowie, Malcolm. *Proust among the Stars*. New York: Columbia University Press, 1998.
Boym, Svetlana. *Common Places: Mythologies of Everyday Life in Russia*. Cambridge, MA: Harvard University Press, 1994.

Boym, Svetlana. *The Future of Nostalgia*. New York: Basic Books, 2001.

Bracewell, Wendy, ed. *Orientations: An Anthology of East European Travel Writing*. Budapest: CEU Press, 2009.

Briggs, Julia. *Night Visitors: The Rise and Fall of the English Ghost Story*. London: Faber, 1997.

Brown, Karen McCarthy. *Mama Lola: A Voodoo Priestess in Brooklyn*. Berkeley and Los Angeles: University of California Press, 1991.

Bruner, Edward M. *Culture on Tour: Ethnographies of Travel*. Chicago: University of Chicago Press, 2005.

Buell, Lawrence. "Introduction: In Pursuit of Ethics". *PMLA* 114 (1999): 7–19.

Burns, Peter M. "Social Identities and the Cultural Politics of Tourism". In *Tourism and Social Identities: Global Frameworks and Local Realities*, edited by Peter M. Burns and Marina Novelli. Oxford: Elsevier, 2006, pp. 13–39.

Butcher, Jim. *The Moralisation of Tourism: Sun, Sand . . . and Saving the World?* London: Routledge, 2003.

Buzard, James. *The Beaten Track: European Tourism, Literature, and the Ways to "Culture": 1800–1918*. Oxford: Clarendon, 1993.

Cabezas, Amalia L. *Economies of Desire: Sex Tourism in Cuba and the Dominican Republic*. Philadelphia: Temple University Press, 2009.

Calarco, Matthew. "Thinking through Animals: Reflections on the Ethical and Political Stakes of the Question of the Animal in Derrida". *Oxford Literary Review* 29 (2008): 1–16.

Călători străini despre țările române. 10 vols. Bucharest: Romanian Academy, 1968–2001. New series, 6 vols. Bucharest: Romanian Academy, 2004–10.

Călinescu, George. *History of Romanian Literature*. Milan: NAGARD, 1982.

Carra, Jean-Louis. *Histoire*. Jassy: Société Typographique des Deux-Ponts, 1777.

Carrigan, Anthony. "'Hotels are Squatting on My Metaphors': Tourism, Sustainability, and Sacred Space in the Caribbean". *Journal of Commonwealth and Postcolonial Studies* 13, no. 2 and 14, no. 1 (2006–7): 59–82.

Carrigan, Anthony. *Postcolonial Tourism: Literature, Culture, and Environment*. London: Routledge, 2011.

Carrigan, Anthony. "Preening with Privilege, Bubbling Bilge: Representations of Cruise Tourism in Paule Marshall's *Praisesong for the Widow* and Derek Walcott's *Omeros*". *ISLE: Interdisciplinary Studies in Literature and Environment* 14, no. 1 (2007): 143–59.

Carver, Robert. *Paradise with Serpents: Travels in the Lost World of Paraguay*. London: Harper Perennial, 2007.

Cernovodeanu, Paul. "Contributions to Lord Paget's Journey in Wallachia and Transylvania". *Revue des études sud-est européennes* 11, no. 2 (1973): 275–85.

Chalk, Peter. "Liberation Tigers of Tamil Eelam's (LTTE) International Organization and Operations: A Preliminary Analysis". *Commentary* 77 (1999) <www.fas.org/irp/world/para/docs/com77e.htm> .

Chambers, Ross. *The Writing of Melancholy: Modes of Opposition in Early French Modernism*. Chicago: University of Chicago Press, 1987.

Chatwin, Bruce. "The Nomadic Alternative". In *Anatomy of Restlessness*. London: Jonathan Cape, 1996, pp. 13–20.

Chi, Robert. "Toward a New Tourism: Albert Wendt and Becoming Attractions". *Cultural Critique* 37 (1997): 61–105.

Chishull, Edmund. "Un călător englez necunoscut în România la 1702". Translated by Caterina Piteșteanu. *Buletinul Societății Regale Române de geografie* 41 (1922): 280–81.

Chishull, Edmund. *Travels in Turkey and Back to England*. London, 1747.

Choi, HwanSuk Chris, and Ercan Sirakay. "Sustainability Indicators for Managing Community Tourism". *Tourism Management* 27, no. 6 (2006): 1274–89.

Ciobanu, Veniamin. "Imagini ale străinului în cronici din Moldova şi Ţara Românească (secolul XVIII)". In *Identitate/alteritate în spaţiul românesc*, edited by Alexandru Zub. Iaşi: Universitatea A. I. Cuza, 1996, pp. 57–64.

Cioranescu, Alexander. "Le Serdar Gheorghe Saul et sa polémique avec J. L. Carra". *Societas Academica Daco-Romana. Acta historica* 5 (1966): 33–71.

Cipăianu, George. "Opţiunea occidentală a românilor". In *Călători români în Occident*, edited by Nicolae Bocşan and Ioan Bolovan. Cluj: Presa Universitară, 2004, pp. 37–45.

Clark, Steve, ed. *Travel Writing and Empire: Postcolonial Theory in Transit*. London: Zed, 1999.

Clifford, James. *The Predicament of Culture: Twentieth-century Ethnography, Literature, and Art*. Cambridge, MA: Harvard University Press, 1988.

Clifford, James. *Routes: Travel and Translation in the Late Twentieth Century*. Cambridge, MA: Harvard University Press, 1997.

Clifford, James. "Traditional Futures". In *Questions of Tradition*, edited by Mark Phillips and Gordon J. Schochet. Toronto: University of Toronto Press, 2004, pp. 47–61.

Clifford, James, and George Marcus, eds. *Writing Culture: The Poetics and Politics of Ethnography*. Berkeley and Los Angeles: University of California Press, 1986.

Constantine, David. *Early Greek Travelers and the Hellenic Ideal*. Cambridge: Cambridge University Press, 1984.

Coulter, Gerry. "Baudrillard and Hölderlin and the Poetic Resolution of the World". *Nebula* 5, no. 4 (2008): 345–67.

Cronin, Michael. *Across the Lines: Travel, Language and Translation*. Cork, Ireland: Cork University Press, 2000.

Cronin, Michael. *Translation and Identity*. London: Routledge, 2006.

Crystal, David. *Language Death*. Cambridge: Cambridge University Press, 2000.

Dalnekoff, Donna Isaacs. "A Familiar Stranger: The Outsider of Eighteenth-century Satire". *Neophilologus* 57 (1973): 121–34.

Dalrymple, William. "Introduction". Locations 124–287. In *The Best Travel Writing 2010: True Stories from around the World*, edited by Sean O'Reilly, James O'Reilly, and Larry Habegger. London: Amazon Media 2010. Kindle e-book.

Dalrymple, William. *Nine Lives: In Search of the Sacred in Modern India*. London: Bloomsbury, 2010.

Darnton, Robert. *Mesmerism and the End of the Enlightenment in France*. Princeton, NJ: Princeton University Press, 1968.

Davies, Martin. "Review of *Paradise with Serpents*, by Robert Carver". *Independent*, 8 October 2009.

De Botton, Alain. *The Art of Travel*. London: Penguin, 2003.

Debaene, Vincent. *Adieu au voyage: l'ethnologie française entre science et littérature*. Paris: Gallimard, 2010.

Del Gizzo, Suzanne. "Going Home: Hemingway, Primitivism, and Identity". *Modern Fiction Studies* 49, no. 3 (2003): 496–523.

Deletant, Dennis. *Romania Observed*. Bucharest: Encyclopedic, 1998.

Deletant, Dennis. "Romanians". In *Imagology: The Cultural Construction and Literary Representation of National Characters*, edited by Manfred Beller and Joep Leerssen. Amsterdam: Rodopi, 2007, pp. 223–26.

Deleuze, Gilles, and Félix Guattari. *A Thousand Plateaus: Capitalism and Schizophrenia*. [1980] Trans. Brian Massumi. London: Continuum, 2004.

Delfini, Alex, and Paul Piccone. "Modernity, Libertarianism and Critical Theory: Reply to Pellicani". *Telos* 112 (1998): 23–47.

DeLoughrey, Elizabeth M. *Routes and Roots: Navigating Caribbean and Pacific Island Literatures*. Honolulu: University of Hawaii Press, 2007.

Derrida, Jacques. "The Animal That Therefore I Am (More to Follow)". Trans. David Wills. *Critical Inquiry* 28 (2002): 369–418.

Derrida, Jacques, *Given Time: 1. Counterfeit Money*. [1991] Trans. Peggy Kamuf. Chicago: University of Chicago Press, 1992.

Derrida, Jacques. *Specters of Marx: The State of Debt, the Work of Mourning, and the New International*. Trans. Peggy Kamuf. New York: Routledge, 1994.

DeSilva, K. M. *A History of Sri Lanka*. Delhi: Oxford University Press, 1981.

Di Biase, Carmine G., ed. *Travel and Translation in the Early Modern Period*. Amsterdam: Rodopi, 2006.

Djuvara, Neagu. *Le pays roumain entre Orient et Occident*. Paris: Publications Orientalistes de France, 1989.

Dobrizhoeffer, Father Martin. *An Account of the Abipones: An Equestrian People of Paraguay*. Asunción, 1784.

Doggett, Scott, and Joyce Connolly. *Dominican Republic and Haiti*. Melbourne: Lonely Planet, 2002.

Dolby, Nadine. "A Small Place: Jamaica Kincaid and a Methodology of Connection". *Qualitative Inquiry* 9, no. 1 (2003): 57–73.

Dollé, Marie. *Victor Segalen, le voyageur incertain*. Croissy-Beaubourg: Éditions Aden, 2008.

Donnell, Alison. "She Ties Her Tongue: The Problems of Cultural Paralysis in Postcolonial Criticism". *Ariel* 26, no. 1 (1995): 101–16.

Döring, Tobias. *Caribbean-English Passages: Intertextuality in a Postcolonial Tradition*. London: Routledge, 2002.

Drace-Francis, Alex. "Constantin 'Dinicu' Golescu and His *Account of My Travels*: Eurotopia as Manifesto". *Journeys, The International Journal of Travel and Travel Writing* 6, nos. 1–2 (2005): 24–53.

Drace-Francis, Alex. *The Making of Modern Romanian Culture*. London: I. B. Tauris, 2006.

Dreyfuss, Joel. "A Cage of Words". In *The Butterfly's Way: Voices from the Haitian Dyaspora in the United States*, edited by Edwige Danticat. New York: Soho, 2001, pp. 57–64.

Drysdale, Helena. *Mother Tongues: Travels through Tribal Europe*. London: Picador, 2001.

Dubow, Jessica. "'From a View on the World to a Point of View in It': Rethinking Sight, Space and the Colonial Subject". *Interventions* 2, no. 1 (2000): 87–102.

Duppé , Claudia. "Tourist in Her Native Country: Kapka Kassabova's *Street without a Name*". In *Facing the East in the West: Images of Eastern Europe in British Literature, Film and Culture*, edited by Barbara Korte, Eva Ulrike Pirker, and Sissy Helff . Amsterdam: Rodopi, 2010, pp. 423–36.

Durrell, Gerald. *The New Noah*. [1955] London: Penguin, 1968.

Dutton, Denis. "Jean Baudrillard". *Philosophy and Literature* 14 (1990): 234–38.

Duval, David Timothy. "Cultural Tourism in Postcolonial Environments: Negotiating Histories, Ethnicities and Authenticities in St Vincent, Eastern Caribbean". In *Tourism and Postcolonialism: Contested Discourses, Identities and Representations*, edited by Colin Michael Hall and Hazel Tucker. London: Routledge, 2004, pp. 57–75.

Eagleton, Terry. *After Theory*. London: Allen Lane, 2003.

Eagleton, Terry. *Figures of Dissent: Reviewing Fish, Spivak, Žižek and Others*. London: Verso, 2002.

Edmond, Rod. *Representing the South Pacific: Colonial Discourse from Cook to Gauguin*. Cambridge: Cambridge University Press, 1997.

Edmond, Rod, and Vanessa Smith. "Editors' Introduction". In *Islands in History and Representation*, edited by Rod Edmond and Vanessa Smith. London: Routledge, 2003, pp. 1–18.

Ehrenreich, Barbara. *Nickel and Dimed: Undercover in Low-wage USA*. London: Granta, 2002.

Ehrlich, Gretel. *In the Empire of Ice: Encounters in a Changing Landscape*. Washington, DC: National Geographic, 2010.

Ehrlich, Gretel. *This Cold Heaven: Seven Seasons in Greenland*. [2001] New York: Vintage, 2003.

Eliade, Pompiliu. *Histoire de l'esprit publique en Roumanie*. 2 vols. Paris: Hachette, 1905–14, vol. 2, pp. vii–xiii.

Evans, Walker, and James Agee. *Let Us Now Praise Famous Men* (1939). French edition: *Louons maintenant les grands hommes*. [1972] Paris: Plon, 1993.

Fabian, Johannes. *Time and the Other: How Anthropology Makes Its Object*. [1983] New York: Columbia University Press, 1986.

Faifer, Florin. *Semnele lui Hermes*. Bucharest: Minerva, 1990.

Fantini, Alvino E. "Language: Its Cultural and Intercultural Dimensions". Adapted from "Language, Culture and World View: Exploring the Nexus". *International Journal of Intercultural Relations* 19 (1995): pp. 3–15.

Fennell, David A. *Ecotourism: An Introduction*. London: Routledge, 1999.

Ford, Paul. *AIDS and Accusation: Haiti and the Geography of Blame*. Berkeley and Los Angeles: University of California Press, 1992.

Forsdick, Charles. "Edward Said, Victor Segalen and the Implications of Post-colonial Theory". *Journal of the Institute of Romance Studies* 5 (1997): 323–39.

Forsdick, Charles. "Said After Theory: The Limits of Counterpoint". In *Post-Theory: New Directions in Criticism*, edited by Martin McQuillan, Graeme Macdonald, Robin Purves, and Stephen Thomson. Edinburgh: Edinburgh University Press, 1999, pp. 188–99.

Forsdick, Charles. *Travel in Twentieth-century French and Francophone Cultures: The Persistence of Diversity*. Oxford: Oxford University Press, 2005.

Forsdick, Charles. *Victor Segalen and the Aesthetics of Diversity: Journeys between Cultures*. Oxford: Oxford University Press, 2000.

Fortunati, Vita, Rita Monticelli, and Maurizio Ascari. "Foreword". In *Travel Writing and the Female Imaginary*. Bologna: Patron Editore, 2001.

Foster, Kevin. *Lost Worlds: Latin America and the Imagining of Empire*. London: Pluto, 2009.

Frank, Joseph. *The Widening Gyre: Crisis and Mastery in Modern Literature*. New Brunswick, NJ: Rutgers University Press, 1963.

Freire Gomes, Plinio. "Blank Variations: Travel Literature, Mapmaking, and the Experience of the Unknown in the New World". In *Unravelling Civilisation: European Travel and Travel Writing*, edited by Hagen Schulz-Forberg. Oxford: P.I.E./Peter Lang, 2005, pp. 66–89.

Fremantle, Tom. *The Road to Timbuktu*. London: Robinson, 2005.

French, Jennifer L., and Thomas Wigham. "The Mournful Cry of the Urutau". *Midwest Quarterly* 50, no. 1 (2008): pp. 32–42.

Freud, Sigmund. "Mourning and Melancholia". In *The Standard Edition of the Complete Psychological Works of Sigmund Freud*, edited by James Strachey. [1915] London: Hogarth, 1957, vol. 14, pp. 243–58.

Freud, Sigmund. "The Uncanny". In *The Standard Edition of the Complete Psychological Works of Sigmund Freud*, edited by James Strachey. [1919] London: Hogarth, 1955, vol. 17, pp. 217–52.

Gane, Mike. "America, the Desert and the Fourth World". In *Baudrillard: Critical and Fatal Theory*. London: Routledge, 1991, pp. 178–92.

Gauch, Suzanne. "A Small Place: Some Perspectives on the Ordinary". *Callaloo* 25, no. 3 (2002): 910–19.

Geertz, Clifford. *Available Light: Anthropological Reflections on Philosophical Topics*. Princeton, NJ: Princeton University Press, 2000.

Geertz, Clifford. "From the Native's Point of View". In *Meaning in Anthropology*, edited by Keith H. Basso and Henry A. Selby. Albuquerque: University of New Mexico Press, 1976, pp. 221–37.

Geertz, Clifford. *The Interpretation of Culture*. New York: Basic Books, 1973.

Georgescu, Vlad. *Political Ideas and the Enlightenment in the Romanian Principalities*. Boulder, CO: East European Monographs, 1971.

Georgescu, Vlad. *The Romanians: A History*. Trans. Alexandra Bley Vroman. [1984] London: I. B. Tauris, 1991.

Gibson, William. "Chishull, Edmund (1671–1733)". *Oxford Dictionary of National Biography*. Oxford: Oxford University Press, 1993, vol. 11, pp. 493–94.

Gikandi, Simon. "Between Roots and Routes: Cosmopolitanism and the Claims of Locality". In *Rerouting the Postcolonial: New Directions for the New Millennium*, edited by Janet Wilson, Cristina Sandru, and Sarah Lawson Welsh. London: Routledge, 2010, pp. 29–45.

Gimlette, John. *At the Tomb of the Inflatable Pig*. London: Arrow, 2003.

Gimlette, John. "Pink pigs in Paraguay—Shiva Naipaul Prize, 1997", author's blog, (1 March 2010) <http://blogs.spectator.co.uk/books/2012/08/pink-pigs-in-paraguay-shiva-naipaul-prize-1997/>).

Glenny, Misha. "'Mum, Why Is Everything So Ugly?'", *Guardian*, 5 July 2008.

Glissant, Édouard. "Le chaos-monde, l'oral et l'écrit". In *"Ecrire la parole de nuit": la nouvelle littérature antillaise*, edited by Ralph Ludwig. Paris: Gallimard, 1994, pp. 111–29.

Goff, Stan. *Hideous Dream: A Soldier's Memoir of the US Invasion of Haiti*. New York: Soft Skull, 2000.

Gold, Herbert. *Best Nightmare on Earth: A Life in Haiti*. London: Flamingo, 1994.

Goldsworthy, Vesna. *Inventing Ruritania*. New Haven, CT: Yale University Press, 1998.

Golescu, Dinicu. *Însemnare a călătorii mele* (1826). Cited in the preface to *Scrieri*, edited by Mircea Anghelescu. Bucharest: Minerva, 1990, pp. 101–2.

Gössling, Stefan. "Tourism and Development in Tropical Islands: Political Ecology Perspectives". In *Tourism and Development in Tropical Islands: Political Ecology Perspectives*, edited by Stefan Gössling. Cheltenham: Edward Elgar, 2003, pp. 1–13.

Grace, Sherrill E. *Canada and the Idea of North*. Montreal: McGill-Queen's University Press, 2007.

Granado, Alberto. *Traveling with Che Guevara: The Making of a Revolutionary*. New York: Newmarket, 2004.

Greene, Graham. *Travels with my Aunt*. London: Penguin, 1969.

Griffin, Patrick. "Fathers and Sons in Nineteenth-century Romania". PhD diss., University of Southern California, 1969.

Guevara, Ernesto. *The Motorcycle Diaries*. London: Verso, 1995.

Guida, Francesco. "Un libro «italiano» sui paesi romeni alla fine del settecento". In *Italia e Romania*, edited by Sante Graciotti. Florence: L. S. Olschki, 1998, pp. 344–65.

Hall, C. Michael. "Power in Tourism: Tourism in Power". In *Tourism, Power and Culture: Anthropological Insights*, edited by Donald V. L. Macleod and James G. Carrier. Bristol: Channel View, 2010, pp. 180–99.

Hall, Stuart. "Gramsci's Relevance for the Study of Race and Ethnicity". *Journal of Communication Inquiry* 10, no. 2 (1986): 5–27.

Hammond, Andrew. *The Debated Lands*. Cardiff: University of Wales Press, 2007.

Hamre, Bonne. "South American's Last Frontier" <http://gosouthamerica.about.com/cs/southamerica/a/ParGranChaco.htm>.

Haneş, Petre V. *Un călător englez despre Români. O scriere englezească despre Principatele Românetradusă în româneşte de Constantin Golescu*. Bucharest: L. Alcalay, 1920.

Harbsmeier, Michael, ed. *Stimmen aus dem äussersten Norden: Wie die Grönländer Europa für sich entdeckten*. Stuttgart: Jan Thorbeke Verlag, 2001.

Hardt, Michael, and Antonio Negri. *Empire*. Cambridge, MA: Harvard University Press, 2000.

Hare, John. *The Lost Camels of Tartary: A Quest into Forbidden China*. [1998] London: Abacus, 1999.

Harrison, David, and Martin Price. "Fragile Environments, Fragile Communities? An Introduction". In *People and Tourism in Fragile Environments*, edited by Martin F. Price. Chichester: Wiley, 1996, pp. 1–16.

Hau'ofa, Epeli. *Kisses in the Nederends*. Auckland: Penguin, 1987.

Hemingway, Ernest. *Green Hills of Africa*. [1935] London: Arrow, 1994.

Heppner, Harald. "Introduction". In *Romania and Western Civilization*, edited by Kurt W. Treptow. Iasi: Center for Romanian Studies, 1997, pp. 1–19.

Heppner, Harald, ed. *Die Rumänen und Europa*. Vienna: Böhlau, 1997.

Heywood, Colin. "Paget, William, Seventh Baron Paget (1637–1713)". *Oxford Dictionary of National Biography*, new ed. Oxford: Oxford University Press, 2004, vol. 42, pp. 383–84.

Holban, Maria. "Autour de l'*Histoire de la Moldavie et de la Valachie* de Carra". *Revue historique du sud-est européen* 21 (1944): 155–230.

Hölderlin, Friedrich Johann. "Patmos". In *Hölderlin: Poems and Fragments*. Oxford: Alden, 1990, p. 34.

Holland, Patrick, and Graham Huggan. *Tourists with Typewriters: Critical Reflections on Contemporary Travel Writing*. [1998] Ann Arbor: University of Michigan Press, 2000.

Hout, Syrine Chafic. *Viewing Europe from the Outside: Cultural Encounters and Critiques in the Eighteenth-century Pseudo-oriental Travelogue and the Nineteenth-century "Voyage en Orient"*. New York: Peter Lang, 1997.

Huggan, Graham. *Extreme Pursuits: Travel/Writing in an Age of Globalization*. Ann Arbor: University of Michigan Press, 2009.

Huggan, Graham. *Interdisciplinary Measures: Literature and the Future of Postcolonialism*. Liverpool: Liverpool University Press, 2008.

Huggan, Graham. *The Postcolonial Exotic: Marketing the Margins*. London: Routledge, 2001.

Huggan, Graham, *Extreme Pursuits: Travel/Writing in an Age of Globalization*. Ann Arbor: The University of Michigan Press, 2009, pp. 137–147.

Huggan, Graham, and Helen Tiffin. "Green Postcolonialism". *Interventions* 9, no. 1 (2007): 1–11.

Huggan, Graham, and Helen Tiffin. *Postcolonial Ecocriticism: Literature, Animals, Environment*. London: Routledge, 2010.

Huyssen, Andreas. *Twilight Memories: Marking Time in a Culture of Amnesia*. London: Routledge, 1995.

Ingold, Tim. *The Perception of the Environment: Essays in Livelihood, Dwelling and Skill*. London: Routledge, 2000.

Institute of Peace and Conflict Studies, "*Drug-trafficking and Abuse in Sri Lanka*" <http://www.ipcs.org/print_article-details.php?recNo=1115>.

Ioncioaia, Florea. "Veneticul, păgînul şi apostatul. Reprezentarea străinului în Principatele Române (secolele XVIII–XIX)". In *Identitate/alteritate în spaţiul românesc*, edited by Alexandru Zub. Iaşi: Universitatea A. I. Cuza, 1996, pp. 30–49.

Ionescu-Ruxăndoiu, Liliana. *Dialog şi naratiune în proza românească*. Bucharest: Romanian Academy, 1991.

Iorga, Nicolae. "Contribuţii la istoria literaturii române în veacul al 18-lea si al 19-lea. Scriitori bisericeşt". *Analele Academiei Române. Memoriile secţiunii literare*, 2nd. ser., 28 (1905–6), 196.

Iorga, Nicolae. *Histoire des relations anglo-roumaines*. Iaşi: Neamul Românesc, 1917.

Iorga, Nicolae. *Istoria literaturii românești în secolul al XVIII-lea*. 2 vols. Bucharest: Ed. Didactică și Pedagogică, 1969.

Islam, Syed Manzurul. *The Ethics of Travel: From Marco Polo to Kafka*. Manchester: Manchester University Press, 1996.

Israel, Heinz. *Kulturwandel grönländischer Eskimo im 18. Jahrhundert*. Abhandlungen und Berichte des Staatlichen Museums für Völkerkunde Dresden 29. East Berlin: Akademie-Verlag, 1969.

Iyer, Pico. "Kapka Kassabova author webpage" <http://www.kapka-kassabova.com/street.html>.

Iyer, Pico. *The Global Soul*. London: Bloomsbury, 2000.

Jelavich, Barbara. *History of the Balkans*. 2 vols. Cambridge: Cambridge University Press, 1983.

Jezernik, Božidar. *Wild Europe*. London: SAQI, 2004.

Jones, Gail. "Mourning, Australian Culture, and the Stolen Generation". In *Imagining Australia*, edited by Judith Ryan and Chris Wallace-Crabbe. Cambridge, MA: Harvard University Press, 2004, pp. 159–71.

Jones, Owain. "(Un)ethical Geographies of Human-non-human Relations: Encounters, Collectives and Spaces". In *Animal Spaces, Beastly Places: New Geographies of Human-animal Relations*, edited by Chris Philo and Chris Wilbert. London: Routledge, 2000, pp. 266–73.

Kaplan, Caren. *Questions of Travel: Postmodern Discourses of Displacement*. Durham, NC: Duke University Press, 1996.

Kassabova, Kapka. "Bloodaxe books, author webpage" <http://www.bloodaxebooks.com/personpage.asp?author=Kapka+Kassabova>.

Kassabova, Kapka. "Author webpage, books". <http://www.kapka-kassabova.com/books.shtml> .

Kassabova, Kapka. *Geography for the Lost*. Highgreen: Bloodaxe, 2007.

Kassabova, Kapka. "Interview and Poems: 'Refugees', 'Coming to Paradise', 'Immigrant Architectures', 'My Life in Two Parts', 'In the Shadow of the Bridge'". In *Creativity in Exile*, edited by Michael Hanne. Amsterdam: Rodopi, 2004, pp. 135–41.

Kassabova, Kapka. "Pisatelkata emigrantka Kapka Kassabova: Balgariya ne e geografsko myasto s prazni kashti za anglichanite". *Kapital* (28 August 2008) <http://www.kapka-kassabova.com/>.

Kassabova, Kapka. "Poet Kapka Kassabova on Talk Talk". <http://www.youtube.com/watch?v=ZDQ95KHN4a4>.

Kassabova, Kapka. *Street Without a Name: Childhood and Other Misadventures in Bulgaria*. London: Portobello, 2008.

Kassabova, Kapka. "From Bulgaria with Love and Hate: The Anxiety of the Distorting Mirror, A Writer's Perspective". In *Facing the East in the West: Images of Eastern Europe in British Literature, Film and Culture*, edited by Barbara Korte, Eva Ulrike Pirker, and Sissy Helff . Amsterdam: Rodopi, 2010, pp. 67–78.

Kearney, Robert M. "Sri Lanka: The Politics of Communal Violence". *Newsweek* (Asian ed.) 17 May 1985.

Kellner, Douglas. *Jean Baudrillard: From Marxism to Postmodernism and Beyond*. Stanford, CA: Stanford University Press, 1989.

Kellogg, Frederick. *A History of Romanian Historical Writing*. Bakersfield, CA: C. Schlacks, 1990.

Kempadoo, Kamala. *Sexing the Caribbean: Gender, Race, and Sexual Labor*. London: Routledge, 2004.

Kempadoo, Kamala, ed. *Sun, Sex, and Gold: Tourism and Sex Work in the Caribbean*. Lanham, MD: Rowman and Littlefield, 1999.

Keown, Michelle. *Postcolonial Pacific Writing: Representations of the Body*. London: Routledge, 2005.

Khatibi, Abdelkebir. *La Mémoire tatouée*. Paris: Denoël, 1979.

Kidd, Stephen. "Land, Politics and Benevolent Shamanism: The Enxet Indians in a Democratic Paraguay". *Journal of Latin American Studies* 27, no. 1 (1995): 43–75.

Kincaid, Jamaica, *A Small Place*. London: Virago, 1988.

King, Jane. "A Small Place Writes Back". *Callaloo* 25, no. 3 (2002): 885–909.

Kiossev, Alexander. "The Dark Intimacy: Maps, Identities, Acts of Identification". In *Balkan as Metaphor: Between Globalization and Fragmentation*, edited by Dusan Bjelić and Obrad Savić. Cambridge, MA: MIT Press, 2002, pp. 165–90.

Klarreich, Kathie. *Madame Dread: A Tale of Love, Vodou and Civil Strife in Haiti*. New York: Nation, 2005.

Kogălniceanu, Mihail. *Scrisori din vremea studiilor*, edited by P. Haneş. Bucharest: Tipografiile Române Unite, 1934.

Korte, Barbara, Eva Ulrike Pirker, and Sissy Helff, eds. *Facing the East in the West: Images of Eastern Europe in British Literature, Film and Culture*. Amsterdam: Rodopi, 2010.

Koshar, Rudy. *German Travel Cultures*. Oxford: Berg, 2000.

Kostova, Ludmilla. "Degeneration, Regeneration and the Moral Parameters of Greekness in Thomas Hope's *Anastasius*". *Comparative Critical Studies* 4, no. 2 (2007): 177–92.

Kostova, Ludmilla. *Tales of the Periphery*. Veliko Tŭrnovo: St. Cyril and Methodius University Press, 1997.

Kovats-Bernat, J. Christopher. *Sleeping Rough in Port-au-Prince: An Ethnography of Street Children and Violence in Haiti*. Gainesville: University Press of Florida, 2006.

Kristeva, Julia. *Black Sun: Depression and Melancholia*. Trans. Leon S. Roudiez. New York: Columbia University Press, 1989.

Kroes, Rob. "America and the European Sense of History". *Journal of American History* 86, no. 3 (December 1999): 1135–55.

Kuehn, Julia, and Paul Smethurst, eds. *Travel Writing, Form, and Empire: The Poetics and Politics of Mobility*. London: Routledge, 2008.

LaCapra, Dominick. *Representing the Holocaust: History, Theory, Trauma*. Ithaca, NY: Cornell University Press, 1994.

Law, John, and Annemarie Mol. "Situating Technoscience: An Inquiry into Spatialities". In *Translation and Identity*, edited by Michael Cronin. London: Routledge, 2006, pp. 40–58.

Leach, Michael. "Don Eduardo Is Sleeping: A Return to New Australia, Paraguay". *Overland* 169 (2001): 90–97.

Leask, Nigel. "Byron and the Eastern Mediterranean: *Childe Harold II* and the 'Polemic of Ottoman Greece'". In *The Cambridge Companion to Byron*, edited by Drummond Bone. Cambridge: Cambridge University Press, 2004, pp. 99–117.

Lemny, Stefan. *Jean-Louis Carra (1742–1793). Parcours d'un révolutionnaire*. Paris: L'Harmattan, 2000.

Lentin, Alana. "The Problem of Culture and Human Rights in the Response to Racism". In *Resituating Culture*, edited by Gavan Titley. Strasbourg: Council of Europe, 2004, pp. 94–99.

Levin, Stephen. *The Contemporary Anglophone Travel Novel: The Aesthetics of Self-fashioning in the Era of Globalization*. London: Routledge, 2008.

Levinas, Emmanuel. *Difficult Freedom: Essays on Judaism*. Trans. S. Hand. Baltimore, MD: Johns Hopkins University Press, 1990.

Levinas, Emmanuel. *Is It Righteous to Be? Interviews with Emmanuel Levinas*. Edited by Jill Robbins. Stanford, CA: Stanford University Press, 2001.

Levinas, Emmanuel. *Otherwise than Being or Beyond Essence*. Trans. Alfonso Lingis. The Hague: Martinus, 1981.

Levinas, Emmanuel. *Totality and Infinity*. Trans. Alfonso Lingis. Pittsburgh: Duquesne University Press, 1969.

Lévi-Strauss, Claude. *Tristes Tropiques*. Paris: Plon, 1955.

Lewis, Paul. "Untitled review of *El Paraguay bajo los Lopez: Algunos ensayos de historia social y política*, by Jerry Wilson Cooney and Thomas Wigham". *Hispanic American Historical Review* 76, no. 4 (1996): 824–25.

Lezard, Nicholas. "Danube Blues" (14 February 2009) <http://www.guardian.co.uk/books/2009/feb/14/street-without-name-kapka-kassabova>.

Lidchi, Henrietta. "The Spectacle of the 'Other'". In *Representation: Cultural Representations and Signifying Practices*, edited by Stuart Hall. London: Sage, 1997, pp. 66–99.

Lindsay, Claire. "Beyond *Imperial Eyes*". In *Postcolonial Travel Writing: Critical Explorations*, edited by Justin D. Edwards and Rune Graulund. Houndmills: Palgrave Macmillan, 2011, pp. 17–35.

Lindsay, Claire. *Contemporary Travel Writing of Latin America*. London: Routledge, 2010.

Lingis, Alphonso. *The Community of Those Who Have Nothing in Common*. Bloomington: Indiana University Press, 1994.

Lippit, Akira Mizuta. "Magnetic Animal: Derrida, Wildlife, Animetaphor". *MLN* 113 (1998): 1111–25.

Lisle, Debbie. *The Global Politics of Contemporary Travel Writing*. Cambridge: Cambridge University Press, 2006.

Llewellyn Smith, Julia. *Travels Without My Aunt: In the Footsteps of Graham Greene*. London: Penguin, 2001.

Lopez, Barry. *Arctic Dreams: Imagination and Desire in a Northern Landscape*. [1986] London: Harvill, 1999.

Lynge, Aqqaluk. "Introduction". In Hans Egede Saabye, *Journal in Greenland 1770–1778*. Hanover, NH: International Polar Institute Press, 2009.

Lynge, Aqqaluk. *The Right to Return: Fifty Years of Struggle by Relocated Inughuit in Greenland*. Nuuk: Forlaget Atuagkat, 2002.

Lynge, Aviaaja. "Mental Decolonization in Greenland". *Inter-Nord* 21 (2011): 273–76.

MacCannell, Dean. *The Tourist: A New Theory of the Leisure Class*. [1976] Berkeley and Los Angeles: University of California Press, 1999.

MacDonald, Kenneth Iain. "Ethics—Issues of". In *Literature of Travel and Exploration: An Encyclopedia*, edited by Jennifer Speake. New York: Fitzroy Dearborn, 2003, vol. 1, pp. 401–3.

Malaurie, Jean. *Les Derniers Rois de Thulé: Avec les Esquimaux Polaires face à leur destin*. [1955] Paris: Plon, 1989.

Malaurie, Jean. *Hummocks: Journeys and Inquiries among the Canadian Inuit*. [1999] Trans. Peter Feldstein. Montreal: McGill-Queen's University Press, 2007.

Malte-Brun, Conrad. *Précis de la géographie universelle*. 29 vols. Paris: 1810.

Mancaş, Mihaela. "Structura naraţiei în perioada romantică". In *Structuri tematice şi retorico-stilistice in romantismul românesc*. Bucharest: Romanian Academy, 1976.

Manceron, Gilles. *Segalen*. Paris: Lattès, 1992.

Marino, Adrian. *Littérature roumaine—littératures occidentales*. Bucharest: Tiintifică şi Enciclopedică, 1981.

Marino, Adrian. "Vechi complexe româneşti". *Observator cultural* 76 (2001): 0–48.

Mauss, Marcel. *The Gift: Forms and Functions of Exchange in Archaic Societies*. [1925] London: Routledge and Kegan Paul, 1969.

Mazilu, D. H., ed. *Cronicari munteni*. Bucharest: Univers Enciclopedic, 2004.

Mazilu, Dan Horia. *Noi şi ceilalţi*. Iaşi: Polirom, 1999.

McCarthy Brown, Karen. *Mama Lola: A Voodoo Priestess in Brooklyn*. Berkeley and Los Angeles: University of California Press, 1991.

Meethan, Kevin. "Introduction: Narratives of Place and Self". In *Tourism, Consumption and Representation: Narratives of Place and Self*, edited by Kevin Meethan, Alison Anderson, and Steve Miles. Wallingford: CABI, 2006, pp. 9–23.

254 *Bibliography*

Michelson, Paul E. "Romanians and the West". In *Romania and Western Civilization*, edited by Kurt Treptow. Iaşi: Center for Romanian Studies, 1997, pp. 11–24.
Mihăilescu, Vintilă. "Orientalism după Orientalism". *Dilema veche* 5, no. 221 (2008): 12-33.
Miller, Richard B. *Casuistry and Modern Ethics: A Poetics of Practical Reasoning.* Chicago: University of Chicago Press, 1996.
Minson, Jeffrey. *Questions of Conduct: Sexual Harassment, Citizenship, Government.* Basingstoke: Macmillan, 1993.
Mitu, Sorin. *National Identity of the Transylvanian Romanians.* Trans. Sorana Corneanu. Budapest: CEU Press, 2001.
Morand, Paul. *New York.* Paris: Flammarion, 1930.
Morris, Jan. "Introduction". In Herbert Gold, *Best Nightmare on Earth: A Life in Haiti.* London: Flamingo, 1994, p. 9.
Mort, Graham. "Finding Form in Short Fiction". In *Short Circuit: A Guide to the Art of the Short Story*, edited by Vanessa Gibbie. London: Salt, 2009, pp. 33–95.
Moura, Jean-Marc. *La Littérature des lointains: histoire de l'exotisme européen au XXe siècle.* Paris: Champion, 1998.
Moura, Jean-Marc. *Lire l'exotisme.* Paris: Dunod, 1992.
Mowforth, Martin, and Iian Mun. *Tourism and Sustainability: Development and New Tourism in the Third World.* 2nd ed. London: Routledge, 2003.
Moynagh, Maureen. *Political Tourism and Its Texts.* Toronto: University of Toronto Press, 2008.
Muecke, Stephen. "Discourse, History, Fiction: Language and Aboriginal History". *Australian Journal of Cultural Studies* 1, no. 1 (1983): 71–79.
Murray, David. *Indian Giving: Economies of Power in Indian-white Exchanges.* Amherst: University of Massachusetts Press, 2000.
Naipaul, V. S. *The Middle Passage: Impressions of Five Societies.* [1962] London: Picador, 2001.
Nettle, Daniel, and Suzanne Romaine. *Vanishing Voices: The Extinction of the World's Languages.* Oxford: Oxford University Press, 2000.
Newsham, Brad. *Take Me with You.* London: Bantam Books, 2002.
Nixon, Rob. "Environmentalism and Postcolonialism". In *Postcolonial Studies and Beyond*, edited by Ania Loomba, Suvir Kaul, Matti Bunzl, Antoinette Burton, and Jed Esty. Durham, NC: Duke University Press, 2005, pp. 33–51.
Nixon, Rob. *London Calling: V. S. Naipaul, Postcolonial Mandarin.* New York: Oxford University Press, 1992.
Nora, Pierre. "Between Memory and History: Les Lieux de Mémoire". *Representations* 26 (1989): 7–25.
Norris, Christopher. *Uncritical Theory: Postmodernism, Intellectuals, and the Gulf War.* Amherst: University of Massachusetts Press, 1992.
Nyman, Jopi. *Men Alone: Masculinity, Individualism, and Hard-boiled Fiction.* Amsterdam: Rodopi, 1997.
Nyman, Jopi. *Postcolonial Animal Tale from Kipling to Coetzee.* New Delhi: Atlantic, 2003.
Onion, Charlie. "Review of *At the Tomb of the Inflatable Pig*, by John Gimlette". *WAG Magazine*, 15 March 2004.
Ortiz, Fernando. *Cuban Counterpoint.* Trans. Harriet de Onis. New York: Knopf, 1947.
Palsson, Gisli. *Writing on Ice.* Hanover, NH: University Press of New England, 2001.
Parry, Jonathan, and Maurice Bloch, eds. *Money and the Morality of Exchange.* Cambridge: Cambridge University Press, 1989.
Patapievici, Horia-Roman. "Calmul discuţiei, seninatatea valorilor". *Idei in dialog* 1 (2004): 22–44.
Patapievici, Horia-Roman. *Flying against the Arrow: An Intellectual in Ceauşescu's Romania.* Trans. Mirela Adăscăliţei. Budapest: CEU Press, 2003.

Pattullo, Polly. *Last Resorts: The Cost of Tourism in the Caribbean*. London: Cassell, 1996.

Payton, Brian. *In Bear Country: A Global Journey in Vanishing Wilderness*. London: Old Street, 2007.

Pensky, Max. *Melancholy Dialectics: Walter Benjamin and the Play of Mourning*. Amherst: University of Massachusetts Press, 1993.

Petro, Pamela. *Travels in an Old Tongue: Touring the World Speaking Welsh*. London: HarperCollins, 1997.

Phelan, James. "Rhetoric/Ethics". In The Cambridge Companion to Narrative, edited by David Herman. Cambridge: Cambridge University Press, 2007, pp. 203–216.

Phillips, Thomas. "Heaven and Hell: The Representations of Paraguay as a Utopian Space". *European Journal of American Culture* 27, no. 1 (1998): 15–27.

Picard, Michel. "Cultural Heritage and Tourist Capital: Cultural Tourism in Bali". In *International Tourism: Identity and Change*, edited by Marie-Françoise Lanfant, John B. Allcock, and Edward M. Bruner. London: Sage, 1995, pp. 180–95.

Picard, Michel. "Cultural Tourism, Nation-building, and Regional Culture: The Making of a Balinese Identity". In *Tourism, Ethnicity, and the State in Asian and Pacific Societies*, edited by Michel Picard and Robert Everett Wood. Honolulu: University of Hawaii Press, 1997, pp. 60–77.

Pippidi, Andrei. "Pouvoir et culture sous Constantin Brancovan". *Revue des études sud-est européennes* 26, no. 4 (1988): 285–94.

Polezzi, Loredana, ed. "Translation, Travel, Migration". Special issue, *The Translator* 12, no. 2 (2006): 169–88.

Popescu, Mircea. "La vendetta dell'abate". *Societas Academica Dacoromana. Acta historica* 1 (1959): 281–90.

Porter, Dennis. *Haunted Journeys: Desire and Transgression in European Travel Writing*. Princeton, NJ: Princeton University Press, 1991.

Potts, Rolf. *Marco Polo Didn't Go There*. Palo Alto, CA: Traveler's Tales, 2008.

Pratt, Mary Louise. "Fieldwork in Common Places". In *Writing Culture: The Poetics and Politics of Ethnography*, edited by James Clifford and George E. Marcus. Berkeley and Los Angeles: University of California Press, 1986, pp. 27–50.

Pratt, Mary Louise. *Imperial Eyes: Travel Writing and Transculturation*. London: Routledge, 1992.

Ragsdale, Hugh. "Evaluating the Traditions of Russian Aggression: Catherine II and the Greek Project". *Slavonic and East European Review* 66, no. 1 (1988): 91–117.

Rajasinghan, K. T. "Sri Lanka: The Untold Story". *The Island* (Colombo), 23 May 1985.

Rallet, Dimitrie. *Suvenire şi impresii de călătorie*. [1858] Critical ed. Edited by Mircea Anghelescu. Bucharest: Minerva, 1979.

Ramey, Lynn. "Monstrous Alterity in Early Modern Travel Accounts: Lessons from the Ambiguous Medieval Discourse on Humanness". *L'Esprit Créateur* 48, no. 1 (2008): 86–89.

Richards, Greg, and Julie Wilson. "Developing Creativity in Tourist Experiences: A Solution to the Serial Reproduction of Culture?" *Tourism Management* 27, no. 6 (2006): 1209–23.

Richards, Thomas. *The Imperial Archive: Knowledge and the Fantasy of Empire*. London: Verso, 1993.

Ridon, Jean-Xavier. "Pour une poétique du voyage comme disparition". In *Autour de Nicolas Bouvier: Résonances*, edited by Christiane Albert, Nadine Laporte, and Jean-Yves Pouilloux. Geneva: Zoé, 2002, pp. 120–35.

Roa Bastos, Augusto. *Son of Man*. [1960] Trans. Rachel Caffyn. Madrid: Debolsillo, 1980.

Rojek, Chris, and John Urry, eds. *Touring Cultures: Transformations of Travel and Theory*. London: Routledge, 1997.

Roman, Denise. *Fragmented Identities*. Lanham, MD: Lexington, 2003.

Rosello, Mireille. *Postcolonial Hospitality: The Immigrant as Guest*. Stanford, CA: Stanford University Press, 2001.

Ross, Kristin. *Fast Cars, Clean Bodies: Decolonization and the Reordering of French Culture*. Cambridge, MA: MIT Press, 1995.

Russo, Alecu. "La pierre du tilleul". In *Scrieri*. Bucharest: Minerva, 1908, pp. 130–31.

Ryan, James R. "Hunting with the Camera: Photography, Wildlife and Colonialism in Africa". In *Animal Spaces, Beastly Places: New Geographies of Human-animal Relations*, edited by Chris Philo and Chris Wilbert. London: Routledge, 2000, pp. 201–23.

Sahlins, Marshall. "Goodbye to Tristes Tropes: Ethnography in the Context of Modern World History". *Journal of Modern History* 65, no. 1 (1993): 1–25.

Said, Edward W. *Culture and Imperialism*. New York: Knopf, 1993.

Said, Edward W. *Orientalism: Western Conceptions of the Orient*. [1978] London: Penguin, 1995.

Sarner, Eric. *La Passe du Vent: Une Histoire Haïtienne*. Paris: Payot, 1994.

Sartre, Jean-Paul. *Situations III*. [1945] Paris: Gallimard, 1949.

Scheiner, Corinne. "Teleiopoiesis, Telepoesis, and the Practice of Comparative Literature". *Comparative Literature* 57, no. 3 (2005): 239–45.

Schlunke, Katrina, and Anne Brewster. "We Four: Fictocriticism Again", *Continuum* 19, no. 3 (2003): 393–95.

Schrift, Alan D., ed. *The Logic of the Gift: Toward an Ethic of Generosity*. London: Routledge, 1997.

Schweitzer, Albert. *Humanisme et mystique*. Selected and presented by Jean-Paul Sorg. Paris: Albin Michel, 1995.

Scott, David H. T. *Semiologies of Travel: From Gautier to Baudrillard*. Cambridge: Cambridge University Press, 2004.

Sebald, W. G. *Austerlitz*. [1999] Trans. Anthea Bell. New York: Random House, 2001.

Sebald, W. G. *The Emigrants*. [1992] Trans. Michael Hulse. London: Harvill, 1997.

Sebald, W. G. *The Rings of Saturn*. [1995] Trans. Michael Hulse. London: Harvill, 1998.

Sebald, W. G. *Vertigo*. [1990] Trans. Harriet de Onis. London: Harvill, 1999.

Segalen, Victor. "La Queste à la Licorne". In *Œuvres complètes*, edited by Henry Bouillier. Paris: Laffont, 1995, vol. 2.

Segalen, Victor. *Essay on Exoticism: An Aesthetics of Diversity*. [1955 as *Essai sur l'exotisme*] Trans. Yaël Schlick. Durham, NC: Duke University Press, 2002.

Segalen, Victor. *Les Immémoriaux*. Paris: Mercure de France, 1907.

Segalen, Victor. *Peintures*. [1916] Paris: Gallimard, 1983.

Segalen, Victor. *Stèles*. [1912] Paris: Gallimard, 1973.

Segalen, Victor. *Equipée*. [1929] Paris: Gallimard, 1983.

Segalen, Victor. *Le Fils du Ciel*. Paris: Flammarion, 1975.

Senders, Stefan, and Allison Truitt, eds. *Money: Ethnographic Encounters*. Oxford: Berg, 2007.

Sennett, Richard. *The Conscience of the Eye: The Design and Social Life of Cities*. New York: Norton, 1990.

Shacochis, Bob. *The Immaculate Invasion*. London: Bloomsbury, 1999.

Sharrad, Paul. *Albert Wendt and Pacific Literature: Circling the Void*. Manchester: Manchester University Press, 2003.

Shehade, Raja. *Palestinian Walks: Notes on a Vanishing Landscape*. London: Profile, 2007.

Sheller, Mimi. *Consuming the Caribbean: From Arawaks to Zombies*. London: Routledge, 2003.

Shields, Rob. "Fancy Footwork: Walter Benjamin's Notes on Flânerie". In *The Flâneur*, edited by Keith Tester. London: Routledge, 1994, pp. 61–80.

Simons, John. *Animal Rights and the Politics of Literary Representation*. Basingstoke: Palgrave, 2002.

Smart, Barry. "Europe/America: Baudrillard's Fatal Comparison". In *Forget Baudrillard?*, edited by Chris Rojek and Brian S. Turner. London: Routledge, 1993, pp. 47–69.

Smith, Mick, and Rosaleen Duffy. *The Ethics of Tourism Development*. London: Routledge, 2003.

Snyder, Gary. *The Practice of the Wild*. Emeryville, CA: Shoemaker and Hoard, 1990.

Soja, Edward. *Thirdspace: Journeys to Los Angeles and Other Real-and-imagined Places*. Cambridge, MA: Blackwell, 1996.

Søltoft, Pia. "Ethics and Irony". In *The Concept of Irony*, edited by Robert L. Perkins. Macon, GA: Mercer University Press, 2001, pp. 265–88.

Spalding, Linda. *The Follow*. London: Bloomsbury, 1998.

Spanos, William. "Bill Spanos in Conversation", with Robert Kroetsch and Dawn McCance. *Mosaic* 34, no. 4 (2001): 1–19.

Spivak, Gayatri Chakravorty. *Death of a Discipline*. New York: Columbia University Press, 2003.

Sprinker, Michael, ed. *Ghostly Demarcations: A Symposium on Jacques Derrida's Specters of Marx*. London: Verso, 1999.

Steinbeck, John. *Travels with Charley: In Search of America*. London: Penguin, 1997.

Still, Judith. *Feminine Economies: Thinking against the Market in the Enlightenment in the Late Twentieth Century*. Manchester: Manchester University Press, 1997.

Stoyanova, Olya. "Kapka Kassabova i vyatarat na promenite [Kapka Kassabova and the Wind of Change]", *Dnevnik* (11 September 2008) <http://www.dnevnik.bg/razvlechenie/2008/09/11/548878_kapka_kasabova_i_viaturut_na_promenite/>.

Strachan, Ian Gregory. *Paradise and Plantation: Tourism and Culture in the Anglophone Caribbean*. Charlottesville: University of Virginia Press, 2002.

Sugnet, Charles. "Vile Bodies, Vile Places: Traveling with *Granta*". *Transition* 51 (1991): 70–85.

Szerszynski, Bronislaw, and John Urry. "Visuality, Mobility and the Cosmopolitan: Inhabiting the World from Afar". *British Journal of Sociology* 57, no. 1 (2006): 113–131.

Tappe, E. D. "Documents Concerning Rumania in the Paget Papers". *Slavonic and East European Review* 33, no. 80 (1954): 201–11.

Thacker, Brian. *The Naked Man Festival and Other Excuses to Fly around the World*. Sydney: Allen and Unwin, 2004.

Theroux, Paul. *The Great Railway Bazaar*. London: Penguin, 1975.

Thomas, Evan, "War and Remembrance". *Time* (international ed.) 17 December 1984.

Thompson, Carl. *Travel Writing*. London: Routledge, 2011.

Thomsen, Mads Rosendahl. *Mapping World Literature: International Canonization and Transnational Literature*. London: Continuum, 2008.

Thomson, Ian. *Bonjour Blanc: A Journey through Haiti*. London: Hutchinson 1992.

Thornton, Thomas. *The Present State of Turkey*. London: Joseph Mawman, 1807.

Thornton, Thomas. *Starea de acum din oblăduirea geograficească, orăşenească şi politicească a Principatelor Valahiei şi Moldaviei*. Buda: Royal University Press, 1826.

Throsby, David. *Economics and Culture*. Cambridge: Cambridge University Press, 2001.

Todorova, Maria. *Imagining the Balkans*. New York: Oxford University Press, 1997.

Trencsényi, Balázs, and Michal Kopeček, eds. *Discourses of Collective Identity in Central and Southeast Europe*. 2 vols. Budapest: CEU Press, 2006–7.

Trivedi, Harish. "The Postcolonial or the Transcolonial?" *Interventions* 1, no. 2 (1999): 269–72.

Tyler, Stephen A. "The Poetic Turn in Postmodern Anthropology: The Poetry of Paul Friedrich". *American Anthropologist* 86, no. 2 (1984): 328–36.

Verdery, Katherine. "Moments in the Rise of the Discourse on National Identity, Seventeenth through Nineteenth Centuries". In *Românii în istoria universală*, ed. A. I. Cutza. Iaşi: Universitatea A. I. Cuza, 1988, pp. 25–60.

Virilio, Paul. *Esthétique de la disparition*. [1980] Paris: Galilée, 1989.

Volovici, Leon. "Polonii şi Ţara Leşească în literatura română". *Anuar de lingvistică şi istorie literară* 28 (1981–82): 57–64.

Walcott, Derek. "What the Twilight Says". In *What the Twilight Says: Essays*. [1970] New York: Farrar, Straus and Giroux, 1998, pp. 143–59.

Wallraff, Gunter. *Lowest of the Low*. London: Methuen, 1988.

Wendt, Albert. *Leaves of the Banyan Tree*. Auckland: Longman, 1979.

Wheeler, Sara. "In Stroessner's Shade". *Guardian* 29 September 2007.

Wheeler, Sara. *The Magnetic North: Notes from the Arctic Circle*. London: Jonathan Cape, 2009.

White, Kenneth. "Celtisme et Orientalisme". In *Regard, espaces, signes: Victor Segalen*, edited by Eliane Formentelli. Paris: L'Asiathèque, 1979, pp. 211–21.

White, Kenneth. *Segalen: théorie et pratique du voyage*. Lausanne: A. Eibel, 1979.

Wilentz, Amy. *The Rainy Season: Haiti since Duvalier*. New York: Simon and Schuster, 1989.

Williams, Raymond. *Politics and Letters*. London: New Left, 1979.

Wolf, Andreas. *Beiträge zu einer statistisch-historischen Beschreibung des Fürstenthums Moldau*. Sibiu: Hochmeister, 1805.

Wolfe, Cary. *Animal Rites: American Culture, the Discourse of Species, and Post-humanist Theory*. Chicago: University of Chicago Press, 2003.

Wolff, Larry. *Inventing Eastern Europe*. Stanford, CA: Stanford University Press, 1994.

Wyschogrod, Edith. *An Ethics of Remembering*. Chicago: University of Chicago Press, 1998.

Yamashita, Shinji. *Bali and Beyond: Explorations in the Anthropology of Tourism*. Trans. J. S. Eades. New York: Berghahn, 2003.

Youngs, Tim. "Making It Move: The Aboriginal in the Whitefella's Artifact". In *Travel Writing, Form, and Empire: The Poetics and Politics of Mobility*, edited by Julia Kuehn and Paul Smethurst. London: Routledge, 2009, pp. 148–66.

Youngs, Tim. "White Apes at the Fin de Siècle". In *Writing and Race*, edited by Tim Youngs. London: Longman, 1996, pp. 166–90.

Zhao, Weibing, and J. R. Brent Ritchie. "Tourism and Poverty Alleviation: An Integrative Research Framework". In *Pro-poor Tourism: Who Benefits? Perspectives on Tourism and Poverty Reduction*, edited by Colin Michael Hall. Clevedon: Channel View, 2007, pp. 55–67.

Zub, Alexandru. "Europa in der rumänischen Kultur". In *Die Rumänen und Europa*, ed. Harald Heppner. Vienna: Böhlau, 1997, p. 275.

Zub, Alexandru. "Political Attitudes and Literary Expressions Illustrative of the Romanians' Fight for National Dignity". *Synthesis* 4 (1977): 17–33.

Contributors

Jan Borm is coauthor of *Réforme et Révolutions: Hommage à Bernard Cottret* (Les Editions de Paris—Max Chaleil, 2012) and *Savoir et pouvoir au siècle des Lumières* (Les Editions de Paris—Max Chaleil, 2011). He lectures in French at the University of Versailles, France.

Anthony Carrigan lectures in the School of English at the University of Keele, England. He specializes in postcolonial literatures and cultures, focusing on globalization, economic development and environmental change. He is author of *Postcolonial Tourism: Literature, Culture, and Environment* (Routledge, 2011). His current research project on postcolonial literature and disaster addresses the social and environmental dimensions of various post–World War II crises.

Michael Cronin holds a personal chair in the Faculty of Humanities and Social Sciences at Dublin City University, Ireland. His publications include *Translating Ireland: Translation, Languages and Identity* (Cork University Press, 1996), *Across the Lines: Travel, Language, Translation* (Cork University Press, 2000) *Translation and Identity* (Routledge, 2006), *The Barrytown Trilogy* (Cork University Press Ireland into Film series, 2007), *Translation Goes to the Movies* (Routledge, 2009) and *The Expanding World: Towards a Politics of Microspection* (Zero, 2012).

Alexander Drace-Francis lectures in Modern European History at the School of History in the University of Liverpool, England. He publishes mainly on the post-1700 cultural history of Romania and Southeastern Europe. He is author of *The Making of Modern Romanian Culture* (I. B. Tauris, 2006). He has worked with Wendy Bracewell on an AHRC-funded project studying East European images and ideas of Europe through travel texts. With Bracewell, he edited a bibliography and a comparative historical introduction to East European travel writing (CEU Press, 2009).

Charles Forsdick is James Barrow Professor of French at the School of Cultures, Language and Area Studies at the University of Liverpool, England. He is author of *Travel in Twentieth-century French and Francophone Cultures: The Persistence of Diversity* (Oxford University Press, 2005) and *Ella Maillart: "Oasis interdites"* (Le Cippe. Zoé, 2008), coauthor (with Feroza Basu and Siobhan Shilton) of *New Approaches to Twentieth-century Travel Literature in French*, vol. 10, *Genre, History, Theory: Travel Writing across the Disciplines* (Peter Lang, 2006) and coeditor of *Transnational French Studies: Postcolonialism and Litterature-monde* (Liverpool University Press, 2010).

Corinne Fowler lectures in the School of English at the University of Leicester, England. She is author of *Chasing Tales: Travel Writing, Journalism and the History of Ideas about Afghanistan* (Rodopi, 2007) and coauthor of *Postcolonial Manchester: Diaspora Space and the Devolution of Literary Culture* (Manchester University Press, 2013). She leads an Arts Council–funded project called 'Grassroutes: Contemporary Leicestershire Writing' and directs the Centre for New Writing at the University of Leicester.

Graham Huggan is Professor of Commonwealth and Postcolonial literatures at the School of English at the University of Leeds, England. His research spans the field of comparative postcolonial literary and cultural studies. He has interests in ecocriticism, travel writing, short fiction and film. Recent publications include *The Postcolonial Exotic: Marketing the Margins* (Routledge, 2001), *Postcolonial Ecocriticism: Literature, Animals, Environment* (Routledge, 2010; coauthored with Helen Tiffin) and *Extreme Pursuits: Travel/Writing in an Age of Globalization* (University of Michigan Press, 2009).

Syed Manzurul Islam is author of *The Ethics of Travel: From Marco Polo to Kafka* (Manchester University Press, 1996), which explores the extent to which it is possible for the traveler to encounter those who are different from himself and examining the consequences of such encounters. He also writes fiction and has authored a collection of short stories, *The Mapmakers of Spitalfields* (Peepal Tree, 1997) and two novels: *Burrow* (Peepal Tree, 2004) and *Song of our Swampland* (Peepal Tree, 2010).

Gillian Jein lectures in French at the School of Modern Languages at the University of Bangor, Wales. Her research interest is in urban cultures, exploring the relationships among space, ideology and practices of urban life in France, including graffiti and street art, as understood through the ethics of space, power and identity. She is the author of *Urban Crossings: Alternative Modernities in French Travel Writing, 1851–2000* (Anthem, 2013) and coeditor of *Aesthetics of Dislocation in French and Francophone Literature and Art: Strategies of Representation* (Edwin Mellen, 2009).

Ludmilla Kostova is Professor of British literature and cultural studies at the University of Veliko Turnovo, Bulgaria. She has published extensively on eighteenth-century, romantic and contemporary literature in English as well as on travel writing and representations of intercultural encounters. Her book *Tales of the Periphery: the Balkans in Nineteenth-Century British Writing* (Veliko Turnovo: St. Cyril and St. Methodius University Press, 1997) has been frequently cited by specialists in the field.

Laurie Hovell McMillin is Professor of rhetoric and composition at Oberlin College. Her research interests include cultural studies, nonfiction prose, South Asian culture and religion and Tibetan studies. Her published work includes *Buried Indians: Digging up the Past in a Midwestern Town* (University of Wisconsin Press, 2006) and *English in Tibet, Tibet in English: Self-Presentation in Tibet and the Diaspora* (Palgrave Macmillan, 2001).

Jopi Nyman is Professor of English at the Univerity of Eastern Finland. He is the author of *Mobile Narratives: Travel, Migration and Transculturation* (Routledge, 2013) and coauthor of *Locality, Memory, Reconstruction: The Cultural Challenges and Possibilities of Former Single-Industry Communities* (Cambridge Scholars, 2012), *Mapping Appetite: Essays on Food, Fiction and Culture* (Cambridge Scholars, 2007) and *Under English Eyes: Constructions of Europe in Early Twentieth-century British Fiction* (Rodopi, 2000).

Alasdair Pettinger is an independent scholar based in Glasgow. His research interests include transatlantic abolitionism and representations of 'race' in the mid-nineteenth-century, travel writing and the cultural history of vodou. He is author of 'Irresistible Charms and Colonial Discourse' (PhD. Thesis, University of Essex, 1998) and the editor of *Always Elsewhere: Travels of the Black Atlantic* (Continuum, 1998). He has published articles in *New Formations*, *Studies in Travel Writing* and the *Journal of African Travel Writing*.

Index